The Author William R. Young, Galgorm, Co. Antrim

FIGHTERS OF DERRY

THEIR DEEDS AND DESCENDANTS

BEING A CHRONICLE OF EVENTS IN IRELAND DURING THE
REVOLUTIONARY PERIOD
1688-1691

BY

WILLIAM R. YOUNG

With a biographical sketch of the author by

GORDON LUCY

Second edition, illustrated

 BooksUlster

First printed in Great Britain for Eyre and Spottiswoode, Publishers Limited,
London, 1932

Second, illustrated edition published by Books Ulster, 2016

Typographical arrangement © Books Ulster

Photographic images of St. Columb's Cathedral, the Guildhall and Bishop's Gate
courtesy and copyright of Roger Bradley (Ulster Photography)

Cover image from an unattributed print of the 1920s/30s

ISBN: 978-1-910375-08-2

BIOGRAPHICAL SKETCH OF THE AUTHOR

The Right Hon. William Robert Young (1856–1933)

William Robert Young was a member of an extremely influential and well-known County Antrim family. His father was John Young of Galgorm Castle, Ballymena, who was a prominent figure in the linen industry and the first Presbyterian to be appointed to the Irish Privy Council. His mother was Grace Charlotte Savage who came from an Anglo-Norman family long associated with the Ards peninsula in County Down. She was the daughter of Lieutenant-Colonel Patrick Savage of the 13th Light Dragoons.

Young was educated at Harrow (which he left in 1875, having played for the Football XI in 1873–4) but did not progress to Oxford or Cambridge. Instead, he travelled extensively on the Continent before entering the family firm of J. & R. Young, flax and yarn merchants, of which his father was the head.

On 28 August 1893 he married Mary Alice Macnaghten, the eldest daughter of the Right Hon. Sir Francis Edmund Macnaghten of Dundarave (the third baronet). Mary Alice was an enthusiastic and accomplished photographer. Between 1890 and 1915 she took over a thousand photographs, most of which are of her family and life on the estate at Galgorm. William and Mary Alice had one child—Hilda Grace Young—who was born on 22 June 1896. In 1924 she married Lieutenant-Colonel Arthur O'Neill Cubitt Chichester. Their elder daughter, Rosemary Hilda, married John Warden Brooke, the future 2nd Viscount Brookeborough, of Colebrooke, in 1949.

Two of Young's brothers and one of his sisters also led noteworthy lives. Rose Maud Young (1865–1947) was a scholarly enthusiast for the Irish language and a close friend of Douglas Hyde, the founder of the Gaelic League. Henry George Young (1870–1956) had a distinguished career in the Indian Army and attained the rank of brigadier-general. Between 1921 and 1951 he was serjeant-at-arms in the Northern Ireland Parliament. George Charles Gillespie Young (1876–1939) was the MP for Bannside in the Northern Ireland House of Commons from 1929 until his death. He was also the Orange County Grand Master of Antrim.

Young was eminent in local commercial and public life. He was High Sheriff of County Antrim in 1920 (a position his father had already held twice) and a Deputy Lieutenant for the county. Like his father he was a staunch unionist and was politically active from the mid 1880s onwards, both as an organiser and a platform speaker. He became an honorary secretary of the Ulster Unionist Council and played a leading role during the third Home Rule crisis, especially in Mid-Antrim, succeeding his father as chairman of Mid-Antrim Unionist Association. He was a close ally of Sir Edward Carson.

In 1921, Viscount FitzAlan of Derwent, the last Lord Lieutenant of Ireland, travelled to Galgorm to invest him as a member of the Irish Privy Council. FitzAlan's journey was made to spare Young the inconvenience of leaving his home while incapacitated due to illness.

Young's magnum opus—*Fighters of Derry: Their Deeds and Descendants, Being a Chronicle of Events in Ireland during the Revolutionary Period, 1688–91* (London, 1932)—was a product of the ill-health which afflicted him for more than a decade. His obituary in the *Northern Whig* of 13 September 1933 explains:

> 'When chronic illness confined him to the house he took up literature as a recreation, and compiled a strikingly interesting history of the Siege of Derry, which is generally conceded to be the most detailed as well as the most vivid story of the attack on and defence of the city which has yet been written.'

The *Belfast News Letter* obituary observed:

> 'Mr Young wrote a delightful history of the Siege of Derry, a volume pronounced by the critics to be one of the best ever compiled'.

More recently, Dr William Roulston of the Ulster Historical Foundation has described Young's substantial and impressive tome as 'the best single source' of information on those who were involved in the siege and on events during the Williamite War in general, adding that the book 'contains a fascinating overview of Irish society in the late 17th century, particularly the settler community in northwest Ulster'.

Gordon Lucy,
2016

CONTENTS

LIST OF ILLUSTRATIONS

The Siege of Londonderry from a contemporary Dutch print

TO THE MEMORY OF

RANDAL MARK KERR

EARL OF ANTRIM,

BUT FOR WHOSE FRIENDSHIP AND UNSELFISH INTEREST IT
WOULD NEVER HAVE REACHED COMPLETION, AND TO THOSE
FRIENDS ASSOCIATED WITH HIM,
THIS BOOK
IS AFFECTIONATELY DEDICATED

"A People, who take no pride in the noble achievements of remote ancestors, will never achieve anything worthy to be remembered by remote descendants."

LORD MACAULAY'S "HISTORY OF ENGLAND," VOL. III, P. 224.

"We stand upon our guard, and do resolve, by the blessing of God, rather to meet our danger, than to expect it."

EXTRACT FROM GUSTAVUS HAMILTON, ENNISKILLEN. LETTER OF JAN. 23, 1689, ADDRESSED TO:—

THE EARL OF MOUNTALEXANDER, THE VISCOUNT MASSEREENE, AND DIVERS OTHERS OF THE NOBILITY AND GENTRY OF THE NORTH-EAST PART OF ULSTER.

PREFACE

THE Siege of Derry is an epic of which any Province may be proud. There for 105 days of fierce bombardment, ceaseless attack and counter-attack, pestilence, and famine, the Ulster Scot held doggedly to the crumbling bastions, hurling defiance in the teeth of the armies of his legitimate sovereign, and of the French and Irish generals who in turn were in command. Lord Macaulay in his immortal prose (Vol. III of his "History of England") has left us a never-to-be-forgotten description of this Homeric struggle, and Dr. Witherow has (in his "Derry and Enniskillen") given us a graphic story of the events. The history of the great Defence and the honour of the Defenders are safe in such hands: but it has occurred to me that the present-day generation of Ulstermen, of all political creeds, whether Protestant or Roman Catholic, would be interested in a work giving short sketches of the men who played prominent parts in this great epic and subsequent campaign down to the fall of Limerick, with particulars of their family, antecedents, and present representative. There is scarcely an Ulsterman whose ancestry, direct or through a female line, has not some hereditary touch with participants in those memorable events. May I confess that, as an Ulster Scot and strong Unionist, my original idea was to confine these sketches to the Defenders of the Maiden City, but, while pursuing my researches among all available data, I soon found that such a limitation would eliminate many a name held in honour and respect for splendid services and sacrifices on behalf of their legitimate sovereign by a large section of that Ulster of which I am so proud? The reasons leading to this conclusion are shortly summarized. For the first time, in centuries of their history, the Irish had found themselves, so they fondly imagined, on the rightful, and therefore winning, side. Their chosen King and leader was the monarch of the three kingdoms. In his Catholicism they had seen their ancient faith restored, and by his prerogative they were again in possession of estates taken by the Anglo-Scot settlers at the time of the Plantation. Though foiled at Derry and beaten at the Boyne (where a gallant Irishman is said to have exclaimed "Change Kings and we'll fight you again!"), they fought desperately on at Athlone and Aughrim to the walls of Limerick, where they again and again proved the worth of an Irish soldier. There can to-day be nothing but sympathy and admiration for the thousands of Irishmen who, after Limerick, rather than accept extinction in their own land, elected to become exiles and serve in the armies of Spain and France, where the Irish Brigades in many a hard-fought battle proved themselves second to none, while their officers, in many cases, served with such distinction as to found families once ranking among the grandees of Spain, or high in the nobility of other continental countries.

My "Sketches" are therefore divided into two parts.

Part I.—Of those who directly or indirectly were responsible for the Defence, viz.:

    (1) The leaders of the County Associations, who with their levies took part in the Preliminary operations and contributed much of the man power for the Defence.

    (2) The Apprentice Boys and those responsible for "the shutting of the gates" on the 8th Dec., 1688.

    (3) The actual Defenders during the 105 days' siege.

    (4) The leading men of Enniskillen, who did much for the Defence.

    (5) Those engaged in the Relief of the city.

Part II.—Officers in the Army of Investment, where nearly every Jacobite officer was serving at some period during the long siege, with special references to subsequent services (after Limerick) in the Irish Brigades of France and Spain.

In submitting this work to the public, I must express my thanks to the many kind friends who made its publication possible, to the representatives of families mentioned in the sketches, who supplied me with data, and in particular to the Very Reverend the Deans of Derry and Dromore, Mr. Thomas U. Sadleir, of the Office of Arms, Dublin, and Mr. H. C. Lawlor, of Belfast, for their invaluable assistance.

WILLIAM R. YOUNG.

Galgorm,
  Co. Antrim.
    July 1932.

INTRODUCTION

HOW little do we know of the greatest siege in the history of the British Isles? Those weary months of war at Derry. There have been few prolonged sieges, and they were chiefly in the days of the Civil War. Cornwall was proud of Sir John Arundel aged "nearly twice four score," who valiantly held out at Pendennis Castle for five months. Nottingham is immortalized by sweet Mistress Lucy Hutchinson, with her fervid adoration of a gallant husband. Hull made a name for Sir John Hotham, but, like Nottingham, was never seriously invested. Latham House, where an indomitable woman held the foe with desperate sorties, must not be forgotten. Most famous of all, Lord Winchester's defence of Basing; truly, a magnificent affair. One's blood warms as the stately pages of Clarendon spread before us the detailed story. And what to a schoolboy can match the tale of Pomfret Castle; how the gallant defenders escaped death by bricking themselves in till the besiegers had departed? It is certainly the great Clarendon at his best.

Basing and Pomfret are not to be put in comparison with Derry. It was a city, poorly walled, mustering only twenty serviceable guns, but covering a large area and containing a considerable population.

It was a peculiar siege. In most instances like Breda, where the valiant Dutch held the Spaniard, or in modern times like Paris in 1870, the inhabitants of a country held their town against a foreign invader. In such cases, the attacking forces have usually been in the predicament of keeping open lines of communication and being themselves surrounded by a hostile population. At Derry all this was reversed. Its army and population were alien alike in race and creed, while the investing forces were mostly native Irish, Catholic in religion, with some French levies in addition. The great advantage of the Jacobites lay in the fact that the bulk of the country people were with them (settlers of English or Scottish origin being powerless to act), and that communications with headquarters at Dublin were never in danger, the only possible menace being from Enniskillen on the flank.

So far the tale of the investment has only been half told by local historians. Mr. Young now presents the story of what happened both within and without the city: a chivalrous Ulsterman tells of the heroic Walker and his men, and also chronicles the splendid deeds of the attacking Jacobites. He not only narrates his history in the aggregate, but he has traced as far as possible the career of every individual that was present, even in some cases to the latest generation. He has also dealt with the principal participants in the events leading up to the fall of Limerick, and has drawn on the unique MS. entitled "A List of the Refugees at Chester 1689" in the Library of Trinity College, Dublin, which former writers had completely ignored. But in the main his work is a triumph of local knowledge and local study, as he sets down in his own refreshingly direct way the tasks and toils, so cherished by their descendants, of the "Fighters of Derry."

THOMAS U. SADLEIR.

July 1932.

INTRODUCTORY CHAPTER

JAMES II. had not been many months on the throne of England before Protestant Ulster was much perturbed by his fanatical efforts for the restoration of a Catholic supremacy in the Three Kingdoms. As early as 1685, a royal favourite and Roman Catholic, Colonel Richard Talbot (a member of the old Irish family of Malahide), had been dispatched to Dublin to command the Irish Army, independently of the Protestant Viceroy, the Earl of Clarendon. His instructions were to cashier the Protestant officers and organise a Catholic Army. So well did he carry out his mission that in 1687 the Earl of Clarendon was recalled, and Talbot, raised to the peerage as Earl of Tyrconnell, appointed in his stead as Lord Deputy. (It was not until some two years later that he was advanced to a Dukedom and made Viceroy.) Unperturbed by any interference, Tyrconnell now proceeded to purge the Executive, as he had done the Army, of Protestant officials, while the charters of all cities and corporations were revoked, and new ones granted in which care was taken that Catholic influence should preponderate. In this way, in 1688, the Corporation of Derry had been remodelled, and the Celt had taken the place of the Anglo-Scot. John Campsie, the Protestant Mayor, had been replaced by Cormac O'Neill, who, although a Protestant, was a strong supporter of the King, being a cousin of (Rose O'Neill) the Marchioness of Antrim, to whose Shane's Castle estates he was heir, while he held a commission as Lieut.-Col. in one of her brother-in-law the Earl of Antrim's regiments. While Tyrconnell was thus working for his master's ends, his plans were interrupted by an unexpected happening. On the 5th November, 1688, William of Orange landed at Torbay with some 15,000 Dutch troops, being joined at once by the leaders of the Constitutional and Protestant party. The Great Revolution had commenced.

The effect in Ireland was immediate. Tyrconnell found himself obliged, while still pressing forward his muster of Irish levies in Dublin, to send some 3000 men, out of the Irish establishment of 7000, to James' assistance in England. The County Associations of noblemen and gentry of Ulster, formed earlier in the year for mutual protection and defence of the Protestant religion, already at work organising their levies, immediately got into direct communication with William of Orange. This state of tension between the Dublin executive of the legitimate sovereign and William of Orange's supporters in Ulster was suddenly broken by a seemingly trivial event. Lord Mountjoy's Regiment, consisting almost entirely of Protestants, had garrisoned Derry for a considerable time, but had been withdrawn (25th November, 1688) to strengthen King James' army in England. (As a matter of fact, it never crossed the Channel, as will be seen later.) To the horror of the citizens of Derry, it was intimated to the city authorities that this friendly regiment was to be replaced by one of new levies raised by the Earl of Antrim, who was to be appointed Governor. General consternation reigned at the idea of being at the mercy of undisciplined Roman Catholic troops. On the 7th December this was increased to a veritable panic by the arrival of a messenger from George Canning of Garvagh (the agent of the London Company of Skinners) to Tomkins, a leading burgess of the city, bringing him a copy of an anonymous letter addressed to the Earl of Mountalexander, which had been picked up in the street of Comber, Co. Down. This letter was a warning to Protestants in general of a projected attempt at massacre on the coming 9th of the month. Derry had not forgotten the terrible events of 1641, but the news had circulated for barely twenty-four hours when a courier from their neighbour, George Phillips, of Limavady, arrived to warn them of the near approach of Lord Antrim's regiment. The streets were thronged with angry crowds discussing the situation and demanding immediate and decisive action. On the Lord Bishop (Ezekiel Hopkins) attempting to preach moderation, he was interrupted by Irwin (afterwards one of the famous apprentices) with: "My Lord, your doctrine's good, but we can't now hear you out." A few only of the older men sided with the younger in the popular clamour, the most conspicuous of whom were Tomkins and the Rev. John Gordon, Presbyterian minister of Glendermot, a parish just outside the city in Co. Derry.

While things were still in a state of indecision, two advance companies of Lord Antrim's Regiment, who had been ferried across the river, presented themselves at the Ferry Gate, demanding admission. (Lord Antrim had remained for the night with Mr. George Phillips of Limavady.) The city authorities were still undecided, but thirteen gallant apprentices, regardless of consequences, backed by some stalwart friends, like Tomkins and Gordon, took the law into their own hands. Rushing down, they shut the gates in the face of the intruders, who, hearing the cry, "Bring round the big gun," quickly retired to the other side of the river. The apprentice boys of Derry had made history. The die had been cast and the City Fathers committed to an overt act of rebellion.

The names of the thirteen gallant "apprentice boys" are worthy of record, viz. Henry Campsie, William Sherrard, Daniel Sherrard, Alexander Irwin, James Steward, Robert Morrison, Samuel Harvey, William Crookshank, Alexander Cunningham, John Cunningham, Samuel Hunt, James Spike or Spaight, William Cairnes.

A meeting of the citizens was at once held, and resolutions were passed to prepare for a resolute defence. On the 11th December six companies were raised for the manning of the walls, of which the following were appointed officers:—

1st Company:
    Capt. Sam. Norman.
    Lieut. William Crookshank.
    Ensign Alex. Irwin.

2nd Company:
    Capt. Mathew Cocken.
    Lieut. Henry Long.
    Ensign Francis Hunt.

3rd Company:
    Capt. John Tomkins.
    Lieut. James Spaight.

4th Company:
    Capt. Alex. Lecky.
    Lieut. James Lennox.

Ensign Alex. Cunningham.   Ensign John Harvey.

5th Company: *6th Company:*
     Capt. Wm. Jemmett.   Capt. Thomas Moncrieff.
     Lieut. Robert Morrison.   Lieut. James Morrison.
     Ensign Dan. Sherrard.   Ensign Wm. Mackie.

Steps were taken to repair the walls, and subscriptions raised for the purchase of arms and munitions.

While all this was taking place, Lord Antrim, informed by his host, Mr. George Phillips, of the position in Derry, had retired with his regiment to Coleraine, where he awaited further instructions from Tyrconnell. Luckily at this crisis in their affairs the city had the advice and approval of David Cairnes, the possessor of the large estate of Knockmany, Co. Tyrone, at one time a leading citizen of Derry, and law adviser of the Irish Society. Hearing of what had been going on, he had hurried to the scene of action. After taking part in their deliberations, and possessed of their fullest confidence, David Cairnes sailed on the night of the 11th for England, in a vessel of his own, which by lucky chance was in the Lough, to put the position before King William and the Irish Society, and ask for troops, supplies, munitions and arms.

Tyrconnell's fury at "the shutting of the gates" in the face of Lord Antrim's Regiment knew no bounds, and he ordered Lord Mountjoy with six companies of his regiment to proceed to Derry and reduce the refractory city to obedience. To Mountjoy were given powers to negotiate and make terms. The city authorities were already in correspondence with Mountjoy, explaining their action as no rebellion, but justifiable on constitutional lines for their own protection. They explained their readiness to apologise, and to admit Government troops if Protestant.

On the 21st December Lord Mountjoy arrived in Derry. No negotiator could have been more acceptable. He was the head of an old Co. Donegal Plantation family, always on the most friendly terms with the inhabitants of the city. His grandfather, Sir William Stewart, Bart., of Ramelton, had been the first grantee of his large estates. His father, Sir Alexander, 2nd Baronet, had rendered Derry signal service at the time of the 1641 rebellion, and had fallen fighting on the loyalist side at the battle of Dunbar in 1650. Born in 1650, the son and successor to the estate, and 3rd Baronet, had been raised to the peerage as Baron Stewart of Ramelton and Viscount Mountjoy in 1685. With such family antecedents, and his own well-known loyalty to the Crown, although a Protestant, he had been allowed to continue as Master of Ordnance and to retain his regiment. With such a friend the City Fathers of Derry had little difficulty in coming to the following arrangement with Mountjoy, which the latter undertook to have confirmed by Tyrconnell: (1) Derry was to make humble apology, and be pardoned for the past. (2) Two companies of Lord Mountjoy's Regiment, conditional on the men being Protestant, were to be admitted as garrison of the city. (3) These two companies were to be commanded by Lord Mountjoy's Lieut.-Col. [Lundy], a

Scotch Episcopalian, who was to be installed as Governor, and (4) the six companies raised by the city were to be allowed to retain their arms and share the garrison duty with the two companies to be admitted. Having thus set things in order, and Lundy with his two companies being installed in the city, Mountjoy returned to Dublin.

Tyrconnell, while more than ever determined on wreaking vengeance on such refractory subjects, dissembled his rage and pretended satisfaction. Mountjoy was assured that the arrangement would be carried out, and was requested as a special favour to the Viceroy to go on a special mission to James II., then at Louis XIV.'s Court in Paris (James had left Whitehall on the 18th December). In spite of many warnings from friends, Mountjoy fell into the trap. Sailing in the same ship with him to France was an emissary of Tyrconnell's bearing secret instructions to Louis XIV.'s Ministers to have Mountjoy arrested as a traitor and placed in the Bastille. There the unfortunate nobleman remained for some three years, being exchanged in 1692 for a leading Jacobite prisoner, General Richard Hamilton, of whom more will be said later. How far James II. was responsible for this mean transaction will never be known. At all events, after his exchange in 1692 Lord Mountjoy joined King William's army as a volunteer in Flanders, where he fell fighting against the French at Steinkirk in the same year.

David Cairnes, who had sailed on December 11th, owing to storm and contrary winds did not reach London until late in January. He was most graciously received in audience by His Majesty at Whitehall, and promised every possible support for his Derry friends. To the results of his mission I will return later.

In January 1689, while Derry, with Lundy in command, was feverishly preparing for the great struggle now inevitable, and while Tyrconnell was organizing Ireland for a fitting reception for James II. and raising musters for his projected attack on Derry, the situation may be roughly described as follows:—

In Ulster Tyrconnell's forces consisted of 2000–3000 men under Col. Gordon O'Neill, at Charlemont Fort on the Blackwater, two regiments quartered at Lisburn and Belfast, Lord Antrim's regiments holding Carrickfergus and Coleraine, and two flying columns not exceeding some 1500 men each, commanded respectively by Sir Patrick Sarsfield and Lord Galway, operating in Connemara and on the borders of Ulster. Until the great offensive was opened from Dublin these forces were merely marking time. The Protestant inhabitants had already begun to centre in Derry and Enniskillen, where Gustavus Hamilton was organising his levies. The County Associations raised by the noblemen and gentry for mutual protection and defence of the Protestant religion had for some months been busily engaged in the raising of men and organisation. Generals for each county with a county council were appointed, while a supreme council, or Consult, sat at Hillsborough, Co. Down, to co-ordinate and direct operations.

On the Co. Antrim Council were:—

> Viscount Massereene, appointed General.
> Sir William Franklin, Bart., Belfast.
> Arthur Upton, Castle Upton.
> Davis or Davies, Carrickfergus.
> Harrison, Lisburn.
> Shaw, The Bush, Antrim.

On the Co. Down Council were:—

> The Earl of Mountalexander, appointed General.
> Sir Arthur Rawdon, Bart., Moira.
> Sir Robert Colville, Newtown.
> James Hamilton, Bangor.
> James Hamilton, Tullymore.

On the Armagh Council were:—

> Sir Nicholas Acheson.
> Capt. Poyntz of Acton.
> Capt. Middleton.

The Monaghan Council had for leader Lord Blayney, of Castle Blayney.

The Londonderry and Donegal Council nominated Col. Lundy, Governor of Derry, as their General, while the *Tyrone Council* appointed Major Gustavus Hamilton, already organising forces in Enniskillen, to command.

The Supreme Council or Consult, which was in continual session at Hillsborough, consisted of the following members:—

> Earl of Mountalexander, representing Co. Down.
> James Hamilton of Tullymore, representing Co. Down.
> Arthur Upton, Castle Upton, representing Co. Antrim.
> William Cunningham, representing Co. Londonderry.
> — Johnston, representing Co. Monaghan.
> Capt. Poyntz, representing Co. Armagh.
> (See Reid's "History of the Presbyterian Church of Ireland," Vol. II. p. 359.)

At the beginning of March defence preparations were well forward. The following regiments had been raised by their respective colonels, and officered by local gentry, having in some instances among them Protestant officers of experience cashiered by Tyrconnell from the Irish establishment: a regiment of Dragoons, Down and Antrim, commanded by the Earl of Mountalexander; a regiment of Dragoons, Down, commanded by Sir Arthur Rawdon, Bart., and the following nine infantry regiments:—

Co. Down Infantry Regt., commanded by:—

Sir John Magill, Gillhall.
Sir Robert Colville, Newtown.
James Hamilton, Tullymore.
James Hamilton, Bangor.

Co. Antrim Infantry Regt., commanded by:—

Col. Clotworthy Skeffington, eldest son of Viscount Massereene.
Sir William Franklin, Bart., Belfast.
William Leslie, Ballymoney.
Arthur Upton, Castle Upton.
Archibald Edmunston, Red Hall.

The following were among the other regimental units of the Ulster Protestant County Associations: Viscount Charlemont's regiment at Dungannon, under command of Major Rev. George Walker; a regiment raised by Col. Stewart, also at Dungannon; 200–300 Dragoons raised by Capt. William Stewart, of Killymoon, in the neighbourhood of Cookstown; Lord Blayney's force, 500–700 men at Armagh; the Earl of Kingston's flying squadron of 500–700 men, operating round Ballyshannon.

The Hillsborough Consult, aiming at thorough co-ordination of all their efforts, had kept in close touch with all the counties, and particularly with Lundy in Derry, who was looked upon as Commander-in-Chief. While Lundy advocated the concentration of all forces in and around Derry for its defence, the Consult were strongly in favour of attacking the Dublin force on its march and of preventing any investment of the city. To the latter course Lundy at last consented, promising everything, and doing nothing when the situation arose.

At last, early in March, Tyrconnell's force for the punishment of Derry was on its way north. It consisted of 5000–7000 men under command of General Richard Hamilton. News soon reached Hillsborough of its approach. On the 11th of March it lay for the night at Newry, Co. Down. On the 14th, Sir Arthur Rawdon, having collected every available man, met the enemy at Dromore in the same county. So disastrous was the result that the engagement has gone down in history as the "Break of Dromore." On his retreat Sir Arthur Rawdon's force was augmented to some 3000 men, with which he retired to Coleraine, pursued by Hamilton, who delayed long enough to burn Hillsborough Castle and sack Lisburn, while in his further progress Antrim Castle, the seat of Lord Massereene, was looted and committed to the flames.

Bad indeed as the effect of Dromore was on the supporters of King William, more grievous still was Hamilton's prompt circulation of Tyrconnell's proclamation offering pardon and protection to all rebels in arms who immediately surrendered, and exempting by name the following conspicuous leaders, viz. the Earl of Mountalexander, the Earl of Kingston, the Viscount Massereene, Sir Robert Colville, Sir Arthur Rawdon, Bart., Col. Clotworthy Skeffington, John Hawkins, Robert Sanderson, Francis Hamilton, Sir John Magill. The effect of this proclamation was electrical, many of the leaders of the party flying for safety across the Channel or seeking the protection of Major Gustavus Hamilton's camp.

After the "Break of Dromore" and early successes, Hamilton pressed on after Rawdon to Coleraine, where he intended to cross the Bann and continue his advance on Derry. On his way to Coleraine Rawdon had been joined by Lord Blayney at the head of some 500—700 men from Armagh. Ordered by Col. Lundy to retire on Derry, Lord Blayney had preferred a union with the forces of the Hillsborough Consult. He had successfully avoided Col. Gordon O'Neill's forces at Charlemont Fort, and crossed the Bann at Toome. Coleraine they found held by local levies under the command of Sir Tristram Beresford, Bart., Col. Canning of Garvagh, Col. Blair of Agivey, and several local gentry. Immediate preparations were made for resisting the impending attack. On the 27th March Hamilton attacked, but was driven back with the loss of some 760 men. Foiled in his attempt to take Coleraine, where he had expected to cross the Bann, Hamilton was obliged to retire and seek a means of crossing the river between that place and Toome. To prevent this, Rawdon, who had had the bridge at Portglenone demolished and all boats removed, now transferred his forces to the left bank, splitting up his men into the following units, of which Sir Arthur Rawdon was in command at Moneymore:—

Col. Skeffington, Toome.	Sir John Magill, Kilrea.
Major Mitchelburn, Newferry.	Col. Canning, Magherafelt.
Col. Edmunston, Portglenone.	Col. Blair, Agivey,

while Sir Tristram Beresford was left with sufficient strength to hold Coleraine. Notwithstanding all their efforts, the river passage was forced near Portglenone on the 7th April by a detachment commanded by Col. Nugent, a younger son of the Earl of Westmeath, and the rest of Hamilton's army were soon across. Desultory skirmishing ensued, in which Capt. James Magill, a son of Sir John Magill, and several other officers were killed, the result being immediate retreat across the mountains to Derry, where the wearied men arrived on the 9th or 10th April, with the enemy on their heels. With the forcing of the Bann Coleraine became untenable, and its garrison and inhabitants withdrew to Derry.

While all these events were taking place Derry had been greatly cheered, as a first result of David Cairnes' mission to England, by the arrival on the 21st March of a

special emissary from King William in the person of Capt. James Hamilton.[1] Capt.
James Hamilton brought arms for 2000 men, 400 barrels of powder and £500, while
he conveyed a letter from the Secretary of State, the Earl of Shrewsbury, thanking
the Corporation in the King's name for what had been done, promising immediate
dispatch of 2000 men to strengthen the garrison, and confirming Col. Lundy in his
appointment as Governor of the city. The next day, March 22nd, William and Mary
were publicly proclaimed as Joint Sovereigns and the Oath of Allegiance was taken
by all officers and those in authority. On the 21st March the famous "Declaration
of Union," whereby "each and all mutually promised and engaged to stand by one
another, and not to leave the kingdom or desert the public service until their affairs
were in a settled and secure position," was signed by all officers then in Derry and the
prominent men in the city. When Sir Arthur Rawdon and his county associates arrived
in the city their signatures were appended to the same Declaration on the 10th April.
While on the 10th April this second edition of the "Declaration of Union" was being
signed and a council of war held in the city, David Cairnes returned from his mission
with the welcome news that the Fleet was already on its way with reinforcements of
2000 men, and that King William, urgent on a strenuous defence, would support
them in every possible way.

Things could not have been in a more critical state. The populace, the garrison
and the county leaders were all suspicious of Col. Lundy's half-hearted actions, but
Cairnes' influence succeeded in bringing about some semblance of concord. Added
to Hamilton's advance on the city, James II., who had landed at Kinsale on the 12th
March and spent a fortnight in Dublin, was now on his march north via Omagh at
the head of Tyrconnell's levies.

On the 13th April Hamilton was before the city, luckily on the opposite bank
of the Foyle, there a mighty river of some 1000 yards in width. Finding a crossing
impossible, Hamilton was forced to march some twenty-five miles up the river and
effect the passage above the junction of the Finn and Mourne near Lifford. Lundy's
conduct during the few days 13th to 15th April revived the old suspicions. His forces
had indeed been ordered out to prevent the crossing of the Finn, but hardly had they
taken up the required position before they were ordered to retire. Col. Murray, at the
head of a small detachment, had retarded the enemy for a few hours at Cladybank,
but receiving no support was obliged to join in the general withdrawal. This was on
the 15th April. Lundy himself was among the first to re-enter the walls, and by his
instructions the gates were shut in the face of late arrivals from the front, to prevent
the enemy effecting an entrance at their heels. Among those so shut out was the gallant
Col. Murray, who with his troops passed the night at Culmore Fort. On the very day
of these disastrous happenings the British Fleet arrived in Lough Foyle with the promised reinforcements of 2000 men. The garrison was as much cheered as Hamilton was

---

[1] Capt. James Hamilton succeeded in 1704 as 6th Earl of Abercorn.

dismayed by the sight of their masts. Communications were at once opened between Lundy and the officers in command. After several consultations in secret conclave between the commanding officers of the relieving force and Lundy, who alleged the city to be unprovided for defence and untenable, it was resolved that the Fleet with these reinforcements should return to England. Of course the proposed withdrawal was soon well known. It was arranged that all officers of the garrison wishing to avail themselves of a free passage should accompany the Fleet. Many had already made their way to the ships, but late on the 16th the enraged people proceeded to take forcible steps to prevent more desertions, one officer at least being killed by an angry mob. On the 18th April the Fleet, to the consternation of the populace, dropped down the Foyle to Greencastle, sailing the next day to England. David Cairnes, who shared to the full in the indignation of the populace and garrison against the Governor and his false statements regarding the city, again sailed on the 18th April to lay the true facts of their position before King William. Notwithstanding the withdrawal of the Fleet and the desertion of so many leaders, the garrison and populace were as determined as ever on a stout defence. What they wanted was a daring leader.

Col. Murray and his troops had spent the last two days at Culmore Fort. On the morning of the 18th they presented themselves at the gates, still closed to them by Lundy's instructions, but Murray was admitted by James Morrison, captain of a gate. Once among the admiring populace Murray became the popular hero. At the head of his followers he invaded the council chamber, where Lundy and some selected officers were actually negotiating terms of surrender with emissaries dispatched by James. Having protested in the strongest measure, and frightened Lundy into the dread of a popular outbreak, Murray proceeded to take possession of the city gates, replacing the guards appointed by Lundy with men of his own on whom he could depend. King James had arrived that morning at Hamilton's camp, and was on his way at the head of a considerable force to accept the surrender of the city from Lundy. Thanks, however, to Murray's intrepid action, when the King did arrive at the gates there were no Lundy and no keys. Instead of that, some shots were fired, a few men dropped close to the King and the Royal force hurriedly retired to their camp. Once saved by the gallantry of apprentice boys, the city was again saved by the intrepidity of Col. Murray.

All was consternation in the Irish camp. The immediate surrender of the city had been expected. James II. had been accompanied by some 500 French troops and two distinguished generals, Pusignan and de Maumont, who expressed a firm opinion that a place so poorly fortified, manned and munitioned must yield at once to a resolute attack. In Derry there was exaltation, but all were fully alive to the danger of their position. Col. Lundy[1] succeeded in escaping in disguise at night and making his way to Scotland.

---

[1] See Part I, No. 1.

On the 19th April James again opened negotiations with the rebel city through the Earl of Abercorn,[1] who, having completely failed in his object, was courteously escorted back through the lines by Col. Murray. The same day an enthusiastic meeting was held in the city for organising the Defence. Owing to the number of refugees who had flocked there for protection, there were at least 30,000 people, chiefly women and children, within the walls, of whom about 7000 were fighting material. These 7000 consisted of the companies raised by Derry for its own defence, of the remnants of Cos. Antrim and Down regiments brought in by Sir Arthur Rawdon, of the Coleraine levies (Sir Tristram Beresford, Col. Canning and Col. Blair's units), who came in after the evacuation of that town, of Lord Charlemont's Regiment, a portion of which under command of Major Rev. George Walker and Col. Stewart had by Lundy's command come in from Dungannon, of units raised by neighbouring landlords,[2] and of Col. Francis Hamilton's Regiment of Co. Tyrone. The first business was the nomination of a new Governor. The position was unanimously offered to Col. Murray, but refused on the plea of want of experience in the management of civil affairs. Major Henry Baker, a Protestant officer cashiered by Tyrconnell, who had proved his worth as an officer under Sir Arthur Rawdon in the retreat from Dromore to the city, was then appointed Governor, and Major Rev. George Walker of Lord Charlemont's Regiment was appointed Assistant Governor. The 7000 men were then divided into the following eight units or regiments:—

Sir Arthur Rawdon's Dragoons, commanded by Major Henry Baker.
Lord Charlemont's Regiment, commanded by Major Rev. George Walker.
The Coleraine Regiment, commanded by Major Parker.
Col. Skeffington's Regiment, commanded by Major Mitchelburn.
A regiment commanded by Col. Hamill.
Francis Hamilton's Regiment, commanded by Col. Whitney.
Col. Canning's Regiment, commanded by Major Crofton.[3]
The Horse, commanded by Col. Murray, who was to command in the field.

On the 20th April James II. had left the camp and gone to Dublin so as to be in time for the opening of his Parliament early in May. He left the command of the investing army in the hands of Pusignan, de Maumont and General Richard Hamilton. On the 23rd Culmore Fort, commanding the river approach to the city, garrisoned by some 200–300 men, under Capt. William Adair,[4] fell without a shot to a cavalry

---

[1] See Part II, No. 7.
[2] Kilner Brazier of Rath, Col. Forward of Castle Forward, John Cowan of St. Johnston, Col. Murray, Phillips of Limavady and Col. Hamill of Strabane.
[3] All the above names are subjects of Individual Sketches, Part I.
[4] Of the Ballymena family.

raid made by the Duke of Berwick, a natural son of James II.[1]

Although the story of the siege is now left to what is given in the individual sketches, I give herewith a rough diary of siege events to enable the reader to follow the incidents in the individual sketches:

Diary of Siege Events.

April	15.	Hamilton's army crossed the Finn.
„	17.	Hamilton's army in camp before Derry (Donegal side).
„	18.	King James repulsed at gates.
„	18.	Colonel Murray entered the city as a popular hero.
„	18.	Lundy fled in disguise.
„	19.	Baker and Walker elected Governors of City.
„	19.	Earl of Abercorn's attempt to negotiate terms of surrender.
„	20.	James II. left the Irish camp for Dublin.
„	21.	First sally of the garrison. General de Maumont killed.
„	23.	Culmore Fort surrendered.
„	25.	Pennyburn fight. General Pusignan killed.
May	6.	First Windmill Hill fight. General Ramsay killed.
„	18.	Clegyan Fight.
June	4.	Second Windmill Hill fight.
„	11.	English Fleet arrived in the Lough.
„	18.	Boat fight on the Foyle.
„	20.	General Rosen arrived in the Irish camp to take command.
„	26.	Roche's swim from the Fleet and that of Mr. Gimprey a few days later.
„	28.	Earl of Clancarty's attack on gate.
„	30.	Governor Baker's death. Succeeded by Major Mitchelburn.
July	2.	General Rosen exposed defenceless old men, women and children before walls. Threat of garrison to hang their prisoners.
„	25.	Garrison's last sally at Pennyburn.
„	28.	Breaking of boom. Relief ships reach quay.
„	30.	The investing army retreats to Dublin.

James II.'s Parliament, which met in Dublin on May 7th, 1689, and sat for some

---

[1] Part II, No. 13.

three weeks, passed two sweeping and fanatical Acts:—(1) *The Repeal of the Act of Settlement*, practically transferring all estates held by Protestants to Roman Catholic hands. (2) *The Bill of Attainder*, condemning without trial or enquiry to all the frightful penalties of high treason, with confiscation of estates, over 2500 persons, peers, bishops, deans, minor clergy, landowners, merchants and women. The names on this list of attainders were hurriedly furnished by the Jacobite members of Parliament who had thus ample opportunity of paying off old scores. The Bill was divided into five categories:—

Under the First, the attainted were given until the 10th August to surrender and prove innocence.

Under the Second, absentees from Ireland since the 5th November, 1688, were given up to the 1st September, 1689, to surrender and prove innocence.

Under the Third, absentees before 5th November, 1688, were given till the 1st October to surrender and prove innocence.

Under the Fourth, all absentees, being resident in England, were required to signify their loyalty to the Crown by the 1st October, and if proved innocent were to receive a discharge from the Chief Governor of Ireland.

Under the Fifth, absentees by reason of sickness, or nonage, on proving their loyalty before the last day of the first term after their return, were to be acquitted and restored. Meanwhile their estates and personal property were to be vested in the King. A further and drastic clause specially limited the exercise of the King's prerogative of pardon in these attaintures to the 1st November, making still surer the fate of the proscribed. The only speakers who raised their voices against this Bill were the Bishop of Meath in the Upper, and the chivalrous Sir Patrick Sarsfield in the Lower House. Afraid of alienating his Protestant supporters in England, James now attempted to moderate and control the extreme Irish party. Many leading men, including the Earl of Granard, cautiously followed the King. But it was too late, the Bill was passed in both Houses without a dissentient voice, and the King had the mortification of attaching his signature to a measure limiting the Royal Prerogative of Mercy.

To Northerners the chief interest in these 2500 attainders lies in the Ulster names, some 921 in all, comprising seventeen peers of Ireland, two wives of peers, five bishops, six baronets, three deans, thirty-two minor clergy, twelve knights, thirty-one yeomen and 813 officers, landed gentry, merchants and women.

After the Relief Kirke and his troops received a perfect ovation on entering the city. Kirke began well by confirming Mitchelburn in the Governorship, and, while approving the congratulatory address of the citizens to King William and Queen Mary, nominated the ex-Governor the Rev. George Walker to convey it to their Majesties. It was not long, however, before Kirke, by his arrogant and overbearing methods, had alienated the citizens. The guards at the city gates and military posts in the town were all removed and replaced by men of the relief force, while the Ulster regiments, which had borne the brunt of the siege, were formed into new regimental combinations, and many of their officers omitted. So intolerable had he become that, when he left a few months later to join the Duke of Schomberg's camp, there was joy rather than regret, and when in 1691 news came of a cannon ball having taken off his head at Athlone there was no expression of sympathy.

Walker's report of his reception at Court and the promised £10,000 towards the repair of siege damages was some solace to the wounded feelings of the people of Derry. Not only did this grant never materialise, but the long arrears of pay, some £74,000, due to the gallant defenders was never paid, although Cols. Mitchelburn and Hamill paid many visits to London on behalf of the claims of the unfortunate men.[1] Early in 1690 the Corporation had indeed received, by order of the King and Queen, through the Duke of Schomberg, 250 parcels of wheat, four tons of cheese and £500 in cash in lieu of coal for the supply of people in want in the city. Finding themselves neglected by the Government at the end of 1690, some 216 of the leading citizens signed a commission empowering three agents to repair to London and press for compensation for the losses and damages incurred during the siege. The result of this effort was as ineffectual as the claims for £74,000 for arrears of pay. It was well for Derry that she possessed rich and influential friends in the City Companies and Irish Society who stood by her in her troubles.

---

[1] See Sketches in these names.

PART I

INDIVIDUAL SKETCHES

DEFENDERS

INDIVIDUAL SKETCHES

1. **LIEUT.-COL. LUNDY**, Governor of Derry, December 1688 to April 20th, 1689. For particulars of this man's extraordinary behaviour during his governorship of the city, which nearly succeeded in ruining the Protestant cause in Ulster, I would refer the reader to the Introductory Chapter, and for an estimation of his character I would cite the annual burnings to which his effigy is subjected in the maiden city. Whether he was a traitor of the blackest dye, a coward believing the city untenable or merely a weak vacillating man, it is hard to define. There are, however, two circumstances which must be at least considered. Why, when he left Derry in disguise on the night of the 20th April, did he not go to James' camp outside the city instead of flying to Scotland? And why, if he was in treacherous communication with James and his advisers, was his name included in the Dublin Parliament list of attainted in the following May?

He was a Scotch Episcopalian who had obtained a commission as Lieut.-Col. in Lord Mountjoy's Jacobite Regiment. It was Lord Mountjoy who, although a Jacobite and a strong friend of the city, had left him in command of the two companies and made him Governor of Derry.

For some months he lay hid in Scotland, but when William of Orange was firmly established on the throne he was arrested and consigned to the Tower of London. He was eventually tried by court-martial and dismissed the army. He died some years later in obscurity. His signature is attached to the "Declaration of Union."

2. **MAJOR HENRY BAKER**, Governor of Derry, nominated April 19th, 1689, died June 30th, 1689. One of the Protestant officers cashiered by Tyrconnell early in 1688, he took service in one of the regiments raised by the Hillsborough Consult. He took part under Sir John Magill in February 1689 in the abortive attempt to surprise Carrickfergus Castle. He was with Sir Arthur Rawdon at the "Break of Dromore" and through the disastrous retreat to Derry. During these operations he had been distinguished for coolness and gallantry. He signed the "Declaration of Union," and in the critical days of April 10th to April 17th prior to the investment of the city he had been one of the strongest supporters of resolute and decisive action. On the 19th April he was unanimously nominated to the Governorship of the city, vacated by Lundy's flight, while Major Rev. George Walker of Lord Charlemont's Regiment was appointed Assistant Governor. He was also given the command of the remnant of Sir Arthur Rawdon's Dragoons. In all the early sorties of the garrison he was conspicuous in the field, particularly on the 21st April when the French General de Maumont was killed. Walker, Mackenzie and Ash in their authoritative siege accounts pay warm tribute to the admirable manner in which he carried out his responsibility in the field of action

and in the management of city affairs. To the great regret of the garrison he died of
a fever on the 30th June, his place as Governor being filled by Major Mitchelburn,
whose name he had himself proposed on his death-bed.

"Londeriados" commemorates him in the following noble lines:—

> "True to his friend, and faithful to his trust,
> Upright in dealing and to all men just."

Mackenzie in his "Siege" thus records his death: "Governor Baker died greatly
lamented by the garrison, in whose affections his prudent and resolute conduct had
given them a great interest." He was buried in the Cathedral church, and shares with
other illustrious dead in all the monuments erected in honour of the gallant defenders.
Of his family nothing is known, but Graham in a note to his Catalogue conjectures
that he was the grandson of a Capt. Baker serving in the Carrickfergus garrison,
who fell in action the same day as Sir John Chichester fighting the McDonnells at
Altnafracken in 1575. His widow was granted a small annuity in recognition of her
husband's services.

3. **Major Rev. George Walker**, Rector of Donoughmore, Co. Tyrone, Governor
of Derry from April 19th to end of siege. He was also in command during the siege
of the Charlemont Regiment, which, as Major, he had brought into the city before
the investment. His book "Walker's Siege" is one of the standard authorities on the
great defence.

In approaching the history of this great man, for he was undoubtedly great, it is not
my intention to go into his exact position as Governor, or enter into the controversy
of his fairness to all the other actors in the stirring events, as given in his account of
the siege. On these points the readers of Walker, Mackenzie and Ash must judge for
themselves. His monument, Bible in hand, standing on the ramparts of Derry and
the place he holds in the history of the times are sufficient attestation of the part he
played and of the city's appreciation of the services he rendered.

He was of a Nottinghamshire family. His father was inducted into the incumbency
of Baldoney, Co. Derry, in 1630, transferred to Cappagh in 1636 and to Kilmore in
1663, where he died in 1667. The son was born about 1618, and educated in Glasgow.
After taking Holy Orders he was for some years curate of the parish of Dungannon,
until in 1662 he was appointed to the Rectory of Donoughmore, the parish of which
he was still incumbent at the Revolution. When the Revolutionary crisis of 1688 was
approaching and the Ulster counties were organising their several associations for
mutual protection and the defence of Protestantism no one in Co. Tyrone was more
energetic than George Walker. He had much to say in the raising of Lord Charlemont's
Regiment, commanding as their Major the companies in garrison for some months
at Dungannon, which he brought into the city just before the investment. With his

regiment he had taken his full share in the abortive efforts, so frustrated by Lundy's treachery or incapacity, to prevent Hamilton's approach to the city (April 13th to 17th). Such a reputation had he made in the handling of his regiment that on the 19th April after James' repulse at the gates and Lundy's flight, he was appointed Assistant Governor. In the reorganisation of the city forces he was at the same time confirmed in the command of the Charlemont Regiment.

It is unnecessary to say more of Walker's doings in the field than that he was present in all actions. Whatever may have been the case afterwards, or whatever the subsequent recriminations and rivalry, during the siege itself the two great Churches, Episcopal and Presbyterian, worked together in complete harmony. United or alternate services were of almost daily occurrence in the Cathedral, which Protestants of all denominations flocked to attend, regardless of the denomination of the preacher. Of these preachers, Walker himself, and the Rev. John Mackenzie, Presbyterian minister of Derryloran, were the most frequent occupiers of the pulpit, while the latter was the Presbyterian Chaplain to Walker's own regiment. On this happy and desirable relationship "Londeriados" comments as follows:—

> "The church and Kirk did jointly preach and pray
> In St. Columba's church most lovingly,
> Where Doctor Walker to their great content
> Spoke stoutly 'gainst a Popish Government.
> Master Mackenzie preached on the same theme
> And taught the Army to fear God's great name."

On the very afternoon of the relief (Sunday, April 28th), when an excited throng awaited the arrival of the "Mountjoy" and "Phœnix" on the quay, Walker was preaching to a crowded audience in the Cathedral, urging them "to fight the good fight." In the historical picture of "The Relief," standing prominently among the starving spectators on the quay, is depicted the gaunt figure of Governor Walker, waiting for the consummation for which he had so gallantly struggled.

When Kirke made his entry into the city Walker and his colleague Col. Mitchelburn handed over the reins of office. Kirke immediately appointed Mitchelburn to the Governorship, while, at his instigation, Walker was rightly entrusted with the conveyance of an address of congratulation on the relief to the King and Queen in London. This address is signed by some 145 of the principal officers of the garrison and leading citizens, the first signatures being of the two Governors, Walker and Mitchelburn. Walker's progress to and from London was a continuous ovation, and his reception in the capital a public manifestation of admiration for the heroic defence of Derry and a recognition of the service rendered in thereby preserving Ulster for the Protestant Crown. Among other marks of exceptional honour he was received seated by the House of Commons and presented with a strongly-worded resolution of thanks. Entertained at banquets by the Irish Society and City Companies, he was made a D.D. of the Universities of Oxford, Cambridge and Glasgow. His crowning distinction was his reception at Hampton Court by the King and Queen, where, after being graciously received and thanked for the magnificent Defence of Derry, he was presented as a personal gift with £5000. "And do not think, Doctor," said his Majesty, "that I offer you this sum as payment for your services. I assure you that I consider your claims on me as not at all diminished." Although urged by his friends to appear at these functions in military uniform, Walker had the good sense to prefer the quieter garb of his clerical calling, in which he is depicted in his famous portrait by Kneller, the Court Painter of the day.

During his stay in London his time was fully occupied in pressing on the Government the claims of Derry for compensation for war losses. Of the £10,000 originally promised nothing was again heard, nor indeed was any other allowance made. With the Irish Society and City Companies his persistent advocacy must have had much to do with the generous assistance accorded to the city and citizens in their time of stress. He also busied himself in writing and preparing for the press his story of the "Siege," a work which was greedily bought up by the public and ran through many editions.

On his return to Ireland he again took up the clerical duties of Donoughmore parish, but he was not long back before William of Orange's landing at Carrickfergus brought him to Belfast, where he was the leader of the Episcopalian clergy in their presentation of an address of welcome to the King, from whom he had a most gracious reception. It would appear that while in England he had been promised by the King the Bishopric of Derry, as soon as it became vacant (by resignation or death). Ezekiel Hopkins, Bishop of Derry, had fled to London on the shutting of the gates, and had since been officiating in a small London incumbency, but retaining his titular designation. His removal was a delicate matter and consequently Walker's appointment was *in nubibus.* Walker accompanied his sovereign on the march to the Boyne, not improbably invited to do so because of his knowledge of the country. At all events it was only natural that he should desire to be present at the great battle for which he had done so much to prepare the way, and stand again by the side of his old comrades in arms, such as Col. Mitchelburn, who was commanding his old Derry regiment. To the King a few days before the battle news was brought in camp of Hopkins', the Bishop of Derry's, death. Walker was summoned and given the see.

On the fatal day of the Boyne, Walker, who had been watching the advance across the Boyne, saw the Duke of Schomberg fall mortally wounded in the river and rushed down to encourage the men. Struck by a cannon ball, he fell dead. King William, when informed by an attendant of the death of the Bishop at the ford, exclaimed in a fit of irritation: "What took him there?" The King, who himself was ever in the front of battle, should have had more fellow feeling for the fighting prelate! Walker is accused by Macaulay, otherwise so laudatory of his actions, of thrusting himself into military affairs, where he was not wanted. A few days later Dr. Walker's remains (he had not lived to be consecrated Bishop) were laid to rest by his comrades in arms in the church of Castlecaulfield, where they are marked by a fitting monument.

In a letter written by Dr. Tillotson, afterwards Archbishop of Canterbury, to Lady William Russell, widow of the Lord William Russell so cruelly executed by James II., we have, under date September 19, 1689, the following interesting comments on Walker's coming appointment to the Bishopric: "The King besides his great bounty (£5000) to Mr. Walker whose modesty is equal to his merit, has made him Bishop of Londonderry, one of the best Bishoprics in Ireland. It is incredible how much every one is pleased with what His Majesty hath done in this matter, and it is no small joy to see that God directs him so wisely." If Walker had ambitions, and no man is worth much without, his ambitions were all for his country's good. His example as a Protestant clergyman and man of resolute action in times of national crisis will always be remembered by Ulstermen of the same breed and outlook as himself.

Besides the splendid monument in his honour on the ramparts of Derry, his name is perpetuated in the stained glass window unveiled in the Cathedral in 1913 to the memory of the gallant defenders of 1689. Among those who subscribed to this window are Mr. Woolsey Butler, Col. W. F. Story, C.B., Capt. R. H. Story, R.N., Mr. Edwin H. Story, Mr. Edward Doherty. His wife is now known to have been Miss Isabella Berkeley, though as his brother-in-law was Mr. Maxwell, of Finnebrogue, who in fact was married to his sister, it was long thought that her name was Maxwell. The arms of Berkeley are impaled with his on his monument. As a widow she received a small annuity in recognition of her husband's services.

According to Dwyer's "Siege," the Rev. George Walker left four sons, all of whom served in King William's army. Of three of these sons I am able to give the following particulars:—

4. **WILLIAM WALKER**, son of Rev. George Walker, the Governor in Derry during the siege. Both father and son figure among the attainted in James' Dublin Parliament of 1689.

5 and 6. **ROBERT WALKER, GEORGE WALKER**. Both these sons' names figure in the address to King William, a clear indication of their being present during the siege.

7. **COL. JOHN MITCHELBURN**, Governor of Derry from June 30th, 1689, till the end of the siege. A grandson of Sir Richard Mitchelburn of Broadhurst, Sussex. He was a Protestant officer, cashiered by Tyrconnell, and had taken service with the Hillsborough Consult in the Cos. Antrim and Down force, being present with them in the "Break of Dromore," at Coleraine, in the attempt to hold the Bann passage and in the retreat on Derry; in all these actions he particularly distinguished himself by coolness in emer-

gency. Once in the city in the operations preliminary to the investment he was one of the most energetic, not only in the field, but also in the strongest representations to force Lundy into more determined action. After James' repulse at the gates and Lundy's flight he was heart and soul with the citizens in the reorganisation of their forces and preparations for resolute defence. On the 19th April he was appointed to command the remnant of the Skeffington Regiment, which he did with honour and success till the end of the siege. The siege historians Walker, Mackenzie and Ash agree in their eulogies of his conduct as Governor and Colonel of his regiment.

When Major Baker was lying on his death-bed, he was requested by the garrison to nominate his successor in order to avoid any possible friction over the appointment. Baker nominated Mitchelburn, who accordingly became Governor on the latter's death on June 30th. Baker seems to have acted in a most chivalrous spirit, to judge from the following comments in Mackenzie's "Siege." "In May Col. Mitchelburn was suspected by Governor Baker and the garrison. The Governor confined him to his chamber, between whom (the Governor and Mitchelburn) there was some little scuffle when he was apprehended. He continued under the rule of confinement, but was never tried by court martial. What the grounds of suspicion were, it is too tedious to relate."

When the city was relieved and Kirke took over the management of affairs he had enough sense to continue Mitchelburn as civil Governor of the city and in command of his regiment. It is interesting to know that Mitchelburn had served under Kirke at Tangier, and was therefore cognisant of the character of the man with whom he had to deal. Mitchelburn's name comes next to Walker's in the address of congratulation to the King and Queen. This address, as we know, was presented by Walker, who received £5000, while nothing but Royal thanks came to Mitchelburn.

Mitchelburn was present with his old Derry regiment, the Skeffington, at the Boyne, and through the campaign to the surrender of Limerick in 1692. He got little recognition for his services, and was refused the sinecure governorship of Culmore Fort, for which he applied. Returning to Derry after the campaign, he resumed his duties as Alderman of the Corporation, to which he had been elected in 1689. The Irish Society acknowledged his services by a special grant of £100, some slight solatium for his treatment by the Government. He paid frequent visits to London in prosecution of the claims of the soldiers of the garrison for £74,000 arrears of pay. These journeys, involving an expenditure he was unable to meet, landed him in the Fleet Prison, where he spent several weeks. In 1699 he unfortunately fell foul of the Derry Corporation owing to a publication of his in London of the case of the soldiers' claims for arrears of pay which, the Corporation alleged, misrepresented the facts to their detriment. As Mitchelburn refused to retract, apologise or explain, he was disfranchised and expelled from that body. Some years later this passing estrangement ended happily in his restoration to civic honours and a place on the Corporation. In 1704, under the provisions of the "Test Act" of 1703, so very unjust to Presbyterians, who had proved their worth in 1688–9, twenty-two of the very Corporation that had expelled Mitchelburn were themselves driven from office for refusal to conform.

Mitchelburn settled down to a useful life as a citizen. He was particularly ener-getic in his efforts to preserve siege relics. Owing to him the captured flags were given an honoured place in the Cathedral. (In fact he was the beginner of the movement so splendidly carried on to-day by the Very Rev. R. G. S. King, Dean of Derry.) To him also is probably due the annual celebrations on the anniversary of "The Relief."[1] Nicholson, Bishop of Derry in the beginning of the eighteenth century, in his Diary, still extant, mentions Mitchelburn in connection with two such celebrations, thus "Aug. 1, 1718. Col. Mitchelburn's bloddy flag being hoisted the first time on the steeple. In the afternoon great guns." "Aug. 1, 1720. Col. Mitchelburn and Dr. Squire dined with me." Both these entries "Bloddy Flag," firing of big guns, and dinners at the Bishop's Palace indicate an annual celebration on the 1st August.

Mitchelburn died in 1721, and, although the Cathedral would have seemed a most fitting resting place, he was, by his own special desire, buried beside his old friend and comrade in arms Adam Murray in the old churchyard of Glendermot, where the Irish Society have erected a worthy memorial in his honour. In his will of July 21, 1721, the following testament shows that he had not forgotten the city nor its heroic defence: "I, John Mitchelburn of the city of Londonderry being desirous to settle and dispose of what temporal estate it hath pleased Almighty God to bless me with, do make this my last will and testament. I order for maintaining the Flag on the Steeple of Derry fifty Pounds for which I have already given my bond." This red, or bloody flag, emblem of the city's maidenhood, proud record that she had never surrendered to any assault, had flown almost constantly from the Cathedral tower or steeple during the siege. It had been the outward and visible sign to the Fleet, lying in the Lough, of the city's non-surrender. Thanks to Mitchelburn's thoughtful provision the bloody flag still flies on great anniversaries. As long as that flag flies the Defence of Derry will not be forgotten, nor the name of Mitchelburn fade from Ulster memory. His name is commemorated on the base of the massive pillar surmounted by the figure of Walker, on the walls of Derry. Mitchelburn clubs of apprentice boys still march under his banner, and in the Cathedral window unveiled in 1913 in memory of the defenders no one is more entitled to a place of honour than he.[2]

Of his descendants there is no record, the only one subscribing as a connection of his to the Cathedral window being Mr. Solomon F. Darcus of Derry.

---

[1] In regard to date of relief, the facts are as follows: On the 28th July the Boom was broken, and late the same evening the "Mountjoy" and "Phœnix" were at the quay. On the 29th and 30th July the investing army retired to Dublin. The 1st August was the probable date of General Kirke's army entering the city.
[2] To the "Siege and History of Derry," edited by John Hampton and published in 1861, I owe many of the above facts.

8. **Capt. Thomas Ash**, son of John Ash of Corrnerrin, now Ashbrook, Co. Derry. Capt. Thomas was all through the siege, serving with distinction, first as Lieutenant in Col. Parker's Coleraine Regiment, and afterwards as Captain with the latter's successor, Col. Lance. His name is favourably mentioned in Walker's and Mackenzie's accounts. Referring to the second Windmill Hill action "Londeriados" writes in his praise, viz.:—

> "The Irish pressed our trenches on the strand
> Till noble Captain Ash did them withstand."

Capt. Thomas himself kept a diary of the siege, now one of the standard authorities, but this was not published until 1792, when his grand-daughter edited it. It is a valuable chronicle of daily events.

He was one of the witnesses to the Governor's Commission of the 11th July, 1689, appointing Commissioners to treat with the enemy for surrender. He was one of the attainted in James' Dublin Parliament of 1689 and his name is among the signatures to the city's address to King William and Queen Mary after the relief. He served in Col. Mitchelburn's Regiment at the Boyne and through the subsequent campaign, afterwards settling down to the life of a country gentleman at Corrnerrin. He was High Sheriff of County Derry in 1694, and subsequently appointed Lieut.-Col. to the County Regiment of which George Conyngham of Spring Hill was Colonel.

His family, of Saxon extraction, had settled in Ulster at the time of the Plantation, acquiring considerable estates, notably Corrnerrin (Ashbrook) near Derry.

Capt. Thomas Ash figures in the famous picture of the relief of Derry, and he is one of the defenders whose names are commemorated in the memorial window in the Cathedral, unveiled in 1913, to which among others the following of his descendants were subscribers: Col. Beresford-Ash, Capt. and Mrs. Mackey, Mr. H. J. Cooke, Thos. Spoteswode Ash, Mrs. Sidney Lyle, Mrs. John Cooke, Mrs. Tyler.

The present-day representatives of the family through the female line are (1) the Beresford-Ashs of Ashbrook, Co. Derry, who are still in possession of the original family place, (2) Mrs. Sidney Lyle, Derganagh, Ballycastle, Co. Antrim, daughter and heiress of the late Mr. Thomas Ash, Co. Derry.

9. **Henry Ash**, a brother of the above, was another of the city's gallant defenders, serving all through the siege. He was one of the few Protestant burgesses of the city appointed under Tyrconnell's new charter of 1688. He was Mayor of Derry 1696, 1705 and 1709.

10. **Thomas Ash**, of Ashfield, Co. Cavan, was attainted in James II.'s Dublin Parliament, 1689. What family he belonged to I have not been able to trace.

11. **Dr. Joseph Aicken**, author of the poem "Londeriados." The poem was written and published in Dublin by "Joseph Aicken" in 1699. It is dedicated "To the

Worshipful the Mayor, to the Honourable Robert Rochfort Esq., Attorney-General and Speaker of the honourable House of Commons, the Recorder, and to the Aldermen, Burgesses and Freemen of the City of Londonderry." In his dedicatory epistle the author states: "I have seen many narratives of the siege[1] but all far short of the thing; and I may boldly aver that no material passage is wanting in this, having had my information from good hands, besides the advantage of the printed narratives.

I have styled Col. Adam Murray hero and general, which I am sure no man, who knew the particular merits in the siege, will think unjust or unsuitable, especially those who have read the printed narratives." Now almost at the end of the poem itself, when the author was recounting how his hero Murray was severely wounded in the last sortie of the garrison (July 25th, 1689) there are the lines:—

> "His wound was great, but by the mighty skill
> Of Dr. Aicken, and Hermann, he grew well
> In seven weeks time. This was our last sally."

All this indicates that Joseph Aicken, the author, was the Dr. Aicken of the poem, and that "the information from good hands" was derived from his own siege experience. Be that as it may, to the author we owe much, not only for the supply of incidents and descriptions of battles Homeric in their style, but also for the mention of names and details otherwise lost. The verse is certainly not of the highest order, but what is wanting in polish is amply atoned for in vigour and incident. In the Sketches I make frequent use of quotations from this graphic source marked "Londeriados."

Aicken's poem was for years lost to the world, until in 1790 a mutilated copy was discovered in an old house in Armagh, believed to have been the residence of Capt. John Coghran, one of the defenders of Derry.[2] A few years later a perfect copy of the 1699 edition was discovered.[3] This work (Aicken's) has the additional merit of giving names of generals and officers of the investing force, all of whom can be identified in D'Alton's King James' Army List or in the Jacobite accounts of the campaign. "Londeriados" is a valuable contribution to Ulster history, and priceless to the descendants of those who took part in the great struggle.

12. **Rev. John Mackenzie,** Presbyterian minister of Derryloran (Cookstown). He was all through the siege of Derry in the dual capacity of fighter and Presbyterian Chaplain to Governor Walker's Charlemont Regiment. In 1690 he published his "History of the Siege," which, with Walker's, are the standard authorities. Although differing in slight detail they are in complete accord in all essentials. How these two representatives of two great Churches were the most frequent occupiers of the

---

[1] Presumably Mackenzie's "Siege," published 1690, and Walker's "Siege," published 1699.
[2] See Sketch under his name.
[3] Hampton's "Siege and History of Derry," p. 475.

Cathedral pulpit during the siege is told under Walker,[1] where the well-known lines from "Londeriados" are quoted. Referring to preaching in the Cathedral "Londeriados" has a further allusion:—

> "Though all the houses in the town were slap'd
>   By dreadful bombs, Columba's church escap'd,
>   Wherein great store of ammunition lay
>   And where the Church, and Kirk did jointly pray.
>   In all Columba's church no damage's found
>   Yet the bombs tore the dead out of the ground."

The effectiveness of Mackenzie's services, and the confidence of the garrison in him, are proved by his being one of the six commissioners appointed to treat for surrender on the 12th July with a like number of the enemy. The negotiations ended in nothing, but the names of the Derry six are interesting, viz. Col. Hugh Hamill, Col. Thomas Lance, Capt. Robert White, Capt. William Dobbin, Mathew Cocken, Rev. John Mackenzie.

Mackenzie died in Cookstown in 1696 in his forty-ninth year.[2] The Rev. John Mackenzie's name is among the defenders commemorated in the Derry Cathedral window unveiled in 1913, to which his descendant Miss Caroline Mackenzie is a subscriber.

13. **The Rev. James Gordon**, Presbyterian minister of Glendermot, stands out so conspicuously in the shutting of the gates on December 8th, in the preparations for defence, and in the relief that he is worthy of more than passing notice among the defenders.

Appointed to the Ministry of Glendermot, just outside the city boundaries, in 1680, he had for years been closely interested in its public affairs. For his aiding and abetting of the apprentice boys on "the closing of the gates" on the 8th December, see Introductory Chapter. On the following day Mackenzie (p. 165) gives this mention of a further service rendered by the reverend gentleman: "Having appeared on a hill near the city with some 20 or 30 horse, in conjunction with some 50 or 60 boys led by George Cook, a butcher of the town, so frightened Lord Antrim's Regiment (although having no design of disturbing them) that their retreat was precipitated to Coleraine." Before the investment of the city Mr. Gordon retired to Greenock; but if we can credit this story,[3] and there seems no reason to doubt it, Mr. Gordon's interest in the fate of the city brought him back to Lough Foyle, where Kirke's fleet was lying inactive (July 1689). With the help of an old friend, Capt. Browning of the "Mountjoy," as determined as himself for prompt action, Gordon obtained an interview with Kirke.

---

[1] See No. 3, Part I.
[2] Reid's "History of the Presbyterian Church."
[3] As told in Reid's "History of the Presbyterian Church," pp. 386–7.

The interview began by Gordon saying that he had heard of the General's threat to hang him at the yard-arm for interference. To which Kirke replied by accusing the minister of using opprobrious language in calling them cowards for not attempting the impossible. Gordon retorted that it was possible. "Aye," said Kirke, "but who will venture?" "I will venture for one," replied Gordon, and Capt. Browning said he would venture, and another (evidently Capt. Douglas of the "Phœnix"). The result, according to this account, was the subsequent attack, breaking of the Boom and relief of the city, Gordon being detained meantime as a hostage on the General's ship.

The gist of the above tale was conveyed by Gordon to some members of the Cardross congregation (to which he was appointed minister in 1692), from whom it was reported to a Mr. Wallace, his successor, and so to the historian Woodrow, who chronicles it. We do not hear of Gordon again in Ulster.

14. **Col.** or **Capt. John Chichester**, of Dungannon, mentioned in "Londeriados":—

> "From Dungannon brave Chichester was sent
> With Caulfield the Lord Charlemont's regiment."

This Chichester was the second son of Col. John Chichester of Dungannon, brother of the first Earl of Donegall. His branch of the family were the owners of the large Dungannon estates granted at the Plantation. He took part in all the operations round Derry preliminary to the investment. While Lundy was plotting the surrender of the city and was summoning to his council of war only those officers in his secret confidence, Chichester was one of those refused admittance.[1] A few days later, April 18th, when the relieving force, believing in Lundy's assertion that the city was untenable, departed for England, Chichester was one of many officers of the garrison availing himself of the offer of a free passage in the Fleet.

In the Treasury Records there is still to be seen a petition addressed by him to King William (May 1689) in which he complains of Lundy's refusal to admit him to the council of war, of his watch and pistols being taken from him by the captain of H.M. frigate in which he had sailed, as payment for his passage, and asks for military employment in the coming campaign in Ireland.[2] The petition is endorsed by King William "will satisfy him as occasion requires." As his death is recorded in the same year in the Duke of Schomberg's camp near Dundalk, it is evident that he got the desired employment. The history of the Chichester family in Ulster is most interesting. Among the officers who came over in 1574 with the Earl of Essex to push their fortunes in Ulster were three brother Chichesters of the ancient Devonshire house of that name, viz., in seniority, (1) Arthur, (2) John and (3) Edward. All won distinction serving as constables and governors of Carrickfergus Castle, while filling other high

[1] Harris.
[2] That of the Boyne.

posts. John, who had been knighted, lost his life in a fight with the Macdonnells of the Glens at Attnafracken near Redhall in 1597. But it was Arthur who laid the foundations of the afterwards great house of Donegall. This extraordinary man had a remarkable career. He had served in the army of France, being knighted by Henry of Navarre on the field of battle. He had been a naval captain under Sir Francis Drake in the destruction of the Armada, and had been with the Fleet in the Cadiz venture. He had played his part in the long Tyrone war, ending in the submission of the Earl of Tyrone at Mellifont in 1603. In 1604 he had been appointed Lord Deputy of Ireland and it was during his ten years of office that he was primarily responsible for carrying into effect the Ulster Plantation of Anglo-Scot settlers on the escheated territories of the fugitive earls of Tyrone and Tyrconnell. Out of the escheated lands of the Earl of Tyrone, he secured large estates for himself round Dungannon. Out of the O'Neills of Clannaboy's territories he became owner of a large area, now the Belfast estate of the family, and out of Sir Cahir O'Dogherty's confiscations he secured the Barony of Innishowen in Co. Donegal which gave the family their territorial title of Earl and eventually Marquess of Donegall. He had been created in 1612 Baron Chichester of Carrickfergus and Admiral of Lough Neagh. On relinquishing the Lord Deputyship in 1614 he was for many years Lord High Treasurer of Ireland before settling down at the magnificent mansion of Joymount, Carrickfergus, which he had himself erected. Dying unmarried in 1634 he was buried in the old church of St. Nicholas, Carrickfergus, his estates devolving under his will on his surviving brother Edward, who was created in 1637 Baron and Viscount Chichester of Carrickfergus. This Viscount Chichester died in 1647, leaving two sons:—

(1) Arthur, succeeding as 2nd Viscount, raised to the Earldom of Donegall in 1647. He died without male issue in 1674, when the earldom passed to his nephew Arthur, the eldest son of

(2) John of Dungannon. The second son of this John of Dungannon was Col. John Chichester, the subject of this sketch, from whom descend in direct male line the Chichester-O'Neills of Shane's Castle, now represented by Shane, 3rd Baron O'Neill.

15. **The 2nd Earl of Donegall** figures among the lists of attainders in James II.'s Dublin Parliament in 1689, as also

16. **The Countess of Donegall**, or more properly Letitia, the Dowager of the first Earl (see below). This Dowager Countess had married as second husband

17. **Sir William Franklin, Bart.**, of Moverne, Bedfordshire, who, with his wife, appears to have represented the interests of the Donegall family in Co. Antrim during the stirring times of the Revolution. It was this Franklin who raised and commanded

a regiment of the Chichester tenantry, and who led them at the "Break of Dromore" and through the retreat on Derry. He and his Countess have no further mention than in the list of attainted in James' Dublin Parliament of 1689, where he is described as Sir William Franklin, Bart., of Belfast, Co. Antrim. When King William passed through Belfast on his way to the Boyne, he was lodged by special orders from the Duke of Schomberg in the Chichester Castle of Belfast, but there was no Chichester or Franklin to do His Majesty honour.

18. **Sir William Stewart, 3rd Bart.**, of Ramelton, Co. Donegal, Viscount Mountjoy, by creation of 1685. His grandfather Sir William Stewart, Bart. (creation 1623), of the same stock as the royal house of Scotland, had been the original grantee of the large Ramelton estate at the time of the Plantation. His son, Sir Alexander, 2nd Bart., had distinguished himself on the Royal side during the civil war, losing his life in Cromwell's overwhelming victory at Dunbar in 1650. His son, Sir William, the 3rd Bart., born a few weeks after his father's death, was raised to the peerage in 1685 as Viscount Mountjoy, and about the same time given command of a regiment and made Master of the Ordnance. Though a Protestant, and closely bound by hereditary friendship with the Protestant colonists in Co. Donegal and citizens of Derry, his loyalty was so well known that Tyrconnell the Viceroy allowed him to retain his regiment.

A reference to the Introductory Chapter will show how Mountjoy, in his desire to serve Derry in her misfortunes after "the shutting of the gates," landed himself for three years in the Bastille, and brought about his outlawry. After his long sojourn in the Bastille, in 1692 he was exchanged for General Richard Hamilton, the Jacobite, who had been a prisoner in England since the Boyne. Such treatment forced him to change his views and on his release he joined King William's army in Flanders as a volunteer, falling at the battle of Steinkirk a few months later. Lord Mountjoy left two sons, both of whom were serving in the Derry defence, probably having entered the city as officers of the two companies of the Mountjoy regiment commanded by Lundy, viz.:—

19. **William Stewart**, Lord Mountjoy's eldest son, of whom "Londeriados" has the following mention:—

> "… young Lord Mountjoy's Dragoons
> Advanced next, raised in his Father's towns,
> For near to Newtown Stewart in Tyrone
> The neighb'ring gentlemen were all his own.
> The false Lundy under Dunbarton bred
> His Father's regiment thither led."

William was one of the officers of the garrison signing the "Declaration of Union" April 10th, 1689, and his signature is attached to the city's address to King William after the relief. His name also figures among the attainders in James II.'s Dublin Parliament 1689. He succeeded as 2nd Viscount after his father's death at Steinkirk in 1692.

20. **MAJOR ALEXANDER STEWART**, Lord Mountjoy's second son. Serving all through the siege, he was several times mentioned[1] for conspicuous gallantry in sorties. He was one of the witnesses, July 11th, 1689, to the appointment of the garrison's six commissioners to treat for surrender with the enemy. His name was also on the list of the attainted in James II.'s Dublin Parliament, 1689.

When the direct descendants of the 1st Viscount died out with the death of the 3rd Viscount, who had been created Earl of Blessington, the title became extinct, but the Baronetcy created in 1623 devolved on the line of Thomas Stewart, the second son of Sir William, 1st Baronet of Ramelton. This line is represented to-day by the 11th Baronet, Sir Henry Jocelyn Urquhart Stewart, Fort Stewart, Co. Donegal.

21. **THE RIGHT REV. EZEKIEL HOPKINS**, Bishop of Derry 1685–1690. In the troublous scenes following on "the shutting of the gates," Dec. 8th, 1688,[2] rather than burden his conscience by participation in any action infringing on the Divine right of Kings, the Bishop fled to Raphoe, and thence a few days later to London, where, although retaining his episcopal title, he officiated regularly in a small church until his death in 1690. His successor in the bishopric was, as we know, the famous Governor of Derry, Rev. George Walker, who did not live to be consecrated, his place being filled by a noted divine, the Rev. William King, D.D., author of the standard work "The State of the Protestants in Ireland under King James' Government."

Bishop Hopkins, in his short occupancy of the see, is said to have spent considerable sums in repairing and beautifying the Cathedral. One of his daughters married in 1693 Col. Thomas Stewart, an ancestor of the present Baronet of Fort Stewart.

22. **WILLIAM CAULFEILD, 2ND VISCOUNT CHARLEMONT**, and 6th Baron Charlemont of Castlecaulfeild. The first of the family in Ulster was Sir Tobias Caulfeild, so greatly distinguished in the long Elizabethan struggle against Hugh, Earl of Tyrone. At the Plantation he received grants of large estates round Castlecaulfield in the counties Armagh and Tyrone. He was Governor of Charlemont Fort on the Blackwater, and created Baron Charlemont in 1620. Dying in 1627 without issue, he was succeeded under special remainder, in title and estate and also in the Governorship of Charlemont Fort, by a nephew, the 2nd Baron.

At the beginning of the 1641 rebellion Charlemont Fort was surprised and taken by Sir Phelim O'Neill, all the occupants, including Lord Charlemont, being put to the sword. He was succeeded by his brother Robert as 3rd Baron, and a few years later by yet another brother, William, as 4th Baron. This 4th Baron was created a

---

[1] Mackenzie's "Siege."
[2] See Introductory Chapter.

Viscount in 1665 and on his death was succeeded by his son William (above) as 5th Baron and 2nd Viscount.

Like all the other great Ulster Protestant landowners in their several counties and districts he was particularly energetic in preparing, by organisation and levying of men, to meet the threatened danger. Chiefly at his instance, and from among his tenantry, the Charlemont Regiment was raised, with headquarters at Dungannon. We all know how a few days before the investment Walker, acting under Lundy's orders, marched the regiment to Derry, and how he commanded it there during the siege. This regiment, after serving with distinction at the Boyne and through the subsequent campaign, had the honour of being incorporated in the Royal Army, where it bore an honoured name. General Hamilton's march to the investment of Derry was so overwhelming in its success that all the county landlords not already in Enniskillen or Derry were forced to seek safety across the Channel. The exodus at this time was marked.

"Londeriados" has the following reference to the Charlemont Regiment in the gathering for the protection of the city: "With Caulfeild, the Lord Charlemont's Regiment." Whether this means Lord Charlemont, or one of his cousins, Capt. Thomas Caulfeild, as that great authority Graham suggests in "The Catalogue," in "Ireland Preserved," is not stated. Lord Charlemont was among the attainted in James II.'s Dublin Parliament of 1689.

The Charlemont family have another siege connection through the marriage in 1728 of Alice, daughter and co-heiress of John Houston, of Craigs, Co. Antrim, and Castlestewart, Co. Tyrone, with the Hon. and Rev. Charles Caulfeild, second son of the 2nd Viscount Charlemont, through whose line the title descends. The present Countess of Ranfurly, only daughter and heiress of the 7th Viscount Charlemont, has the same descent. The present and 8th Viscount Charlemont, Drumcairn, Co. Tyrone, the Minister of Education for Northern Ireland, is the present representative of this old family.

23. **Capt. Thomas Caulfeild**, the seventh son of 2nd Viscount Charlemont, an officer in the Charlemont Regiment, who served with it in the operations preliminary to the investment of Derry.

24. **Sir John Skeffington, 2nd Viscount Massereene** of Lough Neagh and of Antrim Castle, Vice-Admiral of Lough Neagh.

The first of the name in Ireland was Sir William Skeffington, who, coming over to Dublin in 1539 as an official of the Crown, rose subsequently to the Lord Deputyship of Ireland. His grandson, the family having meanwhile acquired considerable estate in Co. Antrim, was created a Baronet by Charles I. His son, Sir Richard Skeffington, 2nd Baronet, died in 1647, leaving a son, Sir John Skeffington, 3rd Baronet, who married the only daughter and heiress of Sir John Clotworthy, Bart., of Antrim Castle, was created in 1660 for great services rendered at the restoration of Charles II. Viscount

Massereene, of Lough Neagh, and Vice-Admiral of Lough Neagh. On the 1st Viscount's death in 1665, his son-in-law, Sir John Skeffington, succeeded, under special remainder of the patent, as 2nd Viscount. The union of two such family interests and large estates made him one of the most influential Protestant noblemen in the county, if not in Ulster, at the time of the 1688 revolution. In the formation of County Associations for mutual defence and protection of Protestant interests, in the raising of regiments and in the creation of a central consultative committee at Hillsborough, no one showed greater energy than Lord Massereene. He was the prime mover in Co. Antrim and in preparing the manifesto, signed by twenty-three noblemen and gentry, to their fellow Protestants. He and his son, Col. Clotworthy, were responsible for the raising of the Skeffington Regiment, which afterwards played such a part in the siege. In spite of all their efforts, Hamilton with Tyrconnell's army from Dublin on his way to Derry found them unready. The "Break of Dromore" and the pursuit through the length of Co. Antrim over the Bann to the walls of Derry were the result. The Skeffington Regiment was present in these disastrous happenings, which included the burning of Antrim Castle. Owing to the treachery of a servant some £3000 worth of silver buried for safety fell into the hands of the enemy. Lord Massereene was some days in the city of Derry, engaged with his regiment in the operations preliminary to the investment. When, however, owing to Lundy's misrepresentations, the relieving Fleet sailed away, believing the city untenable, Lord Massereene, like so many others similarly situated, considering the conditions hopeless, took advantage of the offer of a free passage in H.M. ships. Lord Massereene, it must be remembered, was one of the Ulster leaders exempted from pardon in Tyrconnell's March proclamation, and with his son, before leaving Derry, had signed "The Declaration of Union." They were both also on the list of attainted in James' Dublin Parliament of 1689.

"Londeriados" has the following lines referring to father and son at Derry:—

> "Next unto these brave Skeffington's regiment
> Into camp in gallant order went,"

while Graham in "The Catalogue" in "Ireland Preserved," thus refers:—

> "Here too was brave Lord Massereene
> In William's army serving."

Before leaving for England Lord Massereene had contributed, early in April, a considerable sum to the city for defence preparations.[1]

The list of the original officers of the Skeffington Regiment as raised by Lord Massereene is so interesting that I give it in full, viz.:—

---

[1] Mackenzie.

Col.	Viscount Massereene	Antrim Castle.
Lieut.-Col.	Clotworthy Skeffington	Antrim Castle.
,,	John Houston	Craigs, Co. Antrim.
Capt.	John Dobbin	Drumsergh, Co. Antrim.
,,	John Hamilton	Cloughmills, Co. Antrim.
,,	William Shaw	The Bush, Co. Antrim.
,,	Humphrey Bell	
,,	Henry McCullagh	Antrim, Co. Antrim.
,,	John Anderson	
,,	Edmund Rice	
,,	William Erwin	
,,	John Bickerstaff	Rosegift, Co. Antrim.
,,	Richard Bickerstaff	Rosegift, Co. Antrim.
,,	Thomas Tracey	
Lieut.	Goburn	
,,	Sam. Archer	
,,	Andrew Dunbar	
,,	Richard Kane	Co. Antrim.
,,	John Cunningham	
,,	Joshua Campbell	
,,	Sam. Ferguson	
,,	John McCullagh	Co. Antrim
,,	Francis Boyd	
,,	William Shaw	The Bush, Co. Antrim.
Ensign	Anthony Sherbourne	
,,	Samuel Shellcross	
,,	Richard Jackson	
,,	James Morris	
,,	James Royde	
,,	John Wilson	
,,	John White	
,,	William McCullagh	Antrim, Co. Antrim.
,,	Joseph Wilson	
,,	John Brady	
,,	John Clements	Carrickfergus, Co. Antrim.
,,	Forest Shortridge	
Adjutant	William Crofts	
Chaplain	Rev. John Knox	
Q.-M.	John Hughes	
Surgeon	Thomas Adair	

Mate   John Thompson[1]

On the reorganisation of the regiment, April 19th, after Lord Massereene's departure, Major John Mitchelburn was given the command and the following officers were appointed to fill vacancies, viz.:

Capt.	James McCormack	Lisburn, Co. Antrim.
„	David Chalmers	
„	Charles Shaw	The Bush, Co. Antrim.
„	Michael Cunningham	
Lieut.	William Gunter	
„	Oliver Ancketell	
„	Edward Ruckne	
„	William Pollok	
Ensign	George Ryford	
„	Chas. Johnstone	
„	John Ruiley	
„	John Young	

The regiment took a prominent part under Mitchelburn all through the siege, at the Boyne and through the subsequent campaign down to the fall of Limerick. Many of these officers are subjects of individual sketches.

In the annals of the siege it is stated that 60 tons of salmon, the property of Lord Massereene, lying for shipment on the quay had been seized by the authorities and used for provisioning the city. An allusion to this drew forth the most interesting explanation from the present Lord Massereene, verified by documents which he kindly produced. It would appear that Lord Massereene had been, prior to the investment, the lessee of the Irish Society's fishery on the Bann at Coleraine and on the Foyle at Culmore and that at the commencement of the siege large parcels of salmon from these fisheries, cured and ready for shipment, were lying in Derry. These fish were worth about £15 per ton. After the relief his Lordship made a claim on the Government for compensation, and in substantiation of his claim was able to submit the following certificate dated March 1691 from officers serving in the Defence of Derry:—

> "That the parcels of salmon 'referred to' during the siege were of great use and benefit for the provision and subsistence both of officers and soldiers of the garrison, during the time the said city was kept, and with much hardship and difficulty defended against the enemy."

The following are the signatures: Col. John Mitchelburn, Governor during the siege, Cols. Richard Crofton, Adam Murray, Henry Monro, William Campbell and

[1] See Hampton's "Siege of Derry," p. 468.

Thomas Blair; Majors John Dobbin, Ant. Schomberg and George Holmes; Capts. James Harrison, Adam Downing, Thomas Lance, Thomas Dickson, Alfred Esmond, Henry Lane, John Fleming, Abraham Hillhouse, Alexander Sanderson, Benjamin Wilkins, William Taylor and Michael Holmes, and Lieuts. Henry Peirce, Robert Lowther,

Allan Stephenson, John Henderson, James Tracey, Robert Walker, Oliver Aplin, Patrick Doran, Francis Buller, John Hunter, Charles Aubery, James Gardiner, Sam. Ervine and James Barr.

On the presentation of his claim, backed by the above certificate, at Whitehall, 1692, Lord Massereene was paid £900 by order of the King.

In 1692 Lord Massereene, as a mark of His Majesty's appreciation of his loyal services, was appointed Governor of the City and County of Londonderry and of the town of Coleraine. This commission, still in the family archives, bears the signature of Lord Sydney, Lord-Lieutenant of Ireland. On the back of this there is a curious endorsement of Lord Sydney's dated June 30th, 1692, ordering the keeper of the Phœnix Park to "kill and give Lord Massereene one fat buck, or if not in season a brace of does."

Lord Massereene died in 1695 and was succeeded by his son.

25. Col. Clotworthy Skeffington, 3rd Viscount Massereene. He was Lieut.-Col. of his father's Skeffington Regiment, with which he took part in all operations from the "Break of Dromore" to the investment of Derry. His experiences were similar to those of his father.[1]

The present representative of this old family is Algernon William John Clotworthy, 12th Viscount Massereene, and Viscount Ferrard, H.M.L. Co. Antrim, of Antrim Castle. For several generations the head of the family had enjoyed the higher honours of an earldom. The fourth and last Earl died in 1816, leaving an only daughter, Lady Harriet Skeffington, who succeeded to the Viscountcy. She married Viscount Ferrard, son and heir of the last Speaker of the Irish House of Commons, who in 1821 was created a Baron of the United Kingdom, under the title of Baron Oriel, in virtue of which the present Viscount has a seat in the House of Lords. The Speaker's wife was at the same date created, in her own right, Viscountess Ferrard, which has descended to her son. Skeffington was assumed as the family name. From this union descend the double Viscountcy of Massereene and Ferrard, borne by the head of the house. Everyone deplores with Lord and Lady Massereene the second burning of their ancient castle and the loss of such priceless and historic relics as the Speaker's chair of the Irish House of Commons.

26. Hugh Montgomery, 2nd Earl of Mount Alexander, Mount Alexander, Co. Down. He was the representative in 1688 of the great Montgomery Plantation

---

[1] For further particulars, see Introductory Chapter.

family with enormous estates and influence. His great-grandfather Sir Hugh, 6th Laird of Braidstane, N.B., had in conjunction with Hamilton (afterwards Viscount Clandeboye) secured large grants from the Crown, sharing under the tripartite treaty with Conn O'Neill of Castlereagh in his vast territory.[1] Sir Hugh was subsequently created Viscount Montgomery of the Ards, and his grandson, the 3rd Viscount, raised to the Earldom of Mountalexander, a title taken from the surname of his wife, a daughter of the Earl of Stirling, whose name he had already given to the great house he had erected near Comber.

What Lord Massereene did in Antrim, Lord Mountalexander did in Co. Down in the way of raising local levies and in preparations to meet Tyrconnell's threatened advance from Dublin. A reference to the Introductory Chapter will tell of the quick sequence of unpleasant events after Richard Hamilton's arrival at Newry, the "Break of Dromore," retreat to Derry, and the flight of so many influential leaders across the Channel. How far Lord Mountalexander was with his men is not clear, but "Londeriados," in his summary of the Protestant muster at Derry, seems to indicate his presence in the undernoted lines:—

> "Thither my Lord Mount Alexander's horse
> And foot advance to join the British force.
> Both horse and foot, the relics of Dromore
> Where they the shock of the Irish army bore
> For he Nor East a general's post obtained
> When at Dromore, the Irish army gained
> The Victory …"

Lord Mountalexander's name figures in the list of attainted in James II.'s Dublin Parliament of 1689. The Earl afterwards held several good appointments under the Crown as a reward for his services during the revolution. Still, on his death, in 1716, he left the property in a seriously crippled condition, and although Mountalexander was in his possession, the Newtown and Comber estates had been sold to Sir Robert Colville of Galgorm Castle for £10,000 and £3000 respectively.

On the death of the 5th Earl of Mountalexander without issue in 1756 the titles became extinct and the remnant of the great property was left to his widowed countess, *née* Mary Angelique de la Cherois, through whom it passed to the old Huguenot family of De la Cherois, of The Manor House, Donaghadee. Scarcely a vestige is to-day to be seen of the great Mansion House of Mount Alexander.

---

[1] See "Montgomery Manuscripts" for full account of this transaction, how they aided Conn in escaping from Carrickfergus Castle, obtained his pardon from King James on conditions, how Sir Hugh's brother, the Rev. George Montgomery, Dean of Norwich and *persona grata* at Court, was their instrumental agent, and how for his pains he was made Bishop of Derry and Clogher and afterwards translated to Meath.

27. **HENRY VINCENT BLAYNEY, 5TH BARON BLAYNEY,** of Castle Blayney, Co. Monaghan.

The first of the name in Ulster had received large grants in Co. Monaghan, including Castle Blayney, at the time of the Plantation. He was created Baron Blayney a few years later.

When the revolution of 1688 was pending the 5th Baron, as the owner of large estates, was one of the most influential landowners of the Province. He was a strong supporter of the Protestant cause, throwing all his energies into the county efforts to prepare resistance to the threatened campaign from Dublin. Lord Blayney, as an old army officer, had been appointed to command the Protestant levies of Co. Monaghan and adjacent districts. He made Armagh his headquarters, whence he kept himself in close communication with Lundy in Derry, the Enniskillen men and the Consult of Hillsborough. He had some 1000 foot and a few hundred horse at Armagh in the spring of 1689 when news was brought of the "Break of Dromore" and Sir Arthur Rawdon's retreat on Coleraine, and at the same time he received orders from Lundy to concentrate on Derry. The difficulty was much increased by the fact that some 3000 Jacobite troops, under Col. Gordon O'Neill, were holding Charlemont Fort. By quick and strategic movement, Lord Blayney succeeded in making his way, with only a slight skirmish, to Toome, where he crossed the Bann into Co. Antrim, and joined Sir Arthur Rawdon on his way to Coleraine. How Col. Richard Hamilton was repulsed before that town, but forced the passage of the Bann, pursuing the Protestants under Rawdon to the walls of Derry, is told in the Introductory Chapter. No one was more active than Lord Blayney in the actions taken by the garrison to prevent Hamilton's investment of the city, but Lundy frustrated all success. Finally, when Lundy, by his declaration that the city was untenable, had induced the relieving Fleet to retire, Lord Blayney was among the many officers who, believing the position hopeless, left with the Fleet for England.

Nothing shows Lord Blayney's importance among the Ulster Protestant leaders more than the fact that he is one of those exempted by name from all hope of pardon in Tyrconnell's Proclamation of March 1689. Lord Blayney was a signer, April 10th, 1689, of the famous "Declaration of Union," and his name is on the list of the attainted in James' Dublin Parliament, 1689.

Referring to the gathering of the Protestant forces at Derry "Londeriados" has the following lines in regard to the choice of leaders:—

> "There Baron Blayney a brave regiment led
>   Which near Armagh, and Blackwater were bred."

and again:—

> "They chose Lundy their general, and did grace
>   The brave Lord Blayney with the second place
>   Next him, Sir Arthur Rawdon, these be they."

The campaign had broken down Lord Blayney's health; he died in England within a short time. After the death of the 12th Baron in 1874 the title became extinct, but a good deal of the property passed by purchase to Lord Francis Hope.

28. **Lord Folliott, 3rd Baron of Ballyshannon.** His grandfather Sir Henry Folliott, the first of the name in Ulster, had acquired by purchase in the early Plantation years from the original grantee the large Ballyshannon estate. The purchase with full manorial rights had been confirmed by the Crown, and Sir Henry created Baron Folliott in 1619. The Folliotts were in an isolated position on the western borders of the Atlantic, but the marriage of the daughter of the 1st Lord Folliott with John King of Boyle Abbey, Co. Roscommon,[1] had brought these two influential Protestant families into the closest relationship.

At the beginning of the revolution Lord Kingston with his regiment of some 500 or 600 horse was holding the Ballyshannon district, supported by his cousin, the 3rd Lord Folliott, with rough levies of foot. After Hamilton's arrival before Derry, with King James in camp before the gates, all Protestant resistance was reduced to the actual defenders within the city and the men of Enniskillen. Where possible there was immediate flight to England as in the case of Lord Folliott.[2]

Lord Folliott was among the attainted in James II.'s Dublin Parliament of 1689.

29. **Capt. John Folliott**, of Ballyshannon, Co. Donegal, an officer serving in Lord Kingston's horse.

30. **Thomas Folliott**, of Ballyshannon, Co. Donegal.

31. **Francis Folliott**, of Ballyshannon, Co. Donegal. His name also figures in the Enniskillen address to King William after the relief. The title is long extinct.

32. **Robert King, 2nd Baron Kingston**, of Boyle Abbey, Co. Roscommon. The first of the family in Ireland was John King, who occupied several important posts and received large grants of land, including Boyle Abbey, during Queen Elizabeth's reign. His son Robert had married a daughter of the 1st Lord Folliott of Ballyshannon. Their son John, by his marriage with a daughter of Fitzgibbon, "the White Knight," had become the owner of Mitchelstown Castle and territory in Co. Cork. This John for services rendered at the Restoration was created, in 1660, Baron Kingston. He died in 1676, being succeeded by his son Robert, the subject of this sketch, as second Baron.

Most of his interests seem to have been outside Ulster, but owing probably to his Folliott relationship he threw himself heart and soul into the Protestant cause. He was in command of some 600 horse operating in the district between Sligo and Ballyshannon. When Hamilton's rapid march through Down and Antrim had made

---

[1] Afterwards Baron Kingston.
[2] See Introductory Chapter, and No. 32, Lord Kingston.

the Protestant position untenable except in a walled town, Lord Kingston was ordered by Lundy, the Governor, to retire on Derry. In attempting to do this he found himself cut off by Hamilton's advancing army. Seeing no possible escape, he was obliged on 14th April, 1689, to disband his force, instructing every man to shift as best he could for himself. Lord Kingston with several of his officers was lucky enough to find a ship sailing for England from Killibegs, Co. Donegal. Once in England and repairing to Court, he was able to give the King exact information regarding the Ulster position. The following year he landed with William at Carrickfergus, and was present at the Boyne and subsequent campaign. He had been exempted from all hope of pardon in Tyrconnell's proclamation of March 1689, and was among the attainted in James' Dublin Parliament of May 1689. On his death in 1699 he was succeeded by his brother,

33. **JOHN KING, 3RD BARON KINGSTON**, of Boyle Abbey. This third Baron had married the daughter of Florence O'Kane, of the ancient family of Keenaght, Limavady, in 1683, had become a Roman Catholic and with his wife's family espoused the Jacobite side. He was present with James at the Boyne, afterwards accompanying him to France. After Limerick he was attainted with confiscation of estates; he died in 1727. The attainder and confiscation were subsequently reversed, and he was succeeded by his son James, the fourth and last Baron Kingston, on whose death in 1761 the title became extinct.

The present representative of the family is Sir Henry Edwyn King-Tenison, 9th Earl of Kingston, Kilronan Castle, Co. Roscommon, who is descended in the female line from Robert, a younger brother of John, 1st Baron Kingston. The original Barony having become extinct in 1761, the later creations were as follows: Baron 1764, Viscount 1766, Earl 1766. The following were the officers of Lord Kingston's Regiment obliged "to shift for themselves" April 14th, 1689, when he disbanded his men. Several of the names figure later in individual sketches. Majors Owen Vaughan and Thomas Hart, Capts. Hugh Morgan, Percy Gething, — Folliott, Edward Woods, William Ormsby, William Smith, William Griffith, Francis Gore and Francis King, Lieuts. Richard Brook and Adam Ormsby and Cornet Oliver Brookes.

34. **SIR ARTHUR RAWDON, 2ND BART.**, of Moira, Co. Down. The 1st Baronet, Sir George, besides holding the large estate of Moira, Co. Down, had acted as agent for Lord Conway on his great Killultagh estate, residing at Brook Hall, near Lisburn. During his absence serving in the Royalist army in England this house had been burnt to the ground in the 1641 rebellion. Besides his prominent position in Ireland, Sir George had been a welcome frequenter of the Whitehall Court and a favourite of Charles II. Dying in 1684 he was succeeded by his son, Sir Arthur, the subject of this sketch, as 2nd Baronet.

In the troublous years prior to the revolution, no one in Ulster worked harder in the preparations for Protestant resistance. When General Richard Hamilton, on his march from Dublin to Derry, met and defeated the Antrim and Down forces at Dromore, it was Sir Arthur Rawdon who extricated the remnant, and with numbers augmented to some 3000 men commanded an orderly retreat to Coleraine. A reference to the Introductory Chapter will show how Hamilton was repulsed before Coleraine, how Rawdon failed to prevent the crossing of the Bann, and how Rawdon was obliged to retreat before Hamilton to the walls of Derry. In these operations not only was Sir Arthur most conspicuous for gallantry in action, but it was his coolness in danger and foresight in emergency that enabled his command to reach the city. Sir Arthur's health had more or less broken down under the stress, so he could do little more than protest against Lundy's inactivity and urge decisive action. All was of no avail, Lundy was secretly working for surrender, and the hopelessness of the position, in their eyes, was inducing many of the county leaders to retire across the Channel. So Sir Arthur sailed with the withdrawing fleet, 18th April. He never fully recovered his health, dying in 1694. He was one of the signers of the "Declaration of Union" and attainted in James' Dublin Parliament, May 1689. He was also one of those exempted from all hope of pardon in Tyrconnell's proclamation, March 1689.

"Londeriados" has the following reference:—

> "Sir Arthur Rawdon's horse rode to the plains,
> In warlike order, 'bove a thousand men;
> Some of his men strong polished armour bore,
> But he himself a silken doublet wore."

In the thrilling historical novel by Sir S. R. Keightley, entitled "The Crimson Sign," dealing with the Siege of Derry, one of the outstanding characters is a Lady Hester Rawdon, but I can find no other mention of such a lady. Sir Arthur Rawdon was buried beside his father, Sir George, in the family vault in Hillsborough churchyard. Sir Arthur's son and successor, Sir John, the 3rd Baronet, was created Earl of Moira, 1761, and his son became Marquess of Hastings in 1816. The present representative, through the female line of this old family, is the Countess of Loudoun.

35. **Arthur Upton**, of Castle Upton, Co. Antrim. The first of the family in Co. Antrim was Henry Upton, of the Devonshire family of that name of L'Upton, his mother being a Fortescue of Filleigh, in the same county. Henry was one of the Earl of Essex's officers, accompanying his expedition of 1574 to Carrickfergus. He had received a grant of the Castle Upton estate, and had married a daughter of Sir John Clotworthy, of Antrim Castle. On Henry's death he had been succeeded in the Castle Upton estate by his son, Arthur Upton, the subject of this sketch, who was in possession at the time of the revolution. With his relations the Massereene family, he was one of the most energetic of the Co. Antrim Protestant landlords in organising the

Co. Antrim Association of nobility and gentry for mutual protection.[1] Arthur Upton raised a regiment on his estate, which took part in all the operations from the "Break of Dromore" to the retreat on Derry. Once in Derry, he was one of the signers of the "Declaration of Union" (April 10th) and one of the many protesting against Lundy's inaction. When, however, Lundy's misrepresentation of the garrison's position induced the Fleet to sail to England without landing a gun or a man, he, like many others, believing all hopeless, availed himself of the free passage offered and crossed the Channel.

His name figures in the list of attainted in James' Dublin Parliament, May 1689. He returned to Castle Upton after the revolution, being eventually succeeded in the estate by his fourth but eldest surviving son, viz.:—

36. **Clotworthy Upton**, of Castle Upton, an officer in his father, Arthur Upton's, regiment, with which he served from the "Breakof Dromore" to the retreat on Derry. He accompanied his father across the Channel, but returning to Ireland, he took part in the victorious campaign of King William's army down to the Siege of Limerick, where he particularly distinguished himself by gallantry in leading one of the assaults on the town, in which he was severely wounded and taken prisoner. His name also figures in the list of attainted in James' Dublin Parliament, May 1689. He died in 1735.

37. **Arthur Upton**, another son of Arthur Upton, of Castle Upton, was also an officer in his father's regiment. He was killed in 1690 at the battle of Aughrim.

38. **Oliver Upton**. His name figures among the signatures of the Derry address to King William after the relief. He was probably of the Castle Upton family, but I can find no other indication.

In 1766 the head of the family was created Baron Templetown, and in 1806 Viscount Templetown. The present representative of the family is Henry Edward Montagu Dorington Clotworthy, 4th Viscount Templetown.

39. **Sir George Maxwell**, of Killyleagh Castle, Co. Down, was the son of Sir Robert Maxwell, of Waringstown. He had married the widowed Countess of Clanbrassil, the then owner of Killyleagh Castle and Hamilton estate.[2] He was a leading member of the Co. Down Association for mutual protection and defence of Protestant interests. He had raised a regiment on the Hamilton estate, with which he had been in the "Break of Dromore" and in the retreat to Derry. Once in Derry he was a staunch advocate for decisive action, and was one of the signers of the "Declaration of Union." When Lundy's treachery led to the withdrawal of the Fleet without landing a man or a gun, like many others, deeming the position hopeless, he had taken advantage of a free passage to England.

[1] For regiments raised, etc., see Introductory Chapter.
[2] See "Hamilton Manuscripts."

"Londeriados" has the following reference to him:—

> "Next unto these brave Skeffington's regiment
> Into camp in gallant order went
> From Killyleagh young Sir George Maxwell
> Was to that regiment Lieutenant Colonel."

His name also figures in the list of attainted in James' Dublin Parliament, May 1689.

40. **WILLIAM HILL**, of Hillsborough Castle, Co. Down. The first of the name in Ulster was Sir Moses, who came over as an officer with the Earl of Essex in 1574. While serving under Sir John Chichester at Carrickfergus he was present on the memorable day of Alttnafracken, near Redhall, when the Macdonnells of the Glens, attacking in force, killed Sir John and scattered the force. Sir Moses only escaped by the fleetness of his horse and by swimming the Curran of Larne at Island Magee, where he lay hid till the danger was past. He received considerable grants of land at Hillsborough, and by subsequent purchase of territory from Conn O'Neill, of Castlereagh, laid the foundations of the great estate since enjoyed by his descendants of the Downshire family. In recognition of loyal services at the Restoration, 1660, Sir Moses' son and successor, Arthur, was appointed hereditary constable of Hillsborough Castle.[1]

Arthur's son William was the owner of the estate at the time of the 1688 revolution. He was a prominent member of the Co. Down Association, and his castle of Hillsborough was made the headquarters and centre of deliberations. He raised a regiment among his own tenantry, and was present at the "Break of Dromore." How far he was present with Sir Arthur Rawdon on his retreat to Derry is uncertain, but "Londeriados" has the following mention of his regiment at Derry:—

> "From Hillsborough Squire Hill a regiment sent
> Which into camp in gallant order went."

He was one of the leaders who went across the Channel after Tyrconnell's March proclamation, and was among the attainted in James' Dublin Parliament, May 1689. Hillsborough Castle was burnt by Hamilton after Dromore.

He accompanied William of Orange when he landed at Carrickfergus in 1690, and it was on his way to the Boyne when visiting William Hill at Hillsborough that King William signed the Regum Donum, the great historical charter of the Presbyterian Church of Ireland. Dying in 1693, he has been succeeded by a long line of lineal descendants. In 1717 the head of the family was created Baron Hill of Kilwarlin, in 1751 Viscount Kilwarlin, in 1772 Earl of Hillsborough, in 1789 Marquess of Downshire, the present representative of this old house being the 7th Marquess of Downshire,

---

[1] Which had been built by his father.

Murlough, Co. Down. He is still the hereditary constable of Hillsborough Castle, and till recently disbanded there was no more picturesque sight than this old guard in their quaint mediaeval uniform of the 17th century turning out for church parade on some great occasion.

41. **Major Joseph Stroud**, of Lisburn, Co. Down, a prominent member of the Co. Down Association for mutual protection and defence of Protestant interests, raised a troop of horse at his own charges, with which he was present at the "Break of Dromore" and with Sir Arthur Rawdon in the retreat to Derry. Once in Derry he shared with other county officers in protestations against Lundy's inaction. He was present with Col. Adam Murray at Clady Bank, where they might have stopped the passage of Hamilton's army had Lundy given due support. When so many officers, believing the position hopeless, were sailing with the Fleet for England, April 19th, he too took his departure.

"Londeriados" thus writes:—

> "From Down likewise Major Stroud did bring
> A gallant regiment, which his praises sing."

He figures among the attainted in James' Dublin Parliament of May 1689. In August 1689 he received by order of King William £200 in recognition of his services, and the Duke of Schomberg, Commander-in-Chief in the field, was instructed to give him "a commission for first captain of horse that would fall." On the 2nd September, 1689, he received his commission as Captain in Lord Delamere's regiment of horse, with which he was present at the Boyne.[1]

42. **Sir Nicholas Acheson, 4th Bart.**, of Market Hill, Co. Armagh. Archibald Acheson, the original grantee at the Plantation of the Market Hill estate, was created a baronet in 1628. His great-grandson, Sir Nicholas (above), was in possession of the estate in 1688.

He was prominent in the Armagh Association for mutual protection and defence of Protestant interests. He raised a regiment among his own tenantry, which was probably with Lord Blayney's command at Armagh. Whether this regiment accompanied Lord Blayney in his march via Coleraine to Derry (which is probable) or went direct is uncertain. In any case they were at the muster before Derry as mentioned by "Londeriados" viz.:—

> "From Legocurry the brave Acheson
> 'Mongst which the brave Sir Nicholas Acheson."

He was a signer of the "Declaration of Union," April 10th, and was among the

---

[1] See Dalton's "Army List," Vol. III.

attainted in James' Dublin Parliament, May 1689. He probably accompanied the Fleet, April 19th, with many others in like position to England. He died in 1710, being succeeded by his son Arthur as 5th Baronet. In 1776 the head of the family was raised to the peerage as Baron Gosford of Markethill, to a Viscountcy in 1786 and the Earldom of Gosford in 1806.

The present representative of the family is the 5th Earl of Gosford.

43. **ALEXANDER ACHESON**, of Tonihige, Co. Fermanagh, so described in the list of attainted in James' Dublin Parliament, May 1689. He was an officer in his relative, Sir Nicholas Acheson's, regiment, and served with it in all operations up to the investment. He evidently afterwards took service with the gallant men of Enniskillen, as his signature is attached to the Enniskillen address to King William after the relief.

He was a son of Col. William Acheson of Skea and served as High Sheriff of County Fermanagh in 1703.

In the Derry Cathedral window of 1913, erected to the memory of the gallant defenders, his name is among those so honoured, the subscribing descendants being Canon J. H. Acheson, J. F. Acheson, Fred. Acheson, Robert Crow and Miss K. P. Acheson.

44. **HON. FRANCIS ANNESLEY**, of Castlewellan, Co. Down. The first of the name in Ireland was Robert Annesley, who held several high official posts in the kingdom, acquiring considerable landed estates in Cos. Kerry and Down. His son and successor, Francis, who added considerably to these possessions, was created a baronet in 1620 and raised to the peerage in 1621 as Viscount Valentia.

On Lord Valentia's death his eldest son succeeded to the title and Kerry estates, while to the second son, the Hon. Francis Annesley, the subject of this sketch, was left the Co. Down estate centring round Castlewellan, or Clough-ma-hericat, as it was then styled. Francis was a leading member of the Co. Down Association for mutual protection and defence of Protestant interests. He took part in all their preparations, but after the "Break of Dromore" left for England, as did so many in a like position. His name figures on the list of attainted in King James' Dublin Parliament, May 1689. He was in due course succeeded by his son Francis, whose son William was raised to the peerage as Baron Annesley of Castlewellan in 1756 and Viscount Glerawley in 1766, while to the latter's son and successor, Francis Charles, fell the higher honour of Earl Annesley in 1789. On the death of the 6th Earl, the estates of Castlewellan devolved on his sister, Lady Mabel Sowerby (who assumed the name of Annesley), while the title passed to a distant cousin.

The descendant representatives of Hon. Francis Annesley, the subject of this sketch, are (1) The 7th Earl Annesley, (2) Lady Mabel Annesley, Castlewellan, Co. Down, (3) Richard Arthur Grove Annesley, Anne's Grove, Castletownroche, Co. Cork.

45. **Sir Tristram Beresford, 3rd Bart.**, of Coleraine. The first of the name in Ulster was Tristram, son of Michael Beresford, of Orford, who was appointed by the London City Companies in conjunction with John Rowley as their agent to look after the management of their vast interests in Co. Londonderry at the time of the Ulster Plantation, 1611–1620. This Tristram took up his residence at Coleraine, where he acquired considerable property. He was created a baronet in 1665 and died in 1673, being succeeded by his son, Sir Randal Beresford, as 2nd Baronet, on whose death in 1681 his son, the subject of this sketch, became 3rd Baronet.

Sir Tristram Beresford, 3rd Baronet, with his neighbours George Canning of Garvagh, Col. Thomas Blair of Agivey and several others played a most important part in raising men and repairing the dilapidated walls of Coleraine for defence. Sir Tristram was among the many who found their way across the Channel, but many of his Coleraine levies did yeoman service in the defence of Derry, as will be seen in later sketches.

Returning to Coleraine after the Boyne, Sir Tristram died in 1713. A life-size figure of a recumbent knight in armour marks his grave in the ancient church of Coleraine. He was one of those attainted in James' Dublin Parliament, May 1689. His son and successor, Sir Marcus Beresford, 4th Baronet, by his marriage in 1717 with the daughter and heiress of the 3rd Earl of Tyrone, Lady Catherine de la Poer, brought the large Curraghmore estate, Co. Waterford, into the Beresford family. Sir Marcus Beresford was created Baron Beresford of Beresford and Viscount Tyrone in 1720, Earl of Tyrone in 1746 and Marquess of Waterford in 1789.

The present representative of this old family is the 7th Marquess of Waterford, Curraghmore, Co. Waterford.

46. **Sir John Magill, Bart.**, of Gillhall, Co. Down, a prominent member of the Co. Down Association for mutual protection and defence of Protestant interests, raised a regiment among his tenantry, of which two of his sons, as will be seen in later sketches, were officers. He commanded this regiment in the abortive attempt on Carrickfergus and in operations up to the "Break of Dromore," when it is probable he left for England, leaving his sons to command the regiment in Sir Arthur Rawdon's retreat to Derry. The "Londeriados" reference implies Sir John's absence, viz. "Sir John Magill from Down some forces sent." He was among those exempted from all hope of pardon in Tyrconnell's proclamation, March 1689, and was one of the attainted in James' Dublin Parliament of May 1689.

47. His son, **Capt. James Magill**, was with his father's regiment in Sir Arthur Rawdon's retreat on Derry and fell at Portglenone in a gallant effort to prevent Hamilton's passage of the Bann. News travelled slowly in those days, but it is some-what of a shock to find his name in the list of attainted in James' Dublin Parliament, May 1689, almost a month later!

48. Another son, **CAPT. HUGH MAGILL**, of Kerstown, also an officer in his father's regiment, was with Sir Arthur Rawdon's forces at the "Break of Dromore," and at Coleraine and in the retreat on Derry. Once in Derry he was a signer of the "Declaration of Union" (April 10, 1689). He left Derry before the city was invested. His name figures in the list of attainted in James' Dublin Parliament, May 1689, and he is probably the Capt. Hugh Magill who fell at Athlone, July 1690.[1]

In the list of attainted in James' Dublin Parliament, May 1689, there are also the following members of Sir John Magill's family:—

49. **JOHN MAGILL**, of Mienallan, Co. Down, another of Sir John Magill's sons.

50. **WILLIAM MAGILL**, of Gillhall, son of the Capt. James killed at Portglenone[2] and grandson of Sir John. In 1765, by the marriage of Theodosis, daughter and heiress of Robert Hawkins Magill, of Gillhall, with John Meade, 1st Earl of Clanwilliam, the estates passed into that family.

The present representative of the old family in the female line is the 5th Earl of Clanwilliam, Gillhall, and Montalto, Co. Down.

51. **JOHN MAGILL** of Tullycarn, Co. Down, and

52. **CAPT. HUGH MAGILL**, Co. Fermanagh.

53. **MAJOR ARTHUR NOBLE** of Derryree, Lisnaskea, Co. Fermanagh. Among the gallant defenders of the city throughout the siege no one has more frequent mention for daring venture and gallant achievement in the sorties of the garrison.

In "Londeriados" there is constant reference to his prowess, of which I shall give two instances.

The first describes some instances of the Creggan sortie of the 18th May when the attacking party led by Noble and Cunningham were surprised by Lord Galmoy's cavalry and suffered heavy losses (including Cunningham killed), viz.:—

> "In a few days the Governor sends forth
>   Full fifteen hundred soldiers to the North
>   Of Creggan Burn, and this undaunted Band
>   Noble and Cunningham conjointed command;
>   The Fort toward Inch they seized with matchless force
>   But were surprised by Galmoy's troop of horse.
>   Thirty stout men in the affair were lost,
>   But in brave Cunningham alone a host."

The second describes another sortie:—

---

[1] See "Rawdon Papers," letter of David Campbell to Sir Arthur Rawdon.
[2] See No. 47.

> "Crofton and Bashford did much honour gain,
> By Captain Noble multitudes were slain;
> From Lisnaskea, Fermanagh's pride he came
> And now he's Major Noble of the same."

He was one of the witnesses of the garrison to the Governor's appointment of Commissioners (July 11) to treat with General Richard Hamilton for surrender on terms. After the relief he returned to his Fermanagh home, where he was held in high honour. When he was subsequently appointed Lieut.-Col. of the Fermanagh militia, so endeared was he to his old friends and admirers as "the Major" that he was seldom accorded the higher rank.

On his death in 1731 the flat tombstone in the churchyard at Aghalurcher records his demise as follows:—

> "Here lieth the body of Major Arthur Noble
> Who departed this life the 29th Aug. 1731, aged 77
> He was loyal, active and courageous in the late
> Revolution, in defending Derry 1689 …," &c.

The family came of an old Cornish stock, settling in Fermanagh early in the 17th century. One of the same stock is Mr. Shirley Newcomb Noble, Glassdrummond, Co. Fermanagh.

54. **COL. WILLIAM SHAW**, of the Bush, Co. Antrim. The Shaws are descended from the ancient line of Sauchie, N.B., 1451. John, a cadet of this stock, was owner of Greenock Castle in 1565. He was the father of thirteen children, of whom his daughter Elizabeth became the wife of Hugh Montgomery, the 6th Laird of Braidstanes, who settled in the Ards of Co. Down early in the 17th century, being created in 1622 Viscount Montgomery of the Ards. It was probably this matrimonial connection that influenced Elizabeth's brother John to settle on the Montgomery estate, where he was known as John Shaw of the Ards. This John of the Ards left several sons, among them James and William, who both settled in Co. Antrim, James on the Antrim coast on a property acquired under the Earl of Antrim, where he built the Castle of Ballygalley, and William near the town of Antrim. James of Ballygalley Castle's second son, Col. William of the Bush, is the object of this sketch.

All the Shaws at the time of the revolution were ardent supporters of the Protestant side, but he figures most prominently. He had acquired land near Antrim and built the original house, still well known as "the Bush." He was one of the most energetic of landlords as a member of the Co. Antrim Association, and held a commission in Lord Massereene's Skeffington Regiment, with which he was present in all operations up to the retreat of Derry. At Portglenone he particularly distinguished himself for gallantry in trying to prevent General Richard Hamilton from crossing the Bann. Col.

William probably sailed for England before the investment of the city. He was in the list of attainted in James' Dublin Parliament, May 1689. Through the Potter family he was ancestor of Baron de Reuter.

55. **PATRICK SHAW**, of Ballygalley Castle, the elder brother of Col. William, was an energetic member of the Co. Antrim Protestant Association, and figures among the attainted in James' Dublin Parliament of May 1689.

56. **HENRY SHAW**, of Ballyvoy, near Ballycastle, Co. Antrim, was a grandson of Col. William of the Bush. He held a commission in the Skeffington Regiment and was attainted in James' Dublin Parliament, May 1689.

57. **CHARLES SHAW**, of Co. Antrim, was another member of this family holding a commission in the Skeffington or Mitchelburn Regiment.

58. **WILLIAM SHAW**, of Gemmeway, Co. Antrim, probably in the neighbourhood of the town of Antrim. He held a commission in the Skeffington Regiment, was a member of the Co. Antrim Association and was in the list of attainted in James' Dublin Parliament of May 1689.

59. **WILLIAM SHAW**, of Co. Down, so described in the Act of Attainder in James' Dublin Parliament of May 1689, was a member of the Co. Antrim Association.

60. **JAMES SHAW**, of Belfast, was another member of the Co. Down Association and was in the list of attainted in James' Dublin Parliament of May 1689.

The above sketches, Nos. 54–60, show the prominence of the Shaws of the Bush and Ballygalley in Co. Antrim affairs in 1688.

The Shaws of the Bush and of Ballygalley were for generations honourably connected with these two places in county affairs. Col. William Shaw of the Bush[1] is mentioned in a letter memorandum of 1730 of Shane O'Neill's, of Shane's Castle, as "his old comrade who died in 1719."[2]

Since the death of William Henry Shaw in 1887 "the Bush" has passed through several hands, being now the property of Mr. H. D. M. Barton, who maintains the hospitable traditions of the old Shaws. Ballygalley Castle, the picturesque Scottish keep on the Antrim coast, has also long passed from the family, but is to-day in the possession of Capt. Moore, who is a distant connection through the female line. To Mrs. Leslie (*née* Aimé Berry, a descendant of Col. William Shaw of the Bush, and wife of Col. Leslie of the Rifle Brigade) I am indebted for pedigrees and most of the above information.

61. **SQUIRE JOHNSON**, of Glasslough, Co. Monaghan, so described by "Londeriados,"

[1] See No. 54.
[2] See Hill's "McDonnells of Antrim," p. 294, quoting from MS. in Glenarm Castle archives.

viz.:—

> "From Glasslough, Monaghan, and Caledon
> A thousand foot were brought by Squire Johnson."

The number of men under his command is fair attestation of his importance, and the number of Johnsons attainted in the counties of Monaghan, Fermanagh and Armagh is further proof of the influence of the name,[1] many of whom were evidently officers in his regiment.[2] Of Squire Johnson's Christian name I am uncertain, but presume it to be Richard, a signer of the "Declaration of Union," April 10, 1689. In any case the reader will be able to form his own opinion after perusal of the sketches of many other members of this large family connection. The Border family of Johnson had settled in considerable numbers in the counties enumerated in the three or four decades following the Ulster Plantation.

62. **Baptist Johnston**, Co. Monaghan, was second in command of a unit raised by Mathew Ancketell of Ancketell Grove, and present with the latter in the skirmish of Drumbanagher, 1689, when the latter lost his life. He afterwards saw considerable service on the Protestant side.

The present-day representatives of the family are Henry G. Johnston, Fort Johnston, Co. Monaghan, and Col. Baptist Johnston, of Toronto.

63. **William Johnston**, of Co. Monaghan, so described in the list of attainted in James' Dublin Parliament of May, 1689, was probably one of the officers of Squire Johnson's Regiment. He died in 1753, and was buried in Armagh Cathedral.

64. His brother, **Alexander Johnston**, was also in the list of attainted and probably an officer in Squire Johnson's Regiment. In all likelihood he is the Alexander Johnston specially honoured among the gallant defenders of Derry in the memorial window unveiled in the Cathedral in 1913, the descendant subscribers being Henry A. Johnston and H. Stott Johnston. The family is still represented by the Johnstons of Kilmore, Co. Armagh, to which belonged the celebrated Irish architect Francis Johnston.

65. **Capt. John Johnston**, of Drumconnell, Co. Armagh, figures in the list of attainted in James' Dublin Parliament of 1689 as of Londonderry, where he was serving as an officer in Squire Johnson's Regiment.

He is one of the gallant defenders of the city whose name is commemorated in the Derry Cathedral window of 1913, the descendant subscribers being Col. James McCalmont, M.P., Henry A. Johnston and Col. W. Coke Verner.

[1] See this and following, Nos. 62–83.
[2] Please note, the name of this old stock of Annandale on the Scottish Border was then as now variously spelt Johnson, Johnston and Johnstone.

66. **Capt. Joseph Johnston**, Co. Monaghan, another officer of Squire Johnson's Regiment, is mentioned by Mackenzie for good patrol work in the beginning of the siege, and his death is recorded from the effects of a bomb. He was on the list of attainted in James' Dublin Parliament of 1689.

67. **Walter Johnston**, of Mellick, Fermanagh, so described in James' Act of Attainder, 1689, in which his name figures, as also two of his five sons, viz.:—

68. **Francis Johnston**, of Derrycholaght, Fermanagh, and

69. **James Johnston**, of Co. Fermanagh.

70. **Francis Johnston**, of Monaghan, a son of the Francis of sketch No. 68, also figures in the list of attainders in James' Dublin Parliament, May 1689.

The Walter Johnston of Mellick, Fermanagh, was High Sheriff of the county in 1678, and was evidently a man of importance from the number of attaintures in his family. Mellick was evidently the old designation of Magheramena Castle, where the family have resided for generations, the present representative being James Cecil Johnston, Magheramena Castle, Co. Fermanagh.

71, 72, 73. These are three attaintures of the name of Johnston in Co. Down in James' Dublin Parliament, 1689, viz.

71. **George Johnston**, of Co. Down.

72. **Hugh Johnston**, of Rademon, Co. Down, ancestor of the Right Hon. R. G. Sharman-Crawford, P.C.

73. **Thomas Johnston**, of Co. Down.

74. **Andrew Johnston**, Co. Fermanagh.

75. **Robert Johnston**, Aghamee, Co. Fermanagh.[1]

76. **Robert Johnston**, Co. Fermanagh.[1]

77. **Thomas Johnston**, Co. Monaghan.[1]

78. **James Johnston**, Co. Monaghan.[1]

79. **William Johnston**, Co. Monaghan.

80. **Archibald Johnston**, Co. Armagh.

---

[1] Of the above it is to be presumed that the following signers of the Enniskillen address to King William after the relief are one and the same, viz. Thomas, two Roberts and James Johnston.

In addition to the above the following Johnston names figure on the Derry and Enniskillen addresses to King William after the relief, viz.:—

On the Enniskillen address:

81. **HENRY JOHNSTON.**

On the Derry address:

82. **THOMAS JOHNSTON.**

83. **JOSEPH JOHNSTON.**

84. **GEORGE JOHNSTON** of Glynn, Co. Antrim, one of the leading members (1688) of the Co. Antrim Association for mutual protection and defence of the Protestant religion, was probably present with the county forces in the operations up to the investment of Derry. His name figures in the list of attainted in James' Dublin Parliament, 1689.

For over 250 years the family have held prominence in the county. In 1723 William, the son of the subject of this sketch, was High Sheriff of the county, and the same office has lately been held, two hundred years after, by the present representative, General Randal William Johnston, Glynn, Co. Antrim.

85. **CHARLES JOHNSTON**, an ensign in the Skeffington or Mitchelburn Regiment, after the latter had taken over command, served all through the siege. He was probably a member of the family of Glynn.

86. **SQUIRE MOORE**, of Aughnacloy, Co. Tyrone. "Londeriados" records that to the muster of Protestant forces for the defence of Derry:—

> "Squire Moore of Aughnacloy a regiment brought."

William Moore, of Dromont, Co. Tyrone, is the squire referred to, Aughnacloy being the central town of the district, where the Moores held the two large estates of Dromont and Garvey. The officers of this regiment were probably drawn from the Moores of Co. Tyrone, whose names appear in the list of attainted in James' Dublin Parliament of May 1689. These names I now give, with particulars of the services of each in following Nos. 87–93.

87. **COL. WILLIAM MOORE**, of Dromont, who commanded the regiment.

88. **CAPT. WILLIAM MOORE or MOOR**, on the list of attainted, has frequent mention in Mackenzie's "Siege" for gallant conduct in the garrison sorties, and is probably the Moore referred to in the "Londeriados" lines:—

"The gallant Moor of Augher with great might
Cut down the enemy in this bloody fight."

This William Moore, or Col. William of Dromont, was one of the signers as witness to the Governor's commission appointing Commissioners to treat with General Richard Hamilton (July 11th) for the surrender of the city.

89. **James Montgomery Moore**, of Garvey, on the list of attainted, was wounded in one of the Derry sorties. He was Sheriff of Tyrone in 1697.

90. **James Montgomery Moore**, of Garvey, son of No. 89, was also on list of attainted. He was Sheriff of Tyrone in 1701.

91. **John Moore**, of Co. Tyrone, attainted.

92. Another **John Moore**, Co. Tyrone, attainted.

93. **Thomas Moore**, Co. Tyrone, attainted.

In Cavan and Monaghan there were two others of the name attainted, viz.:—

94. **James Moore**, of Garvagh, Co. Cavan.

95. **James Moore**, Co. Monaghan.

The following are the other Moores mentioned in siege annals:—

96. **Patrick Moore** and

97. **Joseph Moore**, signers of the Derry address to King William after the relief.

98. **Robert Moore**, signer of Enniskillen address.

99. **John Moore** and

100. **William Moore**, signers of the Corporation of Derry's commission of 1690 appointing agents to repair to London and press for compensation for losses incurred by the corporation during the siege.

The Moores (or Muirs) were of an old Galloway stock who settled in Cos. Tyrone, Cavan and Monaghan in the early days of the Plantation. In the memorial window in Derry Cathedral, unveiled in 1913 in honour of the gallant defenders, two Moores are so honoured, viz.:—

Defender, James Moore of Garvey.[1] Subscribing descendant, General Sir Alexander Montgomery Moore, K.C.B., of Garvey, Co. Tyrone.

---

[1] See No. 90.

Defender, William Moore of Aughnacloy (the Col. William of Dromont).[1] Subscribing descendants, Judge J. H. Moore, Stuart Hamilton Moore, Godfrey Hamilton Moore, Miss Ethel Moore, Miss Marjorie Moore, Miss Helen Moore, Mrs. Hayes, Miss Hayes.

101. **Capt. Alexander Lecky**, Londonderry. This old family are of the house of Lecky of Leckie, N.B.[2] The above Capt. Lecky was an Alderman and in 1677 Sheriff of the city.[3] In the feverish few months (from the shutting of the gates December 8, 1688, down to the actual investment April 15, 1689) no one took a more active part in the preparations for defence. The confidence of the citizens in him is shown by his selection with James Lenox[4] to proceed to Scotland on a special mission to solicit assistance in arms and munitions (particularly powder, of which they were short). Referring to this mission, and to the zeal shown by the members of the Corporation in useful work, "Londeriados" writes:—

> "Lenox and Lecky, who are aldermen
> For speedy succour into Scotland went.
> Out of our stores, our army clothes received
> Thus all the aldermen themselves behaved."

After the "shutting of the gates" he had been appointed captain of one of the six companies raised for the defence. This captaincy he held all through the siege, being present in all the sorties of the garrison. His signature is attached to the "Declaration of Union." His name is among the attainted in James' Dublin Parliament of May 1689 and he is one of the signers of the city address to King William after the relief, and again in 1690 his signature appears among the burgesses and citizens on a commission authorising and empowering agents to repair to London and press the Government for compensation for the heavy losses incurred during the siege. He was Mayor of the city in 1691 and 1695, and dying in 1717 was buried in the Cathedral, where his son and grandson also lie. In the Cathedral window unveiled in 1913 in memory of the gallant defenders, no name is more rightly entitled to that honourable commemoration than that of Capt. Alexander Lecky.

His descendant representative at that date, Henry Lecky of Agivey, Co. Derry, in 1715 married Mary daughter and co-heiress[5] of Capt. Randal McCollum, Liminary, Glenarm. This Capt. McCollum held considerable estates in perpetuity leasehold at the Causeway and Cushendun under the Earl of Antrim. He was also a sea rover owning a

---

[1] See No. 87.

[2] The estate was sold in 1670, and after passing through several hands is to-day in the possession of "the Youngers of Lecky."

[3] For other particulars see the Cathedral Register of Births, Marriages and Deaths 1642–1703.

[4] See No. 153.

[5] With her sister, who married the then White of Whitehall, Co. Antrim. See sketch of that name.

vessel or privateer of his own. From one of his frequent expeditions he never returned, and his property in 1793 was divided between his two daughters, Mrs. Henry Lecky getting the Causeway portion, on which there was no good residence. Eventually an exchange of property was made between the Leckys and the Macnaghtens, under which the Leckys became owners of the Macnaghtens' old home of Beardiville with surrounding property. Since their coming to Co. Antrim the Leckys have been prominent in county affairs, several of the family filling the office of High Sheriff. The present representative of the family and eighth in descent from the Defender of Derry is Hugh Lecky, of Beardiville, Bushmills, and in 1930 High Sheriff of Co. Antrim.

102. **Edmund Stafford**, of Mount Stafford, Portglenone, Co. Antrim, was the owner of that estate and of Staffordstown in the Feevagh, on the northern end of Lough Neagh at the time of the 1688 revolution.

His great-grandfather, Sir Francis Stafford, had risen to distinction in Elizabeth's service, eventually becoming President of Ulster. He had acquired the large estates inherited by his great-grandson. Sir Francis, who died in 1637, left an only son, Edmund, who died 1644, unmarried, and three daughters (1) Anne, married to John Echlin, son of the Rev. Robert Echlin, Bishop of Down (1613–1635); (2) Martha, married to Sir Henry O'Neill of Shane's Castle; (3) Ursula, married to Sir George Rawdon, 1st Baronet of Moira.

On Edmund's death in 1644 the estates devolved on the issue of Anne, Mrs. John Echlin. By a family arrangement the Ardquin estate of the Echlin family passed to her eldest son Robert,[1] while her second son Francis, who assumed the name of Stafford, inherited the Co. Antrim estate of the Stafford family. This Francis Stafford of Mount Stafford married Sarah, daughter of Sir Alexander McDonnell, 3rd Baronet, of the Cross, near Ballymoney. He was High Sheriff of Co. Antrim in 1667. He left one son, Edmund, who succeeded him, of whom presently, and a daughter, Helen, who married John Macnaghten of Benvarden.

Edmund, the subject of this sketch, was the Stafford in possession of the Co. Antrim estates at the time of the 1688 revolution.

According to Graham's "Catalogue"[2] Edmund accompanied his sister, Mrs. Macnaghten, to Derry for protection before the investment of the city.[3] If so he must have left Derry in time to associate his name so fully with the Jacobite cause that his estates, consisting of twelve townlands at Portglenone and eleven townlands at Staffordstown, were confiscated by King William's Government after the fall of Limerick; of these townlands a considerable portion lying between Portglenone and Ahoghill was granted to Lord Massereene.

---

[1] See Echlin, Nos. 105–108.
[2] See note, p. 300, in Graham's "Ireland Preserved," published 1841.
[3] See No. 104, Edmund Macnaghten.

Edmund, who in his will is described as of Brownstown, Co. Meath, died in 1713, leaving his estates to his wife and son, Francis Edmund (d.s.p. 1723), and failing them to his nephews Alexander Macnaghten[1] and Edmund Macnaghten (also godson) and in default to Bartholomew Macnaghten.[2] On the death of Francis Edmund without issue in 1723 the family representation devolved on Macnaghten of Benvarden, now of Dundarave.[3] The old Mount Stafford house and demesne, now Portglenone, is in the possession of the Alexanders of Portglenone.[4]

103. **MRS. MACNAGHTEN**, of Benvarden, Co. Antrim, *née* Helen Stafford, of Mount Stafford,[5] was the widow of John Macnaghten of Benvarden. She was the mother of two sons:

(1) Alexander, the eldest, of Benvarden, where he was left under other protection during the revolution, and (2) Edmund, ancestor of the Beardiville, now Dundarave family. The younger son, Edmund, b. 1679, a boy of some ten years old, she took with her to Derry. In the historic picture of the Relief of Derry (where mother and son were all through the siege) the mother is depicted, with the child in her arms, cloaked in the Macnaghten tartan.

Nothing further is known of Mrs. Macnaghten. Her son

104. **EDMUND MACNAGHTEN**, of Beardiville. Born in 1679, he was all through the siege.[6] In Graham's Catalogue enumerating the names of those mustering to the defence of the city, he is mentioned as follows:—

> "Macnaghten next came here a boy
> From fair Benvarden blooming."

The Rev. George Hill, the learned author of "The Macdonnells of Antrim," in an interesting article in the *Archaeological Journal* (1860) writes as follows of Edmund Macnaghten: "The patriarchal owner of Beardiville lived until he had entered his 103rd year (born 1679, died 1782) and assisted at family celebrations observed at his younger son coming of age.[7] He (Edmund) remembered the Siege of Derry quite distinctly, and could enumerate the names of tenants on his father's estate present in the maiden city during that memorable time." Edmund lived his long life at Beardiville. He married in his eighty-second year and died in 1782, leaving two sons of whom presently. Edmund's name is, of course, one of the Defenders of Derry commemorated in the

---

[1] See Nos. 103–104.
[2] See Earl of Belmore's family histories.
[3] See No. 103.
[4] See under that name.
[5] See No. 102, Stafford.
[6] See sketch above.
[7] This was Francis, afterwards created 1st Baronet of Dundarave, who was born in 1763.

Cathedral memorial window unveiled in 1913, and among the descendant subscribers are the names of Lord Macnaghten, Hon. Sir Malcolm Macnaghten, K.B.E., Rev. H. A. Macnaghten, Sir Melville Leslie Macnaghten and Mrs. Rowley Hill.

Before continuing the line of Beardiville, it is necessary, in order to make the family history clear, to refer back to Alexander of Benvarden, Edmund's elder brother, and head of the family. This line ended in his grandson John of Benvarden, whose sad story, involving the death of a Miss Knox of Prehen, and his own on the gallows is a tragic incident of 1783. With him the male line of Benvarden became extinct, the representation of the Macnaghten family passing to the Beardiville line. This John had a sister, Jane Macnaghten, who married Lachlan McNeill, of Cushendun, so that their descendant, Lord Cushendun of Cushendun, is the representative in the female line of the old Benvarden stock. Benvarden was sold in 1784, and a few decades later passed into the hands of the Montgomerys, its present owners.

Edmund of Beardiville left as stated two sons, (1) Edmund Alexander (b. 1762), of Beardiville, who represented the County of Antrim for many years in Parliament. He died in 1832, when he was succeeded in the headship of the family by his brother, (2) Francis (b. 1763), who had gone to India early in life. In 1809 he was knighted and appointed a Judge of the Supreme Court of Judicature at Madras, and in 1815 transferred to the more important position of Bengal. He had married the daughter of Sir William Dunkin, another eminent Indian judge. In 1825 Sir Francis and Lady Macnaghten returned to Ireland, taking up their residence at Bushmills House (now Dundarave). In 1836 he was created a baronet. In 1818 the Lyon King at Arms of Scotland[1] had issued a patent to his brother, Edmund Alexander, of Beardiville, recognising him and his heirs of legal blood as chiefs of the Macnaghten clan. This had been done, on the attestation of 400 of the name, under the old custom of tanistry, on the extinction of the main line of Dundarave on Loch Fyne, Argyleshire. The clan had recognised the head of the Irish Macnaghtens, descended from Shane Dhu, third son of Alexander and grandson of Sir Alexander, the chief of the name, who fell at Flodden in 1510, as heirs to the chiefship. On his brother Edmund Alexander's death in 1832 Sir Francis inherited the chiefship as well as the patrimonial estate.

Sir Francis died in 1842, leaving with other issue:

(1) Edmund, who succeeded as 2nd Baronet, of whom later.
(2) William Hay, an officer distinguished in the Bengal service. He was created a baronet in 1839, and was the Sir William Hay Macnaghten, Bart., our special envoy to Cabul, who was assassinated so treacherously in 1841.

Sir Edmund, 2nd Baronet, had been Master in Chancery at Calcutta for many years, but returning after his father's death he settled down at Bushmills, where in the course of a few years he built the present stately mansion on the site of the old

---

[1] The Earl of Kinnoul.

Bushmills House, renaming it Dundarave in honour of the ancient castle of the chiefs of the clan. Sir Edmund, besides taking a leading position in all county affairs, was Parliamentary Representative of Co. Antrim for many years. He died in 1875, leaving with other issue

(1) Francis 3rd Bart., his successor.
(2) Edward, see later as Lord Macnaghten.

Sir Francis had a distinguished career as an officer of the 8th Hussars, which he eventually commanded, serving with them all through the Crimea, at the battles of Alma, Balaclava and Inkermann down to the fall of Sebastopol, and all through the latter part of the Indian Mutiny. On his succession to Dundarave (1875) he was prominent in all county affairs, foreman of the grand jury, High Sheriff in turn, Chairman of the County Council, and H.M.L. Among other issue he had two sons who predeceased him, Edward, who was drowned Mahseer fishing in the Punjaub; Kenneth, who died of typhoid at Khartoum. Dying in 1911, he was succeeded by his brother Edward as 4th Baronet of Dundarave.

He was distinguished at Cambridge as much for academic success as in the athletic field, where he rowed for two years in the University boat, and won the Diamond Sculls at Henley; he was called to the Bar, and soon acquired a large K.C. practice. In 1880 he was returned M.P. for Co. Antrim and after the passing of the Redistribution Bill of 1885, was returned for North Antrim, a seat which he retained until 1887, when he was appointed a Lord of Appeal in ordinary, and created a life peer, taking the title of Lord Macnaghten of Runberry. Runberry, his residence, a house built by himself, is on the rocky coast of North Antrim, near the Causeway. Lord Macnaghten was P.C., G.C.B. and G.C.M.G. He died in 1913, leaving among others the following issue:—

(1) Hon. Edward Charles, 5th Baronet of Dundarave. A prominent K.C. He died in 1914, leaving by his second wife Edith, daughter of Thomas Powell of Coldra, Monmouthshire, two sons, viz.:—
   (*a*) Harry, 6th Baronet, of Dundarave, who fell in action on the glorious 1st of July, 1916, while serving with the Ulster Division in the Great War. He was in his twenty-first year.
   (*b*) Douglas, 7th Baronet of Dundarave, a boy in his twentieth year, who also fell on the Western Front (15th September, 1916), when his uncle
(2) Hon. Francis succeeded to Dundarave as 8th Baronet. (Of Sir Francis presently.)
(3) Hon. Malcolm, K.B.E., a distinguished K.C., until recently M.P. for Co. Londonderry in the Imperial Parliament, when he was appointed a Justice of the High Court in England.

Hon. Sir Francis Macnaghten, 8th Baronet, of Dundarave, is the present representative of the name and chief of the ancient clan. He is the fifth in direct lineal descent from Edmund of the Derry siege, and ninth in descent from Sir Alexander, chief of the clan, who fell at Flodden in 1513. Sir Francis married Beatrice, daughter of Sir William Ritchie, Chief Justice of the Supreme Court of Canada. He has served as High Sheriff of Co. Antrim, of which he is D.L. Hon. Sir Francis and Lady Macnaghten reside at Dundarave, Bushmills, Co. Antrim.

Lineage.—To the chiefs of this ancient clan is more often ascribed a Pictish than a Celtic origin. At all events in the 12th century they were Thanes of Loch Tay, and owners of large territory in the Western Highlands. In 1267 their chief, Gilchrist, was appointed, by Alexander III. of Scotland, hereditary Keeper of Innis Frash (or Frash Eileen) with its ancient castle on Loch Awe, and about the same time was made hereditary Ranger of the Royal Forest of Benbuy, an office which entitles them to the "Roebuck supporters" borne by the chief on his coat of arms. Donald, a grandson of this Gilchrist, figures large in Barbour's poem "The Bruce," where he is spoken of as the Baron Macnaghten of Cowal. This Donald, at first a bitter foe, was so impressed by his knightly feats and gallantry in battle that he became the warmest supporter of "the Bruce." Donald's son Duncan is said to have been one of Lord James Douglas' companions in the latter's journey with the Bruce's heart. Their successor and chief of the clan at the commencement of the 16th century was Sir Alexander Macnaghten, one of that gallant ring of chieftains and nobles of Scotland who fought to the death round their sovereign on the bloody field of Flodden (1513). His son and successor in the chiefship was another Alexander who by his marriage with Anne daughter of Murdock Maclean of Lochbuy by his wife, a daughter of Sorley Boy McDonnell, and sister of Randal McDonnell, 1st Earl of Antrim, was father of three sons, viz.:—

(1) Alexander, chief of the clan, d.s.p.
(2) Malcolm, his successor, as chief of the clan.
(3) Shane Dhu, or John, who came to the North Antrim with his cousin Randal McDonnell (afterwards 1st Earl of Antrim) in the end of the 16th century and in whose descendants the chieftainship of the clan now lies.

Before continuing the history of Shane Dhu and his direct line, I must tell the sad story of the Scottish line of Dundarave on Loch Fyne, the chiefs of the ancient clan. In the end of the 16th and earlier part of the 17th century, their dominant neighbours of Inveraray Castle, the Campbells of Argyle, had been gradually encroaching on the Macnaghten territory, so that by the 1688 revolution their influence had dwindled with their territory. Ardent Jacobites, they were with Dundee in the gallant charge down the pass of Killicrankie, but like many another Highland clan they lost most of the remaining territory in the confiscation that followed. Out again in 1715 and in the '45, practically all that was left was lost. They held on to Dundarave with the tenacity of their race, and it was not until 1818, as already narrated, that the clan nominated the head of the Irish line as their chief.

To return to Shane Dhu (or John). Coming over to Co. Antrim as secretary to his kinsman the Earl of Antrim, he acquired considerable estate under the Earl, building the house of Ballymagarry on the townland of that name, close to Lord Antrim's castle of Dunluce. He died in 1630, being buried in the old graveyard of Bunmairgie, Ballycastle, where there is a monument to his name bearing the following inscription:—

> "Here lyeth the bodie of John Macnaghten
> First secretary to Randal, first Earl of Antrim
> Who departed this mortalitie
> In the year of our Lord God 1630."

His son Daniel succeeded him at Ballymagarry and as Lord Antrim's agent. In 1639 a subsidence of a large portion of the castle into the sea made further residence in Dunluce too dangerous. The Earl of Antrim, by arrangement, transferred his residence to Ballymagarry, giving Macnaghten in exchange a townland at Glenarm, while Macnaghten transferred his household to Benvarden, another of his properties. John, Daniel's son, was the John of Benvarden who married Helen Stafford[1] and whose son Edmund Macnaghten of Beardiville of Derry siege is the subject of this sketch.

105. **ROBERT ECHLIN**, of Ardquin, Co. Down, was the grandson of the Right Rev. Robert Echlin, Bishop of Down, his father being the John Echlin who married Anne Stafford, heiress of the Mount Stafford estate, Co. Antrim. While Robert had inherited the Echlin property of Ardquin, Co. Down, his younger brother Francis had inherited the Mount Stafford property, Co. Antrim, assuming the surname of Stafford.[2]

He married a daughter of the Right Rev. Henry Leslie, Bishop of Down, his grandfather's successor in that see. He is probably the Robert Echlin, described as of Killough, Co. Down, in the list of attainted in James' Dublin Parliament, May 1689.

106. His eldest son **JOHN ECHLIN**, successor at Ardquin, is on the list of attainted in James' Dublin Parliament, May 1689.

107. Another son, **CAPT. ROBERT ECHLIN**, was an officer in the Derry relieving force under General Kirke, particularly distinguishing himself in the operations in the island of Inch, on Lough Swilly. In the subsequent campaign he rose to the rank of Lieut.-Col. in command of the Enniskillen Dragoons.

108. **VERY REV. ROBERT ECHLIN**, Dean of Tuam, another member of this family, was among the list of attainted in James' Dublin Parliament, May 1689. He had been for several years rector of Ardglass in Co. Down.

[1] See Nos. 102 and 103.
[2] See under Stafford, No. 102.

Although Ardquin has passed out of their hands, they are still well known as the Echlins of Echlinville, Co. Down, and a reference to Burke's "Landed Gentry of Ireland" will afford much interesting information about this old Co. Down family.

This Echlinville family are in possession of a priceless and historic heirloom, the silver shaving soap-box, with the Royal arms of England beautifully engraved, of Charles I. This was presented by the unfortunate monarch, just before going to the scaffold, to his dear friend Juxon, Bishop of London, and Juxon, when on his death-bed, handed it over to one of the Echlin family, by whom it has since been reverently treasured.

109. **ARCHIBALD EDMONSTONE**, Laird of Duntreath, N.B., and of Redhall, Co. Antrim.

The Edmonstones of Edmonstone were of ancient Scottish stock; a cadet of the house in 1445 married a daughter of King Robert III. of Scotland and obtained the charter of the lands of Duntreath, Co. Stirling, N.B., of which they have been "the Lairds" to this day. The Laird of Duntreath came to Co. Antrim in 1617, acquiring considerable estate by purchase near Carrickfergus, subsequently confirmed by direct grant from the Crown; he built a house at Redhall, where he settled.

At the time of the revolution (1688) the grandson of the original grantee was in possession of the estates, viz. the Archibald of the present sketch. He was a warm supporter of the Protestant interests, and was appointed Lieut.-Col. of his kinsman Sir Robert Adair's Ballymena Regiment, which he commanded in Sir Arthur Rawdon's retirement to Derry. In the attempt to prevent Hamilton's passage of the Bann at Portglenone Col. Edmonstone was conspicuous for his gallantry. "Londeriados" has this reference to him:—

> "From Ballymanagh the Lord Duntreath's men
> Were the next foot that marched to the plain."

It was on the 10th April that Sir Arthur Rawdon's harassed troops arrived in Derry. So severe had the strain of the retreat been that Edmonstone completely broke down, and died on the 14th April at the fort of Culmore, close to the city. The loss of such a man was deeply regretted by his comrades in arms. Archibald Edmonstone's name, notwithstanding his death, is on the list of attainted in James' Dublin Parliament of May 1689.

For several generations the family continued to reside at Redhall, but in 1784 they sold the estate and demesne to the ancestor of the present Capt. Ker, of Portavo, Co. Down, and returned to Duntreath, which had never left their possession. The return of a family, settled for some 200 years on an Irish estate, to their old ancestral home in Scotland is almost unprecedented. The head of the family was created a Baronet in 1774. The present representative of this gallant defender of Derry is the 5th Baronet,

Sir Archibald Edmonstone, Bart., Duntreath Castle, Co. Stirling, N.B.

Redhall is now in the possession of the Hon. Mrs. McClintock, widow of Admiral McClintock.

110. **PART 1. WILLIAM LESLIE OF PROSPECT** (now **LESLIE HILL**), Co. Antrim. The first of this ancient Scottish house to come to Co. Antrim was Henry Leslie, a grandson of the 4th Earl of Rothes.

He took Holy Orders, and in 1635 was consecrated Bishop of Down in succession to his friend the Rev. George Echlin, the occupier of that see from 1613–1635.

He was translated to Meath in 1660, and died in 1661, leaving three sons.

(1) Robert, Bishop of Dromore 1660, of Raphoe 1661, and of Clogher 1671.

(2) James, of Sheeplands (whose line eventually succeeded to Prospect (Leslie Hill).

(3) William, of Prospect (Leslie Hill).

The third son, William of Prospect, the subject of this sketch, was one of the leading spirits in the Co. Antrim Association for mutual protection and defence of Protestant interests at the time of the 1688 revolution. He raised one of the county regiments, but after the "Break of Dromore," when Hamilton marched through the county and occupied Ballymoney, at his very gates, he was obliged to submit and surrender (see Introductory Chapter). That William submitted only to *force majeure* on Hamilton's occupation of Ballymoney is evident from his being a strong supporter of the established Government of King William and Mary. William Leslie died in 1701, being succeeded by his brother, viz.:

111. **JAMES OF SHEEPLANDS** (mentioned above) now of Prospect (Leslie Hill). He married Jane Echlin, daughter of John Echlin of Ardquin, by his wife Anne Stafford, of Mount Stafford. From this marriage descend the families of Leslie of Ballybay (of whom in a subsequent sketch) and of Leslie Hill.[1] No family for the last two and a half centuries has been more prominent in county affairs than that of Leslie Hill. The number of times a member of the family has filled the office of High Sheriff is proof of this, viz.:—

William Leslie, of Prospect, in 1677.
James Leslie, of Leslie Hill, in 1759.
James Leslie, of Leslie Hill, in 1799.
James Edmund Leslie, of Leslie Hill, in 1854.
James Graham Leslie, of Leslie Hill, in 1907.

The present representative of this old family and direct lineal descendant of Henry, Bishop of Down 1635, and James of Sheeplands is, Senator James G. Leslie, D.L.,

---

[1] This marriage is the old link connecting the families of Dundarave and Leslie Hill. See No. 102, Stafford of Mount Stafford, Nos. 103 and 104, Macnaghten, and No. 105, Echlin.

Leslie Hill, Ballymoney, Co. Antrim.

(For a branch representative of this house in the female line see "Leslie of Ballybay," in Burke's "Landed Gentry of Ireland.")

112. **SIR ROBERT COLVILLE**, of Newtown, Co. Down, and Galgorm Castle, Co. Antrim. His grandfather Alexander Colville, commendator of Culross Abbey, Lord of the Session of Scotland in 1575, left two sons, from the elder of whom descends the line of the Barons Colville of Culross, in the peerage of Scotland. The second son Alexander came to Ulster about 1615. He took Holy Orders, and held in the course of time several good Church livings, among them Ballymoney and Rocavan. As farmer or collector of tithes for the diocese of Connor he amassed considerable wealth, and purchased in 1627 the estate of Galgorm (then the manor of Glenagherty) from Sir Faithful Fortescue.[1] So rich did the Rev. Alexander Colville, D.D., become that he was popularly supposed to dabble in the black arts. During the Cromwellian usurpation he was arraigned before the Ballymena Presbytery to answer a charge of this kind. During the stormy times of Charles I. and Cromwell, he stuck to his Royalist and Prelatist principles. At the end of his life he was on the list of suspects for transportation to Connaught, only escaping by the death of Cromwell. He died and was buried in the vaults of a chapel he himself had built close to the mansion of Galgorm. He was succeeded in his estates by his son Sir Robert Colville, the subject of this sketch. Sir Robert, following his father's lines, continued to add to his landed estates, purchasing, among other properties from the Earl of Mountalexander, the large estate of Newtown (Newtownards), Co. Down, which he made his principal residence.[2] He was three times married. (1) To Penelope, daughter of Francis Hill, of Hillsborough, Co. Down. (2) To Honora, daughter of Thady O'Hara, of Cribilly, Co. Antrim. (3) To Rose, daughter of William Leslie, of Prospect (Leslie Hill), Co. Antrim.

At the time of the 1688 revolution, Sir Robert became one of the leaders of the Co. Down Association for mutual protection and defence of Protestant interests, raising a regiment among his own tenantry. After the "Break of Dromore," and Tyrconnell's proclamation, in which he was one of the leaders exempted from all hope of pardon (see Introductory Chapter), he fled to England. His name is on the list of those attainted in James' Dublin Parliament, May 1689. Returning to Newtown at the end of the revolution, he died there in 1697, being laid to rest in a mausoleum he had built for himself and family in the church of Newtownards. Mr. Edmund Nugent, of Portaferry House, Co. Down, has supplied me with most interesting particulars of the burial places of various members of the Colville family, taken from an unpublished

[1] Glenagherty had been a part of the 60,000 acres granted to Rory Oge Macquillan, who disposed of it to various settlers, among others being Sir Robert Adair, of Ballymena (of whom later). During his occupancy Rory Oge had built and occasionally resided in a castle on an old Dun on the river Maine (in the present Galgorm demesne) of which few traces remain to-day.
[2] Newtown is now the Mountstewart estate of the Marquess of Londonderry.

MS. of his relative, William Montgomery, of Rosemount, author of the "Montgomery Manuscripts," and dated 1701. After highly commending Sir Robert for his example in building two such family mausoleums, Galgorm and Newtownards, he gives the names of those buried in each and elsewhere, viz.: *In the Galgorm mausoleum:* The Rev. Alexander Colville, D.D., and Mrs. Colville. Penelope daughter of Francis Hill, of Hillsborough, Sir Robert Colville's first wife. William, Sir Robert's son by his third wife, Rose, daughter of William Leslie, of Prospect (Leslie Hill).[1]

In the Newtownards mausoleum: Sir Robert Colville and Rose, Lady Colville, his third wife, daughter of William Leslie, of Leslie Hill.

Francis Colville, son by his first wife, Penelope, daughter of Francis Hill, of Hillsborough, lies in Bow Church, London, and another son, Hill, by the same wife, in a church in Dublin. This, William Montgomery quaintly describes as "a melancholy scatterment."

On the death of Robert, the last male descendant of Sir Robert Colville, the Newtown, Galgorm and Kildare estates devolved on his sister, Alicia, who had married about 1721 Stephen Moore, created in 1764 Baron Kilworth of Moore Park, Co. Cork, and in 1766 Viscount Mount Cashell of Cashell. Their son and successor was created in 1781 Earl of Mount Cashell. During this period the Newtown demesne and estates had been sold (about 1760–1770) to the Londonderry family, now the Mountstewart property of the Marquess of Londonderry (see Stewart, Londonderry, 223) and Galgorm had become the residence of an agent, and was rarely visited by the owners. In 1850 in the 3rd Earl's time the great Mountcashell estate in Co. Antrim, with a rental of about £30,000 a year, was sold through the Encumbered Estates Court, and disposed of to many purchasers; the Castle of Galgorm with surrounding estates being bought by Dr. William Young, of Ballymena, in whose family it still remains. On the death of the 5th Earl of Mountcashell a few years ago, the title became extinct, but the family is represented in the female line by Mrs. Holroyd Smyth, Ballynatray, Youghal.

The old mansion of Galgorm is one of the most perfect of the castles built about the time of the Plantation, still preserving its ancient features. An oblong block with massive walls, and remains of the lawns or courtyards in front and in rear (for full description see Lawlor's "Ulster, its Archeology and Antiquities," pp. 167–169). It is supposed to have been commenced by Sir Faithful Fortescue, about 1618, and completed by the Rev. Alexander Colville, D.D., after his purchase in 1627. The house (castle) has the local reputation of being haunted by the ghost of Dr. Colville, who is supposed to have sold his soul to the devil. Queer and uncanny noises are not infrequent, but the present occupiers have no cause for complaint.

---

[1] According to the late Lord Waveney, Spinosa, a daughter of his ancestor, the first Sir Robert Adair of Ballymena, also lies there.

113. **SIR ROBERT ADAIR**, of Ballymena Castle, Co. Antrim, and laird of Dunskey and Kinhilt, Wigtonshire. The first of the name in Ballymena was Sir Robert Adair, laird of Dunskey and Kinhilt in Wigtonshire. He acquired by purchase the large area of the present Ballymena (Adair) estate from Rory Oge Macquillian of the Route (see Macquillan, No. 101, Part II).[1]

The first Sir Robert died in 1626, being succeeded in the estate by his son, the second Sir Robert, who married a daughter of Edmonstone, laird of Dunleith, N.B., and of Redhall, Co. Antrim. Their son, the third Sir Robert, is the subject of the present sketch, and owner of the estate in the 1688 revolution. As a member of the Co. Antrim Association for mutual protection and defence of Protestant interests, he took a leading part, raising a regiment among his tenantry and neighbours. Of this regiment he was Colonel, while the two Lieut.-Cols. were his kinsmen Edmonstone, of Redhall, and Houston, of Craigs. How far he was personally in the operations from the "Break of Dromore" to the retreat on Derry is uncertain; but Edmonstone and Houston, with the regiment, are mentioned for valuable services. Before the investment of Derry he had retired to his Wigtonshire estates. He was one of the attainted in James' Dublin Parliament, May 1689. Returning to Ulster in 1690 he was present at the Boyne, where for gallant conduct he was created a Knight Banneret.

In 1838 the head of the family was created a Baronet, and his son, the 2nd Baronet, was raised to the peerage as Baron Waveney, the peerage becoming extinct on his death in 1886, when the baronetcy devolved on his brother Sir Hugh. The present representative of this old family is the 5th Bart., Sir Robert Shafto Adair, B.L., Ballymena Castle, Co. Antrim, and Flixton Hall, Bungay, Suffolk.

114. **CAPT. WILLIAM ADAIR**, of Ballymena. A brother or cousin of Sir Robert Adair, and an officer in his regiment, which he accompanied to Derry. Once in the city he was ordered with a detachment of men to command the Fort of Culmore on the Foyle, the walls of which were almost in ruins and without armament. On the 23rd April, a few days after the commencement of the investment of the city, the Duke of Berwick at the head of a troop of cavalry presented himself before the place and summoned Adair to surrender. On being allowed to march out with the full honours of war and safe conduct to their homes, Adair capitulated without a shot being fired. This surrender was the subject of much adverse criticism at the time, but the late Lord Waveney, in one of a series of stained glass windows, illustrating the history of his family erected in Ballymena Castle, has cleverly surmounted the difficulty. In the window to Capt. William's memory, over his helmet is a chaplet of laurel, and underneath the

---

[1] Rory Oge's story is a tragic one. Driven out of his ancestral Route by his hereditary foes the Macdonnells of the Glens, Sir Arthur Chichester, Lord Deputy of Ireland, had got him the grant, for himself and tribe of the tuogh of Glenagherty, some 60,000 acres, bounded on the west by the Maine water, on the north by the Clough water, on the south by the Braid, and on the east by the heather hills. In a couple of decades he had disposed of nearly all this vast territory and was reduced to poverty.

inscription: "Defended Culmore, quantum potuit," *i.e.* as long as he was able. Capt. William's name is on the list of attainted in James' Dublin Parliament of May 1689.

115. **Rev. Patrick Adair**, Presbyterian minister of Carrickfergus in 1688. He was a grandson through his mother of the first Sir Robert Adair, of Ballymena. He was an ardent supporter of King William, and was one of the ministers presenting the Presbyterian address of welcome to King William on his landing at Carrickfergus, in 1690. His grandson, William Adair, was a successful London merchant, who on his death in 1782 left £2000 in trust for "the poor freemen of Carrickfergus" (McSkimmin's "Carrickfergus").

116. **Rev. William Adair**, Presbyterian minister, was another of the ministers of his Church presenting the address of welcome to King William on his landing at Carrickfergus in 1690 (Reid's "History of Presbyterian Church of Ireland").

The Adairs of Loughanmore, Co. Antrim. This branch of the Galloway and Ballymena family (always looked upon as near connections by the late Lord Waveney), although they have no direct connection with the siege, are of such importance that they must be mentioned. It is probable that, from their close connection with the Ballymena Adairs, one or more of this branch were officers in Sir Robert's regiment. The name of Loughanmore was probably derived from "Lochan," the style of a farm on the Adair's estate near Stranraer, N.B. The first Adair at Loughanmore was James (described in his will of 1685 as of Donegor); he died in 1686, his son and successor Benjamin (according to the entries in an old family prayer-book, printed in Queen Anne's reign) "natus fuit April Donegor die January 1655," while the fact of the sixth son of this Benjamin is recorded as having the then Lady Adair of Ballymena as one of his godmothers, in 1701. By the marriage of a Summers with the heiress of an old Carrickfergus family, the Crymble estate at Dhoyhill devolved on Charles Adair of Loughanmore in 1797, and has since been in Adair possession. Since the middle of the 18th century the family have occupied a prominent position in the county, many of them filling the office of High Sheriff, among them Henry, D.L., in 1871. This Henry, who fought in a duel in 1840 with an Agnew of Cairncastle, suffered for the remainder of his life from a wheeze caused by a pistol ball penetrating his lung. After Henry's death in 1888 the succession passed in turn to three surviving sisters, devolving on their demise on a distant cousin of the direct line, General Sir William Thompson Adair, K.C.B., Corps of Royal Marines. Both Sir William's father, Sir Charles, and his grandfather had served in this Corps, which Sir William had the honour of commanding before his retirement from the service. Sir William served as High Sheriff in 1916 as a D.L. for the county, and during the troublous times commanded the Co. Antrim U.V.F. Although Loughanmore has passed from the family, the Dhoyhill property is still in the hands of General Sir William Thompson Adair, K.C.B., 39, Hornton Court, London, W. 8.

117. **Capt. George Macartney**, of Belfast, Co. Antrim. High Sheriff of Co. Antrim in 1678 and in 1688; he was the officer who at the head of his troop proclaimed William and Mary in Belfast in 1689. He was one of the attainted in James' Dublin Parliament of May 1689. Capt. George had settled in Co. Antrim in 1649, soon acquiring estate and influence. He was of the old Scottish house of Macartney of Auchinleck, N.B., an estate in which he succeeded his father Bartholomew. Dying in 1691, he left two sons.

118. **James Macartney**, who succeeded to the Auchinleck estate, and returned to Scotland. This James figures as one of the twenty-three of the nobility and gentry of the County of Antrim signing the manifesto calling upon Protestants to arm for self-defence, and

George Macartney who succeeded to his Co. Antrim property. This George was for over fifty years a leading merchant in Belfast, with an influence second to none, being most of that time M.P. for the Borough. To him is in great measure due the foundations of that city's future commercial prosperity. He it was who in 1733 purchased from the O'Haras the castle and estate of Lissanoure in North Antrim, which are still in the possession of his descendants. Dying in 1757, he was succeeded by his son, a third George, who was in course succeeded by his son, a fourth George, better known to the world as Earl Macartney. This distinguished man, almost as great in politics as in diplomacy, which won him world renown, was a leading figure of his times. Having filled the office of Chief Secretary for Ireland he occupied many other great positions, among which were the Governorship of Bengal, and his wonderful Embassy to China. During his busy life, he was honoured with several peerages, being created Baron Macartney of Lissanoure in 1776, created Earl Macartney of Lissanoure, and Viscount Dervock in 1794. Dying in 1806 without issue, the estates, under his will, devolved on his first cousin, Elizabeth Balaguer, a daughter of his paternal aunt, who had married the Rev. Francis Hume (see Hume, No. 120). Their son, again George, assumed the name of Macartney, by which their descendants are still known. The present representative of this ancient family of Auchinleck, N.B., and Lissanoure Castle, Co. Antrim, is Cathanach George Macartney, of Lissanoure Castle, Killagan, Co. Antrim.

Among many priceless treasures at Lissanoure are interesting letters from leading men, statesmen (including the Duke of Wellington) and diplomatists. There are also many momentoes of his Chinese Embassy, and several orders conferred by foreign potentates on the Earl.

119. **Arthur Macartney.** This name figures among the attainted in James' Dublin Parliament (of May 1689) as of Co. Antrim. He may have been a younger son of Capt. George Macartney, or possibly a member of the cadet branch of Blacket, N.B. The last of this old line, George, of Blacket, N.B., came to Ulster about 1630 and settled near the town of Antrim; he left two sons:—

(1) George, who after a distinguished career, died a Major-General, in 1730. He is best known from the untoward incidents of the famous duel in Queen Anne's reign between the Duke of Hamilton and Lord Mohun, to whom George Macartney acted as second. The Duke's second, Col. Andrew Hamilton, of the Scots Guards, openly asserted that after the affair was over, and his principal was lying wounded on the ground, Macartney had thrust at him with his sword. So great was the furore raised by this assertion that Macartney fled to Holland, £500 being offered by the Government, and £200 by the widowed Duchess, for his apprehension.

On George I.'s accession he returned to London and stood his trial. Acquitted of murder, he was sentenced to be branded on the hand, a sentence duly carried out, but with a cold iron (*see* Dalton's "Army List," 1689–1714, Vol. III, p. 45).

(2) Isaac, who succeeded to his father's Antrim property, and was High Sheriff of the county in 1690, from whom descend the line of the Rev. William George Macartney, Vicar of Killead, Antrim, on whose death without issue in 1858 his large estates were devised to his nephew, John William Ellison of Mountjoy, Co. Tyrone, who assumed the additional name of Macartney. His son and successor was the late Rt. Hon. Sir William Ellison Macartney, K.C.M.G., M.P. for South Antrim, 1885–1892; Financial Secretary to the Admiralty, 1895–1900; Deputy-Master of the Mint, 1903–1912; Governor of Tasmania, 1913–1917; of Western Australia, 1917–1920, and High Sheriff of Co. Antrim, 1908.

120. Sir John Hume, 2nd Bart. of Castle Hume, Co. Fermanagh. The Humes or Homes were of the ancient Border stock of Manderston, in Berwickshire. The first of the name in Fermanagh was the grandfather of the subject of this sketch, Sir John Hume, who was the grantee at the Plantation of the estate afterwards called Castle Hume. His son George, a prime favourite with King James, accompanied his sovereign on his accession to the Crown of England to London, shared in his prosperity, and was in course of time created Earl of Dunbar. His influence may have been of use to the family in securing the Fermanagh grant. Although too advanced in years for active service at the time of the revolution, Sir John threw all his energies into the preparations of his and the neighbouring counties for defence of Protestant interests. When the crisis arose he returned to England, but sent his eldest son, Gustavus, with a troop of 200 men, raised on his own estate, to assist the gallant men of Enniskillen. Sir John Hume was on the list of the attainted in James' Dublin Parliament, May 1689.

121. Sir Gustavus Hume, 3rd Bart., who succeeded his father, took a leading part with the men of Enniskillen. He was given (July 1689) a commission as captain in the Enniskillen Regiment of Horse, raised by Col. Wolseley.

122. His nephew, **George Hume** who, serving in Enniskillen, was appointed Quartermaster of Sir John's troop. Both the above officers were afterwards with the gallant Enniskilleners at the Boyne and through the subsequent campaign (*see* Dalton's "Army List," 1689–1714, Vol. III.). Another son of the old Sir John:—

123. **James Hume**, of Knockballemore, Co. Fermanagh, was on the list of attainted in James' Dublin Parliament of May 1689, and is probably the son (no name given) who died on the voyage with Kirke's relief force to the Foyle.

124. **Rev. George Hume**, of Tully, Co. Fermanagh, was on the attainted list in James' Dublin Parliament of May 1689. I can discover no indication of his family. The same applies to:—

125. **Thomas Hume**, of Cavan, on list of attainted in James' Dublin Parliament, of May 1689.

The last of the male line of Castle Hume was Sir Gustavus Hume, on whose death in 1731 without male issue, the estates passed with the marriage of his daughter and heiress in 1736 to Nicolas Loftus, created Earl of Ely. The present representative of the family in the female line is the Marquess of Ely, Ely Lodge, Enniskillen.

126. **George Phillips**, of Limavady, Co. Derry. Although in his ninetieth year at the time of the revolution, no man was of greater assistance in the preparations for defence, or a more staunch defender of the maiden city. He had inherited from his father, Capt. Sir Thomas Phillips, the O'Kane's ancient castle of Limavady, with considerable surrounding estate, and also the direct connection with the citizens of Derry, of which he was a burgess. Sir Thomas Phillips had a remarkable career; coming to Ulster in the Elizabethan wars with Tyrone, he had had various employment in a military capacity, being eventually knighted. During this time he had acquired various small estates, such as the site of the present Portrush, houses in Coleraine, and eight townlands near the present Castledawson (sold by him to the Dawson ancestor in 1633). He was also constable of the castle of Toome, where he had a licence to distil aqua-vitae, and had a grant of the ferries on the River Bann. When the grant of the confiscated O'Kane lands, constituting the whole of Londonderry (in which he had expected a large share for his services) was made to the London Companies, he accompanied as their guide the Company Commissioners sent over to inspect the vast territory. He was in course appointed their surveyor-general and general adviser. He was closely associated with the Companies in the creation of Derry and Coleraine, which grew up under his eyes. From the London Companies he had obtained the grant of the Limavady Castle estate. On Sir Thomas' death his son George, the subject of this sketch, had succeeded to his estates and influence. It was a letter from George Phillips on the 7th December that gave the citizens of Derry warning of the approach of Lord

Antrim's Regiment (see Introductory Chapter). Sending two companies on to enter the city on the eventful 8th December, Lord Antrim passed that night with George Phillips at Limavady. The next morning George Phillips, unaware of what had taken place on the fateful evening of the 8th December, brought Lord Antrim to the city. At the gate Lord Antrim was refused admission, being sent back to rejoin his regiment at Coleraine, while Phillips was taken into the full confidence of the rebellious citizens, so much so, that after having approved of their actions he was nominated Governor. This post he only held a few weeks, until Lord Mountjoy's arrival, and the arrangement made under which Lundy became Governor. In the interval pending the investment (April 15) he brought some 300 of his tenantry to aid in the defence. With these men he was present all through the siege. He is thus referred to in "Londeriados," who mentions the part of his prominence, forty-eight years before, when he had proved a staunch friend of Derry in the great rebellion of 1641.

> "Old Major Phillips, a chief in forty-one
> Had to the City in his old age gone,
> Endured the siege, and with sound wisdom taught
> Our brave commanders, who the Irish fought."

His name is among the attainted in James' Dublin Parliament of May 1689, and does not appear among the signatures to the address to King William, as he had probably retired immediately after the relief to his Limavady estate. There were several sons of his, who also took a prominent part in the defence, viz.:—

127. **PAULETT PHILLIPS.** All through the siege, his name is mentioned as present at the council of war on April 13, when Col. Lundy was so vehemently urged to take more energetic measures to stop Hamilton's advance on the city. He was a signer of the "Declaration of Union" and of the address to King William after the relief. He also figures among the attainted in James' Dublin Parliament of May 1689.

128. **CAPT. THOMAS PHILLIPS.** Probably in Derry all through the siege. His name is among the attainted in James' Dublin Parliament of May, 1689.

129. **DUDLEY PHILLIPS.** One of the defenders of Derry. His name figures on the address to King William after the relief. The Phillips estate of Limavady passed by sale in 1700 to the Rt. Hon. William Conolly, the Speaker of the Irish House of Commons. (See Conolly, No. 1089.)

130. **THE DAWSONS OF MOYOLA PARK**, Co. Derry. Although no Dawson of Castle Dawson (Moyola Park), as far as I can discover, has any direct connection with the siege of Derry, the present owners, the Chichester Clarks, who inherit through the Dawsons, were so closely allied by many matrimonial bonds with families of siege

record, that to preserve the continuity and account for their presence and ownership of Moyola, I must include them. The Dawsons come of an old Westmorland stock. The first of the name in Ulster was Christopher Dawson, of Acorn Park, Westmorland, in 1611, who settled at Drogheda. His son Thomas purchased in 1633 from Sir Thomas Phillips the eight townlands, now constituting the demesne of Moyola Park and Castle Dawson estate (see No. 126, Sir Thomas Phillips). This Thomas Dawson, a Deputy Commissary of Musters, added considerably to his patrimonial estate. He died in 1683, being succeeded by his son, another Thomas. This Thomas was the owner of the estate during the revolution. He probably retired to England. Whatever his action it seems to have been satisfactory to his fellow Protestants, as he was returned M.P. for the borough of Antrim in 1694. He married Olivia, daughter of Arthur Upton, of Castle Upton. Their son having no issue, the property devolved on his uncle, the Right Hon. Joshua, Secretary of State for Ireland in 1710. The town residence of this Joshua is now the Dublin Mansion House, and his name is perpetuated in Dawson Street. Joshua was succeeded by his son Arthur, who married Jane O'Neill, of Shane's Castle. He had a distinguished Parliamentary career as M.P. for Derry County until his appointment in 1742 as a Baron of the Irish Exchequer. Kernahan, in his "County Londonderry of Three Centuries," has the following sarcastic but amusing comment. "Besides being witty and handsome he is remembered better by his drinking song, 'Bumper Squire Jones,' than as a legal luminary."[1] His grandson, the Rt. Hon. George Robert Dawson, M.P. for Derry County (1815–1830), succeeded in course. He married Mary, daughter of Sir Robert Peel, and sister of the great statesman. He afterwards sat for the borough of Hawick, and died in 1856. His son and successor, Col. Robert Peel Dawson, was M.P. and for many years H.M.L. for County Derry. He died in 1877, leaving an only daughter Mary, who had in 1872 married Lord Adolphus Spencer Chichester, younger son of the Marquess of Donegall (see the Chichester sketches), thus making Chichester the name of the owners of Moyola Park and Castle Dawson. On the demise of Lady Spencer Chichester, her husband, Lord Spencer Chichester having predeceased her, their son, Col. Robert Dawson Spencer Chichester, became owner of the estate. He married Dehra Ker Fisher, of the Manor House, Kilrea (see No. 154, Fisher), and, dying in 1921, left an only surviving daughter, Marion, who in 1922 married Capt. James Jackson Lenox Conyngham Clark, R.N., son of the late Col. James Jackson Clark, of Largantogher, H.M.L. Co. Derry, and the name of Chichester Clark was assumed as the family surname.

131. **John Dawson.**

132. **Walter Dawson.**

---

[1] This still famous song was composed by the Baron for Carolan, the harpist, to bring out at a composium at Moneyglass, the seat of Thomas Hamilton Jones.

133. **WALTER DAWSON, JR.**

134. **JOHN DAWSON**, of Co. Monaghan (Killcroe), is among the attainted in James' Dublin Parliament of May 1689. This is evidently the John Dawson, burgess of Armagh (died 1691), and ancestor of the Vesey Dawson family (see Burke's "Peerage" under Earl of Dartrey). His son Walter died in 1704, leaving a son,

135. **CAPT. WALTER DAWSON**, who is also on list of attainted in James' Dublin Parliament of May 1689. By his marriage in 1672 with Frances daughter of Capt. Richard Dawson, of Dawson's Grove, this estate came into possession of the Dartrey main line, who for several generations are styled of Dawson's Grove. Capt. Walter died in 1718.

136. **CAPT. RICHARD DAWSON**, of Dawson's Grove (referred to above), was a retired Cromwellian officer. His name is also among the attainted in James' Dublin Parliament of May, 1689. Capt. Walter Dawson (*see* No. 135) of Dawson's Grove, left an only surviving son, Richard, who married in 1723 a daughter of the Most Rev. John Vesey, D.D., Archbishop of Tuam, hence the future patronymic of Vesey Dawson. In the course of the following generations, Dawson's Grove became Dartrey, and the head of the family was raised to the peerage as follows:—
In 1770 as Baron Dartrey of Dawson's Grove, an Irish peerage.
In 1785 as Viscount Cremorne.
On the death of the original grantee without male issue and succession of a nephew these titles became extinct, and the following took their place in time:—
In 1797, Baron Cremorne of Dawson's Grove (Irish Peerage). In 1866, Earl of Dartrey. In 1847, a Barony of the United Kingdom was conferred.
The present representative of the family is the Earl of Dartrey, Dartrey, Co. Monaghan.
There were the following additional attaintures in James' Dublin Parliament of May, 1689, all probably of the family or connection of the Dawsons of Dawson's Grove, described as follows:—

137. **ISAAC DAWSON**, of Dromany, Co. Monaghan.

138. **LANCELOT DAWSON**, of Killcroe, Co. Monaghan.

139. **WILLIAM DAWSON**, of Killcroe, Co. Monaghan.

140. **ENSIGN THOMAS JACKSON**, of Derry.
"Londeriados," in his muster of the forces for defence of Derry, has the following line:—

"From Tubbermore we Ensign Jackson saw."

This is Tobermore, near Castle Dawson. From other sources we know that Ensign Thomas Jackson resided at Drumbally, Hagan Clark, Tobermore, in the vicinity of the Jackson Clark's estate of Largantogher. The Jacksons, like the Dawsons of Castle Dawson, came from Westmorland, and were connected by association, if not by blood.

The original settlers of the Jackson name came to Ulster in Charles I.'s reign. There were two brothers, viz. Launcelot, at Ballymacarret, in 1639, and Thomas, who obtained about the same time a lien on lands in the vicinity of Coleraine from the Irish Society. Prospering in his undertakings, he acquired considerable estate. He built Jackson Hall, overlooking the river Bann, and married Susannah, daughter of Sir Tristram Beresford, Bart., in 1650 (see No. 45, Beresford). There were three sons of this match: (1) Thomas, the Ensign Thomas Jackson of this sketch. He was a J.P. for Co. Derry in 1677. He served all through the siege, and lost his life at the battle of the Boyne. (2) Samuel, M.P. for Coleraine, 1695–1703. (3) William, M.P. for Co. Derry in 1697.

The last of the three brothers left, among other issue, William, his successor, at Jackson Hall, who left a son Richard, also of Jackson Hall. This Richard sat for thirty-nine years as M.P. for the borough of Coleraine, being Chief Secretary for Ireland in 1777 and a member of the Privy Council. He was married three times, and died in 1790. By his first marriage he had male issue, (1) George, his successor in the estates, M.P. for Coleraine 1791–1796, losing his seat with the Union. He was created a Baronet in 1813 and died at Bruges in 1840. (2) Richard, who died in 1797. By his third wife, Anne, daughter of Charles O'Neill of Shane's Castle, there was issue an only daughter, Anne, who by her marriage in 1802 with the Rev. Nathaniel Alexander (afterwards Bishop of Down, and later of Meath), brought, in the failure of male issue, the representation of the Jackson family into the Alexander of Portglenone line (see No. 176, Alexander).

The old house of Jackson Hall, now termed "the Manor House," still stands overlooking the Bann at Coleraine to attest the former importance of its Jackson owners.

141. **Ensign Richard Jackson** was one of the officers in the Skeffington Regiment at the Siege of Derry (Hampton's "Siege," p. 468).

142. **Mabel Jackson** is among the signers of the Corporation of Derry's Commission of 1690 appointing agents to repair to London and press for compensation for losses incurred during the siege.

143. **Edward Jackson**, described as of Co. Down, is on the list of attainted in James' Dublin Parliament of May 1689.

144. **Clarks of Maghera House**, now Largantogher, Co. Derry. Like the Dawsons of Castle Dawson without direct siege antecedents, but so connected by marriage

with families of the gallant defenders that they have now many links with the epic of Derry. The first of the family to settle in Ulster was John Clark, who came from Lancashire. In 1690 he took a lease of the lands of Fortna Clark and Longfield from the Drapers' Company, and a few years later acquired by purchase from Montgomery, of Grey Abbey, the estate of Maghera (now Largantogher), where the family have resided ever since. He married Jane, sister of the Rev. Fulke White, first Presbyterian minister of Broughshane, Co. Antrim, and ancestor of the famous Field-Marshal Sir George White, V.C., of Whitehall, Co. Antrim (see No. 224, Rev. Fulke White). Their son, Jackson Clark, born 1695, was admitted a freeman of Derry, and died in 1756. The name of Jackson, since so generally adopted by the family as almost to make a hyphened surname, seems to indicate a relationship with the Jacksons of Jackson Hall, Coleraine. At all events, Ensign Thomas Jackson, one of Derry's defenders, was a near neighbour of theirs at Tobermore (see No. 140). His great grandson, James Johnston Clark, D.L., of Largantogher, was M.P. for Co. Derry, 1857–1859. He died in 1891, being succeeded by his son Col. James Jackson Clark, of Largantogher, who was for many years H.M.L. of Co. Derry. Col. Clark married Miss Elizabeth Margaret Lenox-Conyngham, of Springhill, Co. Derry. On Col. Clark's death the representation of the Clarks of Largantogher went to the eldest son of this match, Capt. James Jackson Lenox-Conyngham Clark, R.N., D.S.O., who in 1922 married Miss Marion Chichester, of Moyola Park, when the name of Chichester Clark was assumed. The present representatives of the old families of Dawson of Castle Dawson, Chichester of Moyola Park, and Clark of Largantogher, are: Capt. and Mrs. Chichester Clark, Moyola Park, Castle Dawson, Co. Derry.

For links with Derry, see Nos. 14–17, Chichester. No. 130, Dawsons of Castle Dawson (Moyola). No. 153, Lenox. Nos. 159–161, Conyngham and Lenox Conyngham. No. 224, White of Whitehall.

145. **Mathew Clarke**, is one of the signatures to the Derry address to King William after the relief.

146. **Edward Clarke**, of Co. Monaghan,

147. **John Clarke**, of Armagh,

148. **Samuel Clarke**, of Armagh,

149. **Alderman Clarke**, of Armagh,   } are all on the list of attainted in James' Dublin Parliament.

150. **George Clarke**, of Armagh,

151. **George Clarke**, of Armagh,

There is also on the list of attainted:—

152. ROBERT CLARKE, of Co. Fermanagh, whose name also figures on the Enniskillen address to King William, after the relief, and he was one of the representatives of Enniskillen signing the letter of 13th Dec., 1688, to David Cairnes appealing to Derry for co-operation in the crisis.

153. JAMES LENOX, of Londonderry. One of the most conspicuous of the gallant defenders of Derry, of which he was an alderman. His father, another James, had settled in the city in the early half of the 17th century, and died in 1641. In the chaotic times preparatory to the investment of the city he was a leading spirit in the preparations for defence. After the shutting of the gates (8th December) it was he, who, in conjunction with Norman Jemmett and Thomas Moncrieff, had the forethought to advise the neighbouring gentry of these happenings, and obtain their assistance (MacKenzie). He was selected (9th December) as captain of one of the eight companies raised for defence; an appointment which he held with distinction all through the siege. He was one of the City Commissioners appointed to treat with Lord Mountjoy when the latter was sent by Tyrconnell to arrange terms of settlement. A little later, so great was the city's confidence in him, that he was dispatched with Capt. Alexander Lecky on a special mission to Scotland, to solicit assistance in armaments and munitions, particularly in powder, of which they were short.

"Londeriados" commemorates this mission as follows:—

> "Lenox and Lecky, who are aldermen,
>   For speedy succour into Scotland went,
>   Out of their stores, our army clothes received,
>   Thus all the aldermen themselves behaved."

He was one of the signers (March 1689) of the "Declaration of Union."

After the relief his was among the signatures of the address to King William, and in 1690 he was a signer of the commission authorising two agents of the Corporation to repair to London and press the Government for compensation for the heavy losses incurred during the siege. He was one of the attainted in James' Dublin Parliament, May 1689. He was Mayor of Derry in 1693 and 1697, Sheriff in 1697, and M.P. in 1696–1703.

It was evident that in peace or in war he had the confidence of his fellow citizens. He died in 1723, aged seventy-one, and was buried in the Cathedral, where a fitting monument marks his grave. His son, John, married Miss Rebecca Upton, of the Castle Upton family (a Thomas Upton was Recorder of Derry 1707–1732, which accounts for his connection). Their son, Clotworthy Lenox, married in 1745 Alicia Conyngham, daughter and heiress of George Conyngham of Springhill, Co. Derry, when the additional surname of Lenox was assumed. The siege families of Conyngham and Lenox are now represented by Col. William Arbuthnot Lenox Conyngham, D.L., Springhill, Moneymore, Co. Derry.

154. **JAMES FISHER**, described as of Donegal or Londonderry, was one of the attainted in James' Dublin Parliament, May 1689, and was in Derry all through the siege with his brother Daniel (of whom later). In Graham's Catalogue there is a reference to Fisher, and in a note the brothers James and Daniel are specified.

James was the father of a number of sons, of whom Robert settled at Garvagh. His great grandson, James Ker Fisher, emigrated to the States in the early part of the last century, but returning in the 'eighties he purchased the Manor House, Kilrea, where he resided until his death. His only daughter and heiress, Miss Dehra Ker Fisher, married in 1901 Col. Robert Dawson Spencer Chichester, of Moyola Park. There is only one surviving issue of this marriage, the present Mrs. Marion Chichester Clark, of Moyola. After her husband, Col. Chichester's, death in 1921, and for some time after her daughter's wedding, Mrs. Chichester continued to reside at Moyola, being M.P. for South Derry, in the Northern Parliament. In 1928 she married Admiral Henry Wise Parker, C.B., now in command of the Coastguard and Reserves, and her departure from the North of Ireland, where she had earned such a name for her Parliamentary service, was much regretted by her many friends.[1]

155. **DANIEL FISHER** (James' brother) was all through the siege, and his is among the signatures on the address to King William after the relief.

156. **LIEUT. FISHER** (no Christian name). On July 25, in the last sortie of the garrison before the relief "Lieut. Fisher was killed by a shot from the enemy's 'Drake' (a small cannon) as he was going out."

157. **JOHN FISHER**, described as of Monaghan, was on the list of attainted in James' Dublin Parliament.

158. **GEORGE BUTTLE** (or Buthell), of Glenarm, Co. Antrim. His signature is among those of the twenty-three leading men of the county to the manifesto forming the County Association for mutual protection and defence of Protestant interests. What part he played in the raising of regiments and whether he was present in the preliminary operations we do not know. His name figures in the list of attainted in James' Dublin Parliament, May 1689. His father was the Rev. David Buttle, the first stated minister of the old Presbyterian church of Ballymena, to which he came from Scotland in 1627 and remained until expelled by Bishop Jeremy Taylor in 1662. Even after his expulsion he is said to have continued his ministry in private among the members of the congregation. His name stands first on the memorial tablet recording the list and services of distinguished men who have ministered in the old church of First Ballymena Presbyterian congregation. George Buttle married a sister of William

---

[1] The father of the subject of No. 154, James Fisher, also James, settled in Derry from Scotland about 1650. His name is recorded in annals of the time for zeal displayed in getting the first Presbyterian church erected in the city.

Cunningham (Conyngham), of Springhill, and a son of this marriage, another George Buttle, succeeded in 1721, in default of male heirs, to the estate of Springhill, and assumed the name of Conyngham. The Cunninghams attainted in James' Dublin Parliament (the spelling of Conyngham not being used makes it harder to identify the family to which each belong) are:—

159–161. THE CUNNINGHAMS (CONYNGHAMS), of Springhill, Co. Derry. The first of this family to come over from Scotland was William, who settled at Ballydrum about 1609. His son William, who acquired by purchase in 1658 the lands of Ballydrum (now Springhill), died in 1673. He was the father of William Cunningham of Springhill at the time of the revolution, 1688.

The attaintures in sketches 159, 160 and 161 all apply to William Cunningham of Springhill. No. 159 in his military capacity, No. 160 as owner of Ballydrum (Springhill), Co. Derry, No. 161 as owner of the Coagh estate, Co. Tyrone, purchased by his father in 1663. Col. William Cunningham's sphere of action was not confined to counties Derry and Tyrone, as we find his name among the twenty-three leading men of Co. Antrim signing the manifesto forming the Co. Antrim Association for mutual protection and defence of Protestant interests. In Sir Arthur Rawdon's retreat from the Bann to Derry he did good service in command of the Canning of Garvagh Regiment. Even before this he had been energetic in Belfast, when he had been one of four prominent men writing a letter of warning to the Protestants of Dublin, after the anonymous letter to Lord Mountalexander had been picked up in the streets of Comber, bidding him take precautions against a repetition of 1641. It is probable that, after the investment of Derry, William Cunningham retired to England. He had received a commission as captain from King William in the Skeffington (Mitchelburn) Regiment, with which it is probable he was present at the Boyne after his return. On his death in 1721 he was succeeded by his nephew George Buttle, a son of a sister who had married Mr. George Buttle, of Glenarm, son of Rev. David Buttle, minister of Ballymena Presbyterian church (see No. 158, George Buttle, of Glenarm). George Buttle assumed the name of Conyngham. He died in 1784, being eventually succeeded at Springhill by his daughter Anne, who married in 1745 Clotworthy Lenox (grandson of James Lenox of the siege of Derry) (see No. 153, James Lenox), and the name of Lenox Conyngham was assumed by their son and successor at Springhill, and has been the family surname ever since, viz. George Lenox Conyngham, of Springhill, married Jane Hamilton, daughter of James Hamilton, of Castfefin, and granddaughter of John Hamilton, of Murvagh (Brownhall), Co. Donegal. He died in 1816, being succeeded by his son, Sir William Lenox Conyngham, K.C.B., who married Laura Arbuthnot and, dying in 1906, left a son and successor at Springhill, Col. William Arbuthnot Lenox Conyngham, D.L., who married in 1903 Mina Ethel Lowry, daughter of Col. Lowry, of Rockdale, Co. Tyrone (see Lowry, No. 285). There are issue by this marriage, so that the line of Lenox Conyngham embracing so many links with the great siege will be preserved. The old house of Springhill, with its fine oak panelling, quaint corners, and mediaeval air, is one of the few specimens extant of the country mansion of that period. The house is a mine of antique furniture, its walls are hung with pictures of the past, among them the portraits in oils of Col. William Conyngham (the subject of this sketch), by Lely, and those of Sir Albert Conyngham, of Mount Charles, and his son, Henry Conyngham, of Mount Charles, by the Court painter Kneller, while among the archives of the family are many valuable documents relating to the siege of Derry and its Corporate history, and last, but not least, Col. William Conyngham's commission as captain in the Skeffington (Mitchelburn) Regiment (1689) signed by King William himself.

162. **SIR ALBERT CUNNINGHAM (CONYNGHAM)**, of Mount Charles, Co. Donegal. His name figures among the attainted in James' Dublin Parliament, May 1689. The first of this ancient Scottish family (probably of the same stock as the Conynghams of Springhill, Co. Derry) to settle in Donegal was the Rev. Alexander Conyngham, who held a Church living in 1611, and was later Dean of Raphoe. His grandson, Sir Albert, had nothing to do with the defence of Derry, but Graham writes of his being in residence on his Mount Charles estate at the beginning of the revolution, and exerting such powerful influence that no members were sent to attend James' Dublin Parliament from Co. Donegal except from St. Johnstown, then occupied by James' army investing Derry. (Graham's "Derriana," 1823 edition, p. 119.) He was present at the Boyne in command of a regiment of Dragoons raised by himself, and did good service on the Protestant side in the subsequent campaign. He was murdered by rapparees a few years later in Co. Sligo.

163. Son and successor of the above, **HENRY CONYNGHAM**, of Mount Charles, was also on the list of attainted in James' Dublin Parliament. He served with King William from the Boyne throughout the campaign. For the services of father and son the family were rewarded with the grant of the confiscated estates of Slane Castle, Co. Meath (formerly belonging to the Flemings, Baron Slane). In the course of a few generations the head of the house was raised to the Irish peerage, becoming Baron in 1781, Viscount in 1789, Earl in 1797, and Marquess (U.K.) 1816. The present representative of the family is the 5th Marquess Conyngham, Slane Castle, Co. Meath, and Mount Charles, Co. Donegal.

164. **JOHN CUNNINGHAM**, of Tully, Co. Donegal, so described on list of attainted in James' Dublin Parliament. This may be the signer of the address to King William after the relief. If so, he was all through the siege.

165. **ALEXANDER CUNNINGHAM**, was one of the thirteen gallant apprentice boys

who shut the gates of Derry on the 8th December. On the 9th December he was appointed ensign to one of the eight companies raised by the city for defence. With this company he served through the siege. In recognition of his services he was, after the relief (August 1689), elected a Burgess of the city, and his signature is attached to the Corporation's 1690 Commission. In 1841, a descendant representative, another Alexander Cunningham, was living at Castle Cooley, Bews, Co. Donegal.[1]

"Londeriados" has the following lines, which may refer to his family:—

> "From Lough Swilly, the Stuarts (Stewarts) and Cunninghams
> A party brought, which to our party joins."

The following three names are those of officers in the Skeffington (afterwards Mitchelburn's) Regiment present in Derry during the siege (Hampton's "Siege," p. 468).

166. **LIEUT. JOSEPH CUNNINGHAM**, of the Skeffington Regiment. This may be the Joseph Cunningham, of Kilmacenet, Co. Antrim, one of the attainted in James' Dublin Parliament.

167. **LIEUT. JOHN CUNNINGHAM**, of the Skeffington Regiment. He was all through the siege, and one of the signers of the address to King William after the relief.

168. **CAPTAIN MICHAEL CUNNINGHAM**, of the Skeffington Regiment. He was the owner of the estate of Prehen, Co. Derry side of the Foyle, facing the city, and was one of the most distinguished of the defenders. "Londeriados" mentions him as follows:—

> "From Prehen Capt. Michael Cunningham."

In Mackenzie's "Siege," his name is particularly mentioned for gallantry in many sorties, especially in that of Pennyburn, 25th April, and the second sortie of Windmill Hill on the 4th June (this is confirmed by Walker). His signature is one of those to the address to King William after the relief. He left on his death an only daughter and heiress, who married Robert Harvey, of Mintiagh, Co. Donegal (for their descendants see No. 212, Harvey of Mintiagh, and Malin Head, and No. 214, the Montgomerys of Benvarden). Prehen was sold eventually to the Knoxes, who were the owners for many generations.

169. **CAPT. JOHN CUNNINGHAM**. "Mackenzie" has the following account of this officer's death in the first Windmill Hill sortie of May 6th.

> "About this time our men went out, viz. Capt. Jo Cunningham, Capt. Noble (see No. 53), Capt. Archibald Sanderson (see No. 306), and some others. The enemy's horse

---

[1] Graham's Catalogue, "Ireland Preserved," 1841 edition.

took Capt. Cunningham prisoner, whom after quarter given they perfidiously murdered."

In enumerating the losses of the garrison in this sortie of May 6th, "Londeriados" writes:—

"'mongst whom their valiant Capt. Cunningham, after quarter given."

170. **JAMES ROE CUNNINGHAM** was among the contributors of supplies in the provisioning of Derry before the investment. "Londeriados" has the following mention:—

"James Roe Cunningham & Master Brookes
Gave great supplies as are seen by their books."

171. **JAMES CUNNINGHAM** is mentioned as being very useful to the garrison, at the end of July, by inventing a mixture of starch and tallow which enabled them to eke out their scanty store of provisions a few days longer. His name is among the signatures to the address to King William after the relief, and also to the Corporation Commission of 1690.

172. **ARCHIBALD CUNNINGHAM**,

173. **JOHN HARVEY**, as Trustee of estate of Frederick Cunningham.

$\left.\right\}$ signers of Corporation Commission of 1690.

In Graham's "Derriana" published in 1823, p. 87, there is the following interesting note on Derry Cunninghams.

"There were three families of the name in Derry during the siege, the heads of which were distinguished from each other by patronymics according to the Scottish custom, viz. Alderman Jack, Jew Jack, and Merchant Jack. From the former of these are descended Conyngham McAlpine of Dublin, the late Conyngham McCrae of Lifford, the Balls of Shannon, and the Sproules, lately resident in Strabane."

174. **COL. JOHN CUNNINGHAM.**

175. **COL. SOLOMON RICHARD.**

These were the two Colonel's commanding the two English regiments which arrived in the Foyle on April 15th, but which, owing to the machinations of Lundy, sailed back to England on the 18th without even landing the stores and munitions so badly required for the defence of the city.

Both these officers were subsequently tried by court-martial and cashiered.

176. **Capt. Andrew Alexander**, of Londonderry, was one of the attainted in James'
Dublin Parliament, under the above description. What part he took in the actual
defence we are not told, but he was conspicuous in all the preliminary operations.
He was a prominent citizen at the time of the revolution, and owner of the estate of
Ballyclose, near Limavady, which he had purchased from the Phillips family. He was
the ancestor of the Alexanders of Portglenone, of Caledon (Earls of Caledon), as will
be seen in course of this sketch. In the Derry Cathedral window unveiled in 1913 to
commemorate the gallant defenders his name is among those so honoured, among the
descendant subscribers being Miss Eleanor Alexander, daughter of the late Archbishop
of Armagh, the late Major John Alexander Montgomery of Benvarden, Major Francis
James Montgomery, of Benvarden, and Mrs. Elizabeth Ferguson Montgomery, of
Benvarden. The family is supposed to have been of Irish origin, and to have migrated
to Cantire, becoming an important clan under the Macdonells, Lords of the Isles. A
certain William Alexander, recognised as head of this clan, was created Earl of Stirling
in 1631. Although probably allied in blood, no kinship between this Earl and the
Irish Alexanders has so far been proved. The first of the name in Ulster was John of
Eredy, Co. Donegal, where he settled in 1613. He left, among other issue, Andrew of
Ballyclose (the subject of this sketch). He left three sons, the eldest of whom, John,
his successor at Ballyclose, purchased the estate of Gunsland, overlooking the Foyle
just outside Derry, the name being eventually changed to Boomhall. Dying in 1747,
he was succeeded by his eldest surviving son, Nathaniel of Boomhall, credited with
building the mansion of that name, who more often resided in his large house in the
Diamond of the city. He married Elizabeth, daughter of William McClintock, of
Dunmore, Co. Donegal. Among the issue of this match were two sons, (1) Robert,
the eldest, ancestor of Alexanders of Portglenone, (2) James, ancestor of the Earl of
Caledon.

(1) Robert, entered the service of the East India Company and went abroad. He
     died in 1790, leaving a son, Nathaniel, his successor, who took Holy Orders.
     In 1802 he married Anne Jackson, daughter of the Rt. Hon. Richard Jack-
     son, of Jackson Hall, Coleraine, by his third wife, Anne, daughter of Charles
     O'Neill, of Shane's Castle (see No. 140, Jackson, of Jackson Hall). Nathaniel
     was enthroned Bishop of Down in 1804, and translated to the more import-
     ant see of Meath in 1823. About 1800, before his elevation to the bishopric,
     Nathaniel had bought the old Mount Stafford demesne from the trustees of
     Hutcheson, late Bishop of Down, and while he was rebuilding the house, part
     of which is still existing in the present mansion of Portglenone House, he and
     his wife resided at Shane's Castle with her cousin, Earl O'Neill. The Bishop
     (Nathaniel) died in 1840, his wife having predeceased him in 1827. They
     left an only son, Robert, who succeeded at Portglenone. He was also in Holy

Orders, Rector of Ahoghill, and Archdeacon of Connor. He left two sons: (1) Nathaniel his successor at Portglenone, for twelve years, 1841–1852, M.P. for Co. Antrim. (2) Robert, of whom later (his son succeeding him). On Nathaniel's death in 1853 he was succeeded in turn by his two sons Robert and John, then minors, whose trustees found the property so involved that they sold the demesne of Portglenone. On the elder son Robert coming of age he came about the same time into a fortunate legacy, which enabled him to repurchase the family place. On Robert's death he was succeeded by his brother John, known as the Admiral, in kindly reference to a few months' service as a midshipman in the Navy. Both brothers were D.L.'s, and served as High Sheriff for Co. Antrim. On John's death in 1901 the succession went to his first cousin Robert Arthur Alexander, son of Robert, the grandson of the Bishop already mentioned. The present representative of Capt. Andrew Alexander of Derry, and of the Alexanders of Portglenone, is the above Robert Arthur Alexander, D.L., of Portglenone House, Co. Antrim, who married Miss Emelia Nicholson, of Balrath, Burry, Co. Meath.

(2) James Alexander, second son of Nathaniel of Boomhall (above). While his elder brother Robert, ancestor of the Portglenone, finally went to India (as already narrated), James took up his residence at Boomhall, Co. Derry. He married Anne, daughter of James Crawford, of Crawfordsburn, Co. Down. He was M.P. for the County of Derry 1774–1784, and held many important Government posts. He was created Baron Caledon of Caledon in 1790. He was created Viscount Alexander in 1797, and Earl of Caledon in 1800 (for further particulars, see Burke's "Peerage"). The present representative of this branch is the 5th Earl of Caledon, Caledon House, Co. Tyrone.

There are many other descendants of the Alexanders of Boomhall, among whom the most prominent are, (1) The family of the most distinguished prelate of his day, the late Rev. William Alexander, Archbishop of Armagh, whose wife, Mrs. Alexander, has enriched our hymnals with so many simple and charming verses, and whose daughter, Miss Eleanor Alexander, has made herself a name in the literary world for fascinating and graceful writing. (2) The Alexanders of Fork Hill, Co. Armagh, descended from the fourth son of the Rev. Nathaniel, Bishop of Meath. (3) The Alexanders of Upavon, Kent. (4) The Alexanders of Melfort, Co. Cavan, in direct descent from the Boomhall stock. (5) The Alexanders of Sutton Place, Surrey, descended from the fourth son of the Bishop of Meath. (For further information see Burke's "Peerage and Landed Gentry.")

There are several other families related through the female line, such as the Montgomerys of Benvarden, to which reference will be made in due course.

177. **WILLIAM MONTGOMERY**, of Rosemount (Greyabbey) (see, for head of family, No. 26, the Earls of Mountalexander). This was the author of the Montgomery

Manuscripts. Born at Aughantain, Co. Tyrone, in 1633, where his grandmother (a Stewart) was living, he was a mere boy when the rebellion of 1641 broke out. As he lived until about 1706 his own memoirs, his accounts of the Earls of Mountalexander, and narrations of the various cadets of the house of Braidstone during the 1641 rebellion, the Cromwellian times, the Restoration and the revolution of 1688, in all of which he took a prominent part, form priceless historical data. These accounts of the Earls of Mountalexander, and of the various cadets of the house appear to have been handed over when written (about 1701) to the then representatives in question. While several have been lost, the De la Cherois, of Donaghadee, the Montgomery, of Rosemount, and others were able to furnish the Rev. George Hill with the material of the Montgomery Manuscripts, 1603–1706, published in 1869, annotated by him. If the text is valuable, Hill's copious notes on members of the Montgomery and leading Ulster families of that period make it doubly so. It is to this work that I owe much of my information concerning the cadets of Braidstone conveyed in this and following sketches. William's father, Sir James Montgomery, was the third son of Sir Hugh, 1st Viscount Montgomery, of the Ards. From his father, the 1st Viscount, he received the lands of Greyabbey (Rosemount) in 1629, legally confirmed by grant from his brother, the 2nd Viscount, in 1638, when the estate was erected into the manor of Rosemount. Into Sir James' wonderful and adventurous life there is no space to enter (see Montgomery Manuscripts). He was killed in 1651 by a piratical attack on the merchant vessel in which he was sailing from Edinburgh to London, and was succeeded by his only son, the William of this sketch. An ardent Royalist like his father, he did his little bit for the restoration of Charles II. and in the same year (1660) married Lady Catherine Montgomery, a daughter of the Earl. In his memoir William writes of the great honour paid him on his wedding day by six Hughs, cadets of Braidstone attending as his bridegroomsmen. Hill in his notes states that these were probably

Hugh of Ballylesson.	Hugh of BallymacClady.
Hugh of Ballymagown.	Hugh of Ballyskeogh.
Hugh of Tullynyng.	Hugh of Ballyhenry.

William served in many important positions, filling the office of High Sheriff of Down, and for some years M.P. for Newtown. In the 1688 revolution he had a commission in the Earl of Mountalexander's Horse, and after the "Break of Dromore" accompanied his lordship to England. The revolution over, he returned to Down, and it was probably from 1690 to 1701 that the bulk of his interesting Manuscripts was compiled. He was one of the attainted in James' Dublin Parliament. After William, the author's, death (about 1706) the estate passed to his son, viz.:—

178. **JAMES MONTGOMERY**, of Rosemount, who had held a commission in the Earl of Mountalexander's Regiment during the revolution, and had been attainted in James'

Dublin Parliament. In 1717 he sold the Rosemount estate to his kinsman, William Montgomery, of Maghera and Gransheogh (of whom presently in No. 180), in whose family it has since remained. He died in 1728, but although he left male issue, there was none alive to claim the Montgomery Viscountcy to which this line was entailed on the death of the fifth and last Earl of Mountalexander in 1747.

179. **ROBERT MONTGOMERY**, of Rosemount, Co. Down, so described, is on the list of attainted in James' Dublin Parliament, but which of the many kinsmen of the house, I have been unable to trace.

180. **CORNET WILLIAM MONTGOMERY**, of Gransheogh, so described, is among the attainted in James' Dublin Parliament. In 1688 this representative of the cadet branch of Gransheogh (or Granyshaw) was living at Maghera in Co. Derry, which was sold in 1717 when they became the owners of Rosemount.

When the original grantee of the huge estate, Sir Hugh, the 1st Viscount Montgomery of the Ards, came over to settle in 1605, he brought with hi him several cadets of his Braidstone house, with promises of sub-grants on his territory. Among these was his kinsman, John Montgomery, a grandson of the 5th Laird of Braidstone, who was given the townland of Gransheogh (or Granyshaw). He was a few years later murdered with his wife, family and servants by woodkernes (Irish outlaws), who, expelled from their tribal lands by the settlers, and driven to the woods, were compelled to live by pillage. The eldest son, Hugh, badly wounded and left for dead, managed to survive. Brought up and looked after by his Montgomery relatives, he eventually took up his residence at Gransheogh, and a few years afterwards received from his cousin, George Montgomery, Bishop of Derry, the lease of the Church lands of Maghera, Co. Derry. Hugh, his son, held both properties of Gransheogh and Maghera, at the latter of which he resided. His son William is the subject of present sketch. He held a commission first as Cornet, and then as Captain in the Earl of Mountalexander's Regiment during and after the revolution. He resided, like his father, at Maghera, where he was visited in 1701 by the author of the Montgomery Manuscripts. His son William of Gransheogh and Maghera, in 1717 bought from his cousin, James Montgomery, of Rosemount, the property of that name, now styled Greyabbey.[1] He was succeeded by his son William of Greyabbey, born 1734, died in 1799, whose descendants, the representatives of the old Braidstone lairds of Gransheogh and Rosemount, are now represented by General Robert Arthur Montgomery, D.L., Greyabbey, Co. Down.

181. **HUGH MONTGOMERY**, of Ballymagowan, Co. Down, held a commission as captain during the revolution in the Earl of Mountalexander's Regiment. He was attainted

---

[1] About the time (1717) when the above purchase of Rosemount was made, William sold the Maghera property to John Clark, whose descendants, the Clarks of Largantogher (to which the name was changed) are still the owners. (See No. 144.)

in James' Dublin Parliament. He built and resided in the house of Ballymagowan (later known as Springvale). His father, the Rev. James Montgomery, was of the house of Hazelhead, N.B., cadets of Braidstone. On coming to Co. Down about 1640, he was appointed Curate of Newtown, and Chaplain to the Earl of Mountalexander. He died in 1647, when his son Hugh (above) succeeded to his property. Hugh left several sons, but of their descendants little is known.

The original Ballymagowan Manuscript was given to Hugh Montgomery (above) and from him passed in course to a descendant, viz. the Rev. William Montgomery, Presbyterian minister of Ballyeaston, Co. Antrim, where he was ordained in 1759 and died in 1809. A grandson of his was the late Mr. B. W. D. Montgomery, of the Ulster Club, Belfast, so well known in that city for his many activities, commercial and Unionist.

182. **John Montgomery**, of Creboy, Co. Down. Described among the attainders as of Carrickboy, evidently in error for Creboy. The original settler in Co. Down was Patrick Montgomery, laird of the small estate of Blackhouse, N.B., and a cadet of Braidstone. He did Sir Hugh Montgomery such good service in 1605, by providing his own vessel for Conn O'Neill's escape from Carrickfergus Castle to Scotland, that he was rewarded with the grant of the townland of Creboy, near Donaghadee, on his death in 1629. He left two sons, Hugh, who died in 1630, and John, who fell on the Royalist side at Dunbar in 1650. The latter left a son, Patrick, who disposed of most of the Blackhouse, N.B., estate in 1663, and lived at Creboy. His son John, the subject of this sketch, held a commission in the Mountalexander Regiment in 1688. In 1716 he sold his Creboy property and returned to Scotland, to live on the remnant of his Blackhouse estate (see Montgomery Manuscripts).

183. **Hugh Montgomery**, of BallymacClady, Co. Down, was attainted in James' Dublin Parliament. Undoubtedly a cadet of the house of Braidstone, and probably an officer in the Mountalexander Regiment, during the revolution. I have not been able to classify him among the many Hughs mentioned in the Montgomery Manuscripts.

184. **Col. Hugh Montgomery**, of Ballylesson, Co. Down, was on the list of attainted in James' Dublin Parliament. He held a commission as captain in the Mountalexander Regiment, and afterwards as colonel in King William's army. He was present in all the operations to prevent Hamilton's investment of Derry and was a signer (10th April) of the "Declaration of Union," while he was one of the most vehement in protesting against Lundy's actions at a council of war. He was a sharer in the misfortunes of the Cladyford crossing. "Londeriados" gives him the following mention:—

"Next Montgomerys foot of Ballylesson."

Col. Hugh's grandfather, the Hon. George Montgomery, was the third son of the 1st Viscount Montgomery, of the Ards, to whom his father had granted several townlands, styled Dunbrackley, in the neighbourhood of Lisburn. This estate was subsequently erected into the manor of Ballylesson. Here the family resided. Hugh (above) was twice married, the second wife being the widow of the 4th Lord Blayney. There was a son by each wife, but there was no surviving male of this line in 1757 on the death of the 5th Earl of Mountalexander, to claim the Viscountcy, so we may presume this cadet branch to be extinct.[1]

The Montgomerys of Derryburke, Co. Fermanagh.

George Montgomery, Bishop of Derry, afterwards of Meath, which latter he held in conjunction with Clogher, from about 1618 till his death in 1650. In the see of Clogher, as in Derry, he found scope in the Church lands for the plantation of Anglo-Scotch tenants, bringing over several of his own Braidstone kinsmen. Among these, and perhaps the most prominent, was Hugh Montgomery, who with his wife, children and effects was settled at Derryburke, near Enniskillen. He left one son, Nicholas, of Derryburke, born about 1615, died 1706. He left four sons, of whom the eldest, Hugh Montgomery, succeeded to Derryburke, but after his marriage with Catherine, daughter and heiress of Richard Dunbar, of Derrygonnelly, transferred his residence there, and was styled of Derrygonnelly (see No. 191, Dunbar of Derrygonnelly). He is on the list of attainted in James' Dublin Parliament. He was one of the gallant men of Enniskillen and a signer of the address to King William aftefter the relief. He left among other issue (1) Nicholas, who married Angel, daughter and heiress of William Archdale, of Castle Archdale, where, assuming the surname of Archdale, they resided. (For continuance of this line see No. 198, Archdale of Castle Archdale); (2) Hugh, from whom descends the lineal line of the Montgomerys of Derryburke and Derrygonnelly now represented by General H. M. de Fellenburg Montgomery, D.L., Blessingbourne, Fivemiletown, Co. Tyrone.

There were two other of Nicholas of Derryburke's sons on the list of attainted in King James' Dublin Parliament, viz.:—

185. **ROBERT MONTGOMERY**, of Derryburke.

186. **THE REV. ANDREW MONTGOMERY**, Rector of Ballymore, Carrickmacross, who was also a signer of the address.

187. **JOHN MONTGOMERY**, of Croghan, Co. Donegal, was among the attainted in James' Dublin Parliament. The first member of this family in Co. Donegal was brought in by George Montgomery, Bishop of Derry, during his occupancy of that

---

[1] The subject of this sketch may be mixed up with the Hugh of Derryburke (see No. 189).

see, and planted in Church lands at Castle Doe, of which he was made incumbent, viz. the Rev. Alexander Montgomery, of the Hazelhead cadet branch of the Braidstone house. His son Major John Montgomery's will was proved in 1679. He left several sons, of whom the above John secured the estate. From this John's brother Alexander descended the Monaghan and Leitrim families, of which the following were attainted in James' Dublin Parliament, viz.:—

188. **Hugh Montgomery**, described as of Co. Monaghan.

189. **Capt. Hugh Montgomery**, described as of Co. Leitrim. This family is to-day represented by Richard Johnston Montgomery, of Beaulieu, Co. Louth, and by The Montgomerys, of Killee, Co. Cork. (See Burke's "Landed Gentry of Ireland.")

190. **William Montgomery** is among the signatures to the Derry address to King William.

191. **The Dunbars of Derrygonnelly**, Co. Fermanagh. Among the first settlers at the Plantation was John Dunbar, later Sir John, whose original small proportion was supplemented by purchase in a couple of generations to the large estate of Derrygonnelly, near Enniskillen. The Dunbars were of ancient Scottish stock, descended from the Earls of Dunbar. Their ancestor the 7th Earl had married a daughter of King Robert the Bruce. Their immediate branch had been settled at Mochram in Wigtonshire.

In 1696 the author of the Montgomery Manuscripts paid a visit to his kinsman Nicholas of Derrygonnelly (of which he gives a most interesting account on p. 489). If proof were required of the royal ancestry of the Dunbars, it was to be found in the wonderful sword shown to him, which Sir John had brought with him from Scotland. The author describes it "as double-edged, of excellent metal," inscribed on one side of the blade, "Robertus Bruschius, Scotorum Rex, 1310." So fine was the temper that no Irish smith could have forged it. Unfortunately, this marvellous weapon has vanished. By the marriage of Hugh Montgomery (see No. 188) with the daughter and heiress of Richard Dunbar, the Derrygonnelly estate passed into the Montgomery family. The representation of the Dunbar line now rests through female descent in the houses of Archdale, of Castle Archdale, and Riverdale and Montgomery, of Blessingbourne.

There are several Dunbars mentioned in the list of attainted in James' Dublin Parliament, in siege records, etc., whom I presume to have been descendants of the first settler, viz:—

192. **Thomas Dunbar**, Enniskillen, Co. Fermanagh.

193. **John Dunbar**, Killoe, Co. Fermanagh.

194. **JOHN DUNBAR**, Ballinure, Co. Fermanagh. The three above were among the attainted.

195. **PHILIP DUNBAR**. His signature is among those on the Derry address to King William after the relief.

196. **CAPT. DUNBAR**, without Christian name, is mentioned (by Mackenzie) for conspicuous bravery in preventing Hamilton's troops crossing the Bann, and (by "Londeriados" and Walker) for energetic action in the sorties of the garrison.

197. **LIEUT. ANDREW DUNBAR**. Served through the siege as an officer of Col. Mitchelburn's Regiment (see Hampton's "Siege," p. 468).

198. **WILLIAM ARCHDALE**, of Castle Archdale. The Archdales, of Castle Archdale and Riverdale. The first of the name in Co. Fermanagh was John, who came over from Norfolk in 1615, and obtained a grant of lands forming the nucleus of the Castle Archdale estate. His grandson William was High Sheriff of the county in 1667, and on the list of attainted in James' Dublin Parliament, where he is described as of Bummininver, Co. Fermanagh. This is the William of this sketch. He married Elizabeth, sister of Henry Mervyn, of Trillick, Omagh, acquiring a certain amount of Mervyn land, and the connection is marked by the use of Mervyn next the surname (see No. 199). By this marriage there were two sons and a daughter, Angel. The early death of the sons left Angel the sole heiress, and by her marriage about 1720 with Nicholas Montgomery, of Derrygonnelly, who assumed the surname of Archdale, the old name was preserved. From their son Mervyn Archdale descend the two families of Castle Archdale and Riverdale, of which the present representatives are Edward Archdale, of Castle Archdale, and the Rt. Hon. Sir Edward Mervyn Archdale, Bt., M.P., Riverdale. Sir Edward Archdale is the popular Minister of Agriculture in the Northern Government. For some forty years he has been zealous in his Parliamentary duties, first in the Imperial and latterly in the Northern House, attending to the interests of the people he represents. No honour was more deserved, or more appreciated by his many friends of all classes and creeds in Ulster, than the baronetcy lately conferred on him by his gracious Majesty.

199. **AUDLEY MERVYN**, of Trillick, Omagh. The Mervyns were not among the Plantation settlers in Co. Tyrone. Their near relations, Sir George Touchet, 18th Baron Audley, and his son, Sir Mervyn Touchet (Lord Audley's wife and Sir Mervyn's mother was a daughter of Sir James Mervyn), of Forthill, Wiltshire, getting large grants of land round Omagh. Here they settled in 1615, bringing their relative Audley Mervyn over to join them in later years. In 1616 Lord Audley was created Lord of Castlehaven, being succeeded in 1617 as second Earl by his son, Sir Mervyn. This second Earl or his son was very prominent on the confederate side at the time of the 1641 rebellion.

By the commencement of the 1688 revolution, the Audleys had disappeared, and Audley Mervyn was the representative landowner of the large estates in their, as well as his own, interests. His son Henry, who was M.P. for Augher in 1686 (and after the revolution M.P. for Co. Tyrone 1692 and 1695 and High Sheriff in 1716), took a prominent part as representing the men of Enniskillen in the negotiations between the city of Derry and Tyrconnell's agent Lord Mountjoy. After the temporary settlement and Mountjoy's departure he remained in Derry during the preliminaries of the investment, and after Lundy's treachery accompanied the retiring fleet to England.

"Londeriados" mentions Audley, evidently in error for his son Henry, in the following lines:

> "Then Audley Mervyn from Omagh was sent
> To join our forces with a regiment."

Audley Mervyn, the subject of this sketch, was among the attainted in James' Dublin Parliament, being described as of Trillick, Co. Tyrone, while two other members of his family figure on the same list, viz.:—

200. **HENRY MERVYN**, described as of Omagh, Co. Tyrone, and

201. **GEORGE MERVYN**, described as of Co. Tyrone. On the demise of Audley and Henry Mervyn, the latter leaving no male issue the succession went to sisters of the latter, viz.:—

(1) Elizabeth, by her marriage with William Archdale added the bulk of the Mervyn estate to Castle Archdale (see sketch Archdale No. 198).
(2) Deborah, who married James Moutray of Favour Royal, Co. Tyrone (see No. 202, Moutray).

202. **JAMES MOUTRAY**, of Favour Royal, Co. Tyrone. His name is on the list of attainted in James' Dublin Parliament, under clause IV, which indicates his having withdrawn to England before the outbreak of the 1688 revolution.

The Ridgeway settler in Co. Tyrone, afterwards created Earl of Londonderry (see that name, No. 221), had received large grants at the time of the Plantation. In 1622 Sir James Erskine, a grandson of the Earl of Mar, had purchased from him the Aghamoyle portion of the estate, later created into the manor of Favour Royal. It would appear that Sir James Erskine had obtained from James I., aways impecunious, his Majesty's permission to dispose of an earldom, "on terms," to his choice among the Ulster planters. So Ridgeway got his earldom, and Sir James got his Favour Royal (Hill's "Plantation of Ulster," pp. 475–6). Sir James Erskine had issue a son, Archibald, and a daughter, Anne.

The first Moutray to appear on the scene was Robert Moutray, 9th Laird of Seafield, of Roscobie, in Fifeshire. Arriving in Ulster early in the Plantation era, he married Anne (above), daughter of Sir James Erskine, while their son, John Moutray, married his cousin Anne, daughter and heiress of Archibald, son of Sir James Erskine, thus acquiring the Favour Royal estate. The son of this union is the James Moutray of Favour Royal, in 1688, and subject of this sketch. He was High Sheriff in 1682, and M.P. for Augher, 1692–1695. He married Deborah, sister of Henry Mervyn, of Trillick (see No. 200). Their son, another James, was High Sheriff in 1695. He married Rebecca, daughter of Col. James Corry, of Castle Coole (see No. 289). Since their day successive generations have occupied the old manor of Favour Royal, always of high standing and prominent in county affairs; perhaps the best known and most popular was that outstanding Orangeman and Unionist, the late Anketell Moutray, D.L., of Favour Royal. When in the troublesome times of 1923 he, an old man in his eightieth year, was kidnapped and carried off across the frontier by a band of desperadoes, a wave of hot indignation swept Ulster, and never was greater enthusiasm than when, three weeks later, he was returned unharmed by his trying ordeal. The present representative of the family is his son, Col. Anketell Gerald Moutray, of Favour Royal.

203. **JOHN FORWARD**, of Burt, Co. Donegal, and his son,

204. **CAPT. JOHN FORWARD**, of Burt, Co. Donegal, were both so described in the attainted list of James' Dublin Parliament. The father held considerable estate round Burt, subsequently known as the Castle Forward property. Two days after the shutting of the gates (December 8th), in reply to Derry's urgent appeal, the father sent his son, the captain (styled the "Squire" by "Londeriados") with 200 men:—

> "From Cole Mackletrain (*sic*) from Burt, and Innishowen
> Squire Forward brought horse and foot of his own."

In Derry they remained till the end of the siege, doing gallant service, as commemorated by siege annalists. Capt. Forward, generally designated Colonel, was a signer of the "Declaration of Union," and was present at the stormy Council of War on the 13th April, when Lundy was so vehemently urged to take more energetic action to prevent Hamilton's advance.

Among the records of the English Privy Council is a note of a request forwarded to King William for some royal recognition of Col. Forward's siege services (Graham's Catalogue and notes).

The first of the name in Donegal was the Rev. William Forward, who came over with Lord Strafford during his Viceroyalty (1640) and acquired the nucleus of the Burt estate. He married a daughter of Bramhall, Bishop of Derry (afterwards Archbishop of Armagh) and was Dean of Connor. His son and grandson were the two Johns above, while the latter's son, who succeeded in due course, left an only daughter, Alice, who, by her marriage with Ralph Howard of Shelton Abbey, Co. Wicklow, in

1755 conveyed the Castle Forward estates to that family. Mr. Howard was created Viscount Wicklow in 1785, and the widowed Viscountess, who survived him, was created Countess of Wicklow in 1793. The present Earl of Wicklow, of Shelton Abbey, Co. Wicklow, is her direct descendant and representative of the Forwards, defenders of Derry (see Burke's Peerage).

There is nothing left of the old family in Co. Donegal except the ruins of Castle Forward near Burt, now Wicklow property, to tell the tale of former greatness.

The Ancketells, of Ancketell Grove, Co. Monaghan.

The first of this old Dorsetshire family in the county was Oliver, High Sheriff in 1662. His son and successor,

205. **Mathew**, of Ancketell Grove, was High Sheriff in 1682, and took a prominent part in the Protestant side on the outbreak of the revolution. He was killed in an affair at Drumbanagher on 13th March, 1689. His death is thus described by Mackenzie:

> "We only lost that brave man (Capt. Ancketell) who, after the enemy were routed, was unfortunately shot by a fellow, who lay in a bush."

Although thus disposed of, his name figures on the list of attainted in James' Dublin Parliament, as also that of his brother,

206. **Richard Ancketell**, of Ancketell Grove, attainted.

Mathew was succeeded at Ancketell Grove by his eldest son, William, High Sheriff in 1707, on whose death, his brother,

207. **Oliver Ancketell**, of Ancketell Grove, was also one of the attainted in James' Dublin Parliament, and was probably the same Oliver who held a commission as ensign in Col. Mitchelburn's Regiment during the siege of Derry (Hampton's "Siege," p. 468). Possibly it was this Oliver Ancketell who was M.P. for the borough of Monaghan in 1754. The Ancketells have long held a most prominent position in Co. Monaghan, and it is with the greatest regret that the news of the sale of Ancketell Grove (1930) and the end of the family as resident landowners has been received.

208. **Lieut. Samuel Ferguson** was an officer in Col. Mitchelburn's Regiment, with which he served during the siege. He was probably a member of the prominent Derry family of that name, whose marriage connections give them so many links with the siege. The first Ferguson was the Rev. Andrew Ferguson, Presbyterian minister of Burt, Co. Donegal, in the middle of the 17th century. Among other issue he left a third son, Andrew, who succeeded him as minister of Burt. This Rev. Andrew Ferguson married a daughter of the Rev. John Harvey, Presbyterian minister of Glendermot.

Their son, John Ferguson, who married his cousin, Sarah Harvey, was Mayor of Derry in 1778 and High Sheriff of Co. Tyrone in 1783 (see Harvey, Nos. 209–210). Their son Andrew was Mayor of Derry, 1796 and 1797, and for several years represented the city in Parliament. He married Elizabeth, daughter of Robert Alexander, of Boomhall (see Alexander, No. 175), and was created a Baronet in 1800. He left a son, and four daughters (of whom later), Sir Robert Alexander Ferguson, 2nd Bart., who married Miss Alexander and occupied a most prominent position in Ulster as well as in Derry city and county. He was Mayor of the city in 1830 and M.P. 1830–1835, while he was also H.M.L. of the County of Londonderry. On his death his large estates devolved on his four sisters, viz. (1) Ann, who married Col. William Blacker, of Carrick Blacker (d.s.p.), (2) Sarah, who married Rev. William Knox, of Clonleigh, Co. Tyrone, (3) Jane, who married John Montgomery, of Benvarden, (4) Elizabeth, who married John George Smyly, Q.C., Dublin. For descendant representatives see under the Montgomerys of Benvarden.

The Harveys of Mintiagh and Malin Head, Co. Donegal.

The first of the name in Co. Donegal was Capt. George Harvey (of the Harvey family of Ickworth), who settled at Dunmore in the first or second decade of the Plantation.

His son James Harvey, of Dunmore, died about 1667, leaving with other issue two sons, (1) David, who died in 1704, from whom was the line of Mintiagh, (2) Robert from whom the line of Malin Head.

Dealing first with the Mintiagh line, the David above was the father of

209. **DAVID HARVEY**, a gallant defender all through the siege, and of

210. **THE REV. JOHN HARVEY**, Presbyterian minister of Ballymoney, and afterwards of Glendermot, who figures in list of attainted in James' Dublin Parliament as of Ballymoney, whose daughter married Andrew Ferguson (see No. 208), while David (above, No. 209), who married the daughter and heiress of Capt. Michael Cunningham, of Prehen, a gallant defender (see No. 170), left a large family, from whom descend the line of Mintiagh. There are still lineal representatives of this family (see Burke's "Landed Gentry of Ireland," 1910 edition), but the old demesne of Mintiagh was sold in 1879 and close connection with the county severed.

Malin Head Line.

The Robert above was the fourth son of James Harvey, of Dunmore, and particularly distinguished himself during the siege.

211. **ROBERT HARVEY**, Storekeeper of the garrison during siege. "Londeriados" has the following references to this gallant defender, viz.:—

> "To settle quarters and to regulate
> The stores, over which Harvey a merchant set."

and again:—

> "Harvey a tanner was a leading man
> And John his son, now their Chamberlain."

212. **JOHN HARVEY** (the son) seems to have been the John Harvey described as of Co. Tyrone in the list of attainted in James' Dublin Parliament. John married three times: (1) Martha Rankin, step-daughter of the famous Capt. Browning of the "Mountjoy"; (2) a daughter of Alexander Lecky of the siege; (3) a daughter of Col. Henry Hart, of Kilderry, Co. Donegal.

He was succeeded by the third son of his third wife, George, born in 1713, High Sheriff of Co. Donegal in 1734. He it was who acquired the considerable estate of Malin Head in Co. Donegal.

For the last two centuries the Harveys have taken a most prominent part in the county. The Malin Head house is full of old portraits and relics of people connected with the siege. The present representative of the old stock is John Harvey, Malin Head, Co. Donegal.

Among the signatures to the Corporation of Derry Commission of 1690 appointing agents to repair to London and press for compensation for siege losses were:—

Robert Harvey,

John Harvey, subjects of Nos. 211 and 212, and

213. **SAM HARVEY**.

214. **THE MONTGOMERYS**, of Benvarden, Co. Antrim. Although the Montgomery male line is without direct connection with the siege, its representation of the old Derry family of Ferguson, with its many marriages with daughters of defenders (Alexander, Harvey, and Cunningham's) gives the family many ties with the historic defence, while Benvarden contains much that is interesting in portraits of members of siege families, and in relics of the siege itself. Burke in his account of the Montgomerys of Benvarden ("Landed Gentry of Ireland," 1910 edition) says: "This family claims to be a branch of the great Scottish house of Montgomery." The cadets of the various Montgomery houses on the Ayrshire coast in the earlier part of the 17th century exploited as traders the coasts of Ulster, each in his own vessel. It would seem that this special Montgomery branch made the harbour of Glenarm their port of entry and subsequent headquarters. Montgomerys were in Glenarm in the Cromwellian times,

for in a list of those to be deported to Connaught (about 1650) still extant there are the names of several Montgomerys of Glenarm. They were the occupiers, late in the 17th or early in the 18th century, of a large house a little distance from the end of the main street at the head of the town. After their leaving, it became for many years the residence of Lord Antrim's agents.

The first of the family of whom we have precise data was Robert Montgomery, born 1711, probably in this very house in which he afterwards resided. His son Hugh, born in 1743, acquired by purchase the Benvarden estate at the end of the 18th century, and died in 1832, leaving with other issue a son, John Montgomery, of Benvarden. He married Jane, daughter of Sir Andrew Ferguson, Bart., of Derry. On the death of this lady's brother, Sir Robert Alexander Ferguson, the 2nd Baronet, she and three sisters became co-heiresses of the large Ferguson estates (see Ferguson, No. 208). Their eldest son and successor, Capt. Robert James Montgomery, D.L., held a commission in the 5th Dragoon Guards, serving with them all through the Crimea, and taking part in the heavy cavalry charge of Balaclava. He was High Sheriff of Co. Derry in 1867, and of Antrim in 1870. He married Elizabeth, sister of Field-Marshal Sir George White, V.C., by whom he had, among other issue, his successor (1892), the late Major John Alexander Montgomery, D.L., an officer of the old Antrim Militia, who served on the Reserve of the Ulster Division during the Great War. He was High Sheriff of the county. He married Elizabeth Ferguson Newland, daughter of the late Canon Newland, Rector of Buncrana, thus doubling the links of siege connections, as this lady was the granddaughter of the Elizabeth Ferguson, wife of John George Smyly, Q.C., one of Sir Robert Alexander Ferguson, Bart.'s sisters and co-heiresses (see Ferguson, No. 208). On Major Montgomery's death in 1928 he was succeeded by their son. The present representative of this family is John A. J. Montgomery, Benvarden.

Mrs. Montgomery, widow of the late Major John, has collected at Benvarden a most interesting set of siege relics, or portraits of members of families connected with the defence; among these are an old Bible of David Harvey's, which he had with him in Derry at the time of the siege, and portraits of Robert Alexander, of Boomhall, of Elizabeth Alexander, wife of Sir Andrew Ferguson, D.L., of Nathaniel Alexander, Bishop of Meath, and of Ann Ferguson, wife of Col. William Blacker, of Carrick Blacker.

This Montgomery sketch should be read in conjunction with No. 176, the Alexander family; No. 208, the Ferguson family; Nos. 208–12, the Harvey family; and No. 168, the Michael Cunningham family, when the Montgomery relationship will be easily seen.

In the memorial window unveiled (1913) in the Cathedral of Derry in honour of the gallant defenders, in connection with those of David Harvey and Capt. Andrew Alexander, the following appear as descendant subscribers: Major John Alexander Montgomery, of Benvarden, Mrs. Elizabeth Montgomery, of Benvarden, Capt. Francis

James, of Milburn, Coleraine, and Miss Eleanor Alexander (daughter of the late Archbishop of Armagh).

215. **ALDERMAN SAMUEL NORMAN**, of Derry, defender, was one of the most prominent of the citizens in incidents leading up to the shutting of the gates, organisation for defence, and in the defence itself. After the shutting of the gates, Norman, with one or two kindred spirits, did good work in warning their country neighbours of the critical position and getting in some bodies of armed tenantry to the assistance of the city. When, on December 10, eight volunteer companies were raised by the city, Norman was appointed Captain of one of these. On Mountjoy's arrival (December 23rd) as Tyrconnell's representative from Dublin, to arrange terms of submission and a settlement, Norman and Mogridge, the town clerk, were appointed by the city authorities to open negotiations (see Introductory Chapter and No. 18, Lord Mountjoy). Norman took his part gallantly at the head of his company all through the siege. His name figures among the signatures of the garrison officers to the "Declaration of Union" (March 1689). He was attainted in James' Dublin Parliament, and after the relief he was in 1690 one of the signers of the commission authorising the appointment by the Corporation of two agents to repair to London and press the Government for compensation for losses incurred during the siege. He died in 1692, and was buried in the Cathedral, where a tablet commemorates his services. In the memorial window in the Cathedral unveiled in 1913, to commemorate the defenders, he is among those so honoured, and his descendant subscribers to this tribute are Charles Norman, D.L., Thomas Norman, T. A. Lee Norman, D.L., Col. Luke Norman, Mrs. Norman, Mrs. Frances Bennett, Mrs. Mary Krause Garfill, Thomas Lloyd Rooke, Henry Rooke, Charles Kough, and Dr. E. F. Kough.

Capt. Samuel Norman had been Mayor of Derry in 1672. His son Charles was Mayor in 1707 and 1713, and M.P. in 1703, 1713 and 1715, while his grandson Robert was M.P. in 1733, all proving the importance of the family in civic affairs. Robert's son Thomas left three daughters, of whom:—

(1) The eldest, Sarah, married Thomas Lee, and the name of Lee Norman was assumed, now represented by Alexander Henry Lee Norman, late of Corballis, Co. Louth,

(2) While the third daughter, Florinda, married her cousin Charles Norman, from which union descend the family of Glengollan, Co. Donegal, now represented by the Normans of Glengollan, Co. Donegal (see Burke's "Landed Gentry of Ireland," 1904 edition).

Glengollan is no longer in the occupation of the family. The sale of Corballis by Mr. Lee Norman, and departure to England is much to be regretted.

Dobbs, of Castle Dobbs, Co. Antrim. On the list of attainted in James' Dublin

Parliament there are two Dobbs (spelt Dobb, evidently in error), viz.:—

216. **JOHN DOBBS**, of Co. Monaghan, whose identity I cannot trace, and

217. **CAPT. RICHARD DOBBS**, Jr., of Co. Antrim. This is the Capt. Richard Dobbs of Castle Dobbs, who was such a prominent member and signed the manifesto of the Co. Antrim Association for mutual protection and defence of Protestant interests in the beginning of the 1688 revolution. His father, another Richard, was then alive, and we may therefore conclude that the family aided in the county organisation of the time, and that possibly one or both took part in the preliminary operations to prevent Hamilton's advance on Derry. The first of the name in Ulster was John Dobbs, who came over from Yorkshire in 1580 as an officer in the Carrickfergus garrison, and was at a later date Deputy Treasurer of Ulster. He was the officer commanding the detachment sent from Carrickfergus to Dunluce Castle to recover the treasure said to have been taken from the wrecked galleons after the loss of the Spanish Armada (1588). Whatever his reception, he brought back no doubloons, and his return was quicker than his going. At all events, at Glenarm Castle there is still to be seen an Armada treasure-chest, but empty. John and a son, Hercules, were lost on a passage to or from England. Another son, John, succeeded, and his son Richard was High Sheriff of the county in 1664, and died in 1701, being succeeded by his son Richard, probably the Capt. Richard Dobbs, jr., of this sketch.

The family acquired considerable property in the neighbourhood of Carrickfergus in the end of the 16th and beginning of the 17th century, and have been in residence at Castle Dobbs for some three hundred years. They have taken a most prominent position in county affairs, filling in almost every generation the office of Antrim High Sheriff, and of Carrickfergus, until the latter was abolished. The present representative of this old family is Major Dobbs, of Castle Dobbs, D.L., Carrickfergus, while the collateral branch of Glenariffe Lodge, Parkmore, is represented by Col. Conway Dobbs, R.E., Glenariffe Lodge, and by his brother, St. Clair Dobbs, D.L., Portnagolan, Cushendall.

218. **LIEUT. COOK**, of Lisnagarvey (Lisburn), defender. "Londeriados" mentions this gallant defender three times. (1) When the citizens of Derry, in public meeting assembled, had been urged by Col. Adam Murray to resist at all costs King James and his advancing army:—

> "Lieutenant Cook, who from Lisburn came,
> Courageously did the same cause maintain."

(2) Referring to one of the sorties of the garrison:—

> "The valiant Cook from Lisnagarvey fought,
> And conquered hundreds, who his ruin sought."

(3) And again:—

> "Lieutenant Cook opposed the enemy,
> And forced their bravest heroes for to fly."

At a great Conservative demonstration in Belfast in 1841 that great, if not the greatest of all Presbyterian divines, the Rev. Alexander Cook, D.D., made the following speech with thrilling effects (extract from authentic Press report of the day):—

"I doubt not I am addressing the descendants of some who were drawn under the walls of Derry. I know (referring to Col. Cairnes, a descendant of the David Cairnes of siege fame) I hold the card of one honoured individual, whose ancestor acted a conspicuous part in its defence, and I wot of another, who had no name to be either honoured or recorded, but at the first outbreak all his family were murdered, but one little child. Driven from a distant part of the County Down, with thousands of starving Protestants, he carried the child in his arms to Derry, and was happily one of those admitted for its defence. But when he mounted guard at night, he had no nurse for his little one, so carried it with him to the Wall, and placing it between the embrasures, where the cannon frowned defiance on James and Slavery (Cheers) Providence protected him in the midst of famine and death, and when in after years, he was questioned how he fared at night for shelter, 'Well enough,' was the reply, 'I had the shelter of my Father's gun.'

"Yes, God protected that motherless and homeless boy, and he who now addresses you is that boy's humble descendant." (Enthusiastic applause.)

Dr. Cook had indeed every reason to be proud, and his own resolute and determined actions, whether for his Church, or for the advantage of the community in general, showed the "No surrender" spirit he had inherited. Although Lieut. Cook's gallantry is unrecorded, Dr. Cook's memory is still revered in the Presbyterian Church of Ireland, and a memorial church and a well-known statue in Belfast are evidence of the appreciation and affection in which his name is held.

219. **Capt. John Cowan**, of St. Johnstown, Derry, defender.
In answer to the appeal for assistance from the citizens of Derry after the shutting of the gates, Capt. Cowan, living some two miles outside, brought a considerable force of armed tenantry into the city. With this company under his command he remained in Derry, doing good service during the siege. He was one of the signers of the "Declaration of Union" and was attainted in James' Dublin Parliament, as was also his brother, or near relative,

220. **Robert Cowan**, who probably also served as a defender during the siege, and may be the Sir Robert Cowan referred to below. On Capt. Cowan's death his estate devolved on his only daughter Mary, who later inherited a large estate from her uncle, Sir Robert Cowan, and marrying Alexander Stewart of Ballylawn, conveyed

the large property to the house of Londonderry. (See No. 222, Col. William Stewart, of Ballylawn, and No. 223, Marquess of Londonderry.)

221. **WINSTON RIDGEWAY, 3RD EARL OF LONDONDERRY** (1st creation 1622). He was an absentee in England during the 1688 revolution and was attainted in James' Dublin Parliament.

His grandfather, Sir Thomas Ridgeway, had secured a considerable portion of land in Co. Tyrone at the time of the Plantation, and had obtained his Earldom of Londonderry in 1622 (it is said by purchase from James I.). On the death early in the 18th century of the 4th Earl (son of the subject of this sketch) without male issue, the title became extinct, but was revived in 1726 by a second creation in favour of Thomas Pitt, who had married Lady Frances Ridgeway, daughter of the 4th and last Earl. This Thomas Pitt, Earl of Londonderry, second creation, was the second son of a remarkable man, viz. Thomas Pitt, a favourite at Court, who had been appointed Governor of Fort St. George, in the East Indies. While there he had the good fortune to buy for some £20,000 the afterwards famous Padogue Diamond, which he sold to the King of France for £135,000. This stone, known as the Pitt, still ranks among the finest in the world. Although Thomas the father died a commoner in 1729 he had lived to see his son Earl of Londonderry. This Earl was succeeded in turn by two sons, but on the death of the third Earl the title again became extinct.[1]

222. **COL. WILLIAM STEWART**, of Ballylawn, Co. Donegal, does not appear to have been in the city during the siege, but as an officer in Lord Mountjoy's Regiment, of which his son Thomas was a captain, he saw considerable service in the subsequent campaign. He was the Stewart of Ballylawn attainted in James' Dublin Parliament.

The first of his family in Donegal was John, of the Garlies Stewart family, who had a grant of Ballylawn in Charles I.'s reign. The Col. William Stewart (above) was the grandson or great-grandson of John.

He left two sons, viz.:—

223. **THOMAS**, of Ballylawn, a captain in Lord Mountjoy's Regiment during the revolution, on whose death in 1747 without issue he was succeeded by his brother, Alexander Stewart of Ballylawn, who married Mary, only daughter of John Cowan, of St. Johnstown (one of the noted defenders during the siege). Mary afterwards inherited a very considerable fortune on the death of her uncle, Sir Robert Cowan, and the estate of Newtown (now known as Mount Stewart), Co. Down, was purchased from Sir Robert Colville. By this marriage there were two sons, viz.:—

---

[1] For present holder of the title, by new creation in 1795, see No. 223, the Earl and Marquess of Londonderry.

(1) Robert, who succeeded to Mount Stewart, and who was raised to the peerage of Ireland as Baron Stewart of Londonderry 1789, Viscount Castlereagh 1795, Earl of Londonderry 1796, and to peerage of U.K. as Marquess of Londonderry 1816.
(2) Alexander, ancestor of Stewart of Ards.[1]

To return to Robert, 1st Marquess of Londonderry. He was the father of that great statesman Viscount Castlereagh, who carried the Union between Great Britain and Ireland. When he came to his untimely end he was succeeded by his half-brother, Charles William, as 3rd Marquess of Londonderry, who in turn was succeeded by his son, Frederick William, 4th Marquess. This was the distinguished soldier and diplomatist, who was one of Wellington's celebrated Generals. He married Frances Anne Emily, only daughter and heiress of Sir Henry Vane Tempest, Bart., by his wife, Catherine Anne, Countess of Antrim in her own right. By this marriage the large Vane estates with Wynyard and a princely position passed to the Londonderry family. In 1833 the Marquess was created in the peerage of the U.K. Earl Vane and Viscount Seaham. Great as the Londonderrys had been in Ulster, this marriage placed them among the greatest of the nobility of the United Kingdom. As Burke in his peerage aptly states: "A pedigree of full 24 descents, a great territorial inheritance, and a name interwoven with the historic events of the Counties of York and Durham combine to entitle the Tempests to a very high place in the roll of the nobility of England."

Of the succeeding Marquesses, all Unionist Ulster owes a debt of gratitude to Charles Stewart, 6th Marquess of Londonderry, for the magnificent stand he took in the forefront of their battle in the Home Rule fight; his name will never be forgotten in the Ulster he loved. As Lord-Lieutenant of Ireland he was at one time dispensing princely hospitality at the Viceregal Lodge in Dublin, while at all times Mount Stewart was kept an open house to his many friends and neighbours. His heart and his purse were always accessible to the calls of the Province, and no man's death came as a greater loss to Ulster. His son and successor, the 7th Marquess, is following in the traditions of his family. As an M.P. he had borne his part in the Home Rule struggle, and since his accession to the title he has taken, not only a prominent place in the House of Lords, but also in affairs of State. As Minister of Education he was for many years in the Cabinet of Northern Ireland, and later a member of Mr. Baldwin's Ministry.

In conclusion, I give a summary of the names of those connected with the Epic of Derry with which the house of Londonderry has blood ties:

(1) Col. William Stewart of Ballylawn.
(2) John Cowan of St. Johnstown, Londonderry.
(3) The Earl of Antrim, on the Jacobite side.

---

[1] See Burke's "Landed Gentry."

224. **THE REV. FULKE WHITE**, of Whitehall, Co. Antrim, was the first Presbyterian minister of the old church of Broughshane, in whose ancient graveyard he and successive generations of his family lie. Settling in Broughshane in 1650 he acquired Whitehall, still in the possession of his family, and in 1690 was one of the ministers selected to present the address of welcome from the Presbyterian Church of Ireland to King William on his landing at Carrickfergus. Of his doings during the Revolution, except the above evidence of his loyalty to the Protestant cause, we have only the following graphic incident related in Witherow's "Siege of Derry": "Leslie (the Rev. Charles Leslie, Jacobite historian of events) tells how Mr. White, Presbyterian minister of Broughshane, had great difficulty in protecting a lady (Mrs. Cormac O'Neill) from being robbed on the 13th Feb., 1689, by forces under the command of Col. Adair and Lieut. Mitchelburn, then on their way to the siege of Carrickfergus. Her only offence was that she was a Roman Catholic, and that her husband was in the Castle they were about to besiege. Mr. White did not leave Mrs. O'Neill till he saw her safe in Shane's Castle in care of Rose O'Neill, Marchioness of Antrim." In explanation of the above, the County Antrim and County Down associations made an abortive attempt in February to surprise Carrickfergus and castle, part of whose garrison consisted of Lord Antrim's Regiment commanded by Col. Cormac O'Neill (a cousin and successor at Shane's Castle of Rose O'Neill, the widowed Marchioness of Antrim). The forces in question who tried to rob Mrs. Cormac O'Neill (who was a daughter of Mr. O'Hara, of Crebilly) were Col. Robert Adair's Ballymena Regiment, evidently on its way to some arranged rendezvous, previous to a combined attack on the castle. Lieut. Mitchelburn was the officer afterwards so famous as one of the Governors of Derry during the siege. This incident, long forgotten, may have been the foundation of the intimacy and friendship subsisting between the O'Neills and Whites for so many generations.

On his death he was succeeded at Whitehall and in the ministry of Broughshane by his son, the Rev. Fulke White, ordained 1716, died 1761, whose great grandson, John White, was High Sheriff of the county in 1860, while his grandson was the distinguished Field-Marshal, Sir George Stewart White, V.C., O.M., G.C.B., &c., D.L., of Whitehall. His gallant leading of the 92nd Gordon Highlanders, when he won his double V.C. at Charasiah and Kandahar, and in many a hard fought action are splendid episodes of war story. His regimental days over, he served in many high posts, among them, military secretary to the Viceroy, General commanding in Burmah, Commander-in-Chief in India, and most important of all Commander-in-Chief in Natal, so memorable for the defence of Ladysmith, and his celebrated words, "Thank God we have kept the flag flying!" After holding the Governorship of Gibraltar he ended a great career as Governor of Chelsea Hospital, where he died. His old friend, and former commanding officer, the great Lord Roberts, most aptly summarised his character when in a speech on parade at Gibraltar he spoke of him "as the brightest living example of the chivalrous Irish soldier and gentleman."

Sir George is survived by his widow, Lady White, of Whitehall, and The Wilderness, Hampton Court, London, by a son, Capt. James Robert White, D.S.O., and by three daughters.

225. **JAMES YOUNG**, of Balluchchule, Co. Donegal, defender, so described in list of attainted in James' Dublin Parliament, served all through the siege. His name is recorded among the witnesses authorising the Governors to appoint commissioners to treat with General Hamilton *re* yielding the city on terms (11th July, 1689). His signature is one of those attached to the address to King William after the relief, and in the records of the Irish Society there is an entry of 1692, ordering a payment of 30*s*. to James Young for beer supplied to Capt. Forward's troop after the shutting of the gates. This troop were among the first of the county contingents to arrive in the city, and were naturally thirsty after a long ride from Burt. Graham, generally accurate, in his notes to the Catalogue in "Ireland Defended," p. 343, states that he belonged to the family of Culdaff. Of this there is some doubt.

Referring to Burke's "Landed Gentry of Ireland" (1894 edition), I find as follows:—

Youngs of Coolkieragh.—The Rev. John Young of an old Scottish stock was Rector of Urney in the middle of 17th century. His son James is the subject of this sketch. James, who died in 1694, left among other issue, John, his successor at Coolkieragh, who left two sons:—

(1) John, from whom descend the line of Coolkieragh, now represented by Richard Ashmore Blair Young, Coolkieragh, Eglinton, Co. Derry.

(2) Thomas of Lough Esk, Co. Donegal, whose grandson William, of Bailieborough Castle, was created a baronet in 1821, and whose son, the 2nd Baronet, was raised to the peerage as Lord Lisgar in 1870, on whose death the title became extinct, but the baronetcy devolved on his nephew, Sir William Muston Need Young, Bart., of Bailieborough Castle.

Youngs of Culdaff, Co. Donegal.—The first of this line in Donegal was the Rev. Robert Young, of an old Devonshire family, inducted Rector of Cloncha in 1640, and of Culdaff in 1668. On his death, about 1668, his son, another Rev. Robert, succeeded to his father's church preferments and estate of Culdaff. Since his time successive generations have been resident at Culdaff, taking a leading and prominent position in county affairs.

The present representative of the family is Robin Young, Millmount House, Randalstown.

There were two of the Young name signing the Enniskillen address to King William, indicating their participation in the gallant doings, viz.:—

226. **MATHEW YOUNG, THOMAS YOUNG.**

227. **JAMES YOUNG**, of Cavan.

228. **JAMES YOUNG**, of Co. Tyrone, and

229. **JAMES YOUNG**, of Co. Monaghan, all attainted in James' Dublin Parliament.

The first Price in Co. Down was Richard Price, an army officer, residing at Newry in 1659. He married Catherine, daughter of James Hamilton, of Bangor. He was Sheriff of Down in 1666. On his death about 1671 his widow married the 4th Earl of Ardglass.[1] Their only son and successor,

230. **NICHOLAS PRICE**, of Hollymount, in 1694 a Lieut.-Col. and in 1707 a Brigadier-General in the army. He was Sheriff of the county in 1694, and M.P. for Downpatrick 1692, 1695, 1703 and 1713. He was one of the attainted in James' Dublin Parliament. He was succeeded by his second son, another Nicholas, the first of the family, styled of Saintfield, who died in 1742. His great-granddaughter, Elizabeth Ann, on whom the estate eventually devolved, married James Blackwood, of Strangford, when the name of Blackwood Price was assumed. Their son, James Charles Blackwood Price, was Sheriff of Down in 1859, succeeded in due course by his son Major James Nugent Blackwood Price of the 60th Rifles, who served as Sheriff of the county in 1902. The family has long been prominent in the county, the present representative being the Rev. Hyde Price, Saintfield, Co. Down.

There were two others of the name among the attainted in James' Dublin Parliament, viz.:—

231. **WILLIAM PRICE**, described as of Donegal or Londonderry.

232. **JOHN PRICE** (yeoman), described as of Co. Cavan. Probably the John signing the Enniskillen address.

233. **THE COUNTESS OF ARDGLASS**, Co. Down, attainted in James' Dublin Parliament, was Catherine, daughter of James Hamilton, of Bangor. As already stated in the sketch of Price of Saintfield, after her first husband, Richard Price's, death about 1671, she had married the 4th and last Earl of Ardglass, on whose death in 1685 she was again left a widow.

The Cromwells (Earls of Ardglass) were of an old Devonshire family. The first of the family coming to Ulster in the 16th century was Thomas Cromwell, son of the 3rd Lord Cromwell of Okeham, whom he succeeded as 4th Lord Cromwell in 1607. He held many important Government posts, among others, the Governorship of Lecale, and acquired by purchase the large estate of Downpatrick centring in and around that

---

[1] See Countess of Ardglass, No. 233.

town. He was created Earl of Ardglass in 1644 and died in 1653.

The 4th and last Earl of Ardglass, who died in 1685, left by his widowed Countess (above) one daughter, who succeeded to the Downpatrick estates and married Edward Southwell. Their descendants held this property for several generations.

234. **Col. Sir Marcus Trevor**, Viscount Dungannon, of Rostrevor, Co. Down, who was one of the attainted in James' Dublin Parliament, was a leading Ulster landowner. He was a zealous loyalist and an ardent supporter of Charles I. and had gained notoriety by wounding Oliver Cromwell at the Battle of Marston Moor. For his services at the time of the Restoration he had been created Viscount Dungannon in 1662. On his death, without male issue, in 1706, the title became extinct, his estate passing to his only daughter Mary, who married William Hill, of Hillsborough, in whose family, that of Downshire, the estate remains. This creation of Viscount Dungannon (1662 and extinct in 1706) must not be confused with later creations.

235. **Capt. William Church**, of Coleraine, defender, figures among the attainted in James' Dublin Parliament. He was killed in one of the garrison sorties on 27th May, 1689, and buried in the city, probably in the Cathedral.[1]

236. Another **William Church**'s signature is attached to the address to King William after the relief, unless Graham has made an error.

237. **George Church**, defender, was a brother of William (No. 235). He served all through the siege and was a signer of the address to King William after the relief.

The Church family had an estate in Co. Derry and for many generations resided at Oatlands, near Coleraine, where they settled early in the 17th century. They no longer possess the property but keep up their connection with the district. Not many years ago a memorial window to one of the family was unveiled in the parish church of Coleraine.

There are at least two representatives of the family, viz. Col. Church, St. Albans, Weymouth; Admiral Church, Bangor, Co. Down.

238. **Capt. William Grove**, of Castle Shannaghan, Co. Donegal, defender. After the shutting of the gates Capt. Grove was among the first of the neighbouring landlords to answer Derry's appeal by bringing in a troop of his own tenantry. In command of these he remained, taking part in the defence until after the relief. He figures in the list of attainted in James' Dublin Parliament.

He lost his life, after the war was over, in the mountains near Newry, from an attack of woodkerne or rapparees.[2]

"Londeriados" thus writes of him:—

---

[1] See Graham's "Ireland Preserved," notes to Catalogue.
[2] Graham, "Ireland Defended," p. 295.

"Grove of Castle Shannaghan had brought
The Kilmacrenan men, who bravely fought.
This valiant man, after the war's slain
When on the Fews he was by Tories ta'en.
He died, lamented for his worth and zeal,
And suffered greatly for the common weal."

The Groves were long in residence at Castle Grove (now Castle Shannaghan) near Kilmacrenan, where they were owners of considerable estate. The estate has long passed from the family, but Capt. William Grove's name is fittingly commemorated in the Cathedral window, unveiled in 1913, to perpetuate the achievement of the gallant defenders. Among descendant subscribers under his name are General Henry Leslie Grove and Mrs. M. E. Boylan.

239. **CAPT. BASIL BROOKE**, of Tullough Galloney, Co. Monaghan, so described in the list of attainted in James' Dublin Parliament.

The first of the name in Ulster was Basil Brooke, a distinguished officer in the Elizabethan service during the Tyrone wars. He was appointed Constable of Donegal Castle, and at the Plantation acquired considerable grants of land in Co. Donegal. He was knighted later on, and dying in 1633 was succeeded in his office as Constable and estates by his son Sir Henry Brooke, who for his services during the rebellion of 1641 received further large grants of estate in Co. Fermanagh. He died in 1672, leaving with other issue two sons, Capt. Basil, the subject of this sketch, and Thomas (of whom presently) attainted in James' Dublin Parliament.

Capt. Basil Brooke succeeded to his father's Donegal property, where the family ultimately made Lough Eske, near Donegal, their headquarters until sold to Major White by the executors of the last Brooke of that line, who died without issue in 1881.

240. The second son of Sir Henry Brooke, the **THOMAS BROOKE** above, succeeded to his father's Fermanagh property, marrying the only daughter of Sir John Cole, a large and prominent neighbouring landlord; a few years later, owing to the death of her only brother without issue, the Cole estate devolved on his wife, and the name of Colebrooke was given to the demesne. Their descendants the Brookes of Colebrooke have always taken a leading position in politics and public affairs in their county and in Ulster. The first baronetcy created in 1762 became extinct, but the second baronetcy, created in 1822, is still in the enjoyment of the family, the present owner of Colebrooke, Co. Fermanagh, being Capt. Sir Basil Stanlake Brooke, C.B.E., M.C., K Bart. Sir Basil served with distinction all through the Great War as an officer in the Royal Fusiliers and 10th Hussars. Besides other medals he wears the Croix de Guerre.

There were two other Brooks (or possibly Brookes) attainted in James' Dublin Parliament, probably descendants of the first Basil Brooke, Constable of Donegal

Castle. The first of these was:—

241. **HENRY BROOKS**, described as of Co. Donegal or Londonderry, and the second was

242. **LIEUT. EDWARD BROOKS**, described as of Co. Donegal or Londonderry. This was one of the Sheriffs of the city and a lieutenant of one of the city companies with which he served all through the siege.

"Londeriados" extols his exertions in the raising of funds and supplies for the defence:—

> "James Roe Cunningham and Master Brooks
> Gave great supplies, as is seen by their Books."

He signed the "Declaration of Union" and also the Corporation's Commission of 1690.

243. **LIEUT. JAMES KERR**, defender. In "Londeriados" there is the following record of his prowess:—

> "Lieut. Kerr, the Laird of Gradon's son
> In the pursuit great reputation won."

He is mentioned by Mackenzie for good service in the sortie of 4th June, and James Carr, probably this Lieut. James Kerr (as Ker, Kerr and Carr were variously spelt in those days), was a signer of the address to King William after the relief.

An old gravestone in Rossory churchyard near Enniskillen gives the names of several Kerrs of Grasskeogh in that parish, going back to James Kerr, probably above, who was serving in "the weighty" horse at the Boyne.[1]

At the centenary celebration of the shutting of the gates held in Derry in 1788 an incident so remarkable is chronicled that I quote it in full[2]:—

"We cannot omit observing that there was one person among the guests, who had been actually present at the siege; he was born the year before the siege, and, while the city was invested, was nursed in a cellar. The company was much struck with the singularity of the circumstance, and the venerable appearance of the old man excited unusual attention."

Graham in his notes to the Catalogue in "Ireland Defended" states that his name was Carr (Kerr?). Unfortunately, nothing more is definitely known, but I presume him to have been a son of the Lieut. James Kerr above.

There were four Kerrs among the attainted in James' Dublin Parliament, viz.:—

---

[1] Trimble's "Enniskillen," Vol. III. p. 1126.
[2] Hampton's "Siege," p. 83.

244. **JOHN KERR**, described as of Co. Fermanagh.

245. **ROBERT KERR**, described as of Omagh, Co. Tyrone.

246. **THOMAS KERR**, described as of Omagh, Co. Tyrone.

247. **THOMAS KERR**, described as of Co. Tyrone.

248. **THE DUKE OF SCHOMBERG.** Of this illustrious General, of his crowning victory and tragic death at the Boyne, so much is known, that in this sketch only a few details of his antecedents and striking career will be given.

His father was the Count Schomberg of an old and noble family in the Palatinate, and his mother a daughter of Lord Dudley. Born in 1609, he was forced by the frequent invasions that devastated the Palatinate to seek refuge, early in life, in Holland, where he laid the foundations of his military renown in the service of the Stadtholders, Frederick William and his son William II., Prince of Orange. On the latter's death in 1650, leaving an infant son, afterwards the famous William III., Prince of Orange, as his successor, he transferred his sword to Louis XIV. of France, in whose service he earned the baton of Field-Marshal in 1676, and a reputation second to none of his celebrated compeers. With the Edict of Nantes, rather than conform to Roman Catholicism, he sacrificed a great fortune, and retired from Louis XIV.'s service. Again adrift, he accepted a high position in the Elector of Brandenburg's army.

When the revolution of 1688 was impending and William of Orange was preparing for his descent on England, Count Schomberg, with the permission of his Elector, offered his sword to William. By no one could the offer have been more appreciated. William was well aware of his reputation and of his value on the field of battle, where he had himself more than once encountered him in Flanders. Joining William at The Hague, Schomberg became the general adviser in all the preparations and in the subsequent expedition.

After the successes in England, the flight of James and William's accession to the throne, Schomberg, who had been welcomed in London as a Protestant hero, was created Duke of Schomberg, with an income of £5000 per annum for himself and heirs. He was sent to Liverpool to command the large army there mustering for descent on the North of Ireland. At the head of this force he landed at Carrickfergus on the 13th August, 1689, just a fortnight after the relief of Derry. Carrickfergus Castle fell a few days afterwards, when Schomberg led his army to Dundalk, where he confronted James for some months: but owing to fever and sickness he was compelled to retire to Belfast, where the rest of the winter and spring of 1690 was spent in more comfortable quarters. Early in the summer of 1690 William landed at Carrickfergus and, joining Schomberg, began the march to the Boyne. Of that eventful day I need not say more here than that, at a critical moment of the day, the gallant old veteran of eighty-one, seeing things going badly in the passage of the river, put himself at the head of some French Huguenots and plunged in, exclaiming "Allons, Messieurs, Voilà vos persécuteurs." He had not gone many yards before he fell into the river, shot dead through the head. At a council of war on the previous night he is said to have differed from the King on the plan of battle, and when the order to attack was brought to his tent the next morning he is said to have exclaimed that it was the first order that was ever sent to him. His death at that junction was looked upon as a national calamity. His body was reverently carried with the victorious army to Dublin, and interred with full military honours in St. Patrick's Cathedral.

Although not directly connected with the defence of Derry Kirke's relieving force had been sent, if not at Schomberg's instigation, with his full approval, while the Duke's letter of the 3rd July to General Kirke, remonstrating at his delay and urging immediate attack at all costs, was probably responsible for the breaking of the Boom of the 28th July. Derry had much reason to be thankful to the Duke. Besides, there was a personal touch, noted on the minutes of the Corporation. On the 19th September, 1689, they had proffered a petition to "His Grace, the Duke of Schomberg, for the poor inhabitants of this city, that remained here all the siege and are now alive in it." In answer, the Corporation received an order from Schomberg (read at their meeting of November) for "the delivering 1000 bushels of wheat, and 1000 bushels of peas for the poor ancient inhabitants of the city as have survived the siege," and another on 4th February, 1690, for 250 parcels of wheat and four tons of cheese pursuant to an order of the King and Council, all to be admitted free of duty, while His Majesty made a special allowance of £500 to provide coal.[1]

Nothing, perhaps, is more striking evidence of the feeling in England for this Protestant hero who had sacrificed so much than his reception by the House of Commons at Westminster before going to Ireland on his last campaign. He had the unprecedented honour of remaining "seated" and "covered" inside the bar of the house, and "after a short space standing up uncovered."[2] The Duke of Wellington, after Waterloo, received the like honour.

249. His son **MEINHARDT, COUNT SCHOMBERG**, his successor as 2nd Duke of Schomberg, was in the command of troops at the Boyne and well avenged his father's death by a relentless pursuit of the flying enemy. He served all through the campaign down to the fall of Limerick in 1691.

Walker's "Siege" has the following allusion to a Captain Shomberg in an affair of June 1689: "By the contrivance of our Governor (Walker) and Col. Mitchelburn, and the directions and care of Captain Shomberg . . . we countermine the enemy before the Butcher's Gate." From this reference Graham in his notes to the Catalogue in

---

[1] Extracts from minutes of Corporation.

[2] Harris.

"Ireland Defended" assumes the Captain in question to have been Count Schomberg, the Duke of Schomberg's son. If so, the son of such an illustrious man would have been definitely named. There is evidently some confusion with

250. **ANTHONY SHUMBERG**, who got his commission as Major in 1691 in Mitchelburn's Regiment,[1] who is probably the same as

251. **ANTHONY SHOBURN**, an ensign in the same regiment in 1689 and a defender.

252. **CAPT. THOMAS KEYS**, of Cavanacor, Co. Donegal, and his brother,

253. **FREDERICK KEYS**, of the same, were both among the defenders through the siege. They held commissions in Col. Baker's, afterwards Col. Crofton's, Regiment.

A note in Dalton's "Army List"[2] informs us that Capt. Thomas Keys, who was in London after the relief, lately in the Derry garrison, received three months' pay from the War Office to enable him to join the Duke of Schomberg's army in Ireland. Both these officers signed the Derry address to King William after the relief.

The family had been in possession of Cavanacor for some time previous to the siege. Local tradition[3] affirms that King James dined in the house while on his way at the head of his army to Derry, and that for this reason the residence was spared in the general burnings of all Protestant property on the army's retirement to Dublin after the relief.

In 1823 by the marriage of Mary, daughter and heiress of William Keys, with Benjamin Geale Humfrey the estate of Cavanacor passed to that line, the present owner (1894)[4] being Major Benjamin Geale Humfrey, of Cavanacor, Ballindrait, Co. Donegal.

254. **HUMFREY OF CAVANACOR**, Co. Donegal. The Humfrey family settled in Wicklow in 1655 and were subsequently in Carlow.

By the marriage in 1823 of Benjamin Geale Humfrey with Mary, daughter and heiress of William Keys, the estate became the Humfreys'[5] and is now in the possession (1894) of their grandson, Major Benjamin Geale Humfrey, of Cavanacor, Ballindrait, Co. Donegal.

An obituary notice[6] recording the death of a Miss Humfrey, of Cavanacor, aged ninety-eight, states that King James on his way to Derry (1689) lunched under a sycamore tree (still standing) on the lawn before the house.[7] The obituary notice further

---

[1] Dalton.
[2] 1689–1714, Vol. III. p. 168.
[3] Graham's "Ireland Defended."
[4] See No. 254.
[5] See No. 253.
[6] "Belfast Newsletter," December 29th, 1923.
[7] This is another version of the local tradition as already given in No. 253, Keys.

states that the distinguished Admiral, Sir Roger Keyes, of Zeebrugge fame, is closely related to the old family of Cavanacor.

Among the attainted in James' Dublin Parliament were several Humphreys (Humfreys?), viz.:—

255. **THOMAS HUMPHREY**, described as of Co. Cavan.

256. **JOHN HUMPHREY**, described as of Co. Fermanagh.

257. **THOMAS HUMPHREY**, described as of Co. Fermanagh.

258. **WILLIAM HUMPHREY**, described as of Co. Fermanagh.

259. **WILLIAM BLACKER**, of Carrick Blacker, Co. Armagh, defender.

In the list of attaintures of James' Dublin Parliament there is the name of George Blacker, jr., described as of Londonderry, evidently a mistake of the compilers of the list for William, the eldest son and heir of George Blacker, of Carrick Blacker, who found himself in Derry under peculiar circumstances. He was conveying his family to the safe refuge of that city when, intercepted by James' advancing army, he was compelled to go on as an unwilling emissary to try to induce the city to surrender. On his arrival there, he spent his first few weeks in confinement, but was afterwards admitted to full confidence, and was among the gallant defenders all through the siege.[1]

He was present at the Boyne, and to him was relegated the duty of escorting the body of the late Governor of Derry, the Rev. George Walker, to Castlecaulfield and of seeing him interred with military honours in the parish church. He served with distinction in the subsequent campaign until the fall of Limerick (1692). He married a lady of the Castle Stewart house, hence the constant recurrence of that Christian name in the line of his descendants.

Among the subscribing descendants under the name of William Blacker to the memorial window in Derry Cathedral, unveiled in 1913 to commemorate the gallant defenders, are Col. Stewart Blacker of Carrick Blacker, Maxwell V. Blacker-Douglas, Edward Carew Blacker, Ralph de la Poer Beresford, Miss Juliet Reeves.

The family are of ancient Danish descent.

BLACKER OF CARRICK BLACKER. According to Burke's "Landed Gentry of Ireland" (1894 edition), the first of the name to settle in Co. Armagh was Valentine Blacker, who came from Yorkshire in 1660, and purchased, from Sir Anthony Cope, of Loughgall, the manor of Carrickblack (henceforth Carrick Blacker). Dying in 1677, he was succeeded by his son George Blacker, the owner of Carrick Blacker in 1688–9, described by Burke as a firm adherent of the Royal House of Stuart. He was Sheriff of Co. Armagh in 1684. On his death his son William Blacker succeeded to Carrick Blacker, the subject of this sketch. From him a long line of lineal descendants, prominent in

---

[1] Mackenzie, p. 209.

their county and in public affairs, have resided at Carrick Blacker.

The present representative of this old stock is Col. Stewart Blacker, D.L., of Carrick Blacker, Co. Armagh. Col. Blacker took a prominent part in the Great War. He was chiefly responsible for raising a battalion of the Ulster Division, which he took out and commanded on the Western Front for two years, until the War Office forced him, on account of advancing years, to give place to a younger man. Returning home, he had enough remaining energy to command with efficiency a battalion of the Ulster Division Reserve until the Armistice.

260. **ENSIGN HENRY SWANZY**, of Avelreagh, Clontibret, Co. Monaghan. He held a commission (1689), still in the possession of the family, in Col. Arthur Upton's Regiment, being ensign in Capt. James McCormick's (of Lisburn) company. With this regiment he was present, under Sir Arthur Rawdon, in the preliminary operations from the "Break of Dromore" to the retreat on Derry, where he took part in the gallant defence.

He was the son of Mr. Henry Swanzy, of Blaris, Co. Down.[1] He was born in 1666 and after the revolution he settled at Avelreagh, Clontibret, Co. Monaghan, and died in 1742. His family were in possession of Avelreagh until 1919.

Family records, it is pleasant to note, tell of the kindly interest taken by the Uptons in the welfare of relatives of officers serving in their old regiment. As late as 1763 this hereditary feeling was shown by Lady Templetown, at that time administering her son, a minor's, estate in Cos. Antrim and Monaghan. A portion of the lands in Co. Monaghan were let on most favourable terms to a relation, Mr. Wildman Swanzy.

The defender of Derry is represented in direct descent by the Rev. Canon Thomas Erskine Swanzy, M.A., Vicar of All Saints, Lincoln, and by the Very Rev. Henry B. Swanzy, M.A., Dean of Dromore and Vicar of Newry, Co. Down, to whom I am indebted for the above particulars.

261. **COL. PARKER**, of Coleraine, defender. He was Lieut.-Col. of Sir Tristram Beresford's Regiment, which, after the latter's withdrawal to England, he commanded in the early weeks of the siege. "Londeriados" has the following line:—

"Then Parker brought a regiment from Coleraine."

Writing of the garrison's successful sortie on the 25th April Mackenzie relates the following untoward incident:[2] "This night, Major (Col.?) Parker left this city and deserted their Majesties' service here, on this occasion a rearguard of foot had been left to defend our men from a party of the enemy, which we on the walls saw coming on them. These Major Parker was too slow or negligent in bringing off, according to his orders, whereby they were exposed to great danger from the enemy. For this misbe-

[1] Afterwards of Kilmore, Co. Monaghan.
[2] Mackenzie, p. 222 in Hampton's "Siege."

haviour he was threatened with a court-martial, which he took this course to avoid," viz. desertion to the Jacobite camp. This is the same Parker who afterwards rendered his name so infamous by being concerned in the atrocious plot to assassinate King William at Kensington.[1] "Londeriados" comments on this as follows:—

> "But Colonel Parker for some policy
> Fled the same night unto the enemy.
> His Coleraine regiment, Col. Lance obtains
> Who in the present service honour gains."[2]

262. **COL. THOMAS LANCE**, of Coleraine, defender, an officer in Sir Tristram Beresford's Regiment, with which he served all through the siege. After Col. Parker's desertion on the 25th April he succeeded him as commanding officer.[3]

"Londeriados" refers to him: "Then Capt. Thos. Lance from Coleraine." In Ash's "Diary" we are told how seven men of his regiment were killed by a chance bomb falling on the house (Harper's) where they were quartered.

He was a signer of the address to King William after the relief. After General Kirke's arrival in the city, his regiment was amalgamated with Col. Monro's, to whom the joint command was given, while Col. Lance was relegated to the command of a force newly organised by General Kirke. Owing to the privations of the siege his health broke down and he died on the 11th September, 1689, in the city, where he was buried.[4]

263. **LANCELOT VANCE.** There is a curious monument in the old graveyard at Coagh, Co. Tyrone, over the burying place of John Vance, of Coagh, born 1712, died 1799. "In the inscription he is stated to be the second son of another John Vance, the first lessee of these lands at Coagh, whose father was Dr. Lancelot Vance surgeon, and afterwards Col. of the Coleraine regiment in the siege of Derry, where he died of excessive fatigue within the walls of Derry, during the memorable siege 1689." "Erected by Robert Anstruther Balburnie Vans, grandson of the first named John Vance." He is further stated to have been of the family of Vans, of Bamburragh, Wigtonshire. In regard to the command of the Coleraine regiment, a not unnatural confusion between the names Vance and Lance probably occurred in the century between the siege and the erection of the monument.[5] The solution is to be found in the record of another member of the family of Vans, of Bamburragh (?), Wigtonshire, whose record I find in Dalton's "Army List," 1689–1714, of which I give the extract below, viz.[6]:—

---

[1] Harris, "Life of King William," p. 207.
[2] See No. 262, Col. Lance.
[3] See under No. 261, Col. Parker.
[4] Mackenzie, and Graham's "Derriana." See No. 261, Col. Parker; No. 263, Lancelot Vance.
[5] See No. 261, Col. Parker, of Coleraine Regiment; No. 262, Col. Lance, of same.
[6] Vol. III. pp. 206–207.

264. **COL. PATRICK VANCE OF BAMBURRAGH,** Wigtonshire, held a commission as Captain in Lord George Hamilton, afterwards Earl of Orkney's, regiment of Enniskillen foot in 1691. In an application to the Duke of Marlborough in 1706 for further military employment, he summarises his services as follows: served in France sixteen years, afterwards in the revolution, and later in 1691 obtained a captaincy in the Enniskillen Regiment, commanded by the Earl of Orkney, in which capacity he served till the reduction of Ireland, when the regiment was broke. In answer to this, he was given a commission as 2nd Lieutenant in Col. Townsend's Regiment, and was later appointed Lieut.-Col. in another regiment. Later on his name figures in 1714 as Lieut.-Col. on the half-pay list.

The above officer was son of Sir John Vans, of Bamburragh, Wigtonshire, succeeding eventually to that estate. He was the first M.P. for Wigtonshire after the Union with England.[1]

265. **CAPT. REV. CHRISTOPHER JENNY,** D.D., defender, Rector of Ardboe and Ardtrae, Co. Tyrone, Prebendary of Mullaghbrack. Coming into the city a few days before the investment he soon became as prominent in the defence as in the organisation, and was accorded the rank of captain, serving in that capacity all through the siege. He was among the witnesses signing the garrison's commission authorising the Governors to appoint commissioners to treat for surrender of the city with General Richard Hamilton on the 11th July. He was a signer of the address to King William after the relief. He was attainted in James' Dublin Parliament.

He was, by the Governors' orders, sent on a deputation, consisting of himself, "C. White, C. Dobbin, C. I. Hamilton, and Jo. Fox (Knox), to wait on General Kirke, still in Inch (Aug. 1), to give him an account of the raising of the siege, to carry him our thanks, and desire him to come and receive the garrison."[2] A few Sundays after the relief he preached before General Kirke, choosing as his text, "When thou goest forth against the enemy then keep thee from every wicked thing."[3]

His daughter, Mary, married the Ven. and Rev. William Ussher, whose daughter, Mary Jenny Ussher, by her union with the Rt. Hon. John Staples of Lissan, brought the siege descent into the Staples family.[4]

266. **FRANCES JENNING** (or **JENNY**). Her signature is appended to the Corporation of Derry's Commission of 1690. She was probably a relative of the Jenny family.

267. **DAVID CAIRNES,** of Knockmany, Co. Tyrone, defender. No man was more conspicuous or useful in the city from the closing of the gates down to the investment,

---

[1] Dalton's "Army List," 1689–1714, Vol. III. pp. 206, 207.
[2] Walker's "Siege."
[3] Ash's "Diary."
[4] See Staples.

or afterwards in London as the representative of the garrison at King William's Court during the siege, than David Cairnes. Of these services full details are given in the Introductory Chapter.

Before proceeding further a few particulars of the family antecedents will be of interest. Alexander Cairnes, laird of Orchardston in Kirkcudbrightshire, a cadet of the ancient house of Cairnes of that ilk, settled in Co. Donegal in 1609. He left three sons, John, Robert and David, who in 1640 acquired in joint purchase the large manor of Killyfaddy in Co. Tyrone.

1. The eldest of these, John, at one time M.P. for Augher, left two sons, William and Alexander, from the daughter of the latter of whom the property of this line eventually devolved on the family of Westenra, Lords Rossmore, the present representatives of the Cairnes of Co. Monaghan in the female line.
2. Robert, who died without issue, leaving his estates to his brother David.
3. David, who left two sons, viz.:—
    (*a*) William, who resided at Killyfaddy and was the father of William, the apprentice boy of Derry siege, of whom presently.
    (*b*) David, defender of Derry and subject of this sketch, who resided on the Knockmany portion of the Killyfaddy estate's.[1]

In 1680 David had taken up the practice of law in Derry and was elected a Burgess. Henceforth his time was divided between Knockmany and Derry. His appointment a few years later as law agent to the Irish Society and marriage with Miss Edwards of an old Plantation family added considerably to his growing importance and influence. This influence, in the critical days pending the revolution, he had used to the full in the neighbouring counties and in the city itself in organising the beginnings of Protestant resistance. His actions therefore in supporting the shutting of the gates, the organisation of defence, and resistance at all costs were what the citizens and garrison had expected of a man in whom they had implicit confidence.[2] "Londeriados" thus refers to his first journey to Court:—

> "The learned Councillor Cairnes to London hies
> To move the Court to send us fresh supplies.
> Their Majesties, like tender parents, sent
> Two regiments and stores for the intent
> . . . .
> Richards and Cunningham the regiments led
> The stores were landed, but the Colonels fled."

His name, of course, figures in the list of attainted in James' Dublin Parliament.

---

[1] For further particulars, see Lawler's "History of the Family of Cairnes."
[2] See Introductory Chapter.

Returning to the city immediately after the relief he threw himself energetically into repairing the ravages of war, pressing for compensation for the siege losses of the city, and demanding payment of the huge arrears of pay due to the garrison. Like all the prominent defenders (except Walker) David Cairnes never received any payment from the Government for his heavy losses and expenditure. The appreciation of the city was, however, shown in his election as first M.P. of the constituency after the siege, but this he had to resign in 1704, after the passing of the Test Act, to which he refused to conform. In 1715 he was appointed Recorder of the city. He died in 1722 and was buried in the Cathedral, where an imposing mural tablet was subsequently erected by the Irish Society to his memory. His name is also recorded in the Cathedral window unveiled in 1913 in memory of the gallant defenders. The massive pillar, crowned by the figure of George Walker, which Derry erected at the beginning of last century in memory of its siege heroes, has five great names, Walker, Cairnes, Mitchelburn, Baker and Murray, inscribed on the base.

David Cairnes left no surviving male issue. His only son had been killed in a duel in England in 1719. He left a daughter, Jane, who married her cousin, Thomas Edwards, of Castle Gore, now represented by the Edwards and Gores of Raveagh.[1]

268. **WILLIAM CAIRNES** (the younger), of Killyfaddy, defender, was one of the thirteen apprentice boys who immortalised their names and made history by the shutting of the gates on the 7th December, 1688. He was appointed a lieutenant in one of the city regiments, with which he served all through the siege, and afterwards held a commission in King William's army, being present at the Boyne and in the subsequent campaign.

This William was the son of William the elder of Killyfaddy, and nephew of David.[2] He died at Killyfaddy in 1740, without issue, the estate passing under his will to John Elliott, the grandson of his sister Mary, when the name of Elliott-Cairnes was assumed.98a Among the representative descendants of this marriage are the Cairnes of Drogheda, the Bellinghams of Castle Bellingham, and the Lawlors, of Belfast, of whom Mr. H. C. Lawlor has, at his residence, Killyfaddy, Windsor Avenue, Belfast, many interesting portraits of siege celebrities and documents relating to those great events.

269. **COL. JOHN CAIRNES**, of Claremore, Co. Tyrone, defender. No name has more frequent mention by all authorities for conspicuous gallantry during the siege. Of him "Londeriados" writes:—

> "Cairnes in our centre stood firm as a rock
> And ne're was moved by their mighty shock."

And again:—

---

[1] See Lawlor's "History of the Family of Cairnes."
[2] For full particulars see No. 267, David Cairnes.

"Near to the Lough Lieutenant Colonel Cairnes
Receives his standing, who great honour earns."

He was among the attainted in James' Dublin Parliament. His exact relationship to David and William Cairnes of Nos. 267 and 268 is not traceable, but he was undoubtedly of that family.[1]

270. **JOHN CAIRNES**, of Agharononan, Co. Tyrone, so described, was among the list of attainted in James' Dublin Parliament. I presume him to have been of the same family. Earl Cairns, Lord Chancellor of England, was descended from a cadet branch of this family, long settled in Co. Down.

271. **ADAM LOFTUS, 2ND VISCOUNT LISBURNE.** He was the second holder of the Viscountcy conferred on his father in 1683, and was a descendant of the celebrated Adam Loftus, Archbishop of Dublin in the previous century, now represented in that line by the Marquess of Ely.

He was attainted in James' Dublin Parliament. According to the historians of the campaign[2] he landed with the Duke of Schomberg at Carrickfergus, was present at the Boyne, and all through the campaign until killed before Limerick. "A man of excellent parts, who has shown himself very diligent and forward on all occasions, since the beginning of the war."[3]

On his death the peerage became extinct. It is not to be confused with the 1695 Earldom of Lisburne conferred on the Vaughan family which they still enjoy.

272. **THE DOWAGER VISCOUNTESS LISBURNE**, mother of the above, was also on the list of attainted in James' Dublin Parliament.

273. **BENNET SHERARD, 2ND BARON SHERARD**, of Leitrim. He was one of the Irish peers attainted in James' Dublin Parliament, but I can find no other fact connecting him with the revolution in Ireland.

His father had been created Baron in 1627 by Charles I. The late representative of the family (1907) was the 11th Baron Sherard, of Glatton, Selton, Hants, who died in 1931.

Other Sherards directly connected with the siege are:—

274. **DANIEL SHERARD**, defender. He was one of the thirteen apprentice boys responsible for the shutting of the gates on 7th December, and was a few days later appointed ensign of a city company, with which he served all through the siege, and as Lieut. Daniel Sherard his name is among the attainted in James' Dublin Parliament.

[1] See Lawlor's "History of the Family of Cairnes."
[2] Harris and Story.
[3] Story.

275. **WILLIAM SHERARD**, defender. He was another of the thirteen apprentice boys.

276. **ROBERT SHERARD**. His signature is appended to the Corporation Commission, while John Harvey signs the same by proxy for—

277. The orphans of **MRS. HUTTON SHERARD**.

278. **CAPT. BALDWIN LEIGHTON**. This officer appears to have been the accredited agent between William of Orange and the Consult of Hillsborough, representing the forces raised by the Protestant county associations of Northeast Ulster. On the 10th January, 1689, after an interview at Hillsborough, he sailed from Belfast with important messages to King William at Whitehall, and on the 9th of the following March he returned to the Hillsborough Consult with promises of support, and regular commissions, with the King's sign manual, for the officers of all the regiments raised or in process of raising.[1]

It would appear that his brother, Edward Leighton, an important Shropshire landlord, was one of William's staunchest supporters, and in his confidence, which accounts for his brother's presence on the scene of action. This Edward, probably in recognition of the family services, was created a baronet in 1693, and is now represented by Sir Richard Baldwin Leighton, 9th Bart., of Luton, Shropshire.

279. **GEORGE CANNING**, of Garvagh, Co. Derry.

The Canning family were sprung of an old Wiltshire stock and for several generations had been prominent among the City of London merchants. On the Ulster Plantation and advent of the City Companies in Co. Derry, George, the grandfather of the above, had come over as the representative of the Ironmongers' Company to look after their interests and take possession of the estates round Garvagh allocated to them.[2] George Canning, who died in 1646, his son William having been killed when the rebels attacked Garvagh in 1641, was succeeded by his grandson, George Canning, the subject of this sketch.

No agent or landlord occupied a more influential position in Co. Derry at the time of the 1688 revolution. It was his timely warning of the approach of Lord Antrim's Regiment, sent through Phillips of Limavady, that apprised the Corporation of their danger and led to the shutting of the gates. In subsequent events, both in city and country, he took a leading part.[3] He raised from the tenantry of the Garvagh estate the regiment of that name, which, under his command, shared with the garrison of Coleraine in repulsing Gen. Richard Hamilton's attack. A few weeks later, after Hamilton's passage of the Bann at Portglenone, Coleraine was evacuated, and the whole

---

[1] Harris, p. 196, and Mackenzie.

[2] In process of time the Garvagh estate, at first held under long lease from the Ironmongers' Company, became the property of the Cannings by purchase.

[3] See Introductory Chapter.

of Sir Arthur Rawdon's force, of which Canning's Regiment formed part, compelled to retire on Derry.

Once in the city he took a leading part in the efforts to prevent Hamilton's advance, but when these failed owing to Lundy's treachery he retired with many others to England. During the siege, Major Crofton was given the command of the Garvagh Regiment, which he led with distinction.

Col. George Canning was among the attainted in James' Dublin Parliament. Returning to Ireland after the relief, he died at Garvagh in 1711.

Stratford, his son and successor, is remarkable in so far that from his three sons descend the line of three distinct peerages, viz.:—

1. From George, the eldest, another George, Prime Minister of England, whose son, created Earl Canning, was Viceroy of India (earldom extinct 1862).
2. From Paul, the second, the line of Garvagh (barony created in 1818), of which the present representative is Leopold Ernest Stratford Canning, 4th Baron Garvagh, and
3. From the third, Stratford, the famous man who as British Ambassador for seventeen years at Constantinople (1841–1858) did so much to ensure the success of British policy and arms in the Crimean campaign. He was created Viscount Stratford de Redcliffe, but dying without issue in 1862, the title became extinct.

280. **MAJOR JOHN HILL**, of Derry, defender. Samuel Hill, a Cromwellian officer, settled in the North of Ireland, left two sons,[1] the elder of whom, the subject of this sketch, was a signer of the "Declaration of Union" and served as an officer of the garrison during the siege.[1] His brother,

281. **CAPT. JONATHAN HILL**, also served as an officer of the garrison during the siege.[1]

All through the 17th century the family held a prominent position in the city and county of Derry, several of them representing the borough in Parliament. Hugh Hill, M.P., of St. Columbs, was in 1779 created a baronet, the present representative being the 6th Baronet, Sir Henry Blyth Hill, Bart., of St. Columbs, Co. Derry.[1]

282. **JAMES HILL**, of Co. Cavan, was attainted in James' Dublin Parliament.

283. **CAPT. OLIVER McCAUSLAND**, of Strabane, defender. In the list of attainted in James' Dublin Parliament there are two of this name, viz. Oliver McCausland of Rash, Co. Tyrone, probably the Oliver above, and

284. **ANDREW McCAUSLAND**, of Clanaghmore, Co. Tyrone, who was probably, if

---

[1] See Burke's Peerage.

not an ancestor, closely related to Col. Robert McCausland, of Fruit Hill (Drenagh), the first of the family living there (he died in 1734), who had property near Cappagh, Co. Tyrone. This Robert McCausland was befriended by the Rt. Hon. William Conolly, of Castletown and Limavady, and acquired considerable estate in Co. Derry; hence the Christian name of Conolly borne in subsequent generations of the McCausland family.

The only mention of the name in connection with the siege is Mackenzie's statement that when Lord Mountjoy, as Tyrconnell's representative, was on his way to the city, after the shutting of the gates, to open negotiations for surrender or making of terms, Capt. Oliver McCausland, of Strabane, was employed as a messenger to warn the Corporation of his approach, but (as Graham in his "Ireland Preserved" notes) "although he carried the message, he did not regret that the answer was 'No Surrender,' " and that he served under the command of Col. Mitchelburn at the siege of Derry. In his will, Capt. Oliver McCausland refers to Col. Robert, of Fruit Hill, as cousin while appointing him an executor and legatee.

The present representatives of this old family are Col. R. A. C. McCausland, Woodbank, Garvagh, Co. Derry, Maurice McCausland, H.M.L. (Co. Derry), Drenagh (Fruit Hill), Limavady, Co. Derry.

With regard to the origin of the family and their coming to Ireland, Burke's "Landed Gentry of Ireland," 1904 edition, has the following account: "This is a junior branch (which emigrated to Ireland temp. James VI.) of the ancient Scottish house of MacAuslane of Buchanan, which sprung from John MacAuslane (or the son of Auslane), who acquired the lands of Buchanan, on the Lennox, and from whom they descended in direct male succession to Sir Walter MacAuslanes of Buchanan." The heir male is stated to have migrated to Ireland *temp.* James VI. He had two sons, of whom the elder, Andrew, was grandfather of the Col. Robert McCausland of Fruit Hill (Drenagh) above.

285. **JOHN LOWRY**, of Co. Tyrone. The first of the name in Co. Tyrone was James Lowry, who came from Scotland early in the 17th century and died in 1665, being succeeded by his son, the subject of this sketch, John Lowry, of Ahenis, Co. Tyrone, who with his second wife,

286. **MRS. JOHN LOWRY** (*née* Jane, daughter of William Hamilton of Ballyfatton, see that name) was present all through the siege, where John Lowry died. John Lowry is on the list of attainted, as is also his son,

287. **JOHN LOWRY**, jr., who d.s.p. 1698. John Lowry, the subject of No. 285, was succeeded by a son, Robert, who left with other issue two surviving sons:

1. Galbraith, who by his marriage with the daughter and heiress of John Corry, of Castle Coole (1733), brought that property into the Lowry family, when

the surname of Lowry-Corry was adopted.[1] Galbraith's son and successor, Armar Lowry Corry, was created a Baron in 1781, Viscount Corry in 1789 and Earl of Belmore in 1797. The present representative of the family is the 5th Earl of Belmore, Castle Coole, Enniskillen.[2]

2. From the Rev. James, the second son of Robert (above) and brother of Galbraith, descend the Lowrys of Pomeroy and Rockdale.

288. **Humphrey Lowry**'s name is among the signatures to the Corporation of Derry's 1690 Commission.

289. **Capt. James Corry**, of Castle Coole, Enniskillen. His father, John, acquired the Castlecoole property by purchase in 1656, and was Sheriff of the county in 1666. Dying in 1683, he was succeeded by his son, the Capt. James of this sketch.

When the revolution broke out he was a most energetic supporter of the men of Enniskillen, but after a time, like many another in like plight, he retired across the Channel. During his absence Castlecoole was burnt, for which he afterwards got some compensation from the Government. His name figures among the attainted in James' Parliament, and also among the signatures to the Enniskillen address to King William.

By the marriage of his granddaughter and heiress (1733), Sarah, to Galbraith Lowry the estate passed to that name, when the surname of Lowry-Corry was assumed, the present representative being the 5th Earl of Belmore, Castle Coole, Enniskillen.[3]

The other attaintures of the name, probably of this family, in James' Dublin Parliament were:—

290. **Nathaniel Corry**, of Glaan, Co. Monaghan.

291. **Isaiah Corry**, of Glaan, Co. Monaghan.

292. **Samuel Corry**, of Glaan, Co. Monaghan.

293. **Walter Corry**, of Co. Monaghan.

294. **William Corry**, of Co. Donegal or Londonderry.

The Corrys were so closely associated with Enniskillen that it is only natural to find three others of the name in addition to Capt. James Corry signing the address to King William from that town after the relief, viz.:—

295. **John Corry**, Capt. James Corry's son and successor at Castle Coole, who was later Sheriff of the county and for a long period M.P. for Enniskillen and the county.

[1] See No. 289, Corry.
[2] See Burke's Peerage and the Earl of Belmore's family histories.
[3] See Burke's Peerage and Nos. 285–288, Lowry.

296. **Hugh Corry**.

297. **George Corry**.

Note.—In giving the attaintures in James' Dublin Parliament I omitted that of

298. **Capt. James Corry**, of Ballyclanara, Co. Monaghan, evidently a duplication of Capt. James, of Castlecoole, but in order to account for the whole list of names given in Harris I include it.

In the memorial window in Derry Cathedral, unveiled in 1913 in honour of the gallant defenders of the siege, John Lowry, of Ahenis, Co. Tyrone, is one of those so commemorated, among the subscribing descendants of the Lowry Corry families being the Earl of Belmore, Lord Rathdonnell, Capt. Edward Lowry, the Rev. F. G. McClintock (Dean of Armagh), Judge G. H. Moore, Stuart Hamilton Moore, Miss Ethel Moore, Miss Marjory Moore, Miss Helen Moore, Mrs. Hayes and Miss Hayes.

The Vaughans of Co. Donegal and Derry.

Sir John Vaughan was a grantee at the time of the Plantation of considerable estate at Buncrana, Co. Donegal. In 1611 he was appointed Governor of Derry, which post he held until his death in 1641, being knighted during his tenure of office. During his governorship the original church or cathedral was built, Sir John being himself the architect. An old tablet in the cathedral belfry has the following quaint inscription:—

"Anno Domini   Caroli Regis
1633   9

"If stones could speake
Then London's praise
Should sounde, who
Built this church and
Citie from the ground."[1]

Sir John Vaughan's descendants held a prominent position in the city of Derry and Co. Donegal for many generations. In the muster of the Protestant forces before the city for its defence prior to the siege "Londeriados" has the reference:—

"The Vaughans likewise brought forth of their own
Some independent troops from Innishowen."

These took part in the long siege. Among the attainted in James' Dublin Parliament are:—

---

[1] "Ordnance Surrey of the County of Londonderry," 1837.

299. **George Vaughan**, of Buncrana, Co. Donegal.

300. **Capt. George Vaughan**, of Co. Donegal or Londonderry.

301. **Charles Vaughan**, of Armagh.

The following of the names are also mentioned by annalists of the times:—

302. **Major Vaughan** as an officer holding a commission in Lord Kingston's Regiment until its disbandment, when cut off from Derry by Hamilton's advance.

303. **Lieut. Robert Vaughan**, an officer in Col. Sir Albert Conyngham's Regiment of Enniskillen Horse, commission 1689.[1] He was also a signer of the Enniskillen address to King William.

The Vaughan family is extinct in the male line. On the death of George Vaughan of Buncrana early in the 18th century, the property passed to his three daughters, co-heiresses, one of whom, Mariana Vaughan, by her marriage with George Hart, of Kilderry, brought the bulk of the Buncrana estate into the Hart family, who now represent the Vaughan name.[2]

The Saundersons of Castle Saunderson, Co. Cavan.

The first of the name in Ulster was Alexander Saunderson from Scotland, who in 1613 obtained a grant of the Tullylagan estate, erected later into the manor of Castle Saunderson. He was High Sheriff in 1622, and died in 1633, leaving two sons (1) Archibald, (2) Robert.

Dealing with the elder of these sons first, viz. Archibald, who died in 1657, succeeded to Tullylagan; he left a son:

304. **Alexander**, of Tullylagan, who with his son and successor, another

305. **Alexander**, were both conspicuous in the defence of Derry. "Londeriados," writing of either father or son in reference to one of the garrison's sorties, says:—

> "Saunderson of Tullylagan in Tyrone
> With bravery great reputation won."

Mackenzie in his "Siege" has many references to father and son, in one of which he mentions for conspicuous service "Capt. Alexander Saunderson, junior, whose father, Capt. Alexander Saunderson, was very useful in garrison." Both these names are on the list of attainted in James' Dublin Parliament as of Tullylagan, Co. Tyrone. Capt. Alexander Saunderson (I presume the junior) was one of the signers of the address to

[1] Dalton's "Army List," 1689–1714, Vol. III.
[2] See Nos. 715–725, Hart of Kilderry.

King William after the relief, and a letter is quoted from him in Hampden's "Siege" under date April 1690, written in London, strongly dissenting from certain aspersions cast on Governor Walker in Mackenzie's "Siege." That Capt. Alexander was in London at that time is proved in Dalton's "Army List," 1689–1714, Vol. III. p. 168, where his name is given among the officers of the Derry garrison, then in London, who received an advance of three months' pay from the War Office to enable them to report immediately in the Duke of Schomberg's camp in Ireland.

Another Saunderson whose precise family connection I have been unable to trace was

306. Capt. Archibald Saunderson, mentioned several times by Mackenzie, and whose name is on the address to King William after the relief.

Having disposed of the three gallant defenders of the Tullylagan Saundersons, I will now return to (2) Robert, the second son of the first settler, Alexander. This Robert lived at Portagh, Co. Cavan (afterwards Castle Saunderson), and dying in 1675, left, with other issue,

307. Robert, his successor at Castle Saunderson.

In the threatening period before the outbreak of the revolution no one took a more leading part in the county's Protestant organisation for resistance than Col. Robert Saunderson (he soon held a commission as such in King William's army). "Harris" in his history narrates how he rode into the town of Cavan "on the 8th Jan. 1689 with a body of four score horse," and that finding a Bench of Jacobite magistrates dispensing justice at Quarter Sessions, he entered the Court House, and mounting the Bench, demanded by what commission they sat there? On their reply "by King James'," he told them that the authority was not good while the laws were unrepealed, and ordered them to return home. Tyrconnell, the Viceroy, was furious at such an insult to the Royal authority, and threatened severe punishment, of which the only effect was the arming of every Protestant. So prominent had Col. Robert Saunderson made himself that in Tyrconnell's Proclamation of March 1689 he was one of the leaders exempted from pardon. He was attainted in James' Dublin Parliament. Since his day, successive generations, in occupation of Castle Saunderson, have held a prominent position in their county and Ulster.

The late Colonel, the Rt. Hon. Edward Saunderson, for many years led the Ulster Party in the Imperial House of Commons, where he earned from friend and foe alike an unrivalled reputation for chivalry in action, adroitness in debate, marvellous repartee, and resource in critical moments. Few leaders have had such a hold on the affection of Ulster, and no death has been more universally regretted.

The present representative is A. D. Saunderson, Bagnor Manor, Newbury.

Among the subscribing descendants to the memorial window, unveiled in 1913 in honour of the defenders of the siege, under the name of Saunderson are the following names: the late Edward Sclater of Hillsborough, Mrs. McCormick Goodhart, Robert Hall McCormick, Leander Hall McCormick.

308. MAJOR-GENERAL JOHN PERCY KIRKE, reliever of Derry.

Nothing in connection with the siege strikes the enquirer as more extraordinary than the selection of an officer of such antecedents for the command of the relieving force. Of his brutal and domineering character King William and the Duke of Schomberg must have been fully aware. An experienced and gallant officer, some twenty years of his military career had been passed in garrison at Tangier in command of the Paschal Lambs, a regiment so designated from the emblem on their standards, which was intended to convey the Christianity of their origin to the Moslems in the country where they were quartered. Thoroughly imbued with the cruelties which warfare in such a barbarous country engendered, Kirke, when Tangier was abandoned, brought his Paschal Lambs back to England. It was not long before Monmouth's rebellion gave him the opportunity of showing the people of the West of England the true character of his Lambs. With the infamous Judge Jeffreys on the Bench, and Kirke, as soldier policeman, guarding the prisoners, there was little mercy or justice. Execrated by the populace, this well-assorted pair were honoured and advanced by James, and yet, when William landed at Torbay, Kirke was one of the first to desert the Jacobite cause.

Everyone knows how Kirke at the head of his expeditionary force of men, arms and munitions, borne by a fleet of thirty sail, anchored off Greencastle in Lough Foyle in the middle of June; how Derry, cheered by the masts, expected immediate relief, while the hopes of the besiegers sunk to zero; how weeks passed, and Kirke still lay idle in the Lough, and how, after strong remonstrance from King William and the Duke of Schomberg, the Boom was at length broken and Derry relieved on the 28th July.

In spite of his criminal dilatoriness in making the attempt at relief, he was received with acclamation when he entered the city and took over command. A few weeks of his arbitrary rule, and overriding of the old and tried officers was enough for that independent population, who were more than delighted when, in the autumn, Kirke and his men marched off to join the Duke of Schomberg's army.

He was at the Boyne. The following year (1691) he was killed at Athlone, and when the news circulated in Derry of his head being taken off by a cannon ball, few were the expressions of regret.

His character was redeemed by his gallantry, and by the fact that he had absolutely refused to become a Roman Catholic at King James' instance.

Stronges, of Tynan Abbey, Co. Armagh.

The Stronges are descended from the old family of Strang or Strong of Balcaskie,

Co. Fife, N.B. The first of the name in Ulster was

309. **MATHEW STRONGE**, who was attainted in James' Dublin Parliament, being described as of Clonlea, Donegal or Londonderry. He was settled at Strabane in 1670, at Clonlea in 1683, and was warden of Lifford in 1713. He is said to have been granted a lease of lands in Co. Derry by the Goldsmiths' Company in recognition of siege services. Dying in 1716 he was succeeded by his son,

310. **CAPT. JAMES STRONGE**, who was in the city all through the siege, and was attainted in James' Dublin Parliament. His signature is attached to the Corporation's Commission of 1690. Strong's Orchard, some 80 perches outside the city walls, is mentioned by Walker as a place selected by the besiegers as a position for their big guns.

Capt. James Stronge's son, the Rev. James Stronge, was Rector of Tynan, and from him descend the family of Tynan (a baronetcy being conferred in 1803), of whom the present representative is the 6th Baronet, Sir Walter Lockhart Stronge, Bart., Tynan Abbey, Co. Armagh.

In the memorial window unveiled in 1913 in Derry Cathedral to commemorate the gallant defenders, Capt. James Stronge is among the honoured, the descendant subscribers being the late Sir James Henry Stronge, Bart., Charles E. Stronge, D.L., and Lord Rathdonnell.

The late Baronet, the Rt. Hon. Sir James Henry Stronge, Bart., was Grand Master of the Orangemen of Ireland, and took a most prominent part in public affairs and in the politics of Ulster. When his only son and heir, James Mathew Stronge, lieutenant in the Royal Irish Fusiliers, fell in action on the Western Front in 1917, the greatest sympathy was felt for the Tynan family.

Among the attainted in James' Dublin Parliament were:—

311. **JAMES STRONG**, described as a yeoman, Cavan.

312. **JOHN STRONG**, described as a yeoman, Cavan.

313. **CAPT. HENLY**, an officer in Sir Arthur Rawdon's force. When Hamilton forced the passage of the Bann at Portglenone and Rawdon was obliged to retire on Derry, Henly, supposed to be mortally wounded, was left on the ground.[1] He was, however, given quarter, and recovered.[2]

314. **DR. HERMAN**, defender, mentioned in "Londeriados" as one of the two doctors (the other being Dr. Aicken) who attended and cured Col. Adam Murray when severely wounded in the last sortie of the garrison at the end of the siege.[3]

[1] Mackenzie.
[2] Witherow.
[3] See No. 11, Aicken.

315. **Capt. Humphrey Bell**, an officer in the Skeffington Regiment.[1] So enraged were the people of the city after Lundy's treachery and the desertion of so many officers to the Fleet, that they fired on several on their way to the Lough, killing Capt. Bell on the 19th April, 1689.[2]

There were two others of the name among the attainted, viz.:—

316. **John Bell**, described as of Co. Cavan.

317. **Andrew Bell**, described as of Co. Cavan.

318. **Capt. Charleton**, defender, an officer who had been with the garrison all through the siege. He deserted to the enemy's camp on 28th July, on the eve of the relief.[3]

The following Charltons (so spelt), probably of same family, were on the list of attainted:—

319. **Charles Charlton**, described as of Co. Fermanagh.

320. **Randall Charlton**, described as of Co. Tyrone.

321. **Capt. Carleton** was one of the captains of Col. Adam Murray's famous Horse, so eulogised by "Londeriados" as "the Borderers," who so ably followed their impetuous leader.[4] It is incredible that he can be the same as No. 318.

322. **William Charlton** (or **Carleton**), described as of Co. Leitrim, figures among the signers of the Enniskillen address to King William, indicating his participation in their gallant doings.

323. **Quartermaster Murdach**, defender. The only mention of this brave man is in the following eulogy of "Londeriados," which makes one wonder that his gallantry escaped the notice of Walker and Mackenzie.

> "Murdach, our general's quartermaster's slain
> Who in all actions did much honour gain;
> For he could six or seven at least withstand,
> And could effect a desperate command;
> Though he be slain, his name will never die
> While Derry's siege is told in poetry."

324. **Joseph Bennett**, defender. He was secretary to the Corporation of Derry previous to the investment of the city, but on the 19th April he was sent to London

[1] List of officers in Hampden's "Siege," p. 468.
[2] Mackenzie in Hampden's "Derry," p. 210.
[3] Mackenzie in Hampden's "Derry," p. 248.
[4] See No. 411, Col. Adam Murray.

to interview King William and press for immediate succour.[1] "Londeriados" thus refers to his mission:—

> "Mogridge was secretary to this power[2]
> For Bennett was to England sent before
> To give their Majesties an information
> Of what had happened since the siege formation.
> He to their camp (the Jacobite) as a deserter flies
> And in a few days himself from thence conveys
> And tells our case unto their Majesties."

No wonder he was received as a genuine deserter, for as Walker puts it, "our men were ordered to fire upon him that the enemy might think he had deserted us." In spite of the perils he accomplished his mission. On the minutes of the Irish Society under date 13th August, 1689, it is recorded that in consideration of Mr. Joseph Bennett's great services, for which his Majesty had already given him a commission as Captain in an infantry regiment, their treasurer was ordered to pay him £10.

In the journal of the English House or Commons, August 1689, in the enquiry into the charges against Col. Lundy, it is recorded that Mr. Bennett in his evidence stated that Lundy on the day of the Cladyford retirement was one of the first that fled into the city before Hamilton's advance, "bidding the men shift for themselves."[3]

Two of the name signed the address to King William, viz.:—

325. **Robert Bennett**, defender.

326. **Thomas Bennett**, defender.

327. **John Mogridge**, defender. In the first few days of the investment, when the previous holder of the office, Joseph Bennett,[4] was sent on a special mission to London, he was appointed to succeed him as Secretary or Town Clerk to the Corporation—an office which he filled during the siege to the general satisfaction. He had previously filled the post of Clerk of the Crown and had taken a leading part in the negotiations with Lord Mountjoy after the shutting of the gates and in the subsequent arrangement. He had been Secretary to the Council of War of 17th April when Lundy, planning the surrender of the city, had advised the Colonels of the two regiments lying in the Lough that the city was untenable, and secretly arranged for their retirement to England. It was Mogridge's timely divulging of this secret that so exasperated the people, and enabled Col. Adam Murray to frustrate the surrender plot.

After the relief he was in 1690 appointed secretary to the deputation sent by the

---

[1] John Mogridge, see No. 327, being appointed in his stead.
[2] The Corporation.
[3] Hampton's "Derry."
[4] See No. 324.

Corporation's Commission to repair to London to press the Government for compensation for siege losses, and was given £10 for his expenses.[1] On 7th November, 1690, the Irish Society for his services in bringing them a letter from the Corporation of Derry made him a grant of £10.

In connection with King William's grant of £500 to the poor of the city made through the Duke of Schomberg in February 1690,[2] Mogridge was ordered to repair to Belfast (17th February, 1690) and receive this £500, taking with him "Two honest men as a guard on his return from thence."[3]

328. **James Mogridge** of Derry, defender, probably of the family of John Mogridge,[4] was one of the signers of the Corporation's 1690 Commission.

329. **Lieut. McPhedris**, defender. In recording the losses of the garrison in the sortie of 21st April, Mackenzie gives the names of Lieut. McPhedris and Cornet Brown,[5] while Walker only mentions Lieut. McPhedris. "Londeriados" enumerates the fallen officers thus:—

> "On our side not a few, Cornet Brown's slain
> And the valiant Lieutenant Phetrix then."

Several various spellings, but all indicative of the same McPhedris.

In the list of attainted in James' Dublin Parliament there is evidently the same surname, again differently spelt, viz.:—

330. **William McFetrick**, of Carnglass, Co. Antrim, evidently one of the same family.

331. **Cornet Brown**, defender.[6] He was killed in the Pennyburn Mill sortie of April 21st.[7]

332. **William Brown**, defender, adjutant in Col. Baker's Regiment all through the siege. Mackenzie writes of him as "industrious and dexterous" and that "when the supply of iron bullets ran short he manufactured good substitutes of brick with outsides of lead."[8]

333. **Capt. Francis Nevil**. How he became implicated is not narrated. It would

---

[1] Hampton's "Siege."
[2] See No. 249, Schomberg.
[3] Hampton's "Derry."
[4] No. 327.
[5] See No. 331.
[6] See No. 329 above.
[7] "Londeriados" and Mackenzie.
[8] See No. 386, Rev. David Brown, Minister of Urney.

appear that King James passed a night or nights at Montgevilin Castle, near Derry, as the guest of Archdeacon Hamilton,[1] whom he sent on the 17th April to arrange terms of surrender with Col. Lundy.

As "Londeriados" records:—

> "Archdeacon Hamilton by King James is sent
> Into the city with this compliment,"

the compliment being full pardon for the past, if immediate surrender. The same evening the Archdeacon, accompanied by Capts. Nevil and Kinnaston,[2] was sent back to continue the surrender negotiations by Col. Lundy. They had access to King James, and while the Archdeacon and Kinnaston returned to the city, Nevil remained in the Jacobite camp. The next day, 18th April, after King James had met with the warm reception at the gate, Lundy, though the "No Surrender" party had gained the upper hand, again sent the Archdeacon back to apologise for the firing, which he assured his Majesty was an act of an unauthorised rabble. The sequel is well known.[3]

Of Nevil, "Londeriados" has the following reference to these proceedings:—

> "The ingenious Nevil and the said Divine
> Went to the King to tell him they would sign
> In a few days, to hasten which the King
> The Irish army 'fore the town did bring—
> Delays are dangerous, and he pushes on
> The town to sign the capitulation."

It is evident that Nevil after these events took protection and remained in the Jacobite camp during the siege. After the relief he returned to the city, and left behind him a most interesting map of Derry at the time of the siege, in which are depicted, not only the walls, &c. of the city, but also the positions of the enemy's guns and of the various regiments of the investing army.[4]

He was a signer of the Corporation's Commission of 1690.

334. **Capt. Charles Kinnaston**, defender. For his participation in Lundy's surrender negotiations, see Sketch No. 333 Capt. Francis Nevil.

He was in the city all through the siege, and was a signer of the address to King William after the relief.

---

[1] A cousin of the Earl of Abercorn with the King, and of Capt. James Hamilton in the city. See No. 1094, Archdeacon Hamilton.

[2] See No. 334.

[3] Mackenzie.

[4] Dwyer's "Siege," p. 73.

The Breaking of the Boom.

335. Capt. Micaiah Browning, of the "Mountjoy." Nothing perhaps in the story of the siege is more thrilling than the rush of the "Mountjoy" on the terrible Boom. We can picture the captain, sword in hand, standing by the wheel and commanding operations until killed by the fatal shot. We can see the arrival of the "Mountjoy" and the "Phœnix" at Derry's quay. We can almost hear the acclamations of the starving populace, and we can sympathise with the captain's weeping widow, who was meeting a dead husband.

It is well known how, with Derry *in extremis*, Kirke for some six weeks had kept his Expeditionary Force and his Majesty's battleships lying inactive in the Lough. Kirke had pronounced the Boom "unbreakable," and even after receiving peremptory orders from King William and the Duke of Schomberg late in July for immediate action he still hesitated. At last after continued remonstrance from the captains of the three victuallers (merchant ships carrying provisions) who volunteered for the perilous service, the "Mountjoy," Capt. Browning, the "Phœnix," Capt. Douglas, and the "Jerusalem" were permitted to undertake the venture; while H.M.S. "Dartmouth" was ordered to engage and demolish Culmore, thus to a great extent fending the three victuallers from heavy fire when attacking the Boom.

About 6 p.m. on the afternoon of the 28th July, with wind and tide favourable, the ships sailed for their objectives, being met by a heavy fire from the shore guns. How the "Dartmouth" carried out her part of the programme, demolishing the Fort of Culmore, will be seen in No. 345, Capt. Leake, R.N. Culmore successfully passed, the "Mountjoy," under a storm of shot and shell, steered right at the Boom; the impact was terrific. She recoiled and ran aground. A wild cheer rang from the Irish, who thought she lay at their mercy. Rushing down to the shore to finish their work, they were utterly unprepared for the broadside which the "Mountjoy" fired into them, and fled in consternation. The broadside had the effect of floating the "Mountjoy" into deep water. Meantime, the long boat of H.M.S. "Swallow," towed behind for the purpose, "well barricaded and provided with seamen to cut the boom," dashed on the obstacle. The impact of the "Mountjoy" had already so shattered the Boom that a few minutes' dexterous use of their axes rendered the river free. But Capt. Browning was dead; and so shaken was the "Mountjoy" that pride of place in leading up the river was now given to the "Phœnix" of Coleraine, closely followed by the former.[1] The further progress up the river, anxiously watched from the city walls, and under continuous fire from the pursuing enemy was slow, but at 10 o'clock in the glowing twilight of that summer evening the "Mountjoy" and the "Phœnix" were dropping to their moorings by Derry's crowded quay and the city was relieved.[2]

---

[1] The "Jerusalem," a much smaller vessel, did not reach the city until next day.

[2] The above description is collated from the narrations of Witherow and Mackenzie, and in minor

Capt. Micaiah Browning was a Derry man and his wife was in Derry throughout the siege,[1] but other evidence seems to connect the name with Co. Fermanagh and Enniskillen, viz.:

336. **Capt. William Browning**, of Co. Fermanagh, so described, was among the attainted in James' Dublin Parliament, while the following were prominent in defence of Enniskillen and signers of the Enniskillen address to King William:

337. **William Browning**. He was one of the eight signers of Enniskillen's letter of 13th December, 1688, to David Cairnes appealing to Derry for co-operation in the impending crisis.

338. **John Browning**.

339. **James Browning**.

340. **Mrs. Browning**, defender. This was the wife of Capt. Micaiah Browning.[2] She was a widow, Mrs. Margaret Rankin, with a daughter, Martha Rankin, when she married Capt. Browning. Both these ladies were all through the siege. In the great historical picture of the relief the pathetic figure of Mrs. Browning has a front place. In recognition of her husband's gallantry and death in action, she had the honour a few months later of being graciously received at Whitehall by their Majesties and presented with a handsome diamond necklace. Her name was put on the Civil List, from which she drew a small annuity. A portrait of this lady, "in full dress, ornamented by the Royal present," is still in the possession of her relatives, the Harveys, of Malin Head.[3]

341. **Martha Rankin**, defender, Mrs. Browning's daughter, Capt. Browning's stepdaughter, married John Harvey, of the Malin Head line, in 1685, so that mother and daughter had many friends in the city during the siege.

In the memorial window unveiled in 1913 in Derry Cathedral in honour of the defenders Capt. Micaiah Browning is among those so commemorated.

342. **Lieut. Rankin**, defender, served all through the defence, and is referred to by "Londeriados" in his description of the Pennyburn sortie of the 21st April, viz.:—

> "Lieutenant Rankin hewed the Irish down
> And in that battle gained much renown."

343. **Alick Rankin**, possibly the above, was a signer of the address to King William after the relief, while

---

details more particularly from Reid's "History of the Presbyterian Church," Vol. II. pp. 386-389.

[1] See No. 340, Mrs. Browning.

[2] No. 335.

[3] Dwyer's "Siege."

344. **JOHN RANKIN** was among the signers of the Corporation's Commission of 1690. (In Nos. 340 and 341 Mrs. Browning, Mrs. Margaret Rankin, and her daughter Martha Rankin are mentioned.)

The family have for generations been closely connected with the city and county, where many of the name are still to be found.

345. **CAPT. LEAKE**, R.N., of H.M.S. "Dartmouth." This gallant officer, afterwards so distinguished in the annals of the British Navy as Admiral Sir F. Leake, was ordered to accompany the "Mountjoy," the "Phœnix" and the "Jerusalem" in their attack on the Boom (see No. 335, Capt. Browning), his special instructions being to lie between these merchant vessels and the shore, fending them from the guns of Culmore Fort, which he was, if possible, to demolish. How thoroughly he accomplished this object, with the loss of only one man killed and two wounded, is well known, but the following extract from the official *London Gazette* of the day (as given in Reid's "Presbyterian History," Vol. II. p. 386) is more than interesting: "Captain Leake behaved himself very bravely and prudently in this action, neither firing great or small shot (though he was plied very hard with both) till he came on the wind of the Castle (Culmore) and then beginning to batter, that the victuallers ("Mountjoy" and "Phœnix") might pass under shelter of his guns, he lay between them and the Castle within musket shot, and came to an anchor."

In the memorial window unveiled in 1913 in Derry Cathedral to the defenders of the city the name of Capt. F. Leake of H.M.S. "Dartmouth" is among the honoured, and among the subscribers is his descendant, G. Martin Leake.

346. **CAPT. ANDREW DOUGLAS**, of the "Phœnix," of Coleraine, reliever, commanded his vessel in the breaking of the Boom and relief of Derry. (For full particulars see under No. 335, Capt. Browning of the "Mountjoy.")

347. **LIEUT. DOUGLAS**, defender. The statement (in Walker's "Siege") that this officer was killed in the Windmill Hill action of the 6th May is the only mention of his name.

348. **LIEUT. DAVID MITCHELL**, reliever. This officer has a curious record. At first an officer of the garrison Mackenzie states "that he went away (deserted?) on the 10th May, 1689, and came again into the Lough with Major-General Kirke" and according to the same authority "on the 13th July Col. Walker (the Governor) received a letter from Lieut. David Mitchell out of the ships (the Fleet lying idle in the Lough) by a little boy." Whatever his reasons for going away, it was atoned for by his subsequent conduct.

There were two others of the name serving in the defence, whose signatures are attached to the Derry Commission of 1690, viz.:—

349. **ALEXANDER MITCHELL**.

350. John Mitchell.

351. Robert Lindsay, of Loughrey, Co. Tyrone, defender, was with his family in Derry all through the siege. After the relief he was one of the signers of the address to King William, and of the Corporation's Commission of 1690. He was among the attainted in James' Dublin Parliament, described as of Manor Lindsay, Co. Tyrone.

352. Alexander Lindsay of Cahoo, defender. A younger brother of Robert (above) was the "chirurgeon" or surgeon Alexander Lindsay, whose death is mentioned by Mackenzie when describing the losses and destruction caused by bombs falling night and day on the city, to one of which on the 5th June the "chirurgeon" had succumbed, of whom he writes "as having been very useful to the wounded."

Others of the name whose family relations I have been unable to trace are:—

353. Andrew Lindsay, described on the list of attainted in James' Dublin Parliament as of Castle Murray, Donegal or Londonderry.

354. Sergeant James Linzy (Lindsay), defender, is among the warrant officers of Col. Hamill's Regiment mentioned as being in London after the relief and in the spring of 1690 taking part in the controversy raised by Mackenzie's attack on Walker.[1]

355. George I. Lindsay's name is among the signatures to the Derry Commission of 1690.

356. Matthew Lindsay was one of the signers of the Enniskillen address to King William.

The Lindsays of Loughrey, Co. Tyrone, were among the earliest of the Plantation grantees, the first settler of the family being Robert who came to Loughrey in 1611, where the family, taking a prominent place in the county, resided until the estate and demesne were sold at the end of last century.

Among the descendant representatives of this old stock are Rev. William O'Neill Lindesay and Mrs. Robert Francis Harrison, of Dublin.[2, 3]

357. Major Breme, defender. Like the "chirurgeon" Alexander Lindsay,[4] he was

---

[1] Hampton's "Siege," p. 459.

[2] See under No. 955, Harrison.

[3] "Londeriados," in naming the leading persons at the muster of the Protestant forces before Derry, mentioned the Laird of "Dunrod." Dunrod in Renfrewshire was for generations the property of the family. From a note in the Montgomery Manuscripts, p. 364, we get the information that Alexander Lindsay, the last Laird of Dunrod, had sold the estate in 1619, and had lived for many subsequent years in extreme poverty in a corner of his old property. He was looked upon by the country people as a warlock or wizard. Could one of the above six sketches Nos. 351–356 have been his grandson and Laird of Dunrod?

[4] See No. 352.

the victim of a bomb or cannon ball on the 5th June.[1] The spelling of the name may be an error for Broom, Broome or Browne. Among the signers of the Corporation's Commission of 1690 were:—

358. Thomas Broom.

359. Elizabeth Browne, and on the new list of Burgesses appointed by Tyrconnell in 1688 the name of Broom occurs twice.

360. Rev. James McGregor, defender. The name is nowhere recorded by any siege authority or in list of names, but from the "History of Londonderry, New Hampshire," presented to the public library of Derry in 1851, it would appear that James McGregor, the founder of that flourishing colony, had been a very young man in Derry during the siege and had discharged from the Cathedral tower the large gun which announced the approach of the vessels for the relief.[2]

His father, Capt. McGregor, lived at Magilligan, Co. Derry, and besides this son left a daughter, Elsbeth, who married Capt. Lachlan McCurdy. The name of McCurdy was well known in Co. Derry, and among their representatives to-day are the McCurdy Greers, of Ballymoney.

During the siege it is not unlikely that he formed that intimate friendship with the subject of No. 361 that led to their association in the great venture narrated under their joint names.

361. Lieut. Mathew Clarke, defender, was an officer in Col. Parker's (afterwards Col. Lance's) Regiment all through the siege. Mackenzie mentions him for good service in many of the garrison sorties, particularly that of the 4th June, when he was badly wounded, "the honourable scar of which (according to Kernahan's 'History of Co. Londonderry for Three Centuries') he carried on his face through life." He was among the signers of the address to King William after the relief, and Dalton's "Army List," 1689–1714, Vol. III. p. 178, informs us that he was one of the officers in London who in the spring of 1690 received three months' pay to enable him to report at once in the Duke of Schomberg's camp in Ireland. In 1697 he was ordained Presbyterian minister of Boveedy (Kilrea). While holding this ministry he published a pamphlet, bearing on a church question of the day, which occasioned considerable controversy.[3] A few years later he resigned his Boveedy charge and was for the rest of his life closely associated with his friend the Rev. James McGregor in his great venture of leading an Ulster party of emigrants to found a colony in North America. Whether he accompanied them when they sailed or joined them later is not clear. At all events, as will be seen, he so identified himself with their fortunes that on McGregor's death

[1] Mackenzie.
[2] Hampton's "Siege," p. 451.
[3] Reid, Vol. III. p. 149.

in 1729 he succeeded as minister of the colony.

In 1718 the Rev. James McGregor (above) at the request of many of his co-religionists in the neighbourhood of Ballymoney and in Co. Derry organised a large band of emigrants to found a colony in North America, and in the same year they sailed under his leadership. The party consisted, not only of single men, but also of married men with their wives and children, among them being those of names still well known in the district, viz. Burnell, Clendinan (Clendenning), Mitchell, Steritt, Anderson, Grigg, Clarke, Nesmith, Weir, Allison, Steele, Stewart, McKien, McCollum and Morrison. Among the wives and children of these emigrants were not a few who had had the terrible experience of being driven under the walls of Derry during the siege, to starve or die by the ruthless French General Rosen. How they made good, establishing a flourishing settlement in New Hampshire, named Londonderry, and how in a few years the towns of Antrim, Coleraine and Belfast grew up under their auspices, in fact a most prosperous community, where the burr of the spinning wheel and the rattle or the shuttle were heard in almost every house, characterising their Ulster origin is told in "The History of Londonderry, New Hampshire," presented to the library of Derry in 1851. The honour of this achievement lies chiefly with the two reverend gentlemen, McGregor, the Founder, and Clarke, his successor in 1729, but much is due to the spirit of the colonists, whose incentive came from the Derry whose name was given to their settlement. It is interesting to know that these emigrants and their descendants have adhered to the Presbyterian faith of their ancestors.[1]

"The History of Londonderry, New Hampshire," alleges that three of these emigrants were in Derry all through the siege, a statement there is no reason to doubt, and therefore accorded, viz.:—

362. **James McKien** of Ballymoney, defender.

363. **Alexander McCollum**, defender.

364. **John Morrison**, defender.

Episcopalian clergymen in Derry during Siege.

Besides those already mentioned, viz. the Governor, Rev. George Walker, Rector of Castlecaulfield in No. 3, Capt. Rev. Christopher Jenny, Rector of Ardboe and Prebend of Mullaghbrack in No. 265 and Rev. William Cunningham, Rector of Killeshandra, there were some fifteen representatives of that Church in the city during the siege, viz. No. 365 to No. 379 below.

365. **Rev. Michael McClenaghan** or **Clenaghan**, Rector of Derry, defender.

---

[1] Hampton's "History of Derry," p. 451, and Kernahan's "History of Co. Londonderry for Three Centuries."

His name figures among the attainted in James' Dublin Parliament and he signed the address to King William after the relief.

366. **REV. SETH WHITTEL** or **WHITTLE**, defender, Rector of Bellaghey, diocese of Derry. On the 17th April Mr. Seth Whittle came into the city on a mission from King James to Col. Lundy for the object of arranging the surrender.[1] On the 19th April he and Mr. George Hamilton were sent by Col. Lundy, "who kept his chamber, afraid of the popular clamour," to the officers sitting in council "to make all the interest they could there to have friends, as he called them, chosen to go to King James, which they earnestly endeavoured." Such, however, was "the exasperation of the multitude on the walls and at the gates," "who threatened to treat any accepting the mission as betrayers of the town, that none of them durst offer to go, and so a stop was put to that dangerous capitulation."[1]

He preached the funeral oration at Governor Baker's funeral on 30th June, and died in the city before the relief.

367. **REV. MOSES DAVIS**, defender, Incumbent of Donaghendry (Stewartstown), diocese of Armagh, 1687–1692, resigning in the latter year. He was in the city all through the siege.[2]

368. **CAPT. REV. JOHN KNOX**, defender, Rector of Glasslough, diocese of Clogher.[2] In the city all through the siege, and evidently of such service to the garrison that besides being appointed chaplain to Col. Mitchelburn's Regiment[3] he was made captain, and was one of four captains sent by the Governor and garrison to interview General Kirke at Inch and congratulate him on the relief. He was attainted in James' Dublin Parliament.

369. **REV. BARTHOLOMEW BLACK**, defender, Curate of Aghalow, diocese of Armagh. In city all through the siege.[2] Signer of Derry address.

370. **REV. THOMAS SEMPILL**, defender, Curate of Donaghmore, diocese of Derry. In city all through siege.[2]

371. **REV. ROBERT MORGAN**, defender, Curate of Cappagh, diocese of Armagh.[2] A signer of the address to King William after the relief.

372. **REV. JOHN CAMPBELL**, defender, Incumbent of Seagoe, diocese of Armagh.[2] Was a signer of the address to King William after the relief.

373. **REV. ANDREW ROBISON (ROBERTSON?)**, defender, Incumbent or Curate of

[1] Mackenzie.
[2] Walker.
[3] Hampton, p. 468.

Stewartstown, diocese of Armagh.[1] In Derry all through siege.

374. **REV. JAMES CHRISTY**, defender, Curate of Monaghan, diocese of Clogher.[1] In city during the siege. He was, 1693–1696, Rector of Aghnamullen in same diocese.

375. **REV. JAMES WALWORTH**, defender, Incumbent of Arigal (Erigal) diocese of Derry.[1] He died in Derry during the siege.

376. **REV. — ELLINGSWORTH**, defender. Merely mentioned as coming from the neighbourhood of Newry and dying during the siege.[1]

377. **REV. RICHARD CROWTHER**, defender, Curate of Comber, diocese of Derry, who died during the siege.[1]

378. **REV. JOHN ROWAN**, defender, Incumbent of Baltiagh, diocese of Derry, who died in the city during the siege.[1]

379. **REV. — JOHNSTON**, defender, mentioned[1] as a clergyman present in the city, without any indication of parish or diocese.

Ministers of the Presbyterian Church of Ireland in Derry during the Siege.

In addition to the Rev. John Mackenzie, of Derriloran, given in No. 12, there were seven ministers of this Church in Derry during the siege, viz. the subjects of following sketches:—

380. **REV. THOMAS BOYD**, defender, minister of Aghadoey, Co. Derry.[2]

381. **REV. WILLIAM CROOKS**, defender, minister of Ballykelly, Co. Tyrone.[2] Referring to Mr. Crooks' preaching in the Cathedral, "Londeriados" has the following line "The same good doctrine" was preached by the learned Mr. Crooks." (See No. 382 for context.)

382. **REV. JOHN ROWAT** (or **RUITT**), defender, minister of Lifford, Co. Donegal.[2] After praising the preaching of the Rev. George Walker and Rev. John Mackenzie at the joint services in the Cathedral "Londeriados" thus refers to the Rev. John Ruit:

> "The Rev'rend Ruit did confirm us still
> Preaching submission to God's holy will.
> He likewise prophesied our Relief
> When it surpassed all human belief.
> The same was taught by the learned Mr. Crooks

---

[1] Walker.
[2] Mackenzie.

And Master Hamilton shewed it from his books.
Then Mills, a ruling elder spoke the same,
Of our Relief, six weeks before it came.
From sunrising to sun setting they taught
Whilst we against the enemy bravely fought.
Thus Heaven assists those actions which proceed
From unity in greatest time of need."

383. **Rev. John Hamilton**, defender, minister of Donagheady,[1] of Strabane.[2] For "Londeriados'" reference to his preaching in the Cathedral see quotation under Rev. John Rowat, No. 382. He died in the city during the siege.[1]

384. **Rev. Robert Wilson**, defender, minister of Strabane, who died in the city during the siege.[3]

385. **Rev. William Gilchrist**, defender, minister of Kilrea, Co. Derry. He died in the city during the siege.[3]

386. **Rev. David Brown**, defender, minister of Urney, Co. Tyrone. He died in the city during the siege.[3]

Dr. Killen in his notes to an edition of Mackenzie's "Siege of Derry," published in 1870, speaks of the Rev. David Brown as being the ancestor of the Rev. John Brown, afterwards minister of Aghadoey, Co. Derry, and of Alexander and William Brown, of Ballymena, who emigrating to the States at the end of the 18th century were the founders of the great house of Brown Shipley & Co. which with their branches in London, New York, Liverpool and elsewhere form a merchant banking concern of world-wide importance. The late Mr. Joseph Bigger, in an article in the *Belfast Newsletter*, 7th June, 1926, entitled "From Ballymena to Baltimore," gives some interesting particulars of the origin of the Browns, and of their marriage connections with the Davisons, of Drumnasole and Knockboy, the Gihons, of Ballymena and Lisnafellan, and the Patricks of Dunminning.

387. **Rev. Alexander Osborne**, of Dublin. He had been the Presbyterian minister of Brigh, Co. Tyrone, but had undertaken the charge of a Dublin congregation shortly before the outbreak of the 1688 revolution. His politics were clearly evinced in his being one of the ministers associated in the address of welcome presented by the Presbyterian Church of Ireland to King William shortly after his landing at Torbay.

Early in 1689, when Hamilton's army was on the eve of marching from Dublin on its way to Derry, and when the Protestants of Ulster were preparing a stubborn resistance, Tyrconnell, the Viceroy, sent Mr. Osborne as his emissary to the Hillsborough

---

[1] Mackenzie.
[2] Reid.
[3] Mackenzie.

Consult to advocate immediate submission. The first intimation of the nearness of the danger seems to have been brought to "The Consult" by Mr. Osborne. He attended a meeting of this body on the 12th March. The leaders had been much cheered by the reception that very day of despatches from King William approving of what they were doing, and of signed commissions for officers in the regiments raised or being raised. Mr. Osborne, instead of advocating submission, supported the Consult in their resistance policy. Meanwhile Hamilton with his Dublin army was upon them, and the "Break of Dromore" on the 14th March ended any hope of successful resistance short of Derry walls. Mr. Osborne has been accused by several contemporary writers of acting as a spy of the Viceroy in his journey to the north, but a vindication published a few months later by the Rev. J. Boyse, a colleague of the Dublin Presbytery, clears his character of any such imputation.[1] Mackenzie, too, takes up the cudgels in support of Osborne's loyalty to the cause. "The real design of his coming," he writes, "was to give them the best information and advice, in order to their defence."

388. **Thomas Osborne**, a brother of the Rev. Alexander Osborne above, was in Enniskillen all through the investment, and was a signer of the Enniskillen address to King William after the relief.

389. **Rev. John Sinclair** of Holyhill, Co. Donegal, Rector of Leekpatrick (Lockpatrick). He seems to have left Derry before the investment, but had brought in a considerable contingent to the city, and had taken an active part in the organisation of the defence. His importance is shown by his signature of the March "Declaration of Union."

"His church was burned by the Jacobite army on their retreat from Derry, and it was only by the timely arrival of a messenger, who had swum across the Foyle with 'a protection' that Holyhill house was saved from a similar fate."[2]

The only other member of this family mentioned is:—

390. **James Sinclair** of Ramelton, Donegal or Londonderry on the list of attainted in James' Dublin Parliament.

The Sinclairs are descended from the ancient house of Sinclair, of Caithness, N.B. The first of the name in Co. Donegal was James, second son of Sir James Sinclair, Bart., of Caithness, N.B., whose son was the Rev. John Sinclair, whose descendants of Holyhill have since held a prominent position in their county.

The family is represented by the widow and sisters of the late William Montgomery Sinclair, of Holyhill and Bonnyglen, Co. Donegal.

391. **Col. Thomas Whitney**, defender, was one of the many Protestant officers

---

[1] Reid, Vol. II. pp. 354–365.
[2] Graham's "Derriana," p. 79.

cashiered by Tyrconnell in his reorganisation of the army prior to the revolution. He came north, offering his services in the Protestant forces then being raised in Ulster, and was appointed Major in Sir John Magill's Regiment. With this regiment he was present at the "Break of Dromore," and in the subsequent retreat on Derry, where he again made himself conspicuous in the endeavour to foil Lundy's treacherous plans. He was one of the signers of the "Declaration of Union." By the 19th April, the day after King James' warm reception at the gates, and Lundy's flight, such a reputation had he earned as a leader of men that in the reorganisation of the garrison he was appointed Colonel of Sir Francis Hamilton's Regiment.

"In the evening of that very day (19th April) a trumpet came to the walls from King James to know why they sent not out commissioners to treat, according to their proposals. The multitude having put a stop to that, Col. Whitney wrote a few lines to excuse themselves to the King."[1] With such a promising beginning it is hard to believe the sequel, which I will leave to Mackenzie to narrate. "About the 27th April Col. Whitney had sold to Capt. D'Arcy some horses which were said to be none of his own. Upon which and other misdemeanours Whitney was confined, and afterwards tried by a council of war, and found no friend to the garrison, for which he was under confinement during the time of the siege."

"Londeriados" has the following terse comment:

> "Whitney's convict, Monroe his post obtained
> Who by his merits had that honour gained."

392. COL. HENRY MONROE, defender, who succeeded Col. Whitney (above) in command of Sir Francis Hamilton's Regiment, was the son or nephew of the famous Scottish General of that name. He is probably the same as the Henry Monro described as of Co. Down in the attainted in James' Dublin Parliament and from whom descended Goldsmith's "Dolly Monroe." He was one of the Protestant officers cashiered by Tyrconnell.

He was a captain in the regiment originally raised by Sir Francis Hamilton. His name has frequent mention for gallantry in action by siege annalists, among others by "Londeriados," viz.:

> "In this great action Colonel Monro
> Cut down the Irish with a mighty blow."

and again when speaking of the second Windmill Hill fight (June 4th), when Col. Nugent led a fierce attack "and brave Monro as quickly him repels."

After the relief of the city he received little recognition for past services in General Kirke's reorganisation of the garrison. His regiment was amalgamated with that of Col. Lance, and while he was given the joint command, with companies for his own

---

[1] Mackenzie in Hampton's "Siege," p. 218.

regimental officers, viz. Capt. Rev. Christopher Jenny, Thomas Ash, Thomas Manson and William Hamilton, "the rest of his officers were broke."[1] He served all through the subsequent campaign and was killed before Limerick in 1691.[2]

393. **LIEUT.-COL. JOHN WIGTON**, of Raphoe, Co. Derry, defender. His name as John Wigton of Raphoe, Co. Derry, figures among the attainted in James' Dublin Parliament. He was with the city forces in all the operations prior to the investment and throughout the siege.

"Londeriados," among other mentions, thus writes of him in the Cladyford engagement:

> "Brave Wigton of Raphoe at the Long Causey
> Opposed their horse, till the foot got away."

In the garrison sortie of the 23rd April:—

> "Baker and Hamil brought forth a big gun
> Strengthened by Lieutenant Colonel Wigton."

394. **CAPT. WILLIAM BEATTY**, of Moneymore, Co. Derry, defender. No one has more frequent mention for gallantry in the constant fighting of the garrison from the 21st April to 30th June.[3] The same authority (Mackenzie) tells of his going away and the why and the wherefore as quoted below:—

On the 30th June "Capt. Beatty also went away, and took protection and lived at Moneymore. But the reason of it was because he had a violent flux, which rendered him useless to the garrison, and he went to try and recover his health; for he had been in all encounters and skirmishes with the enemy before, and ever behaved himself with great integrity and valour."

He lived for many years at Moneymore, where he reared twelve stalwart sons (Graham's "Derriana," p. 116). The same authority tells us of descendants of his living in the earlier part of the 18th century in the Waterside, Derry, and at the Cross, Co. Derry, and relates the following incident as showing the loyalty of a descendant, Mr. James Beatty, a merchant of Newry, whose business necessitated frequent rides on horseback to Dublin. He never crossed the Boyne without alighting from his horse and on his knees returning solemn thanks to God for the great deliverance of this county on that memorable day.

395. **MRS. BEATTY**, of Moneymore, mother of Capt. William Beatty above, would appear from her will dated 8th July, 1689, in which she desires to be buried in Derry, to have accompanied her son to that city and died there during the siege.

---

[1] Mackenzie.
[2] Rawdon Papers.
[3] Mackenzie in Hampden's "Siege," pp. 219, 220, 225 and 226.

396. **Capt. Andrew Adams**, of Strabane, defender, mentioned generally as an officer "very useful to the garrison," and for gallantry in the second Windmill Hill sortie of 4th June.[1]

> "Adams of Strabane, at our cannon was a man
> To Derry's cause devoted."[2]

Among the signatures of those of the Corporation of Derry's Commission of 1690 is the name of

397. **David Adams**, defender, probably a relation.

398. **Robert Baird**, defender, mentioned several times by siege annalists for gallantry in action, particularly in repulsing Lord Clancarty's attack on June 28th on the Butcher's Gate when in conjunction with Capts. Kennedy, Dunbar, Noble, Graham and young Murray, "They did their courage tame."[3]

His name appears joined with that of William Hamill in a petition presented in 1707 to the Irish House of Commons, demanding the huge arrears of pay due to the officers and men of the garrison of Derry during the siege.[4]

399. **Robert Beard (Baird?)**, of Armagh, so described, is on the list of attainted in James' Dublin Parliament.

400. **Capt. Armstrong**, defender, mentioned for gallantry in the second Windmill Hill sortie of 4th June:—

> "Capt. Armstrong came nobly up to fight
> And put their bravest heroes to the flight."[3]

The Armstrongs were a well-known family in Co. Fermanagh. Two of the name were among the attainted in James' Dublin Parliament, viz.:—

401. **Daniel Armstrong**, Co. Fermanagh,

402. **Robert Armstrong**, Co. Fermanagh, while many of the name took part with the gallant men of Enniskillen in their successful operations, the following signing their address to King William:—

403. **John Armstrong**.

404. **Mathew Armstrong**.

---

[1] Mackenzie.
[2] Graham's Catalogue.
[3] "Londeriados."
[4] Hampton's "Siege."

405. **Thomas Armstrong.**

406. **Daniel Armstrong**, while

407. **Capt. Martin Armstrong** particularly distinguished himself in the battle of Lisnaskea as well as in several other engagements.[1]

408. **Lieut. Josias Abernethy**, defender, mentioned for "good service" in the repulsing of the enemy's attack on Windmill Hill on June 4th.[2] This is the only reference to his name, and I therefore infer that he died or was killed before the relief from the following facts, quoted from Dr. Killen's notes to an edition of Mackenzie's "Siege" published in 1870:—

"The Rev. John Abernethy, minister of Moneymore, when he went to London in Jan. 1689, as one of the deputation to present an address of welcome from the Irish Presbyterian Church to King William, sent his wife and children to Derry for protection during his absence."

In Reid's "History," Vol. III. p. 112, we are informed that Mrs. Abernethy lost all her children there during the privations of the siege except John, who prior to the investment had been sent to relations in Scotland. After taking his degree at Glasgow in 1696, this John returned to Ireland and was ordained in 1702 as minister of Antrim, becoming a well-known divine in the Irish Presbyterian Church. It seems, therefore, evident that the Lieut. Josias above was one of Mrs. Abernethy's children who died during the siege.

409. **Tom Barr**, trooper, defender. Of this name we have no information further than the "Londeriados" couplet describing his achievement in the garrison's first sortie of the 21st April, viz.:

> "Tom Barr, a trooper, with one mighty blow
> Cut off the head of an opposing foe."

410. **Isabell Barr**, defender, is one of the signers of the Corporation's Commission of 1690.

411. **Col. Adam Murray**, of Ling, Co. Donegal, defender. His grandfather Gideon, of the house of Murray of Philiphaugh, N.B., had settled at Ling in 1648. His father, John, eighty years of age, was too old for service in the field, so on Adam fell the duty of assisting Derry in her crisis. In a few days he was in the city at the head of a troop of cavalry drawn from the Ling tenantry and neighbours, of the best country material and fighting quality. It has already been told in the Introductory Chapter how he led his troops at Cladyford; how, foiled and unsupported through Lundy's treachery, he was forced to retire on the city; how he was locked outside the gates for the night;

---

[1] See Trimble's "History of Enniskillen."
[2] Mackenzie.

how next day he forced an entrance at the gate; how he made his way into Lundy's "surrender" council of war; how Lundy fled, and how Adam was left supreme, with an enthusiastic populace, to carry out his "No Surrender" policy.

He refused the Governorship of the town offered by acclamation, but accepted command of the forces in the field. How well these duties were carried out is vouched for by Mackenzie and others, although Walker is more sparing of praise. He was the heart and soul of the defence, while he was the leader, and driving force in all the garrison's sorties. Aicken's "Londeriados,"[1] which is dedicated to him, makes him out a veritable hero. Poor as is the verse, the incidents are so full of his achievements that it is frequently quoted in the following account of Col. Adam Murray during the siege. On the 20th April, as arranged by King James, before leaving the camp for Dublin, Lord Abercorn was sent on a final effort to arrange "surrender on terms." Met outside the walls by Col. Murray, to whom he offered £1000 and a colonelcy in a Jacobite regiment, all his proposals were indignantly refused. All ended in Murray "himself conveying the disappointed emissary outside our out-guards."[2] There was nothing now but the ordeal of battle, for which both sides were eager.

De Maimont, a famous French General, had been left in command of the investing army, with which were several other experienced officers and some four to five hundred soldiers of the same nationality. De Maimont and his officers were sanguine of dispersing the inexperienced and untrained garrison of Derry at the first charge, entering the city at their heels, and carrying the fortress by a *coup de main*.[3] If the Irish were not so confident, they had at least little doubt of success. As regards the garrison, Murray, Mitchelburn, Baker and many others were longing for an opportunity of proving the quality of the men they commanded.

On the morning of the 21st April, De Maimont led his forces to the neighbourhood of Pennyburn. Against this array, Murray, Mitchelburn and Baker were not long in showing a bold front. In the successive charges of the horse of both sides such impetuosity was shown that the formations were constantly broken and ranks intermingled. De Maimont and Murray, who had crossed swords early in the day, though eagerly trying to renew the combat, did not meet until late.

> "The Strand once cleared, Murray and Maimont meet,
> Who with dire threat'nings one another greet,
> For they had oft sought one another out
> But still were parted in the bloody rout.
> First they discharged their pistols on the spot;
> In which first firing Murray's horse was shot,
> Yet the brave beast ne'er felt the deadly wound,

---

[1] See No. 11.
[2] Mackenzie.
[3] See Part II. No. 15.

But wheel'd and pranced on the bloody ground;
Redoubled blows they gave with sword in hand,
Which the strong armour scarcely could withstand.
They thunder like the cyclops at the forge,
When they the metal on the anvil urge.
At last their swords in sev'ral pieces flew,
Then with their rapiers, they the fight renew.
The brave Maimont began to falsify
And thought the day his own immediately
He wheel'd his horse, which then began to spurn,
But noble Murray made a quick return;
For under his heav'd arm his sword he thrust
Till at his neck, the purple gore outburst.
His fleeting soul with the free blood expired
And our great hero to the fort retired."[1]

So ended the Homeric conflict, the main facts of which Mackenzie substantiates as follows:

"Col. Murray charged through the Brigade, and had that day three personal encounters with their commander, in the last of which he killed him on the spot, whom the enemy themselves confessed to be Lieut. General Maimont. It was also reported that he killed his brother in the same action."

And yet Macaulay, in his magnificent story of Derry and her defenders, discredits the tale, preferring D'Avaux's version of Maimont being killed by a stray bullet. Now D'Avaux, Louis XIV.'s Ambassador to James' Court, was then in Dublin and could only have had his information at second hand!

The day had proved a thorough vindication of the "No Surrender" policy. The French General, with some 200 men, had been killed, some booty and a standard taken, while the garrison had shown their fighting quality.

On the 15th April in an attack, over the same ground, known as "the Elah sortie," Murray was again successful, inflicting severe loss on the enemy, the French General Persignan, who had succeeded De Maimont in the supreme command, being mortally wounded.

On the 6th May the garrison awoke to find that during the night a considerable force had entrenched themselves with guns in position on Windmill Hill, commanding the defences. Allowed to remain, the city was untenable. Again the garrison rose to the occasion. Led by Murray, an immediate attack was made. It was the bloodiest of all the encounters, but the enemy were swept from their position. General Ramsay, who was in command, and some 200 men were left dead on the field, while many

---

[1] "Londeriados."

prisoners were captured, and five stand of colours remained with the victors. Of these colours two were taken by Col. Mitchelburn and afterwards presented by him to the Cathedral, where the remnants still adorn the sacred edifice. In this fight "Our Gen'ral Murray did wonders everywhere."[1]

In the course of the next few weeks Murray, besides his garrison duty, was faced with a problem of quite another kind. General Hamilton had discovered that Murray's father, an old man of eighty, was still in residence at Ling. Having brought him into camp under escort, he determined on using him to force Col. Murray to surrender the city. So under direful threats the old father was sent into the town to induce Col. Murray to capitulate, under promise of returning if not successful. The old man was unsuccessful, and returning to the camp—

> "To the gen'ral the sad news imparts
> That nought can force his son to quit the town."

General Hamilton, at heart sympathising with the old man, and not to be outdone in chivalry, sent him home under protection:—

> "Where all along he did in safety dwell
> Though by his son the Irish army fell."[1]

On the 4th June the besiegers made a determined effort to regain Windmill Hill, but were repulsed:—

> "The valiant Murray flew from trench to trench,
> And helped our men in many a deadly pinch."[1]

In all succeeding sorties Murray's presence seems to have had an almost magical effect:—

> "The name of Murray grew so terrible,
> That he alone was thought invincible;
> Where ere he came the Irish fled away,
> And left the field unto the English sway."[2]

On the 18th June occurred what "Londeriados" describes as "The Barge of Intelligence Expedition." From the commencement of the investment the enemy had full command of the river; all boats had been destroyed except those in use of the investors. Wishing to reconnoitre a few miles up the river, and if possible to land a messenger to communicate with Enniskillen, Murray had a large barge constructed. In this, with a picked crew of some thirty men, chiefly officers, he set forth on the night of the 18th June. Fired at from both banks, their retreat was cut off by two well-manned

---

[1] "Londeriados."
[2] "Londeriados."

boats. These they at once attacked, capturing one with thirteen prisoners, while the other escaped with heavy loss. In this risky venture Murray "received some shots in his headpiece that bruised his head, and for a time indisposed him for service."[1] But his crew did not escape as well:—

> "At sun rising we land at Ferry Key (Quay)
> And in their boat near thirteen dead men lay."[2]

On the 16th July in the last big sortie of the siege, successful at first:—

> "We them (the enemy) pursued into their trenches strong
> And ne'er bethought us, till were among
> Their strongest body; valiant Murray fought
> And hewed down hundreds, who his ruin sought,
> Till a fierce bullet through his body passed;
> Then we retreated to the town at last.
> Our wounded Gen'ral on his feet came back
> And ne'er complained that he blood did lack."[2]

"He was shot through both thighs, up near the body, which proved so dangerous that he did not recover till near November."[1]

Unable to take further part in the defence he must have learned with supreme satisfaction of the relief, the culmination of his hopes and the vindication of the "No Surrender" policy to which he had devoted himself. His signature is attached to the address of congratulation to King William after the relief.

His indignation must have been great at General Kirke's arbitrary treatment of his old comrades-in-arms of the garrison, and of his requisitioning of his old and trusty charger for personal use. Mackenzie in his graphic account of General Kirke's behaviour comments as follows:—

"Col. Baker, and Capt. Murray's regiments were designed to be joined but (such was the natural indignation of the officers and men) all of Col. Murray's, except a very few, refused, and went off into the country with their carbines and pistols, and the Major General seized their saddles. ... The Major General appointed new captains to most of the companies, leaving them to choose their lieutenants and ensigns, so that a great many of those captains, who had not only raised and armed their companies, almost wholly at their own charge, but had done the greatest service in the defence of the town, were either disbanded or reduced, and their companies given to others that neither expended anything of their fortunes, nor hazarded their lives in that cause. . . . One of these captains took the liberty to complain, but instead of any redress, he was (as himself informed several of us) threatened with the new gallows."

---

[1] Mackenzie.
[2] "Londeriados."

Adam Murray received no recognition for his valuable services. His arrears of pay were never forthcoming. In 1694 he was given a Lieut.-Colonel's commission in Lord Mountjoy's Regiment and drew half-pay until his death.[1] He never entirely recovered, but died in 1706 from the joint effects of wounds and siege privation. He was buried in the old graveyard of the Presbyterian church of Glendermot, where his comrades-in-arms, Colonels Mitchelburn and Hamill, joined him in due course. A century later the Irish Society erected fitting memorials with suitable inscriptions over the graves of these three defenders. Adam Murray also shares in the memorial pillar in honour of her defenders, which, crowned with Walker, Bible in hand, stands on Derry's walls. In the centenary celebration (1788) of the shutting of the gates his great-grandson, James Murray, "carrying the sword, with which his gallant grandfather slew the French General Maimont,"[2] took a prominent place in the procession.

The family in the direct male line from the hero of Derry is extinct, but is represented in the female line by Col. Alexander, Carrickmore House, Co. Tyrone, whose ancestor, Mr. Alexander, of Caw, Co. Derry, married a daughter of Col. Adam Murray. Col. Alexander is in possession of many interesting relics, amongst them a unique set of thirteen buttons, each taken from the coat of one of the thirteen gallant apprentices.

In this sketch I have purposely avoided the vexed question of whether Adam Murray was Church of Ireland or Presbyterian. For my purpose it is sufficient to recognise him as the defender of Protestantism in whom all sections in Derry during the siege had confidence.

412. **Capt. James Murray**, defender, one of Col. Adam Murray's redoubtable captains of horse, sharing in all their actions until killed in the sortie of 16th July, when his Colonel was so severely wounded:—

> "Brave James Murray, a volunteer was slain
> Who in all his actions did applauses gain
> In a few hours Coghran revenge demands
> And in the lines with a battalion stands."[3]

413. **James Murray**, defender. Frequently mentioned as an efficient and useful artillery officer.

> "James Murray from the Northern Bastions
> Near Elah hurt the foes battalions."[3]

414. **Capt. Sam Murray**, defender. An officer in Col. Murray's Regiment. Was one of the officers of the Derry garrison present in London after the relief who received

[1] Dalton's "Army List."
[2] Hampton's "Siege."
[3] "Londeriados."

three months' pay to enable him to report at once to the Duke of Schomberg's camp.[1]

He was one of the garrison officers in 1690 who took part in the controversy regarding Walker's exact position in the garrison during the siege.[2]

415. **HENRY MURRAY**, defender, is among the signers of the address to King William.

416. **CAPT. JOHN COGHRAN**, of Belrath, Armagh, defender, another of the captains in Murray's Horse.

He was conspicuous with his regiment in all the sorties. In that of the 21st April he is credited with killing "the brave Major Taafe,"[3] and in the same action he had his horse shot under him and was wounded in the leg.[4]

After the relief he was one of the signers of the address to King William. After serving all through the war he returned to Belrath, Armagh, where a few years later he fell suddenly dead while walking in one of his fields. "His body was found, with sword half drawn, by an old comrade-in-arms, who is said to have exclaimed, 'Death must have taken him treacherously, for if John Coghran had got but time to draw the remainder of his sword from the scabbard, he would have killed Death himself.' "[5]

In his old Armagh residence about a century ago was discovered the first half-mutilated copy of Aicken's "Londeriados," so often quoted in these sketches.

417. **ROBERT COCHRANE**, as well as the above Capt. John Coghran, were among the witnesses to the document of the 11th July authorising the Governors to open the abortive negotiations for surrender of the city on terms.

The following five of the name (variously spelt) were among the signers of the Corporation of Derry's 1690 Commission:

418. **MARMADUKE COGHRAN**.

419. **THOMAS COCHRANE**.

420. **JEAN COCHRAN**.

421. **ELIZABETH COCHRAN**.

422. **PELLER COGHAN**.

423. **CAPT. STEPHEN HERD** (or **HEARD**), defender, another of the captains in Col. Adam Murray's Horse. Frequently mentioned by siege annalists for good service.

He is one of the attainted in James' Dublin Parliament, described as of Londonderry.

---

[1] Dalton's "Army List," 1689–1714, Vol. III. p. 168.
[2] Hampton's "Derry," p. 459.
[3] "Londeriados."
[4] Mackenzie.
[5] Extract from Stuart's "Armagh" in Graham's Catalogue.

His name is also among the witnesses to the document authorising the Governors of Derry on the 11th July to open the abortive negotiations for surrender, and also on the Corporation of Derry's 1690 Commission. In this latter Commission there were also the signatures of

424. **Stephen Herd**.

425. **James Herd**.

426. **Major Nathaniel Bull**, of Co. Meath, defender, of Col. Adam Murray's Horse, in all of whose actions he greatly distinguished himself. In the 21st April sortie:—

"The second squadron (of Murray's Horse) was led by Major Nathaniel Bull, son of Major Samuel Bull of Co. Meath, who did us very good service by his integrity to the interest of the garrison and his influence on the soldiers to animate their courage."[1]

and in the Elah sortie of the 25th April:—

> "Brave Major Bull did wonders in the fight
> For he beat back the enemy on the right."[2]

427. **Capt. Arthur Bashford** (or **Blashford**), of Co. Monaghan, defender. He was a strong supporter of Col. Adam Murray's opposition to Lundy's surrender, and during the siege has frequent mention in Mackenzie and "Londeriados" for good service in the field.

He was among the attainted in James' Dublin Parliament, described as of Co. Monaghan.

428. **Col. Hugh Hamill**, of Lifford, defender.

Immediately on the news of the shutting of the gates, in answer to Derry's call, Hamill raised among his tenantry and neighbours a considerable force which he led into the city. Commanding these all through the siege, he rendered invaluable services to the defence. With his regiment he took a leading part in trying to prevent Hamilton's army crossing the Mourne and Finn. "All that night (April 14th) Col. Crofton and Col. Hamill (at Lifford) successfully repulsed the enemy, who attempted to pass the ford, killing several with their cannon and small shot,"[3] but owing to Lundy's failure in sending the promised support they were obliged to fall back on the city. In the second Windmill Hill sortie of the 4th June:—

> "Whilst Colonel Hamill does the foe pursue
> Through his cheek a pistol bullet flew."[2]

---

[1] Mackenzie.
[2] "Londeriados."
[3] Harris.

He was among the attainted in James' Dublin Parliament and his signature figures on the address to King William after the relief. He never got any recognition of his services. Being in London in the spring of 1690, he was among the officers of the Derry garrison who received three months' pay to enable them to join the Duke of Schomberg's army in Ireland. (Dalton's "Army List," 1689–1714, Vol. III. p. 168). According to the same authority, in 1694 he was given a captain's commission in Lord Mountjoy's Regiment and was drawing half-pay in 1702.

His whole life after the relief was devoted in association with his brother William (No. 429) (they had been appointed agents for the officers and men of the Derry garrison) to the recovery of their arrears of pay, viz.:—

> Arrears of pay to men in 8 regiments £74,000
> Arrears of pay to officers. £60,000
> Initial equipment of officers and men . . . . $\underline{\quad ? \quad}$
> £134,000

Of this sum £9800 was paid up in 1705 and nothing afterwards. This business entailed frequent visits to London, where he was graciously received by King William at Whitehall. Returning from a visit to Whitehall, Col. Hamill remarked to a comrade: "Was not James a fool to exchange that abode for Robin Cowan's in St. Johnstown?"[1]

Col. Hamill died in 1721, and was buried beside his old comrades-in-arms, Col. Adam Murray and Col. Mitchelburn, in the graveyard of the old Presbyterian church of Glendermot, where a century later the Irish Society erected memorials with suitable inscriptions over the three defenders.

429. **WILLIAM HAMILL** succeeded to his brother's property at Lifford, and continued the ineffectual efforts to recover the Derry garrison's arrears of pay. Queen Anne was so far in sympathy that she gave him a grant of £700 out of her privy purse. In one of William's letters, still extant, he denounces the treatment of the garrison's claims by the Government "as a reproach, and a blemish upon the justice, and even the religion of their fellow subjects."[2]

The name is extinct in the neighbourhood of Lifford.

430. **COL. RICHARD CROFTON**, of Lisdorn, Co. Roscommon, defender, a younger son of Richard Crofton, of Lisdorn. He was an ensign in Lord Berkeley's troop of horse in 1662 and captain in Fairfax's Regiment in 1685. He was among the Protestant officers cashiered by Tyrconnell prior to the revolution. Coming north, his services as an experienced officer were availed of by the county associations in organising their levies.

---

[1] Graham's "Derriana." St. Johnstown was the house in which King James lodged when in camp before Derry.
[2] Dwyer's "Siege of Derry," p. 231.

He was with Sir Arthur Rawdon in the attempt to prevent Hamilton's passage of the Bann, and in the retreat on Derry, when he was in command of the Canning of Garvagh's Regiment. Once in the city he identified himself with the protests against Lundy's inaction, and was among the leading officers signing the "Declaration of Union" (10th April). His name is coupled with Col. Hamill's for good service at Lifford in the effort to stop Hamilton's advance on the 14th April.[1]

On the night of the 17th April, when the gates by Lundy's instructions had been left open to admit the advance of the enemy, Crofton on his rounds discovered the fact, and by his prompt action in doubling the guard and changing the password saved the city.[2] On the 19th April, on the reorganisation of the regiments of the garrison, he was confirmed in his colonelcy of the Canning Regiment, a command he held with honour during the siege, in which he took a distinguished part in all the sorties of the garrison.[3]

His name appears as one of the signatures on the 11th July to the document authorising the Governors to open the abortive negotiations for surrender with the enemy.

After the relief Col. Crofton was one of the signers of the address to King William, and shared with other officers of the garrison in General Kirke's arbitrary treatment. His regiment (the Canning) was amalgamated with that of Col. Mitchelburn, who was given the joint command, while Col. Crofton was reduced. He was in London in the spring of 1690, when his name figures among other officers of the Derry garrison receiving three months' pay to enable them to join the Duke of Schomberg's camp in Ireland. He got a commission as captain in 1694 and was drawing half-pay in 1702.[4] His name also appears in London publications in the controversy then raging as to Col. the Rev. George Walker's exact position as Governor during the siege.

431. **FRANK CROFTON**, defender, a brother of the above, and serving as an officer in his Canning Regiment. He is mentioned for gallantry in the Pennyburn sortie of the 21st April, viz.:—

> "Young Frank Crofton among their forces flew
> And with dire blows a multitude he slew."[5]

432. **JOHN CROFTON**, defender, a signer of the address to King William, a brother of Col. Richard Crofton (No. 430).

He left a diary of the siege, unfortunately lost, but one of his descendants remembers when a boy hearing extracts read, describing how he had to kill his horse in order

[1] Harris.
[2] Mackenzie.
[3] Mackenzie and "Londeriados."
[4] Dalton's "Army List," 1689–1714, Vol. III. p. 168.
[5] "Londeriados."

to feed his men, and how he killed and ate a rat, which he had long kept in a cage.[1]

The representation of Col. Richard Crofton of Lisdorn appears to rest in the male line of the Crofton family of Ireland, viz. in Sir Malby Crofton, 3rd Bart., of Longford House, Co. Sligo.[2]

433. **Col. William Ponsonby**, defender. This William was the second son of Sir John Ponsonby, who came to Ireland with Oliver Cromwell in 1649, and had acquired considerable estate in the south of Ireland. His second wife, a daughter of Lord Folliott of Ballyshannon, was William's mother.

Whether Col. William was present all through the siege is doubtful, but at all events he rendered good service until the investment was complete.

He was one of the four colonels who, when refused admission to Lundy's council of war which was plotting a surrender on the 18th April, protested so vehemently against the proceedings:—

> "Ponsonby brave was here to save
> The threatened walls of Derry.
> His trusty sword made him a lord
> And saved his lands in Kerry."[3]

He was a strong supporter of the Protestant dynasty in William's and Anne's reigns. He was sworn on the Privy Council in 1715, created a Baron in 1721, Viscount Duncannon in 1722 and Earl of Bessborough in 1739. His lineal descendant and representative is the present Earl of Bessborough, Bessborough, Co. Kilkenny.

434. **Col. Thomas Blair**, of Aghadoey (Agivie), Co. Derry, defender, and officer in the Canning Regiment, variously styled in contemporary records Captain, Major and Lieut.-Col. He was with this regiment in all the preliminaries and through the siege. He is first mentioned for repulsing an enemy's attack, when Hamilton was advancing on Derry, at Fagivie (Agivie), in Co. Derry.[4] In the sorties of the garrison his name is constantly mentioned for good service, of which the following are instances. At Pennyburn on the 21st April:—

> "Brave Major Blair the enemies fire sustained
> And in great feats a reputation gained."

And again, on the 25th April, he is associated for commendation with Col. Adam Murray:—

---

[1] A memory of John Crofton's diary, conveyed to me by the kindness of the Very Rev. H. B. Swanzy of Newry, Dean of Dromore.
[2] Burke's Peerage, 1907 edition.
[3] Graham's Catalogue.
[4] Mackenzie.

"Our Gen'ral did wonders everywhere
Assisted by Lieutenant Colonel Blair."[1]

His name was among the attainted in James' Dublin Parliament and he was a signer of the address to King William after the relief. His name is among the officers of the Derry garrison in London in the spring of 1690 who received three months' pay to enable them to report to the Duke of Schomberg's camp in Ireland.[2]

435. **LIEUT. DAVID BLAIR**, defender. Probably a son of Col. Thomas Blair, and an officer in the Canning Regiment, is mentioned for gallantry in the Pennyburn sortie of April 21st.[3]

The Blair family were among the original settlers in the Agivie district, where they held considerable property, and in 1706 Col. Thomas Blair was also a leaseholder on Lord Antrim's Barony of Glenarm. The Blairs were the owners of one of the earliest Bleach Greens in Co. Derry.[4]

The Blairs are extinct in the male line. The Ogilvie Blair Grahams of Larchfield, Co. Down, who owe the Blair to this connection, have some ancient silver inherited from this family.

436. **JAMES BLAIR**, probably of this family, was a signer of the Derry address to King William.

437. **COL. ROBERT WHITE**, defender, one of the Protestant officers cashiered by Tyrconnell prior to the revolution. He got employment as a soldier of experience in Sir William Franklin's Belfast Regiment, with which he served with distinction from the "Break of Dromore" to the retirement on Derry and all through the siege.

He was employed by Lundy (17th April) in his surrender negotiations with King James, but after Lundy's flight threw himself so whole-heartedly into the Protestant cause that he won the confidence of the garrison. After the relief he was one of the deputation sent to Inch (1st August) to congratulate General Kirke on his success. When Kirke reorganised the garrison regiments, their officers and commands, Col. Robert White was given the command of Col. the Rev. George Walker's old regiment.

He died on the 5th August[5] and was interred in Derry, but "his corpse was raised, put into a leaden coffin and carried to England."[6] This statement of Ash's seems to disprove Graham's statement that he was of a Co. Cavan family.

---

[1] "Londeriados."
[2] Dalton's "Army List," 1689–1714, Vol. III. p. 168.
[3] Mackenzie.
[4] For information regarding their importance in the district see the late Dr. Morrison's interesting book, "Modern Ulster."
[5] Walker.
[6] Ash's diary of the siege.

438. **Ensign John White**, of Co. Tyrone, defender, an officer in Col. Mitchelburn's Regiment and all through the siege. He was one of the attainted in James' Dublin Parliament.

439. **Thomas White**, of Co. Cavan, on the list of attainted in James' Dublin Parliament. He was one of the gallant men of Enniskillen, holding a commission as captain (1689) in Col. Lloyd's Enniskillen Regiment and fell at Aughrim.

440. **David White**, of Co. Down, attainted in James' Dublin Parliament.

441. **Nicholas White**, defender, was a signer of the address to King William after the relief.

442. **Francis White**, of Co. Tyrone, defender, so described in the list of attainted in James' Dublin Parliament. He was probably the Francis White who, with other officers at a council of war on the 13th April at Derry, signed a strong remonstrance against Lundy's inaction.

443. **Francis White**, of Co. Cavan, was described as above in the list of attainted in James' Dublin Parliament.

444. **George White** and

445. **Thomas White**, signers of Derry address and probably defenders.

446. **Capt. Barrel**, of Urney, Strabane, defender. The only mention of this name is in reference to "the Elah" sortie of the 25th April, where:—

> "Capt. Barrel from Urney near Strabane
> Did in this action reputation gain."[1]

447. **Capt. Francis Obre**, of Lisburn, defender. First mentioned as an officer commanding a section of the forces of the Antrim and Down Associations sent in the spring of 1689 on the abortive attempt to surprise Carrickfergus Castle and the garrisons of Belfast and Lisburn. He was afterwards with Sir Arthur Rawdon's troops at the "Break of Dromore" and in the retreat to Derry, where he remained all through the siege. He is particularly mentioned[2] for useful service in the Elah sortie of the 25th April, and "Londeriados" thus refers to him on the same occasion:—

> "But Col. Murray and brave Aubrey (sic)
> Opposed the same and caused them back to fly."

His name figures among the signers of the document of the 11th July authorising

---

[1] "Londeriados."

[2] Mackenzie.

the Governors to open the abortive negotiations with the enemy for surrender.

After the relief he was one of the signers of the address to King William, and his name is among the attainted in James' Dublin Parliament.

He was the son of Francis Obre, of Cantilew, Co. Armagh, a property which the family had acquired by the marriage of their ancestor in 1632 with the original grantee of the Plantation. Cantilew is still in the possession of the name.[1]

448. **Hugh Rowley**, of Castleroe, Co. Derry, was one of the attainted in James' Dublin Parliament. His name is of interest as the local representative of the Rowley family who had done so much at the time of the Plantation of the City of London Companies in the county and city of Londonderry.

John Rowley, the first of the family in Ulster, was a leading merchant in London, and in 1610 was sent over along with Tristram Beresford as the City of London agents to view the territory and prepare the way for the Plantation. How well they carried out their mission is a matter of history. This John Rowley was the first Mayor of Derry, 1613, and again in 1623 and 1624. Acquiring considerable property in the neighbourhood of Castleroe, he became a man of great influence. His son and successor, Edward, was Mayor of Derry in 1634, while his son, Sir John, married a daughter and heiress of Sir Hercules Langford, of Summer Hill, Co. Meath, where his descendants have since been represented by the line of that marriage, viz. the Viscount and Barons Langford, Summer Hill, Co. Meath.

449. **Sir Arthur Langford**, of Summer Hill, Co. Meath.

The Langfords had long been closely connected with the town of Carrickfergus and Co. Antrim. The first of the name at Carrickfergus were two brothers, both captains in Elizabeth's and James I.'s services:

1. Sir Roger who obtained a grant from the Crown of Muckamore Abbey about 1620, and in 1580 was appointed Constable of Carrickfergus Castle, being Mayor of the town in 1624.
2. Sir Hercules, Mayor of Carrickfergus, 1614 and 1623. On his death he left his Carrickfergus property to his nephew, Sir Roger's son, another Roger, who was also knighted and Mayor of the town in 1639. The second Sir Roger was father of a second Hercules, who was Mayor in 1631 and High Sheriff, Co. Antrim, 1661. Sir Arthur Langford, probably his son, the subject of this sketch, was M.P. for Co. Antrim in 1716.

The only mention of this name in the critical events of the times occurs in connection with the controversy raging in the spring of 1690 in London with regard to Walker's exact position as Governor of Derry. His taking a leading part in this indicates

---

[1] Burke's "Landed Gentry of Ireland."

a prominence among the supporters of King William. In 1768 a marriage of a Miss Rowley, of Summer Hill, with the then head of the Pakenham family of Pakenham Hall, Westmeath, entitles the descendants of these two families to share with Lord Langford in the representation of this Rowley and Langford stock. The representatives of the above sketches are therefore:—

1. Lord Langford, of Summer Hill, Co. Meath.
2. Marquess of Headfort.
3. The Earl of Longford, Pakenham Hall, Westmeath.
4. Col. Arthur Pakenham, Langford Lodge, Crumlin, Co. Antrim.

With regard to the fourth, it is curious to note that the name of their residence has been for over a century Langford Lodge, while the family is never without a Hercules. The present owner is Col. Hercules Arthur Pakenham, C.M.G., D.S.O., D.L., late of the Grenadier Guards, who commanded a regiment of the Ulster Division in the Great War and is now a senator of the Parliament of Northern Ireland.[1]

450. **THOMAS BAKER**, officer, defender. It is only from his signature to a document, published in London (1690), regarding Walker's exact status as Governor during the siege that we are informed of his serving in the defence.[2]

His name figures among the signatures to the address to King William after the relief. He was one of the Derry officers in London in the spring of 1690 who received three months' pay to enable them to report to the Duke of Schomberg's camp in Ireland.[3]

451. **CHARLES COLQUHOUN**, of Letterkenny, defender.

> "Him (Grove) Charles Colquhoun assisted with some horse
> From Letterkenny and they joined our force."[4]

It is plain that the above brought a body of men to join the contingent which his neighbour, Capt. William Grove, of Castle Shannaghan,[5] led into Derry for the defence. He was attainted in James' Dublin Parliament.

452. **JAMES COLQUHOUN**, of Co. Fermanagh, so described, was among the attainted in James' Dublin Parliament.

Sir John Colquhoun, Laird of Luss, N.B., was one of the original grantees of 1000

---

[1] For further particulars of descent, etc., see Burke's Peerage and "Landed Gentry of Ireland" under names of Lord Langford, Earl of Longford, and Pakenham of Langford Lodge.
[2] Hampton's "Derry," p. 481.
[3] Dalton's "Army List," 1689–1714, Vol. III. p. 168.
[4] "Londeriados."
[5] See No. 238.

acres in Co. Donegal. The above were, in all probability, of his clan.

453. **COMYN**, of Lifford, defender. Local tradition as related in Graham's "Derriana" is so creditable to this old man that I extract the gist of it as follows:—

Comyn was said to have joined Col. Hamill's Regiment when over eighty years old and to have been all through the siege of Derry. On the 18th April, when King James at the head of his army presented himself at the gates sure of immediate surrender, Lundy had given the strictest orders that not a shot should be fired. This was too much for Col. Murray's loyal supporters, the only question among the watchers on the walls being who was to fire the first shot and break the orders of the Governor. Comyn solved the difficulty by claiming the right as the oldest man on the walls to fire the first shot.

> "Comyn's gun made many run
> Amazed was each bye-stander."[1]

In 1820 there were still descendants of Comyn in the neighbourhood of Lifford.[2]

454. **JAMES HOUSTON**, of Garveleigh, Castlederg, defender.

For the preservation of many local traditions (as in the case of Comyn, No. 453) Ulster is indebted to that painstaking author Graham for his Catalogue, in "Ireland Preserved," and "Derriana," published nearly a century ago. From one of these stories derived direct from his descendants I gather what is recounted below.

James Houston residing at Garveleigh, near Castlederg, on the Edwards estate, on the outbreak of the revolution joined the Derry garrison, was present in all the preliminary operations and served all through the siege. An expert marksman, in possession of an ancient and heavy fowling piece, he is said to have shot King James' standard bearer when the Jacobite army was advancing to the city gates on the 18th April. Later in the siege, becoming so weak from an attack of dysentery as to be unable to handle his ponderous weapon, he was assisted and supported to the field by comrades, who loaded and held the gun while he aimed and pulled the trigger. In this manner he killed a French officer riding at the head of his men on the other side of the broad river Foyle.

His name is among the signatures to the address to King William after the relief. Not content with his siege service he was present at the Boyne, Aughrim and Limerick. Returning to Co. Donegal after the campaign he settled at Tinklersford in the parish of Raymochy, where he ultimately died.

Two others of the name, probably relatives, were signers of the Derry Commission of 1690, viz.:—

---

[1] Graham's Catalogue.

[2] Graham.

455. **ROBERT HOUSTON.**

456. **JOHN HOUSTON.**

457. **REV. JOHN KELSO**, Presbyterian minister, of Enniskillen.

No one took a more prominent position in the organisation for, or in the actual defence of, Enniskillen than did this fighting divine.[1] His letter of the 18th December, written on behalf of Enniskillen to David Cairnes as representing the garrison of Derry, is not only evidence of his zeal for the cause but of the confidence placed in him by the men of Enniskillen. In this letter is intimated Enniskillen's approval of the shutting of the gates and Derry's resolute stand, assurance of Enniskillen's support and the hope that they will work together for the common interest. It was men like Kelso whose energies led to the desired culmination in the relief of both these centres and the victory of the Boyne.

Mr. Kelso had been ordained to the charge of Raloo, Co. Antrim, in 1673, being subsequently appointed to Enniskillen. He died shortly after the relief.[2]

458. **LIEUT. ROBERT LOUTHER (LOWTHER)**, defender, an officer in Capt. Nicholas Holmes' company of Col. Baker's Regiment during the siege, a fact gathered from a certificate signed, November 1689, by Governors Mitchelburn and Walker.[3] His name as Capt. Robert Lowder, evidently the same, is among the officers of the Derry garrison in London who in the spring of 1690 received three months' pay to enable them to report to the Duke of Schomberg's camp in Ireland.[4] There are two others of the name Lowther, or Louther, who figure in the list of attainted in James' Dublin Parliament, viz.:—

459. **LANCELOT LOWTHER**, described as of Co. Leitrim.

460. **WILLIAM LOWTHER**, described as of Co. Leitrim.

461. **JOHN LAWDER** (or **LOWDER**), Enniskillen address, son of William Lawder of Drumaleague, Co. Leitrim, was in Enniskillen all through the defence. The present representative of the family is J. Ormsby Lawder, Lawderdale, Ballinamore, Co. Leitrim.[5]

462. **CAPT. NICHOLAS HOLMES** (or **HOMES**), defender, an officer in Col. Baker's Regiment all through the siege.

In the "Barge of Intelligence" expedition of the 18th June, when some thirty officers of the garrison, under the leadership of Col. Adam Murray, made a daring

---

[1] Trimble's "History of Enniskillen."
[2] Dr. Killen's notes to his edition of Mackenzie's "Siege."
[3] Hampton's "Derry," p. 461.
[4] Dalton's "Army List," 1689–1714, Vol. III. p. 168.
[5] Trimble's "Enniskillen," p. 591.

venture up the river, he has the following mention with other officers:—

> "With him (Murray) ascend near thirty officers
> Besides the boys prepared for messengers
> Noble, and Holmes, and the brave Dunbar
> His three companions in the feats of war."[1]

This is fully confirmed by Mackenzie, who praises his gallantry in the enemy's attempt of June 28th to rush the Butcher's Gate.

463. **GEORGE HOLMES** (or **HOMES**), defender, an officer of Col. Lance's Coleraine Regiment, with which he served in the defence.

He was one of the officers signing on the 11th July the document authorising the Governors to open the abortive negotiations with the enemy for surrender.

464. **THOMAS HOLMES**, described as of Co. Monaghan, is among the attainted in James' Dublin Parliament.

465. **JOHN HOMES** (or **HOLMES**). His signature is among those attached to the Derry address to King William after the relief.

466. **CAPT. JAMES GALLAGHER**, defender, an officer in Col. Baker's Regiment all through the siege. The only mention of this name is in Ash's "Diary" viz.:—

"On June 27th James Gallagher's house in Bishop Street, where two barrels of powder were lodged, was hit by a bomb, and 14 people were killed, 6 of Walker's regiment, four horsemen, and four women,"

and that on August 13th, after the relief, he was sent in command of his company, along with four other captains in command of theirs, to relieve a like force at Inch, which by General Kirke's orders were being brought into Derry.

467. **CAPT. ABRAM**, defender. The only reference to this name is that on the 7th June "another bomb fell at Capt. Abram's hill house and smeared it all over with clovey-flowers and broke his chin."[2]

468. **LIEUT.-COL. WILLIAM CAMPBELL**, an officer of the garrison all through the siege. He was conspicuous in the second Windmill Hill action of the 4th June, being thus mentioned:—

> "Col. Monro was posted near the walls
> Brave Campbell's post upon his right hand fells."[3]

---

[1] "Londeriados."
[2] Ash's "Diary."
[3] "Londeriados."

Nothing speaks more of his importance in the garrison than his being selected as one of the pall bearers at the funeral of the Governor, Col. Baker, on the 30th June, the others so honoured being Governors Walker and Mitchelburn, Cols. Lance and Monro, and Alderman John Campsie, ex-Mayor of the city.

His name figures among those signing the document on the 11th July authorising the Governors to open the abortive negotiations with the enemy for surrender on terms. He was a signer of the address to King William after the relief.

469. **LIEUT. JOSHUA CAMPBELL**, defender, an officer in the Skeffington, afterwards the Mitchelburn, Regiment, during the siege.

470. **JOHN CAMPBELL**, a signer of the address to King William after the relief.

471. **CHARLES CAMPBELL**. His signature is among those attached to the Corporation of Derry's 1690 Commission.

Among the attainted in James' Dublin Parliament were the following of the name:—

472. **DAVID CAMPBELL**, described as of Co. Down.

473. **CHARLES CAMPBELL**, described as of Co. Down.

474. **WILLIAM CAMPBELL**, described as of Co. Down.

475. **ROBERT CAMPBELL**, described as of Co. Down.

476. **DAVID CAMPBELL** (yeoman), described as of Co. Cavan.

477. **CHARLES CAMPBELL**, described as of Co. Leitrim.

478. **WILLIAM CAMPBELL**, described as of Co. Tyrone.

The following Campbells were among the men of Enniskillen and signers of the Enniskillen address to King William after the relief:

479. **JAMES CAMPBELL**, and

480. **WILLIAM CAMPBELL**, Enniskillen address.

481. **CAPT. STEPHEN GODFREY**, of Coleraine, defender, an officer of the Coleraine Regiment, commanded by Cols. Parker and Lance in turn. He took part in all the preliminary operations and through the siege.

In enumerating the muster of forces for the defence of the city "Londeriados" has this mention of his name:

"Next him[1] brave Godfrey of Coleraine
Into the city with a company came."

He was a signer of the address to King William after the relief. He was in London in the spring of 1690, when with many comrades of the Derry garrison he became involved in the controversy then raging as to Walker's exact position as Governor during the siege.[2] A little later he was among the officers of the Derry garrison who received three months' pay to enable them to report for service in the Duke of Schomberg's camp in Ireland.[3] Other members of the family were:—

482. **WARREN GODFREY**, defender. His name was among the witnesses to a document of the 11th July authorising the Governors to open the abortive negotiations with the enemy for surrender on terms. Signer of the Derry address.

483. **WILLIAM GODFREY**, of Castleroe, Co. Donegal, figures on the list of attainted in James' Dublin Parliament.

484. **THOMAS GODFREY** and

485. **JOHN GODFREY** are both signers of the Corporation of Derry's Commission of 1690.

486. **CAPT. JOHN CROOKS** (or **CROOKE**), defender, an officer of the garrison all through the siege.

In the enemy's determined attempt to recover Windmill Hill on the 4th June he seems by his initiative to have secured the victory. In this action "our men wondered to find they had spent so many shot and that none of the enemy fell but Captain Crooke observed they had armour on and then commanded to fire at their horses which turned to such good account that but three of these bold men with much difficulty made their escape. We wondered that the foot did not (according to custom) run faster till we took notice that on their retreat they took the dead on their backs and so preserved their own bodies from the remainder of our shot which was more service than they did alive."[4]

His name appears as one of the witnesses to the authority empowering the Governors on the 11th July to open the abortive negotiations with the enemy for surrender on terms. On the 23rd July, a few days before the relief, he was appointed one of the new and special Board of Court-Martial.

487. **CAPT. WILLIAM CROOKS** (or **CROOKE**), defender, mentioned as a volunteer

---

[1] Phillips of Limavady.
[2] Hampton's "Derry," pp. 461, 462.
[3] Dalton's "Army List," 1689–1714, Vol. III. p. 168.
[4] Walker's "Siege."

officer, unattached to any particular regiment, who was conspicuous for general good service. His leg was broken by a bomb and he died from the effects of the wound at the end of April 1689.[1]

488. **Capt. Robert Rogers**, defender, an officer in Col. Hugh Hamill's Regiment, with which he served through the siege. He was a signer of the address to King William after the relief.

Being in London in the spring of 1690 he became involved with other officers of the garrison in the controversy then raging as to Walker's exact position as Governor during the siege.[2] He was one of the officers of the garrison then in London early in 1690 who received three months' pay to enable them to report to the Duke of Schomberg's camp in Ireland.[3]

489. **William Rogers** and

490. **Thomas Rogers** were among the signers of the Corporation of Derry's 1690 Commission.

491. **Capt. Richard Aplin**, defender, and

492. **Ensign Oliver Aplin**, defender, officers in Col. Hugh Hamill's Regiment and all through the siege. They were both in London in the spring of 1690, were involved in the Walker controversy, and received three months' pay to enable them to report to the Duke of Schomberg's camp in Ireland.[3]

493. **Capt. Alexander Watson**, defender. At first a captain in Col. Murray's Horse, he became in the course of the siege Captain of the Gunners and Chief Engineer of the garrison.[4]

> "Watson's made master of th' artillery
> Two hundred gunners, and montrosses there be
> . . . .
> In all attacks our gunners play'd their parts
> For from the walls they tamed the enemy's hearts.
> Eight sakers, and twelve demi culverin
> Discharged their fury daily from within
> Against the enemy's camps on every side
> Which furiously among their forces glide.
> Brave Watson fired upon their strongest ranks
> And swept off files from the enemy's flanks."[5]

---

[1] Mackenzie.
[2] Hampton's "Derry," p. 461.
[3] Dalton's "Army List," 1689–1714, Vol. III. p. 168.
[4] Hampton's "Derry," p. 489.
[5] "Londeriados."

After the relief he was in London in the spring of 1690, was involved in the controversy over Walker, and was one of the officers of the Derry garrison who received three months' pay to enable them to report to the Duke of Schomberg's camp in Ireland.[1]

494. **George Watson**. His signature is attached to the Enniskillen address to King William after the relief.

495. **Quartermaster Edward Curling**, defender. In the various mentions the name is variously given as Curling, Curline and Curlew, all one and the same from the context:—

> "And Curlew did attend the store
> Dividing portions both to rich and poor."[2]

He was Harvey's assistant storekeeper during the siege and later "the storekeeper of provisions" of Col. Lance's Regiment.[3] He was a signer of the address to King William after the relief and his name is on the Corporation of Derry's Commission of 1690. He was in London in the spring of 1690, when he figured in the Walker controversy and as Quartermaster he is among the Derry officers receiving three months' pay to enable them to report to the Duke of Schomberg's camp in Ireland.[4]

496. **Joseph Gordon**, defender, is a signer of the address to King William after the relief.

497. **Col. Joseph Gordon**, of Co. Tyrone, so described, is on the list of attainted in James' Dublin Parliament.

498. **Alexander Gordon**, defender, was one of the few Protestant burgesses of Derry under Tyrconnell's New Charter of 1688.
He was one of the signers of the Corporation of Derry's 1690 Commission.

499. **Lieut. Green**, defender. On the 27th May "Lieutenant Green led one of the parties" in a successful sortie.[5]

500. **Ralph Green** and

501. **Christopher Green** were both signers of the Corporation of Derry's 1690 Commission.

502. **Rev. William Greene**, Killeter, Co. Fermanagh, was one of the attainted in James' Dublin Parliament.

---

[1] Dalton's "Army List," 1689–1714, Vol. III. p. 168.
[2] "Londeriados."
[3] Hampton's "Derry," p. 459.
[4] Dalton's "Army List," 1689–1714, Vol. III. p. 168.
[5] Mackenzie.

503. **THOMAS ADARE (ADAIR)**, defender, surgeon in Col. Mitchelburn's Regiment during the siege.[1] His name is among the signatures to the address to King William after the relief.

His name figures in London in 1690 in the controversy regarding Walker's exact status as Governor during the siege.

504. **CAPT. JOHN ANDERSON**, defender, an officer in Col. Mitchelburn's Regiment during the siege.[1] His name figures in the Walker controversy in London in 1690.

505. **JOHN ANDERSON**, of Co. Leitrim, and

506. **JAMES ANDERSON**, of Co. Cavan, were both among the attainted in James' Dublin Parliament.

507. **QUARTERMASTER W. ANDERSON**, defender, officer in Col. Murray's Regiment.

In London in the spring of 1690 he was one of the officers involved in the Walker controversy, and later received three months' pay to enable him to report to the Duke of Schomberg's camp in Ireland.[2]

508. **LIEUT. DUNLOP**, defender, an officer of the garrison. "Few days passed but (list of officers including Lieut. Dunlop) or some of them went out with small parties, and they seldom returned without doing some execution on the enemy or bringing in some small prey."[3]

According to Trimble's "Enniskillen" a branch of the Ayrshire family of this name, variously spelt Dunlop, Delap and Delapp, settled on Lough Swilly, Co. Donegal, in Elizabeth's reign (or early James I.). From this stock descend the families now represented by (1) the Rev. Canon Robert Delap of Lifford, and Mr. Delap of Monellan, Co. Donegal, and (2) the Delaps of Monasterboice, Co. Louth.

The following members of this family were attainted in James' Dublin Parliament, spelt and described as below:—

509. **JAMES DELAPP**, sen., Enniskillen, Co. Fermanagh.

510. **JAMES DELAPP**, jun., Enniskillen, Co. Fermanagh.

511. **FRANCES DELAPP**, Moylagh, Co. Donegal.

512. **ROBERT DELAPP**, Ballyshannon, Co. Donegal, and

513. **JAMES DELAP**, was one of the defenders of Enniskillen, and a signer of the Enniskillen address.

---

[1] Hampton's "Derry," p. 459.
[2] Dalton's "Army List," 1689–1714, Vol. III. p. 168.
[3] Mackenzie.

514. LIEUT. DALZELL, artillery officer, defender. Referring to the artillery service from the church steeple he is mentioned as follows:

> "Lieutenant D'yell (Dalzell) and some brave seamen
> Did from the walls slay many on the plain."[1]

515. LT.-COL. ADAM DOWNING, of Rosegift, Bellaghey, Co. Derry, defender, mentioned in Graham's Catalogue as serving through the siege. His signature is attached to the document of the 11th July authorising the Governors to open the abortive negotiations for surrender on terms. His name is among the attainted in James' Dublin Parliament.

After the relief of Derry he obtained a commission in King William's army, serving at the Boyne and in the subsequent campaign. He signed the address to King William.

He acquired considerable estate in the neighbourhood of Bellaghey, marrying a Miss Jackson, of Coleraine, and was a Deputy-Governor of Co. Derry. He died in 1719 and lies in a massive vault, erected by himself or his son, in the churchyard of Bellaghey, on which a suitable inscription records his services. He left a son John to succeed him at Rosegift, who left two sons:—

1. The elder of whom, the Rev. Alexander Clotworthy Downing, married the daughter of James Nesbitt, of Tubberdaly, King's Co., the name of Nesbitt in addition to Downing being subsequently assumed by the family.
   The representative of this line through several female descents is Mr. Edward Beaumont Downing Nesbitt, Tubberdaly, King's Co.
2. The second son, Dawson, married Catharine, daughter and heiress of George Fullerton, of Ballintoy Castle, Co. Antrim. Downing Fullerton became the family name and their descendants are still in possession of the castle and property.[2]

The connection of the Downings and Downing Fullertons of Ballintoy with Downing Street and Downing College, Cambridge, is worthy of notice. The Downing family, of whom Col. Adam was a member, were of considerable importance at Charles I.'s Court, and shortly after the Restoration Sir George Downing, 1st Bart., was sent by Charles II. as ambassador to Holland with secret instructions to force the Dutch into a declaration of war, when Louis XIV. of France and England combined were to invade and overwhelm that country. In a few months so unpopular had he made himself that he had to fly for his life. On his return he was sent to the Tower of London. He succeeded, however, in regaining the Royal favour, and dying a rich man, possessing, with other properties, the lands bordering on St. James' Park, on

---

[1] "Londeriados."
[2] See No. 621, Downing Fullerton.

which Downing Street, with the Premier's house and other Government buildings, were subsequently built. He was succeeded in his baronetcy by a son, grandson, and two great grandsons, of whom another Sir George (who died in 1749) left a handsome endowment to found Downing College, Cambridge. It so happened that when this college was being completed in 1795, his relative, Downing Fullerton, of Ballintoy, was dismantling that castle, and the trustees of Downing College purchased the old oak panelling, staircase, etc., which are now incorporated in that building.[1]

516. **Lieut. Dalton**, mentioned as having been the confidential servant of Governor Baker.[2]

> "Lieutenant Dalton was his (Baker's) faithful friend
> And Counsellor, whate'er he did intend."[3]

517. **Lieut. Michael Read (Reid)**, defender, an officer in Governor Baker's Regiment during siege.[4]

In London in the spring of 1690 he was involved in the Walker controversy. He was among the officers of the Derry garrison in London to receive three months' pay to enable them to report to the Duke of Schomberg's camp in Ireland.[5]

518. **Alexander Reid** (or **Read**), defender. A signer of the address to King William after the relief, and also the Corporation of Derry's 1690 Commission.

519. **Major John Read**, described as of Co. Armagh, was among the attainted in James' Dublin Parliament.

520. **Capt. Mulholland**, of Eden, Maghera, Co. Derry, defender. "Londeriados," in his muster of the Protestant forces for the defence of

Derry, records that "Captain Mulholland came from Maghera." The whole of the family must have been there, as the following names evidently of the same stock are among the signers of the address to King William after the relief, a sure indication of their participation in the defence.

521. **Bernard Mulholland**.

522. **David Mulholland**.

523. **John Mulholland**.

Graham in his notes to the Catalogue, published about a century ago, speaks of

---

[1] See *Belfast Newsletter*, 19th October, 1929, special article on Ballintoy and Downing St.
[2] Graham's notes to Catalogue in "Ireland Preserved."
[3] "Londeriados."
[4] Hampton's "Derry," p. 459.
[5] Dalton's "Army List," 1689–1714, Vol. III. p. 168.

this family as still being in possession of their old farmstead of Eden near Maghera. Further enquiry enables me to state that the descendants of the defenders of Derry are to-day (1930) residing on the land for which their ancestors fought.

524. **ROBERT PORTER**, defender. There are many gallant actions recorded of the siege, but none that surpasses the only mention of this name in the fierce Windmill Hill sortie of the 4th June, viz.:—

> "Brave Robert Porter his pike away he threw
> And with round stones nine Irish soldiers slew."[1]

The late Dr. Killen, the historian, in his edition of Mackenzie's "Siege" with notes, published some sixty years ago, referring to this incident states: "There is reason to believe that this Robert Porter was from Burt (Co. Donegal) and probably great-great-grandfather of the Rev. Professor Porter, Belfast Presbyterian College, whose great-grandfather was born in Derry during the siege." This Rev. Professor Porter was afterwards the distinguished President of Queen's College, Belfast. His son bought and resided at Ballygalley Castle (originally built by the Shaw family) on the Antrim coast between Larne and Glenarm, which his descendants only sold at the end of the last century.

525. **DANIEL McNEALE** (or **McNEILL**), defender. His name, described as of Dundrum, Co. Down, is among the attainted in James' Dublin Parliament. A Daniel McNeill figures among the signers of the "Declaration of Union" made in Derry on 10th April, probably the same. He also seems to have been the writer of the letter of 28th June, 1691, from the camp before Athlone quoted in the Rawdon Papers.

526. **REV. ARCHIBALD McNEALE**, of Co. Down, so described in the list of attainted in James' Dublin Parliament, was Chancellor of the church of Downpatrick.

527. **REV. DEAN JOHN McNEALE**, of Down, was so described among the attainted in James' Dublin Parliament. This Dean of Down was ordained by Bishop Jeremy Taylor, was Prebend of Effen, diocese of Limerick, 1669–1683, and appointed Dean of Down in 1683, dying in Downpatrick in 1709, where a monument was erected to his memory in the cathedral.

He was probably the son of the Rev. Daniel McNeale, rector of Billy, Culfeightrin (Ballycastle) and Loughguile in 1661.

528. **JOHN McNEALE**, of Billy, Co. Antrim, so described in the list of attainted in James' Dublin Parliament. He was the representative of the family settled at Currysheskin, Billy, Co. Antrim, for many generations. His branch of the family occupied a leading position in the Route until the middle of the last century, when

[1] "Londeriados."

the estate passed by purchase to a near relative by marriage of the same surname, but differently spelt, Mr. Edmond McNeill, of Cushendun, whose son, Lord Cushendun (Rt. Hon. Ronald McNeill), of Cushendun, the representative of the clan of Taynish, Gygha and Losset (Cantire), also represents, in the female line, the McNeales of Currysheskin. Other representatives, in the female line of this old stock, are the descendants of Col. John McNeill of Parkmount, Co. Antrim, and the Very Rev. Hugh McNeill, Dean of Ripon.

529. CAPT. HUGH MCNEALE, of Clare, Co. Antrim, so described among the attainted in James' Dublin Parliament.

Among the original grantees of large estates on the first Earl of Antrim's territory was this Capt. Hugh's father or grandfather.[1] By the marriage of Capt. Hugh's daughter and heiress with Mr. Boyd, of Ballycastle, the estate passed to that family, the present owner being Miss Boyd, The Manor House, Ballycastle, Co. Antrim.

The McCullaghs of The Grange, Antrim.

When Lord Massereene was organising the Protestant Association of Co. Antrim, and raising his regiment prior to the 1688–89 revolution, he found support and some five officers from his friends and neighbours the McCullaghs, of The Grange, viz.:—

530. CAPT. HENRY MCCULLAGH, defender, who was one of the twenty-three noblemen and gentry signing the Protestant manifesto to Co. Antrim. He was commissioned as captain in the Skeffington, afterwards the Mitchelburn Regiment, with which he served in all the preliminary actions, from the "Break of Dromore" down to the retreat on Derry and through the siege. He died at The Grange in 1720, Shane O'Neill of Shane's Castle thus alluding to his demise: "His old school fellow, and friend of Grange, who died in 1720."[2]

531. CAPT. ARCHIBALD MCCULLAGH, defender, a captain in the Skeffington, afterwards Mitchelburn, Regiment, taking part in all preliminary operations and through the siege.

At Coleraine, when Sir Arthur Rawdon was engaged in repulsing Hamilton's attack on the town, the enemy were directing a heavy gun fire on the bridge across the Bann, which, as the only line of retirement in case of defeat, had to be secured at all costs. In the heat of the action "one of the enemy's shots split the upper beam, and broke the chain (of the bridge) which Capt. Archibald McCullagh with great hazard fastened, the enemy firing very warmly at him."[3] By this deed of gallantry, the passage

---

[1] Hill's "McDonnells of Antrim."
[2] Ibid., p. 350.
[3] Mackenzie.

of the Bann and retreat on Derry were secured when the retirement was made a few days later. Serving all through the siege he is particularly mentioned for good service in the Butcher's Gate sortie of July 16th.[1] After the relief he was one of the signers of the address to King William.

532. **LIEUT. JOHN McCULLAGH**, defender, an officer in the Skeffington, afterwards Mitchelburn, Regiment all through the siege.

533. **ENSIGN WILLIAM McCULLAGH**, defender, an officer in the Skeffington-Mitchelburn Regiment.

534. **LIEUT. ANTHONY McCULLAGH**, defender, of the Skeffington-Mitchelburn Regiment.

All the above officers' names figure in the Walker controversy raging in London in the spring of 1690,[2] and all of them were among the officers of the Derry garrison then in London receiving three months' pay to enable them to report to the Duke of Schomberg's camp in Ireland.[3]

535. **LIEUT. RICHARD KANE**, defender, a lieutenant in the Skeffington, afterwards Mitchelburn's, Regiment with which he served in all the preliminaries and in the siege.

He afterwards fought with distinction in Flanders and died in 1736, while occupying the post of Governor of the island of Minorca, then a British possession. Shane O'Neill, of Shane's Castle, in a letter still extant referring to his death, writes "that his kind friend Brigadier-General Richard O'Kane died in 1736, in Minorca, of which he was chief Governor for the King of England."[4] He was the first of the long line of Governors of British dominions with which Ulster has furnished the Empire, and all the more remarkable at this early date as he was of the ancient Celtic stock.

Richard Kane was really an O'Kane of Keenaght, one of his forbears having settled at Carrickfergus where the family had acquired considerable property, as also at Duneane in Co. Antrim. In his will he left £50 each to the poor of Carrickfergus and Duneane.[5]

536. **QUARTERMASTER ALEXANDER HERON**, defender, of Col. Adam Murray's Regiment, with which he served all through the siege.

His name occurs in the Walker controversy of the spring of 1690.[6] He was one of the officers of the Derry garrison in London receiving three months' pay in the spring

---

[1] "Londeriados."
[2] Hampton's "Derry," p. 459.
[3] Dalton's "Army List," 1689–1714, Vol. III. p. 168.
[4] Hill's "McDonnells of Antrim."
[5] *Ibid.*, where his will is given in full in an appendix.
[6] Hampton's "Siege," p. 459.

of 1690 to enable them to return to Ireland and report to the Duke or Schomberg's camp.[1]

537. **Thomas Gow**, defender. In the Windmill Hill sortie of the 4th June, he "had all the flesh shot off the calf of his leg by a cannon bullet, but, the bone not being broken, he recovered."[2]

538. **Capt. Rickaby**, defender. He was shot in the arm in the sortie of the 10th May.[2]

539. **Two Capts. Closs**. The only reference to these two officers is as follows: "About this time (May 7th) two Captains Closs left us and took protection."[2]

540. **Capt. Robert Gregory**, of Coleraine, defender, in Col. Parker's, afterwards Col. Lance's, Regiment, and his two sons—

541. **Lieut. Gregory** and

542. **Ensign Gregory**, defenders, both in their father's company of Col. Lance's Regiment, and Capt. Robert's brother—

543. **Capt. George Gregory**, defender, of Col. Crofton's (Canning) Regiment. These four Gregorys served all through the siege. Capt. Robert Gregory, in addition to his regimental duties, found employment as one of the chief gunners of the garrison:—

"and Captain Gregory
From the church steeple slays the enemy."[3]

It is pitiable to know of the poverty to which the family were reduced by their siege services, as is to be gathered from the following petition presented by Capt. Robert Gregory to the Lord Justices of Ireland, August 17th, 1716, viz.:—

"That your petitioner and his brother (Capt. George Gregory) did mount the great guns on the steeple of Derry and repaired several of the carriages on the walls thereof. That your petitioner and his two sons, the one his Lieutenant and the other his ensign, were in Col. Lance's Regiment and were very serviceable at the said siege. That your petitioner brought with him (to Derry) 10 large oxen, 22 cows, 20 Barrels of meal, and a horse load of cheese, which he gave among the workmen, and when they had eaten that, he gave them two large horses, which they also eat. The goods and money he laid out among them came to £258, which with his pay as Captain of a Company and one of the chief gunners amounts to £700, for which he never received any reward, till four years ago the Government gave him £50, to prevent himself and

[1] Dalton's "Army List," 1689–1714, Vol. III. p. 168.
[2] Mackenzie.
[3] "Londeriados."

his family from perishing. Your petitioner and his great family, he having a wife and fifteen children, whereof ten are unprovided for, prays for grant of concordatum."

This petition was accompanied by a certificate signed 10th December, 1689, by Governors Walker and Mitchelburn certifying "that Capt. Robert Gregory of Col. Lance's Regiment and Capt. George Gregory of Col. Crofton's Regiment did mount the great guns on the steeple of Derry."

Another petition, undated, to the Lord Justices, states that after the relief Capt. Robert Gregory served the remaining part of the wars of the kingdom in Col. Mitchelburn's Regiment, and prays for assistance for his wife and nine small children "who are in the last necessity."[1]

544. **Capt. James Gledstanes**, of Fardross, Co. Tyrone, defender, accompanied by his brother—

545. **Capt. John Gledstanes**, defender, led a considerable body of his tenantry and neighbours to the assistance of Derry, where they took an active part in the defence.

"Londeriados" states that early in the siege Capt. Gledstanes was appointed on the council of officers to advise the Governors on military matters.

In the Windmill Hill action of the 4th June there is the following mention of the gallant service of these two Captains: "Our men, Capt. James Gledstanes, Capt. John Gledstanes and others next to them left their redoubts, and took the stand with their musquets, pikes and scythes, and fell on them with that vigour that soon spoilt the tune of their huzzas, for few of that party escaped; many of them were driven into the river, and Captain Butler, Lord Mountgarret's son[2] taken prisoner by Captain John Gledstanes."[3]

Capt. James Gledstanes, of Fardross, Co. Tyrone, so described, was one of the attainted in James' Dublin Parliament, and he was one of the signers of the address to King William after the relief.

The Gledstanes family have been in possession of Fardross since early in the 17th century, holding an important position in Co. Tyrone. The present representative of the family is Capt. Ambrose Upton Gledstanes, Fardross, Clogher, Co. Tyrone.

546. **Capt. Edmond Rice**, defender, an officer in the Skeffington, afterwards Mitchelburn, Regiment.[4]

His name is mentioned in Walker's "Siege" for good service, and he was a signer of the address to King William after the relief.

---

[1] The Dublin records having been burned, I am indebted to the Dean of Dromore for obtaining the above copy from Mr. T. U. Sadleir, Temple Mills, Celbridge, Co. Kildare.
[2] See Part II, No. 26.
[3] Mackenzie.
[4] Hampton's "Derry," p. 468.

547. **Capt. John Bickerstaffe** and

548. **Capt. Richard Bickerstaffe**, of Rosegift, Co. Antrim, defenders. Both held commissions in the Skeffington, afterwards the Mitchelburn, Regiment during the siege. Capt. John's name is on the list of attainted in James' Dublin Parliament, and he had been High Sheriff of Co. Antrim in 1682. It was a daughter of one of these Captains from whose marriage with Henry, eldest son of Shane O'Neill, of Shane's Castle, descends the line of the Chichester O'Neills, now represented by Shane, 3rd Baron O'Neill, Shane's Castle, Co. Antrim.

549. **Lieut. William Gunter**, defender, an officer in the Mitchelburn Regiment and through the siege. "Londeriados" mentions his name for good service in the Windmill Hill sortie of May 6th.

550. **Henry Gorges**, of Somerset, Londonderry, so described, figures among the attainted in James' Dublin Parliament. He received a commission as captain (June 1689) in Sir Albert Conyngham's Regiment, with which he served in the Boyne campaign.[1] He was probably the son of Col. John Gorges, who was Mayor of Derry in 1661, and M.P. in 1665.

551. **Hindman, Capt. of the** (Derry) **Guard**, defender. Referring to the arrival of two companies of Lord Antrim's Regiment at the gates on the 8th December, when they were refused admission, "Londeriados" thus mentions Hindman:

> "Then Master Hindman, Captain of the Guard,
> To strengthen whom the neighbours all repaired,
> Attacked this party[2] as the city fired
> Then in disorder, they in haste retired;
> But this retreat such consternation bred
> That some with arms, and some without them fled."

552. **John Hindman**, defender, possibly "the Captain of the Guard," was among the signers of the Corporation of Derry's 1690 Commission.

553. **Capt. Thomas Tracey**, defender, a captain in Col. Mitchelburn's Regiment and all through the siege.[3]

554. **James Tracey**, defender, one of the signers of the address to King William after the relief.

555. **Capt. Hannah**, defender, mentioned for gallantry in the second Windmill

---

[1] Dalton's "Army List," 1689–1714, Vol. III.
[2] Antrim's men.
[3] Hampton's "Derry," p. 468.

Hill sortie of the 4th June "and Capt. Hannah the foe stoutly fought."[1]

556. **LIEUT. ANDREW HANNAGH** (*sic*). The above officer held a commission in Sir Albert Conyngham's Regiment, 1689.[2]

557. **ENSIGN FOREST SHORTRIDGE (SHORTRIX)**, defender. An officer in Col. Skeffington's Antrim Regiment, afterwards Col. Mitchelburn's, and served all through the siege.[3]

He figures in the list of attainted in James' Dublin Parliament as Forest Shortrix, of Co. Antrim.

558. **CAPT. FREEMAN**, defender. "For town Major they chose Capt. Freeman." So writes "Londeriados," referring to his appointment in the reorganisation of the city for defence.

559. **FORBES**, defender.

> "Forbes like thunder among their forces flew
> And with his sword a multitude he slew."

So "Londeriados" in describing his prowess in the Windmill Hill attack on the 6th May.

560. **JAMES FLEMING**, defender. He is mentioned for gallantry in the Windmill Hill attack on May 6th:

> "And Wilson, Sunter, Moore, and Fleming they,
> Attack their trenches, and the enemy slay."[1]

He is probably the James Fleming whose signature is attached to the address to King William after the relief.

561. **RICHARD FLEMING**, defender, was another signer of the address to King William after the relief.

Graham states in his Catalogue in "Ireland Preserved" that their residence at Ballymagorry, Co. Tyrone, was burned by the Jacobite army in their retreat from Derry.

562. **JOHN FLEMING**, defender, and signer of address.

563. **CAPT. WILLIAM RUXTON**, Co. Louth, defender. An officer in Col. Parker's, afterwards Crofton's, Regiment, and was in Derry all through the siege. His name

---

[1] "Londeriados."
[2] Dalton's "Army List," 1689–1714, Vol. III.
[3] List of officers in that regiment. Hampton's "Siege," p. 468.

figures in the Walker controversy in London in the spring of 1690.[1]

Captain William Ruxton was the second son of John Ruxton, of Ardee House, Co. Louth, eventually succeeding to the estate. He was among the attainted in James' Dublin Parliament. His descendants in the direct male line are still in possession of Ardee House, Co. Louth.[2]

564. **LIEUT. MICHAEL BOYER**, defender, and

565. **ENSIGN JOHN BRUSH**, defender. Both of these officers were in Col. Crofton's Regiment serving all through the siege. Their names figure in the Walker controversy in London 1690, and both were among the officers of the Derry garrison then in London who received three months' pay to enable them to join the Duke of Schomberg's camp in Ireland.[3]

566. **ROBERT POOLER**, of Tyross, defender. So Graham in his Catalogue styles this defender of Derry, and in his notes, quoting from Stuart's "Armagh," states that he was one of Col. Murray's best troopers in all his engagements, and that he was killed by almost the last shot of the investing army while watching their departure from the battlements of the city.

567. **LIEUT. GOBURN**, defender, an officer in Col. Mitchelburn's Regiment.[4]

568. **JAMES COLBURN**, defender. His name is among the signatures to the Corporation of Derry's Commission of 1690.

569. **ENSIGN JOHN BRADY**, defender, an officer in Col. Mitchelburn's Regiment who served all through the siege.[4] The following of the name were among the attainted in James' Dublin Parliament:

570. **JOHN BRADY**, described as of Co. Monaghan.

571. **THOMAS BRADY**, described as of Co. Monaghan.

572. **CAPT. WILLIAM WALLACE**, defender, mentioned for good service in the Windmill Hill sortie of the 4th June,[5] and is probably the same as the Lieut. William Wallace described as of Londonderry, figuring among the attainted in James' Dublin Parliament. He signed the address to King William after the relief, and serving in the subsequent campaign he fell before Limerick in 1691.[6]

---

[1] Hampton's "Derry," p. 459.
[2] Burke's "Landed Gentry of Ireland," 1904.
[3] Hampton's "Derry," p.459. Dalton's "Army List," 1689–1714, Vol. III. p. 168.
[4] Hampton's "Siege," p. 468.
[5] Mackenzie.
[6] Rawdon Papers.

Others of the name attainted were:—

573. **Hugh Wallace**, Ravera, Co. Down.

574. **John Wallace**, Ravera, Co. Down.

575. **Robert Wallace**, defender. His signature is attached to the document of the 11th July authorising the Governors to open the abortive negotiations with the enemy for surrender on terms, and is also on the address to King William after the relief.

The following, Nos. 576–587, were officers, in addition to those already mentioned, holding commissions either in the Skeffington Regiment, or in Col. Mitchelburn's Regiment after his succeeding to the command, most of whom, if not all, served through the siege.[1] Of these names I can find no other mention.

576. **Lieut. Samuel Archer**.

577. **Ensign Samuel Shelcross**.

578. **Ensign James Royde**.

579. **Adjutant William Crofts**, and

580. **Quartermaster John Hughes**, all officers of the Skeffington Regiment and through the preliminary operations.

581. **Ensign James Morris**, defender, held a commission in the Skeffington and in the Mitchelburn Regiment during the siege.

582. **Capt. James Chalmers**, defender.

583. **Lieut. Edward Ranke**, defender.

584. **Lieut. William Pollock**, defender.

585. **Ensign George Gyford**, defender.

586. **Ensign John Railey**, defender, and

587. **Ensign John Young**, defender, all officers in the Mitchelburn Regiment during the siege.

588. **Henry Clements**, of Straid, Carrickfergus.

589. **Edward Clements**, of Straid, Carrickfergus. These two brothers were among the twenty-three noblemen and gentry of Co. Antrim whose signatures are attached to

---

[1] List of officers in Hampton's "Derry," p. 468.

the manifesto of Co. Antrim Association calling upon their friends to rally in defence of Protestant interests prior to the 1688–89 revolution. In the raising of the Antrim regiments they took an active part. The Clements were an old family settled in the neighbourhood of Carrickfergus about 1609. The Henry Clements of No. 588 was Mayor of Carrickfergus in 1696, entertaining Dean Swift, then incumbent of Kilroot, at the annual dinner of the Corporation. He died the same year.

590. **ENSIGN JOHN CLEMENTS**, defender, evidently of the same family, held a commission in the Skeffington, afterwards the Mitchelburn, Regiment, serving all through the siege.

591. **DALWAY CLEMENTS**, defender, was in Derry all through the siege, probably an officer in the Mitchelburn Regiment. He was a signer of the address to King William after the relief.

592. **ROBERT CLEMENTS**, of Co. Cavan, so described, was among the attainted in James' Dublin Parliament.

From this Robert Clements descend the family (raised to the peerage as Baron in 1783, Viscount in 1793 and Earl of Leitrim in 1795) now represented by the 5th Earl of Leitrim, Mulroy, Milford, Co. Donegal.[1]

In the counties of Leitrim and Cavan the family held a leading position, several of their members serving as High Sheriffs.[2]

593. **SIR THOMAS NEWCOMEN**, 5th Bart., of Kenagh, Co. Longford, an officer in the Jacobite army, killed in one of the Enniskillen actions in 1689.[3] Of Sir Thomas Newcomen's six sons the following four were fighting on King William's side, viz.:—

594. His second son, **GEORGE NEWCOMEN**, a major in Sir John Edgeworth's Regiment (commission 1689). Was present at the Boyne and through subsequent campaign until killed before Limerick.[4]

595. His third son, **CAPT. THOMAS NEWCOMEN**, defender. In Derry all through the siege, being one of the signers of the address to King William after the relief. He afterwards got a commission as captain in Wolseley's Enniskillen Horse, being present at the Boyne, where he lost a hand. He was on the half-pay list in 1702.[4]

596. His fifth son, **BEVERLEY NEWCOMEN**, was a lieutenant in Col. Hastings' Regiment (1689) and present at the Boyne.

---

[1] Burke's Peerage.
[2] McSkimmin's "Carrickfergus," p. 418.
[3] Dalton's "Army List," 1689–1714, Vol. III. pp. 27, 28. See Part II, No. 313, under this name.
[4] Dalton's "Army List," 1689–1714.

597. His sixth son, **Capt. Charles Newcomen**, held a commission in Col. Wynne's Enniskillen Dragoons. (Dalton's "Army List," 1689–1714, Vol. III. p. 34.) According to the above authority, Capt. Charles' granddaughter was created Baroness Newcomen at the end of the 18th century. According to Debrett, the family had the following honours:—Baronetcy 1781, Barony 1800, and Viscountcy in 1803, all of which became extinct in 1825. Sir Thomas Newcomen, Bart., the father of the four sons mentioned, was the fifth holder of the first baronetcy granted in 1625. It would appear that this Sir Thomas, 5th Bart., although a Protestant and through his second wife, a St. George of Co. Leitrim, closely related to several of the Northern Leaders and their interests, was connected by his first marriage with Tyrconnell. In the spring of 1689 Sir Thomas was in command of a regiment at Lisburn, and Tyrconnell had used him as a means of trying to dissuade his Northern friends from continuing their preparations for resistance. When later in 1689 the Antrim and Down associations almost succeeded in rushing Carrickfergus and Lisburn, Sir Thomas retired with his regiment to Dublin. How he met his death in one of the Enniskillen actions, while four of his sons were fighting for King William, has already been told.[1]

598. **Capt. Sam Wright**, defender, described as of Londonderry or Donegal, figures among the attainted in James' Dublin Parliament, and has frequent mention for good service in the sorties of the siege.

599. **James Wright**, of Co. Monaghan.

600. **James Wright**, of Co. Monaghan.

601. **Sergeant John Wright**, of Co. Monaghan, and

602. **Richard Wright**, of Co. Monaghan, all four so described, among the attainted in James' Dublin Parliament.

603. **John Wright** and

604. **James Wright** were among the signers of the Corporation of Derry's 1690 Commission.

Graham in his notes to his Catalogue ("Ireland Preserved") states that in the middle of the last century there were representatives of this family still living near Ballinrode, Co. Monaghan.

605. **Col. Kilner Brazier** of Rath, Co. Donegal, defender, so described, among the attainted in James' Dublin Parliament.

He was one of the first of neighbouring landlords, when Derry was in danger, to bring a large contingent of his tenantry for the defence of the city. There he remained

---

[1] Montgomery Manuscripts, p. 277 *n.*

until the siege was over. His importance is shown by his being one of the signers of the "Declaration of Union" in March before the investment.

From "The Family History of Hart of Donegal," published 1907, it is to be gathered that the Brazier estate in Co. Donegal was not finally parted with until 1734. Meanwhile the family had become more firmly established in Cos. Limerick and Cork.

After the revolution Kilner Brazier was M.P. for Dundalk 1698–99, St. Johnstown 1703–1713 and Kilmallock 1715 until his death.

The first of the name in Ulster was Paul Brazier, who settled in Coleraine at the time of the Plantation, marrying a daughter of Sir Tristram Beresford, Bart., the ancestor of the Marquess of Waterford. The Brazier family have for generations occupied an important position in Cos. Limerick and Cork, the present lineal representatives of the defender of Derry being the Braziers of Ballyellis, Mallow, Co. Cork, and the Brazier Creaghs, of Creagh Castle, Co. Cork.[1]

606. **Major John Dobbin**, of Carrowdonaghey, Ahoghill, Co. Antrim, defender, an officer in the Skeffington, afterwards the Mitchelburn, Regiment, all through the preliminary operations and the siege, mentioned generally for good and useful sortie service.[2] In the Windmill Hill action of the 6th May:—

> "Major Dobbin led on some valiant men
> Who presently the Irish trenches gain."[3]

He was one of the members of the special court-martial appointed on the 23rd July, and he was a signer of the address to King William after the relief.

607. **Capt. C. Dobbin**, defender, an officer of the garrison all through the siege. He was one of the five captains sent by the Governors to wait on General Kirke at Inch on the 1st August and congratulate him on the relief of the city.

608. **William Dobbin** was a signer of the address to King William after the relief.

609. **Anthony Dobbin**, J.P. Graham, in his notes to his Catalogue in "Ireland Preserved," mentions his coming with the Rev. Andrew Hamilton of Kilskerry to the Irish camp before Derry to visit General Richard Hamilton, and that when there they were witnesses of a savage murder by the Irish soldiers of an old Scottish woman reputed to be a witch.

The Dobbin family[4] were long settled at Carrickfergus. Peter Dobbin was Constable of Carrickfergus Castle in 1400, and the family in subsequent generations acquired considerable property, not only in that town, but also in Co. Antrim. At the time of

---

[1] Burke's "Landed Gentry of Ireland," 1904.
[2] Mackenzie.
[3] "Londeriados."
[4] See McSkimmin's "Carrickfergus."

the revolution they were holders of estates at Ahoghill, Duneane, and Drumseugh, chiefly leasehold on the O'Neill estate. The family were divided in their allegiance, many of them serving in the Jacobite army, of whom later (in Part II, Nos. 136–139).

610. **Capt. Francis Boyd**, defender, mentioned for gallantry in the repulse of the attack on Windmill Hill on 4th June.[1] He was in Mitchelburn's Regiment.[2]

His signature is attached to the address to King William after the relief.

611. **Capt. James Boyd**, defender. A bomb fell on his house (probably the family residence for many generations in Shipquay St.), on the night of 5th June "killing him … but several officers, who were then at dinner, escaped the danger."[1]

He is among the attainted in James' Dublin Parliament, described as Lieut. James Boyd, of Londonderry or Donegal.

The following Boyd (or Boid) signatures are attached to the Corporation of Derry's 1690 Commission:—

612. **Jean Boid**.

613. **Isabel Boid**.

614. **Robert Boyd**.

615. **Helen Boid**.

The Boyd family settled in the city of Derry and Co. Donegal in the 17th century. They are descended from the ancient Scottish family of which the Earl of Kilmarnock was the head. The family, besides their residence in Shipquay Street, were in possession of the estate of Ballymacool near Letterkenny, still the residence of the family, now represented by Mr. William Henry Boyd, who was High Sheriff in Co. Donegal in 1892.[3] The Boyd Carpenters, of whom the late distinguished Bishop of Ripon was the head, are descended from a younger son of the head of this family.

616. **Captain Bacon**, of Magilligan, defender. Among the prominent people attending the Protestant muster before Derry on the eve of the investment, "Londeriados" enumerates "And Captain Bacon from Magilligan." Graham, in his notes to the Catalogue, records the fact that the Rev. Benjamin Bacon, D.D., afterwards Archdeacon of Derry, 1731–1736, and Rector of Tamlaghtard, 1736 until his death in 1772, was his son.

617. **John Henderson**, defender. The only mention of this name is his signature among the witnesses to the Governors' authority of July 11th enabling them to appoint commissioners to treat for the surrender of the city on terms.

[1] Mackenzie.
[2] Hampton's "Derry," p. 459.
[3] Burke's "Landed Gentry of Ireland," 1904.

618. **Lieut. Henry Long**, defender, an officer appointed to one of the city companies, raised after the shutting of the gates, with which he served through the siege. He was one of the leading burgesses who represented the Corporation in the negotiations with Lord Mountjoy.

Mr. Long's house, evidently Lieut. Henry Long's, was hit by a bomb on the 27th April.[1] He was a signer of the "Declaration of Union" and his name figures among the attainted in James' Dublin Parliament. The same bomb that struck his house on April 27th killed

619. **Mrs. Susannah Holding**, "a gentlewoman of eighty years old."[1]

620. **Ralph Fullerton**, defender, one of the signers of the address to King William after the relief.

621. **John Fullerton**, of Ballagh, Co. Antrim, so described, was among the attainted in James' Dublin Parliament.

He was probably of the same family as George Fullerton, of Ballintoy Castle, the marriage of whose daughter Catharine with Dawson Downing, a grandson of Col. Adam Downing, of Rosegift, Co. Derry, led to the surname becoming that of Downing Fullerton, in whose descendants the estate is still vested.[2]

622. **John Buchanan**, Deputy-Mayor of Derry, had been a Burgess of the city for many years previous to the revolution, serving as Sheriff in 1674, and when Tyrconnell, in August 1688, broke the old charter with its Protestant ascendancy and granted a new one with a large majority of Roman Catholics and a small minority of Protestants on the corporate body, John Buchanan, a Protestant, was one of the nominated. Col. Cormac O'Neill, a strong supporter of King James and a personal friend of Tyrconnell's, was nominated Mayor.

In the autumn of 1688, when everything was tending to the revolution, Col. Cormac O'Neill retired from the city to take up his military duties, appointing John Buchanan as his Deputy-Mayor.[3] John Buchanan was immediately faced with the shutting of the gates and the refusal of the people to admit Lord Antrim's Regiment. At public meetings Buchanan attempted to allay the popular clamour:—

> "Upstarts Buchanan, and thus boldly spoke
> 'Take heart good sir, ne'er fear the Irish yoke,
> Receive the Earl of Antrim's regiment:
> In peace and plenty rest yourself content.'"[4]

---

[1] Ash's "Diary."
[2] See No. 515, Col. Adam Downing.
[3] For further account of Col. Cormac O'Neill see in Part II, No. 45.
[4] "Londeriados."

The party of resistance of course carried the day, and Buchanan was of no account. "Londeriados," however, continues his attack. While enumerating the Protestant aldermen for their help he adds

> "Except Buchanan, who's a knave all o'er
> For he had learned to tell his beads before,"

and again, in describing Tyrconnell's Corporation:—

> "For Burgesses and Freemen they had chose
> Brogue makers, Butchers, raps and such as those;
> In all the corporation, not a man
> Of English parentage save Buchanan."

Macaulay, giving as his authority these quotations from "Londeriados," has overdrawn the case when he states "The Corporation (of Derry) had, like the other corporations of Ireland, been remodelled. The magistrates were men of low station and character. Among them there was only one person of Anglo-Saxon extraction and he had turned Papist. In such rulers the inhabitants could place no confidence."[1] The real facts are that the remodelled Corporation, while having a large preponderating majority of Roman Catholics, had a considerable minority of Protestants of Anglo-Saxon extraction. Of this minority, Buchanan, as Deputy-Mayor, and committed to the Jacobite side, was the only Protestant to remonstrate against the exclusion of the Antrim Regiment. This remodelled Corporation disappeared with the investment of the city, their places being filled by the old aldermen and burgesses in whom the city had confidence. Of John Buchanan we hear no more, but the fact that his name is among the signers of the address to King William after the relief and on the Corporation's Commission of 1690, are indications that he remained a Protestant, and had rehabilitated himself with his fellow citizens.

623. **James Buchanan** was a signer of the Corporation's 1690 Commission. Probably of the same family as John Buchanan.

624. **Horace Kennedy**, Sheriff, defender, one of the two sheriffs of the city.[2] These two sheriffs were continued in office under Tyrconnell's new charter of 1688, serving in that capacity during the siege.

He was one of the commissioners appointed by the Corporation to treat with Lord Mountjoy, and was later sent to Scotland to buy arms and munitions.

> "Horace Kennedy went into Scotland
> And moved the Council some relief to send."[3]

---

[1] Macaulay "History of England," Vol. III.
[2] His colleague being Edward Brooke (Brooks), see No. 242.
[3] "Londeriados."

He was one of the signers of the "Declaration of Union" and his name is among the attainted in James' Dublin Parliament.

625. **Capt. John Kennedy**, defender, is mentioned as one of "the six brave Captains" who were particularly distinguished in repulsing Lord Clancarty's attack on the Butcher's Gate (28th June).[1] He had been conspicuous for gallantry in the Pennyburn sortie of the 25th April.[2]

626. **David Kennedy**, defender. Among the volunteer officers who were not "regimented" his name is mentioned as being "frequently out upon service."[2]

The Kennedy family have a long and honourable connection with Derry, the following having filled the office as Mayor:

Horace Kennedy (above), in 1698.
William Kennedy, in 1765.
George C. Kennedy, in 1794.
Thomas P. Kennedy, in 1836.

In the Cathedral memorial window, unveiled in 1913, Horace Kennedy's name figures among the gallant defenders so commemorated, the following being his descendant subscribers: Mr. Horace T. Kennedy, Mr. Charles More Kennedy, Mr. Tristram Kennedy, Mr. Henry Stacey Kennedy Skipton, Mr. George Graham Kennedy, Mrs. Tristram Kennedy, Sir George Young, Bart., Lady Young, Mrs. Kennedy, Mrs. Pete Kennedy, Mrs. James W. Tuke, Mr. Alexander Skipton, Mr. Hardress Waller.

627. **John Cross**, of Co. Tyrone, defender, and

628. **William Cross**, of Co. Tyrone, defender. Both were among the signers of the address to King William after the relief.

The family settled at Dartan in the 18th century and have been there ever since. They take a leading position in Co. Armagh. Mr. William Cross, D.L., of Dartan, was High Sheriff in 1862.[3] In 1887 after the marriage of Sarah Jane Beauchamp Cross, of Dartan, with Arthur Charles Innes, of Dromantine, Co. Down, the name of Cross was assumed by royal licence, so that that family have since been Innes Cross, of Dromantine, Co. Down.[3]

629. **Albert Hall**, defender, a signer of the address to King William after the relief, and of the Corporation's Commission of 1690.

He died in 1701 and was buried in the Cathedral churchyard. His name is among those of the defenders commemorated in the memorial window unveiled in

[1] "Londeriados."
[2] Mackenzie.
[3] Burke's "Landed Gentry of Ireland," 1904.

the Cathedral in 1913. Among the subscribers to this was his descendant, Mrs. A. Alexander Wright.

630. ALDERMAN CRAIG, defender, was one of the Aldermen losing office when Tyrconnell revoked the old charter. However, with the "No Surrender" party in power, he is accorded the old title. So "Londeriados," in enumerating the citizens most prominent in contributing to the preparations for the defence, writes:—

> "Alderman Craig with stores assists the town
> Preaching obedience to the English crown."

631. WILLIAM CRAIGE (or **CRAIG**) was one of the signers of the Corporation's Commission of 1690.

632. ALDERMAN JOHN CAMPSIE, Mayor of Derry during the siege, defender. John Campsie and his son Henry, as burgesses, had been among the Protestant minority appointed by Tyrconnell to the new Corporation (1688) of Derry.[1] John Campsie had been Mayor of the city 1681, 1685, 1686, 1687 and 1688. In the latter year he was displaced under the new charter, being succeeded as Mayor by Col. Cormac O'Neill, who had left John Buchanan as Deputy-Mayor. Once the "No Surrender" policy was in full swing the new corporate body disappeared, and the old aldermen and burgesses resumed office, John Campsie again becoming Mayor, a position he held through the siege.

633. JOHN CAMPSIE, jr., defender, a son of the above. Had been a burgess under the old charter, and Sheriff in 1686.

634. LIEUT. HENRY CAMPSIE, defender, another son of the above. He was another of the Protestant burgesses appointed by Tyrconnell under the 1688 charter.

He was one of the thirteen gallant apprentices who shut the gates on the 7th December, and on the same night received a bad wound in the arm in an attempt to raid arms from the city magazine.

His name is among the signatures to the address to King William after the relief, and to the Corporation's 1690 Commission. He was attainted in James' Dublin Parliament.

The journals of the Irish House of Commons of 1698 record a petition from Lieut. Henry Campsie, praying for relief; on account of his services during the siege of Derry, where he was wounded to the peril of his life, and owing to the poor circumstances to which his family had been reduced, in need of assistance. What the reply was can be imagined.

635. MAJOR CAMPSIE, defender. On the 6th June, during the siege, a bomb fell on

[1] See under John Buchanan, No. 622, for refutation of Lord Macaulay's statement.

Major Campsie's house, "sunk into the cellar, and struck the heads out of two wine hogsheads."[1] No further mention of this name.

The Campsies were an old mercantile family of considerable importance in Derry and surrounding district. Their trading "tokens" are still extant as silent witnesses of their business. Their name is preserved in a townland on the Faryhan river, and in Campsie House on the Co. Derry side of the Foyle opposite Culmore.[2] They must have fallen on evil days, as foreshadowed in Lieut. Henry Campsie's petition, and disappeared.

636. **ALDERMAN ALEXANDER TOMKINS**, defender, was a prominent citizen of Derry, and also a considerable landowner at Tirkearing, Co. Donegal. With Tyrconnell's 1688 charter he had ceased to be an alderman, but his influence in city affairs continued as great as ever. He was a staunch supporter of the apprentice boys in the shutting of the gates, in the preparations for resistance, and in the "No Surrender" party. From his Tirkearing tenantry and neighbours came one of the first contingents in aid of Derry.

> "Alderman Tomkins from Tirkearing sent
> Into the camp a gallant regiment
> Which joined Colonel Murray, as they went
> . . . .
> Alderman Tomkins raised a troop of horse
> And laid in stores against the Irish force."[3]

He was one of the signers of the "Declaration of Union" and stood manfully by the city all through the siege. He was among the attainted in James' Dublin Parliament, and his is probably the signature Alexander E. Tomkins to the address to King William after the relief, but it is possibly another member of the family. With the success of the "No Surrender" policy he had again become Alderman, serving as Mayor in 1713, an office which he had filled in 1683.

637. **CAPT. JOHN TOMKINS**, defender, a son of the above, was appointed to the command of one of the city companies raised after the shutting of the gates, with which he served all through the siege. He is mentioned for good service on 9th December in hastening the departure of Lord Antrim's Regiment from the neighbourhood of the city.[4]

638. **GEORGE TOMKINS**, defender (?). From the fact that he was Mayor in 1706 it is probable that he was in the city during the siege. He was for many years agent for the Irish Society, and M.P. for the city in 1715. He was an executor to Col. Mitchelburn, who died in 1721.

---

[1] Ash's "Diary."
[2] Graham's notes to his Catalogue.
[3] "Londeriados."
[4] Mackenzie.

In the churchyard of the Cathedral there is a tombstone in memory of this George Tomkins.

The family were evidently of great importance, an Alexander Tomkins being again Mayor in 1721. Many of the family were buried in the Cathedral, where an old tablet stands:—

> "Erected 1676
> To the memory of
> John Tomkins and Rebecca his wife
> Alexander Tomkins and Elizabeth his wife
> And of John, Samuel, Rebecca, Elizabeth, Margaret & Fanny
> Children to the said Alexander
> Alexander died 11th day of January 1741"
>
> —(Ordnance Survey County of Londonderry, 1837).

The Tomkins' name has disappeared from Derry, but the family are still represented in the female line by the Beresford Ashes of Ashbrook, and the Knoxes of Prehen, the Tomkins' estate having passed to those families. In the Cathedral window unveiled in 1913 in memory of the gallant defenders, Alderman Alexander Tomkins is among those so honoured, among his descendant subscribers being Miss Hazel H. Knox, Mrs. Cope, Miss Honora T. Galway, Mrs. Carle Galway, Rev. Lindsay Neville Knox, Rev. Canon Andrew Knox, Mrs. S. W. Barton, Waller Barton, Mrs. Robertson Paton, Virginie G. Schiffler (*née* Knox), George Von Schiffler Knox.

639. **WILLIAM BURNSIDE** was another of the Protestant burgesses appointed by Tyrconnell's 1688 charter. There is no other mention of his name.

640. **JOHN BURNSIDE** was one of the signers of the Corporation's 1690 Commission.

641. **HENRY ARKWRIGHT**, defender,

642. **WILLIAM DRAPER**, defender, and

643. **WILLIAM RAGSTON.** These three names are among the signatures to the document of 11th July authorising the Governors to open the abortive negotiations with the enemy for surrender.

644. **ALDERMAN SAMUEL HOBSON**, defender, an Alderman of the old charter, who came into office again with the successful "No Surrender" party.

> "Alderman Hobson with stores of provision
> Supplied the forces of our garrison."[1]

---

[1] "Londeriados."

Described as "Captain Samuel Hobson, of Londonderry," he was among the attainted in James' Dublin Parliament. He died in 1697.[1]

645. **Sergeant Lynn**, defender, killed in the last sortie of July 17th.[2]

646. **John Linn** (or **Lynn**) was a signer of the Corporation's 1690 Commission.

647. **Mathew McClelland**, defender, and

648. **John McClelland**, defender. Both were signers of the address to King William after the relief and may have been the father and son of the following incident in the successful Pennyburn sortie of April 21st:

> "And young McClelland's wounded with a shot;
> The ancient Father did the son revenge,
> Who with the foe did many a blow exchange.
> The tender parents viewed the bloody day
> From off the stately walls by the ship quay;
> For near the walls upon the shore they fought;
> And tender parents their dear children sought,
> The wife her husband; then back to the town
> Our host returned in triumph and renown."[3]

649. **Abigail Cleland (McClelland?)**. Her signature is attached to the Corporation's 1690 Commission.

650. **Capt. James McCormick (McCormac?)**, of Lisburn, defender. Held a commission as captain in Col. Arthur Upton's Co. Antrim Regiment, serving with Sir Arthur Rawdon's force down to the retirement on Derry. During the siege he served in the same rank in Col. Mitchelbum's Regiment.[4]

He is frequently mentioned by siege annalists for distinguished service. Mackenzie thus writes of him, describing events early in May, "Few days passed but Capt. James McCormick with officers (list of names given) or some of them went out with small parties, and seldom returned without doing some execution on the enemy or bringing in some small prey."

His name is among the signatures to the address to King William after the relief. He served with the Mitchelburn Regiment at the Boyne and through the subsequent campaign. Among the attainted were two of the name, as described—

651. **William McCormac (McCormick)**, of Co. Down.

---

[1] Graham's "Derriana."
[2] Ash's "Diary."
[3] "Londeriados."
[4] See list of officers in Hampton's "Derry," p. 465.

652. Capt. William McCormac (McCormick), of Enniskillen, who was greatly distinguished in the many actions round that centre, being a chief instigator of the resistance and defence. His name is among the signatures to the Enniskillen address to King William after the relief. He was the author of a valuable work, still often quoted, entitled "Further Impartial Account of the Enniskillen Men." Whether the two families of Lisburn and Enniskillen are connected or not I am unaware.

From the Capt. James McCormick above are descended a family who have not forgotten the struggle of Derry in their work of usefulness for the Church of England, viz. his great-grandson, the late Canon Joseph McCormick, D.D., Rector of St. James, Piccadilly (1900–1914) and his two sons:

(1) The late Rev. Joseph Gough McCormick, Dean of Manchester, who died in 1924,
(2) The Rev. William Patrick Glyn McCormick, D.S.O., the present Vicar of St. Martin-in-the-Fields,

three Irishmen who have made the voice of Ulster felt in England.

653. Capt. Thomas Moncrieff, defender, a prominent Alderman of the city who had served as Mayor in 1678, 1679 and 1680. He was one of the Protestant burgesses appointed by Tyrconnell's new Corporation of 1688.

He was one of the captains appointed to command a city company raised for defence after "the shutting of the gates." He served all through the siege, and his signature is on the address to King William after the relief, and on the Corporation's 1690 Commission. He was among the attainted in James' Dublin Parliament. After the siege he was again Mayor of the city in 1701 and 1728 (filling the minor office of Sheriff in 1690 and 1715).

654. John Guest, of Belfast, Co. Antrim. The only record of this name is his signature to the manifesto of twenty-three of the nobility and gentry of the county in 1688 calling upon their fellow Protestants to associate in defence of liberty and faith.

According to Dr. Killen (in notes to his edition of Mackenzie's "Siege") Mr. Guest was a leading Belfast attorney.

655. Lieut. Robert Morrison, defender, one of the thirteen gallant apprentices, famous for the closing of the gates on the 7th December. When the town was organised for defence a few days later he was appointed lieutenant to one of the newly-raised companies, with which he served all through the siege.

He was one of the attainted in James' Dublin Parliament.

656. James Morrison, defender, was appointed lieutenant to another of the city companies. He happened to be the officer in charge of the Ship-quay Street gate a few hours after King James' repulse before the gates, when Col. Adam Murray and his troopers, excluded by Lundy, the Governor's, express instructions, demanded admission. He was admitted; an act which entitles James Morrison to a high place in the Derry roll, as Col. Murray was the leader in "No Surrender."[1]

"Londeriados" has a line typical of his actions during the siege:—

> "And Captain Morrison fought the enemy."

657. **Theophilus Morrison**, defender. His signature is attached to the document of the 11th July authorising the Governors to open the abortive negotiations for surrender of the city.

658. **William Morrison**,

659. **Robert Morrison**,

660. **Elizabeth Morrison** and

661. **Henry Morrison** were signers of the Corporation of Derry's 1690 Commission.

662. **William Morrison**, defender. "Londeriados" commends his actions at commencement of the siege as follows:—

> "Morrison and Shennan apothecaries
> Were at vast expense in remedies."

A minute of the Corporation, 19th September, 1689, records his election as Burgess in recognition of siege service.

663. **Adam Morrison**, Coolgarry, Co. Tyrone, was one of the attainted in James' Dublin Parliament.

The above sketches indicate the prominence of the family in Derry during the siege. There are still many of the name in the city and county of whom the most prominent and best known in the last few decades was the late Mr. Hugh Smith Morrison, M.D., D.L., Aghadoey, Co. Derry, for many years M.P. in the Northern Parliament for Co. Londonderry.

664. **Robert Shennan**, defender. See No. 662, William Morrison, for "Londeriados'" allusion to this name.

A minute of the Irish Society, 9th June, 1690, orders "their Treasurer to pay Robert Shennan £5 for medicines supplied to the sick and wounded."[2]

---

[1] Mackenzie.
[2] Hampton's "Siege."

665. Capt. John Maghlin (Macklin), defender, mentioned for gallantry with other officers in repulsing the enemy's determined effort to recapture Windmill Hill on 4th June.[1]

He was a signer of the address to King William after the relief, as was also

666. Robert Maghlin.

667. Lieut. Maghlin, defender. Mentioned for good service in sortie work early in the siege.[1]

668. James Rock, defender. We are told in Ash's "Diary," under date 3rd July, 1689, that "he by the order of the Governor struck the flag on the church (Cathedral) three times and as often hoisted it up, then made a wave, which was done to let the Fleet see our great distress." Walker and Mackenzie both confirm this signalling to the Fleet, without giving the name of the signaller.

669. Alderman Mathew Cocken (Cockayne), defender. Few families were of greater importance among the great mercantile houses of the City of London than that of Cokayne at the beginning of the 17th century. Sir William Cokayne was knighted at Cokayne House (now the City of London Club) on 8th June, 1616, by King James I., whom he had entertained at a princely banquet. Again, in 1620, when Lord Mayor, Sir William banqueted his sovereign with magnificent state. On his death in 1626 he left behind him one surviving son, Charles, who, in 1642, was raised to the Irish peerage as Baron and Viscount Cullen. He left several daughters, all of whom made great matches, viz. with the Earl of Nottingham, Earl of Holderness, Earl of Lindsay, Viscount Faversham, and Earl of Dover.

Sir William Cokayne, the Lord Mayor, had been one of King James' strongest supporters with the city companies in his Ulster Plantation policy. When the arrangements had gone far enough for the allotment of the huge confiscated territory to the individual company or group of companies, it was Sir William who presided at the city meetings, when the shares were drawn by lot, and he was the first Governor of the Irish Society, an association formed by all the city companies interested to manage their concerns in general, such as the proposed towns of Londonderry and Coleraine, and the Fisheries.

The family interest in Londonderry does not seem to have lapsed entirely with Sir William. Among the defenders of the city in the siege of 1689 there is Alderman Mathew Cocken (Cockayne). He had been Sheriff in 1684–85 and had lost his aldermanship with Tyrconnell's new charter of 1688. After the shutting of the gates he was a resolute supporter of the "No Surrender" party, and was appointed a captain of one of the companies raised by the city. As a representative of the Corporation he did

---

[1] Mackenzie.

good work in the negotiations for settlement with Lord Mountjoy, and a few weeks later signed the "Declaration of Union."

During the siege he was one of the Corporation put on a special council to advise the Governors, and "Londeriados" thus writes of his abilities:—

> "Cocken an Alderman in council sate
> He did the Church and State both regulate."

His name was among the attainted in James' Dublin Parliament, and he signed the address to King William after the relief. He died shortly after the siege, and on the minutes of the Irish Society there is an order, 14th December, 1689, "to the Treasurer to pay Mrs. Cocken, the relict of Alderman Cocken, late of Londonderry, being in very low condition, and having a great charge of children, the sum of £10, out of the monies advanced by the 12 companies for the relief of such who suffered by the late siege of Londonderry."

Turning back to Sir William Cokayne's eldest surviving son, Charles, created Viscount Cullen in 1642,

670. His great-grandson, another **CHARLES COCKAYNE**, was the 4th Viscount in 1689, and as such was summoned to James' Dublin Parliament. He failed to attend, but his name does not figure in the list of attainted.[1]

On the death of Borlase, the 6th Viscount, in 1810, the title became extinct; but the representation of the family remains in the line of an elder son of Sir William, another William, whose family have for generations held important positions in the city.

The present head of this old house is Sir Brien Ibrican Cokayne, K.B.E., Baron Cullen, one of the partners of the widely-known firm of Anthony Gibbs and Sons, of London, who served with such distinction as Governor of the Bank of England during the Great War that he was raised to the peerage of the United Kingdom, taking for his title the Barony of Cullen of Ashbourne.

671. **CAPT. THOMAS MANSON**, defender, an officer in Col. Monro's Regiment through the siege, and after the relief transferred to Col. Lance's.[2]

672. **THEOPHILUS MANSON**,

673. **JAMES MANSON** and

674. **WILLIAM MANSON** were among the signers of the address to King William after the relief.

675. **WILLIAM MANSON**, described as of Co. Down, was among the attainted in James' Dublin Parliament.

---

[1] Harris.

[2] Ash's "Siege."

676. **ALDERMAN GERVAIS SQUIRE**, defender, a member of the Corporation who lost his aldermanship with Tyrconnell's 1688 charter. He had been Sheriff in 1662, and Mayor in 1675 and 1676. After the shutting of the gates he was a strong supporter of the "No Surrender" policy:—

> "And Gervais Squire with all his might persists
> In Council, and our troops with stores assists."[1]

He was a signer of the "Declaration of Union," and, with Alderman Cocken, was appointed a representative of the Corporation on the Council to advise the Governors during the siege. After the relief his signature is attached to the address to King William, and to the Corporation's 1690 Commission.

Described as Capt. Gervais Squire, Donaghmore, Co. Donegal, he is one of the attainted in James' Dublin Parliament. He was again Mayor in 1690, dying shortly afterwards.

677. **WILLIAM SQUIRE**, defender, had been Sheriff in 1677. His signature is attached to the Corporation's 1690 Commission. Shortly after his election as Mayor in 1692 he died rather suddenly, his place being filled by James Lenox. In 1724 Mathew Squire, another of the family, was elected Mayor.

Graham, in the notes to his Catalogue, states that in 1843 there were descendants of this family at Manor Cunningham.

678. **JAMES STONE**, described as of Co. Down, attainted in James' Dublin Parliament.

679. **EDMUND STONE**, defender. On 5th June, "in time of parley, Edmund Stone went out to a well near the city walls to draw water, when a treacherous attempt was made on his life by a French officer. He managed to escape, badly, but not mortally, wounded. So meanly base were some of our enemies."[2]

680. **HUGH EADIE** (or **EADY**), defender:—

> "Eady a merchant was at vast expense
> In stores and money for the town's defence."[1]

He was a signer of the Corporation's 1690 Commission.

681. **THOMAS EDY**, described as of Co. Tyrone, and

682. **THOMAS EDY**, also described as of Co. Tyrone, are among the attainted in category IV of James' Dublin Parliament.

---

[1] "Londeriados."
[2] Mackenzie.

683. SAM EWING (EWIN?),

684. JOSHUA EWING (or EWIN),

685. JOHN EWING (or EWIN) and

686. JEAN EWING (or EWIN), are signers of the Corporation's 1690 Commission. It is evidently to one of these names that reference is made regarding preparations for the defence:—

> "Ewin and Wilson gave the same[1]
> And forty merchants, whom I cannot name."[2]

687. JAMES SMITH, defender. Mentioned for good service in the fierce Windmill Hill action of 4th June and on 23rd June "was shot on the Wall near Butcher's Gate, and died immediately."[3]

688. THOMAS SMITH, a signer of the address to King William after the relief.

The following were of the name attainted in James' Dublin Parliament, described as noted:—

689. CAPT. WILLIAM SMITH, of Londonderry.

690. CAPT. RALPH SMITH, of Co. Antrim.

691. CAPT. DAVID SMITH, of Belfast, Co. Antrim.

692. ERASMUS SMITH, of Armagh.

693. ERASMUS SMITH, of Armagh.

694. JOHN SMITH, of Co. Down.

695. ROGER SMITH, of Co. Monaghan.

696. REV. WILLIAM SMITH, of Co. Monaghan.

697. WILLIAM SMITH, of Co. Monaghan.

698. WILLIAM SMITH, of Co. Monaghan.

699. REV. WILLIAM SMITH, of Clenish, Co. Fermanagh.

---

[1] *I.e.* stores and provisions.
[2] "Londeriados."
[3] Mackenzie.

700. **WILLIAM SMITH**, of Greenish, Co. Fermanagh.

There were also among the signers of the Enniskillen address to King William:—

701. **WILLIAM SMITH**, Clenish, Enniskillen.

702. **HENRY SMITH.**

703. **JOSEPH SMITH.**[1]

The above William Smith, of Clenish, Enniskillen, was one of the eight signatories to the Enniskillen letter to David Cairnes of 13th December, 1688, appealing to Derry for co-operation in the coming crisis.

704. **LIEUT. EVINS**, defender. "Londeriados" has two references to this defender, viz.:—

> "Master Mackie and Evins did assist
> And with their substance did our troops subsist."

and again:—

> "Lieutenant Evins praise shall now be told
> Who in all actions was both brave and bold
> Though seventy years of age he stoutly fought
> At several battles, and young soldiers taught
> Until a bullet pierced his hardy breast;
> Yet he returned bravely with the rest.
> To save his life his tender daughter found
> The safest course to suck his bloody wound."

705. **GEORGE EVINS**, described as of Londonderry, figures among the attainted in James' Dublin Parliament.

706. **GEORGE GARNETT**, defender. This name appears among the signatures to the address to King William after the relief. At the centenary celebration of the siege in 1789 a Mr. Garnett, of Co. Meath, was among the descendants of defenders attending the commemoration.[2]

707. **JOHN LAUNDELL**, defender. "Upon the petition of above, retailer, setting forth his services and sufferings in the late siege he was admitted into the freedom of the city Jan. 15, 1691."[3]

---

[1] See Trimble's "History of Enniskillen."
[2] See Graham's notes to the Catalogue in "Ireland Preserved."
[3] Corporation of Derry minutes, from Hampton's "Derry."

708. **LIEUT. ROCHE**, of the relieving force, and

709. **JAMES CROMIE** (or **CRUMY**), of the relieving force.

In the latter half of June (Walker says the 15th, while Mackenzie says the 25th, the date given by Witherow) General Kirke tried to open written communication between the Fleet in the Lough and the besieged garrison by sending messengers to swim up the river. Roche and Cromie volunteered for the hazardous venture. Landing from the Fleet on the Co. Derry side of the River Foyle, the two messengers made their way along the wooded bank to within some three miles of the city. Here, divesting himself of his clothes, with the message tied round his neck in bladders, Roche took to the water, having arranged with Cromie to guard his clothes and promised to bring a boat to bring him to Derry the same night. Cromie was captured by an enemy patrol before Roche returned, interrogated as a spy and doubtless executed. After making his way to Derry, delivering his letter and getting a reply for Kirke, Roche started a day later on his return to the Fleet. His experiences are so graphically described by Graham in "Ireland Preserved" that I quote them almost in full:

"He then swam back to the spot where he had left his clothes, a distance of some three miles, and found they had been taken away. He ran in a state of nakedness, with the letters tied round his neck, pursued by the enemy, and escaped only by taking shelter in a wood, where horsemen could not follow him, but where his sufferings were intense from the lacerations of his body by briars and thorns. Covered from head to foot with blood, he passed through the woods to the Waterside of Derry, where he unfortunately met with a party of Dragoons, one of whom broke his jaw with a halbert, after which he plunged into the river, and, though he was fired at several times, and wounded in the arm, breast and shoulder, he preferred dying in the water to breaking the trust reposed in him. When force was found ineffectual to stop him (now at a safe distance in the river) his pursuers offered him a thousand pounds if he would deliver up the letters he carried; but this he refused to do, and not finding it practicable to proceed to the Fleet, he swam back to Derry, and by preconcerted signals gave notice to General Kirke that he had delivered the letters with an intimation of the length of time, which the city might be expected to hold out."

Roche was subsequently a captain in King William's army and received considerable grants of land in recognition of his gallant service.

Two other of the Cromie (or Crumy) name have mentions in the records of the time, viz.:—

710. **JOHN CRUMY** was a signer of the Corporation's 1690 Commission.

711. **JOHN CROMMY**, of Ballymoney, Co. Antrim, so described, was one of the attainted in James' Dublin Parliament.

712. **McGimpsey**, defender. Although Roche had conveyed General Kirke's message to the garrison, he had failed to carry a written reply back to the General. On the 27th June, a certain McGimpsey, evidently one of the garrison, came to Col. Murray and voluntarily offered to swim down the water with the intelligence. The offer was accepted and a letter written, "representing the great extremity things were reduced to, and with all imaginable earnestness importuning immediate relief."[1] With the letter securely tied in a bladder round his neck, McGimpsey started on his perilous swim. "Whether he was taken alive by the enemy, or was killed by running himself against the boom, as some reported, is uncertain, but within a day or two they hung up a man on the gallows in the view of the city on the other side of the water, and called over to us to acquaint us that it was our messenger."[1]

713. **Lieut. William Crookshanks**, defender, one of the thirteen apprentice boys who made history by the shutting of the gates on the 7th December, 1688. A few days later, when resistance was being organised, he was appointed lieutenant to one of the city companies then raised, with which he served all through the siege. "Londeriados" thus mentions his services:—

> "Lieutenant Crookshank dismounts from our walls
> The enemy's cannon, which upon us falls."

In the middle of June, previous to the swimming episodes, he made a plucky attempt in a specially constructed boat to communicate with the Fleet lying in the Lough. Starting with a volunteer party in the dead of night, he was beaten back "by the enemy's shot from each side the water."[1] His name figures as one of the attainted in James' Dublin Parliament.

In recognition of his siege services he was elected a Burgess of the Corporation in October 1689 and his signature, as "comerarius" (*i.e.* chamberlain), of the city to the Corporation's 1690 Commission, and his appointment as Sheriff in 1692, indicate a rapid advance.

714. **John Crookshanks**, defender, was one of the four Protestant Burgesses appointed on the Corporation under Tyrconnell's 1688 charter. His signature is attached to the Corporation's 1690 Commission, and he became an alderman in 1704.

The family were long and honourably connected with the city of Derry, George Crookshanks being Mayor in 1750.

In the Cathedral memorial window, unveiled in 1913 to commemorate the gallant defenders, Lieut. William Crookshanks is among the honoured, among his descendant subscribers being Major Crookshanks, C.E., C. H. Crookshanks, E. M. Crookshanks, R. Crookshanks.

---

[1] Mackenzie.

The Harts of Kilderry, Co. Donegal.

None of the name was in Derry at the time of the siege but some were closely associated with the supporters of King William in the 1689 revolution and in the assistance given to the besieged city by outside effort.

The Harts were among the original grantees at the time of the Ulster Plantation, when they acquired considerable estate in Co. Donegal. Their prominence in Ulster at the time of the revolution is shown by the frequent mention of their names in different records. These are given below, and a short family history follows to show who each of these was, with a note of their connections by marriage, for which I am much indebted to Col. Hart of Kilderry, for allowing me to read "The Family History of Hart of Donegal."

Among the attainted in James' Dublin Parliament were:—

715. **Capt. Henry Hart**, of Donegal or Londonderry.

716. **George Hart**, of Donegal or Londonderry.[1]

717. **George Hart**, of Donegal or Londonderry.

718. **Lettice Hart** (widow), of Co. Cavan.

719. **Thomas Hart**, of Co. Cavan.

Mackenzie, in his account of the forced disbandment of Lord Kingston's Regiment, mentions among his officers:—

720. **Major Thomas Hart**, and in Ash's "Diary" the following two, without any Christian names, are mentioned as officers sent on the expedition to Inch before the relief, viz.:—

721. **Capt. Hart.**

722. **Lieut. Hart.**

The following were among the signers of the Enniskillen address to King William, the two first named being given commissions as captains in June 1689 in Col. Thomas Lloyd's Regiment of Enniskillen Foot.[2]

723. **Capt. Morgan Hart.**

724. **Capt. George Hart.**

---

[1] Mackenzie.
[2] Dalton's "Army List," 1689–1714, Vol. III.

725. THOMAS HART.

The close connection of the family with Derry will be seen in this short summary. The first of the name in Ulster was Capt. Henry Hart, of an old Devonshire stock, who came over as an officer in Queen Elizabeth's army. Early in 1607 (in King James' reign) he was appointed Governor of Culmore Fort with a grant of 200 acres in the vicinity. He was scarcely in possession before Sir Cahir Doherty's revolt occurred. By an act of treachery when Capt. Henry and Mrs. Hart were visiting at his castle of Doe, they were taken prisoners, and on the threat to kill his wife unless Culmore Fort was delivered into Sir Cahir's hands Capt. Henry was compelled to agree. The attack on, and burning of, Derry quickly followed. Although the revolt was suppressed in a few weeks, suspicion rested on Capt. Henry, and it was not until October 1608 that he was absolved from all blame by an order of the Lord Deputy and Privy Council. At the Ulster Plantation a few years later he acquired large grants of escheated estate, including Culmore, Kilderry (then known as Muff) and Doe Castle. In 1613, when the first charter of the city of Derry was granted, Capt. Henry Hart was among the aldermen appointed. He died in 1637, being buried in the Cathedral church. Among other issue he left two sons, viz.:—

1. George, his successor at Kilderry (Muff House), who married a daughter of George Carey, of Redcastle, and died 1660 (of his issue of the Kilderry main line later).
2. Merrick, who obtained a grant of the lands of Crobert (or Crovert) in Co. Cavan. By his marriage with Letitia Vesey, daughter of the Archbishop of Tuam, there was issue of at least one son, viz.:—

   Thomas Hart, the attainted of No. 717 (and possibly the Major Thomas Hart of No. 720). He was a captain, 1690, in Col. Lloyd's Enniskillen Regiment of Foot and present at the Boyne.[1] His mother Letitia was the attainted widow, viz. Lettice Hart (widow), of No. 718.

To return to the main line of Kilderry. George, who died in 1660, left with other issue

1. Henry, his successor, who married a daughter of Sir Tristram Beresford, Bart., of Coleraine. This was the attainted Capt. Henry Hart of No. 715. Of him and his descendants later.
2. George, the attainted of No. 716. His will is dated 1705. He was in all likelihood the captain of that name holding a commission (1689) in Col. Lloyd's Enniskillen Regiment of Foot.[1]

To return to Henry of Kilderry; his house of Kilderry was in possession of the

---

[1] Dalton's "Army List," 1689–1714.

Jacobites during the revolution, and his youngest son, a baby in arms, was carried off and never again heard of. After the revolution he was appointed in 1696 a Deputy-Governor of the county, and died in 1712. He left among other issue:—

George Hart, born 1685, his eventual successor at Kilderry, by whose marriage with Mariana, daughter and co-heiress (with two other sisters) of George Vaughan, of Buncrana, the larger portion of that estate became the property of the Hart family. Their grandson and eventual successor was another George Vaughan Hart, born 1782. After a distinguished military career, in which he rose to the rank of Brigadier-General, he was appointed in 1820 Governor of the city of Derry (an office long obsolete), which he held until his death in 1832.

The present representative of this family so closely connected with the city of Derry and the counties of Derry and Donegal from the time of the Plantation is his great-grandson, Col. John George Vaughan Hart, D.L., &c., Kilderry, Co. Londonderry.

For further particulars of their marriages with the leading families of Co. Donegal and Derry, see Mrs. Robin Young's interesting history of Donegal families, viz. the Beresfords of Coleraine, the Vaughans of Buncrana, the Careys of Redcastle, the Harveys of Malin Head, the Chichesters, the Youngs of Culdaff, the Sampsons of Burt, and others.

In the Cathedral window unveiled in 1913 in memory of the gallant defenders of the city, among others so commemorated is the name of Hart, the contributing descendants being H. G. Hart and Miss C. Hart.

It should be added that two members of this family held high positions in the Corporation of Derry in the 18th century, viz. Henry Hart, Sheriff in 1718 and Mayor in 1733 and 1734, and George Hart, Sheriff in 1738.

726. **COL. MICHAEL SAMPSON**, of Faughan, Co. Donegal, so described, was one of the attainted in James' Dublin Parliament, while two other Michaels were signers of the Corporation of Derry's 1690 Commission, indicating their presence in the city as defenders, viz.:—

727. **MICHAEL SAMPSON**.

728. **MICHAEL SAMPSON**.

The Col. Michael Sampson (above) served in King William's army at the Boyne and all through the subsequent campaign until killed before Limerick in 1691. His son and successor at Burt and Inch Castle, Col. William Sampson, married one of the daughters and co-heiresses of George Vaughan, of Buncrana.

The first of the family in Co. Donegal was Major Richard Sampson, who at the Plantation acquired considerable estate in the neighbourhood of Burt. On his death in 1652 he was succeeded by the above Col. Michael. The family seems to have become extinct in the male line, but to one of its members, the Rev. George Vaughan Sampson, the author of "Statistical Survey of the County of Londonderry," published in 1813, we are indebted for the preservation of most valuable information.

The Careys (or Carys) of Redcastle and Whitecastle, Co. Donegal.

The first mention of the name is George Carey's appointment as Recorder of Derry in 1613, an office which he held until his death in 1640. He was also M.P. for the city 1613, and about the same time acquired considerable estate under Sir Arthur Chichester at Redcastle in Innishowen. He left six sons:—

729. (i) **Francis**, of Redcastle, one of the attainted in James' Dublin Parliament, whose two sons

730. **Capt. Francis Carey**, of Redcastle, and

731. **Lieut. William Carey** were also among the attainted.

(ii) George, who died in 1669.

732. (iii) **Col. Edward Carey**, of Dungiven, who was attainted.

(iv) Robert Carey, of Whitecastle, who died in 1681, leaving five sons, one of whom was probably

733. **Robert Carey**, of Whitecastle, who figures under that description among the attainted.

(v) Tristram, and
(vi) Henry, of whom nothing is known.

The family appears to be extinct in the male line in Ulster, but has representatives through the female line in many well-known families.

734. **William Gwynn** (**Guine** or **Gwin**).

735. **James Gwynn** (**Guine** or **Gwin**) and

736. **Mary Gwynn** (**Guine** or **Gwin**) were among the signers of the Corporation's 1690 Commission.

Gwynn's Charitable Institution in the city of Derry was opened in 1838 with money left by Mr. John Gwynn, an affluent merchant. He was the son of a tenant farmer near Muff, Co. Donegal, who had made a fortune in the city. It is quite probable that he was descended from one of the above.

737. **WILLIAM STANLEY**, defender, was one of the few Protestant burgesses appointed to the Corporation of Derry under Tyrconnell's 1688 charter, and was a signer of the Corporation's 1690 Commission. The family must have been of considerable civic standing, as Peter Stanley was Sheriff in 1710 and Mayor in 1719 and 1721.

738. **ADAM ALCOCK**, defender. His signature is among those to the address to King William after the relief, and Graham in his Catalogue mentions his name as a defender.

739. **CAPT. ABRAHAM HILLHOUSE**, of Coleraine, defender, so described, is among the attainted in James' Dublin Parliament, and his signature is on the address to King William after the relief.

740. **DUKE FREDERICK OF WÜRTEMBERG**, a brother or son of the reigning Prince of Würtemberg. He landed his command of some 6000 Danes near Carrickfergus shortly before the Boyne, and commanded them through the subsequent campaign down to Limerick. He, with some of his officers, made Galgorm Castle their head-quarters in the winter following the Boyne, while his men were billeted in Ballymena and neighbourhood. The following year, in the attack on Cork, which fell before King William's army, an incident occurred showing the punctiliousness of continental Princes as to due observance of rank. Lord Churchill, afterwards the famous Duke of Marlborough, was in command of the English troops and Commander-in-Chief in King William's absence; when orders were passed by Churchill for an assault on the town, Duke Frederick of Würtemberg, commanding his Danish Brigade, refused to accept orders from an inferior in rank. A compromise was effected by which each was to command on alternate days, the first falling to Lord Churchill, who gave the pass word of "Würtemberg," while on the second day the Duke, not to be outdone in courtesy, reciprocated with "Churchill." So harmony was restored and Cork surrendered.[1] In one of the assaults on the town the Duke of Grafton, said to have been the best of the illegitimate sons of Charles II., fell to the great regret of the victors.[1]

741. **CAPT. FRANK WILSON**, defender. His name is frequently mentioned by siege annalists for useful service. In the May 6th sortie, the attack on Windmill Hill, he is credited by Mackenzie with sharing in the capture of Capt. William Nugent, a son of Lord Westmeath.

He is one of the signers of the address to King William after the relief.

742. **JAMES WILSON** was among the signers of the Corporation's 1690 Commission.

743. **ENSIGN JOHN WILSON** and

744. **ENSIGN JOSEPH WILSON** were officers in the Mitchelburn Regiment, serving through the siege.

---

[1] Harris.

Graham in the notes to his Catalogue states that this family came from Tullywilson, Co. Longford.

The following of the name were attainted in James' Dublin Parliament:—

745. **HUGH WILSON**,

746. **HUGH WILSON** and

747. **JOHN WILSON**, all described as of Co. Tyrone.

In the memorial window unveiled in 1913 in Derry Cathedral to commemorate the gallant defenders Col. Wilson (Captain Frank Wilson of the siege) is among the names so honoured, his contributing descendants being R. E. Follett Jones and James Bristow.

748. **JOHN WILSON**, of Rashie, Co. Antrim, "is supposed to have landed at Carrickfergus 1690 in the suite of King William."[1] Such is, at all events, the family tradition.

He was present at the Boyne and subsequent campaign, settling down afterwards at Rashie, where the family resided for several generations. In the 19th century the head of the family, William Wilson, became the owner of Daramona, Co. Westmeath, where they have since been one of the leading county families. A branch of this family, the Wilsons of Currygrane, in Co. Longford, settled at the latter place about the same time.[1] James Wilson, of Currygrane, Co. Longford, who was Sheriff in 1864, left two sons, the second of whom was that distinguished soldier Field-Marshal Sir Henry Hughes Wilson, G.C.B., &c., who rendered such invaluable service to the Empire in the Great War, and whose assassination a few years ago caused such widespread consternation. It was the *Belfast Evening Telegraph's* obituary notice of his widow Lady Wilson's (*née* a Wray of Ardnamona, Co. Donegal) death that called my attention to this family tradition.

749. **ALDERMAN HENRY THOMPSON**, defender. On 5th June "another bomb killed Mr. Henry Thompson, a Burgess of the city, who showed great zeal for the defence of it."[2] This is confirmed by the graphic lines:—

> "A dreadful bomb through his great body fled
> While he lay sleeping on his fatal bed.
> Thus Alderman Thompson died, and many more."[3]

750. **LIEUT. HENRY THOMPSON**, defender, described as of Londonderry, was

---

[1] Burke's "Landed Gentry of Ireland," 1904.
[2] Mackenzie.
[3] "Londeriados."

among the attainted in James' Dublin Parliament, and was one of the signers of the Corporation's 1690 Commission, as were also

751. **THOMAS THOMPSON** and

752. **CAPT. THOMAS THOMPSON**, defender. The latter was also one of the signers of the document of the 11th July authorising the Governors to open the abortive negotiations for surrender of the city on terms. He was a member of the special court-martial assembled on the 20th July.

753. **WILLIAM THOMPSON** was a signer of the address to King William after the relief.

The family were long of importance in the civic life of Derry, a Hugh Thompson being one of the city Sheriffs as early as 1623.

754. **ROBERT SKINNER**, defender. His name figures among the signatures to the address to King William after the relief.

755. **JAMES SKINNER** was one of the attainted in James' Dublin Parliament.

Referring to the first of these names Graham has the following lines in his Catalogue:—

> "Galtworth, Cathcart and Adair
> Oft weak from want of dinner
> Depressed with care, did oft repair
> To the walls with Robert Skinner."

756. **JAMES GALTWORTH**, defender. Referred to above by Graham's Catalogue, was a signer of the address to King William after the relief.

757. **ALLEN CATHCART**, of Enniskillen, Co. Fermanagh,

758. **JAMES CATHCART**, of Enonisewry, Co. Fermanagh, and

759. **HUGH CATHCART**, of Tullyshanlan, Co. Fermanagh, were all among the attainted in James' Dublin Parliament and signers of the Enniskillen address to King William.

760. **ALEX. CATHCART**, of Enonisewry, Co. Fermanagh, and

761. **ROBERT CATHCART**, of Creaghmore, Co. Fermanagh, were also among the attainted, while

762. **CAPT. MALCOLM CATHCART**, brother of the Allen above, held a commission in one of the Enniskillen foot regiments.

No family played a more important part in the doings of the Enniskillen men than the Cathcarts. Allen and Capt. Malcolm's names figure among the eight signatures of the Enniskillen letter of 13th December, 1688, addressed to David Cairnes in Derry appealing for joint action in the approaching crisis.

The Cathcarts were among the earliest settlers in the Enniskillen district and connected by marriage with all the leading families.[1] Graham in his Catalogue (for quotation, see Robert Skinner, No. 754) refers to one of the name as being a defender in Derry, and out of deference to such authority I include it, viz.:—

763. — **CATHCART**, defender.

764. **CAPT. POGUE** (or **POKE**), defender, is mentioned in the Windmill Hill fight of 6th May for most courageously "cutting down the enemy with his sword" and in "The Barge of Intelligence" venture of 18th June, when they were attacked by two boats, "Londeriados" again writes of his action:—

> "But pilot Pogue with his wide drake[2] them maul'd
> For as they sought to board our barge, then he
> Fired off small shot upon their company."

765. **ALEXANDER POKE'S** (or **POGUE'S**) wife, her mother and brother were all killed by a bomb falling on their house.[3]

It is evident that this Alexander Poke is the Capt. Pogue and pilot Pogue of the former mentions.

Edgar Allan Poe was descended from an Irish family named Pogue.

766. **JAMES HAIRE** (or **HAYRE?**), defender. His signature is attached to the Derry address to King William after the relief.

767. **JAMES HAYRE** (or **HAIRE?**), of Co. Tyrone, and

768. **JOHN HAYRE** (or **HAIRE?**), of Co. Tyrone, so described, are both among the attainted in James' Dublin Parliament.

In the Cathedral window unveiled in 1913 in memory of the Derry defenders, James Haire is one of those so commemorated, his subscribing descendants being the Very Rev. A. Haire Foster, Dean of Clogher, Rev. Canon Armstrong and Mrs. Close Brooks.

769. **GEORGE ELLISON**, defender,

770. **JOHN HOULT**, defender.

---

[1] For further particulars see Trimble's "History of Enniskillen," Vol. II.
[2] Cannon.
[3] Ash's "Diary."

A minute of the Irish Society books of 14th October, 1690, records that upon "petition of the above, setting forth that they had been within the city of Londonderry during the whole siege, and had thereby lost all their subsistence, the Treasurer was ordered to pay them 50/- apiece to enable them to return to their habitations."

771. **RALPH HOULT.** His signature is attached to the Corporation's 1690 Commission.

772. **HENRY PEARSE** (or **PIERCE**?), defender, was a signer of the address to King William after the relief and also of the Corporation's 1690 Commission. A minute in the Corporation books records his being admitted a Freeman of the city of Derry on 2nd November, 1692, in consideration of good services during the siege.[1]

773. **HUGH MONTGOMERY**, defender. Under date of 15th April, 1695, in the minutes of the Irish Society there is an order to pay to the above the sum of £3 in answer to his petition "as a poor ancient man, and a great sufferer in the siege."[1]

774. **JOHN MONTGOMERY.**

775. **JOHN MONTGOMERY.** Two of the name were signers of the Corporation's 1690 Commission.

776. **ALDERMAN JAMES GRAHAM**, defender, is mentioned as follows in the preparations of the city for defence:—

> "Alderman Graham laid to his helping hand
> With stores and money doth the foe withstand."[2]

His importance during the siege is shown by his being one of the signatories on 11th July of the authority to the Governors to open the abortive negotiations for surrender on terms. His name is among the signatures of the address to King William after the relief.

Among the attainted in James' Dublin Parliament there are two James Grahams described as under:—

777. **JAMES GRAHAM**, of Ballashule, Donegal or Londonderry.

778. **JAMES GRAHAM**, jr., of Ballashule, Donegal or Londonderry. The elder may have been the Alderman above.

779. **CAPT. GRAHAM**, defender, was particularly distinguished in the repulse of Lord Clancarty's attack on the Butcher's Gate on the 28th June.[2]

---

[1] Hampton's "Derry."
[2] "Londeriados."

780. Major Graham, defender. "A cannon ball struck Major Graham on the belly as he was leaning over the wall at Shipquay Gate. He died next day," 5th June.[1]

781. John Graham, defender, was a signer of the Corporation's 1690 Commission. The family were of that ancient clan of the Scottish Borderland, many of whom, forcibly expelled in the beginning of the 17th century, had found refuge in Ulster. They were of considerable standing in Derry, a John Graham having been Sheriff in 1662.[2]

Besides the Grahams actually engaged in the siege there were two others on the list of those attainted in James' Dublin Parliament, viz.:—

782. — Graham, described as of Co. Leitrim.

783. Lieut. John Graham, described as of Glasslough, Co. Monaghan, and two among the men of Enniskillen, and signers of that address to King William, viz.:—

784. Francis Graham.

785. James Graham.[3]

In the Cathedral memorial window to Derry's defenders unveiled in 1913, among the names so honoured is that of Augustus Graham (possibly either the Major Graham of No. 780, or Capt. Graham of No. 779), among the descendant subscribers being Miss Ethel Lloyd.

786. Capt. Taylor (Tailor?), defender. Mentioned for good service in the Elah sortie at the end of April.[4]

787. Richard Taylor (Tailor?). His name is among the signers of the Enniskillen address to King William.

788. Councillor Kem, defender. The only mention of this name is that on 4th June Councillor Kem's house was bombed.[1]

789. — Harper. The only allusion to this name in siege annals is that Harper's house was struck by a bomb on 3rd June and many were killed.[1]

There are, however, two of the name among the attainted in James' Dublin Parliament, described as under:—

790. Capt. John Harper, of Ballymena, Co. Antrim.

791. Robert Harper, of Ballymena, Co. Antrim.

---

[1] Ash's "Diary."
[2] See Graham's notes to his Catalogue in "Ireland Preserved."
[3] For further particulars of the name see Trimble's "History of Enniskillen."
[4] "Londeriados."

792. **Rev. John Brisben**. "About the same time (10th May) Mr. John Brisben, a curate, left the town and took protection."[1]

793. **John Logan**, defender, a signer of the address to King William after the relief and referred to in Graham's Catalogue as a defender.

794. **Alexander Logan**, a signatory of the Corporation's 1690 Commission.

795. **Capt. Dixon**, defender, and

796. **Sergeant Neely**, defender. Both these officers were prominent in the garrison's last sortie (of July)[2] and John Dixon, probably the above, was Sheriff in 1697.

797. **John Neely**, Co. Tyrone, attainted.

798. **Warham Jemmett**, defender. Although the official tax collector of the city from the shutting of the gates he was one of the most energetic of the "No Surrender" faction, being appointed a captain of one of the companies then raised. A few weeks later he was one of the city representatives in the negotiations with Lord Mountjoy.[1] Contributing to the funds for providing arms, munitions and supplies for the defence, he is commended in the following couplet by "Londeriados":—

> "Brave Gemmett, the Collector of the town
> For its defence spent great stores of his own."

He figures among the attainted in James' Dublin Parliament and was a signer of the Corporation's 1690 Commission. Transferred to Cork in later years, his daughter Judith, by her marriage with Alderman Brown of that town, was the mother of a son, who was successively Bishop of Killaloe and Cork, and died Archbishop of Tuam in 1782.[3]

799. **Andrew Bailey**, defender,

800. **John Baily**, defender, and

801. **Robert Bailey**, defender. These three names are among the signers of the address to King William after the relief.

This family were settled in Plantation times on the estate of Tirnaskea, near Cookstown, the original mansion being erected in 1632.

Capt. William Bailey, of Tirnaskea, was M.P. for Co. Tyrone in 1798, and the late Mr. Bailey Gage, Secretary of the Irish Post Office, was the owner of this estate.

---

[1] Mackenzie.
[2] Ash's "Diary."
[3] See Graham's notes to his Catalogue in "Ireland Preserved."

802. **ALEXANDER BAILEY**, of Ringdufferin, Co. Down.

803. **JAMES BAILEY**, of Eninsorkey (Innishargie), Co. Down, so spelt and described, were among the attainted in King James' Dublin Parliament.

These were the representatives of the family of Innishargie and Ringdufferin at the time of the revolution, correctly spelt Bailie. A cadet of the ancient Scottish house of Dochfour, N.B., Alexander Bailie had settled at Innishargie about 1600. Alexander, his son and successor of Innishargie left two sons:—

1. John, from whom descend the line of Innishargie; that demesne was sold at the end of the 18th century.
2. Edward, of Ringdufferin, whose descendants have been in possession of that old family property down to the present day.

804. **MATHEW BABINGTON**, of Urney, Co. Tyrone, so described, was attainted in James' Dublin Parliament. He was the grandson of Brutus Babington, Bishop of Derry (see below), and the owner of the estates of Urney, Co. Tyrone, and Castle Doe, Co. Donegal. On his death, shortly after the revolution, leaving two sons, he was succeeded in his estates by his eldest son.

805. **CAPT. WILLIAM BABINGTON**, of Urney and Castle Doe, who (as stated in Burke's "Vicissitudes of Great Families") led a small force to the assistance of Derry after the shutting of the gates, remaining as their leader all through the siege. His signature is on the Derry address to King William after the relief.

In the Cathedral window unveiled in 1913 to commemorate the gallant defenders his name is among those so honoured.

From this son descend the Babingtons of Urney and Greenfort, Portsalon, Co. Donegal, practically extinct in the male line, but now represented by the Bartons of Greenfort, Portsalon, the only daughter and heiress of the last of that house having married, in 1815, Major Barton.

Mathew Babington's second son,

806. **CAPT. RICHARD BABINGTON**, an officer in King William's army, fought at the Boyne and in the subsequent campaign. He had property at Limavady and Lifford. From him descend: the Rt. Hon. Anthony Brutus Babington, K.C., Attorney-General for Northern Ireland, and the Very Rev. Richard Babington, Dean of Cork.

The family were of ancient manorial stock in the county Palatine of Chester. The first in Ireland was the Rev. Brutus Babington, who, after holding many good preferments in England, was appointed Bishop of Derry in 1610 and died in 1611. The subjects of the above three sketches were the grandson and two great-grandsons of this bishop.

The Nesbitts of Tullydonnell, Co. Donegal.

This was an old family settled in the county in early Plantation times. Among the attainted in James' Dublin Parliament were the following, described as under:—

807. **ALEXANDER NESBITT**, of Tullydonnell, Donegal or Londonderry.

808. **JAMES NESBITT**, of Tullydonnell, Donegal or Londonderry.

809. **JOHN NESBITT**, of Tullydonnell, Donegal or Londonderry.

810. **JAMES NESBITT**, of Killygreen, Co. Tyrone, and

811. **PRUDENCE NESBITT**, the wife of John Nesbitt, of Tullydonnell (as stated in a Chancery Bill of 1700), was a signatory of the Derry Corporation's 1690 Commission, indicating her presence in the city during the siege.

In addition Dalton's "Army List" (1689–1714, Vol. III.) records the fact that the following of the name, probably of the Tullydonnell family, held commissions in Col. Sir Albert Conyngham's Regiment, serving at the Boyne and in the subsequent campaign, viz.:—

812. **CAPT. ANDREW NESBITT.**

813. **LIEUT. ALBERT NESBITT.**

814. **CORNET JAMES NESBITT.**

815. **SAMUEL HUNT**, defender, one of the thirteen apprentices who shut the gates on the 7th December, 1688. A day or two after he was appointed ensign to one of the newly-raised city companies, with which he served through the siege. His signature is attached to the address to King William after the relief.

816. **FRANCIS HUNT.** His signature is attached to the Corporation's 1690 Commission.

817. **COL. RICHARD WHALLEY**, defender, one of the Protestant officers cashiered by Tyrconnell when reorganising the army. He got a commission in one of the northern county contingents, retiring to Derry with them. He was one of the signers of the "Declaration of Union" and probably one of the officers retiring to England on 18th April.

818. **HENRY CUST**, defender, a signer of the address to King William after the relief and enumerated among the defenders by Graham in the Catalogue. The same authority states that he subsequently settled at Magilligan.

819. Capt. Henry Hunter. At the beginning of the revolution he was an officer in Col. Sir Francis Hamilton's Regiment at Armagh. He was with that regiment at Derry in the operations preliminary to the siege. A few weeks later he was in Co. Down, where he did good service round Killyleagh. He was subsequently with General Kirke's force in the Foyle, and previous to the relief was sent with a small expeditionary contingent under General Echlin to Inch, where he took part in the repulse of the Duke of Berwick before Ramelton and in saving Letterkenny from an impending attack. He was afterwards at the Boyne and Aughrim, serving down to the fall of Limerick in 1692.

Described as of Londonderry, his name is among the attainted in James' Dublin Parliament. His diary (not published until 1841) is interesting if only for the graphic description of the author's "ten deliverances or escapes from death" in the course of the campaign.[1]

Two members of the family—

820. Margaret Hunter.

821. John Hunter. These signatures are on the Derry Corporation's 1690 Commission.

822. Major Zachariah Tiffin was an officer of the relieving force under command of Cols. John Cunningham and Solomon Richards which lay for some days off Greencastle in Lough Foyle. Major Tiffin with two other officers was dispatched to Derry on the 15th April to give Col. Lundy, the Governor, official intimation of their arrival, and accept his orders in accordance with their instructions. On the same night (15th April) Major Tiffin and his two associates were sent back to the Fleet, with Col. Lundy's written reply to which the following postscript was added:

"Since the writing of this, Major Tiffin is come, and I have given him my opinion fully, which, I believe, when you hear, and see the place, you will join with me that without an immediate supply of money and provisions this place must fall very soon into the enemy's hands. If you do not send your men here some time to-morrow, it will not be in your power to bring them at all. Till we discuss the matter," (Signed) Robert Lundy.

Bad as this was, the verbal message conveyed by Major Tiffin was much worse—its purport being as follows:—

"That there was not above ten days' provisions in the town for 3000 men, although all unnecessary mouths had been put out of it, and though what was in the town for private use was taken to the public stores. Accordingly he (Col. Lundy) ordered Col. Cunningham and Col. Richards to leave their men still on board their ships, and to come with some of their officers to the town, that they might resolve on what was fit to be done."[2]

---

[1] See Graham's notes to his Catalogue in "Ireland Preserved."
[2] Mackenzie.

The following day (16th April) the two colonels, with several officers, including Major Tiffin, attended the memorable Council of War in Derry, at which Lundy presided. This deplorable resolution was confirmed and the Fleet with the two regiments sailed for England on the 18th April, leaving Derry to fight her own battle.

In the autumn of the same year, 1689, a Committee of the House of Commons sat to enquire into the whole matter. Many officers, including Major Tiffin, gave evidence, and on their report Cols. Cunningham and Richards were dismissed from the Service. The report of the Committee and the evidence given can be seen on the minutes of the House. The evidence states that Col. Lundy at the final Council of War was the first to advise the quittance of the town, to which all present agreed, saving Col. Richards, who strongly opposed, saying: "That quitting the town was quitting a kingdom," whereupon another officer, whom he believed to have been Major Tiffin, exclaimed "that he would be hanged for no man's pleasure."[1]

Coming back to Lough Foyle with General Kirke's relieving force, Major Tiffin was given the command of an Enniskillen Foot Regiment (15th July) with which he served with distinction in the engagements round Enniskillen, at the Boyne and down to the fall of Limerick. The regiment he commanded has a fighting history as the 27th of the Line.

823. Lieut. Tubman and

824. Lieut. Berry were both officers in the Co. Antrim Association force which failed in the attempt on Lisburn in February 1689.[2] Major Tubman was the above lieutenant. He was one of the Protestant officers cashiered by Tyrconnell in 1688. Coming North he got a commission in Sir William Franklin's Belfast Regiment, with which he served in the preliminary engagements, and on the latter's retirement to England he was given the command. He was conspicuous in the efforts to stop General Hamilton's advance on the city, and was one of the officers signing the "Declaration of Union." He does not seem to have been in Derry during the siege, but served in the Boyne campaign down to the fall of Limerick.

825. Capt. Richards (afterwards Colonel), an engineer officer with General Kirke's relieving force. Before the relief of Derry he was sent with the expedition operating at Inch on Lough Swilly. He left an interesting MS., only published some sixty or seventy years ago, entitled "The Diary of the Fleet," which is historically of importance as giving several reasons for General Kirke's delay in attacking the Boom.[3]

This Capt. or Col. Richards is not to be confounded with the Col. Solomon Richards of the first relieving force.

---

[1] Hampton's "Derry," giving extract from the *Journal* of the Home of Commons.
[2] Mackenzie.
[3] Graham's "Derriana" and Dwyer's "Siege."

826. **Ensign William Mackie**, defender, was so appointed to Capt. Thomas Moncrieff's company when the city was being organised for defence (10th December, 1688).

827. **Lieut. William Mackey**, of Londonderry or Donegal, so described, is among the attainted in James' Dublin Parliament.

828. **Lieut. Mackie** is specially mentioned for good service at the end of June in countermining to prevent the enemy's undermining of the walls.[1]

829. **Lieut. Mackay**, defender. "Londeriados" mentions him as being among the killed in the Pennyburn sortie of the 21st April:—

> "Lieutenant Mackay fell upon the spot."

There is another allusion to the name as contributing to the preparations for the defence of the city:—

> "Master Mackay and Evins did assist
> And with their substance did our troops subsist."[2]

830. **John Mackay**, of Multo, Co. Antrim, was among the attainted in James' Dublin Parliament.

831. **Josiah Macky** and

832. **Jannett Mackee.** Both these signatures are on the Corporation's 1690 Commission.

The variant spellings of these names as given by the different authorities has made family connection impossible to trace.

833. **James Spike** (or **Spaight**), defender, was one of the gallant apprentices who made history by the shutting of the gates on 7th December, 1688.

In the organisation of the city that immediately followed he was appointed an ensign in Capt. Tomkins' company, with which he served all through the siege. Described as Lieut. John Spieke of Londonderry, his name figures among the attainted in James' Dublin Parliament.

In a note to his "Siege of Derry" Dwyer states "that the Spaights of Limerick have in their veins the blood of the gallant Lieut. Spaight who fought at Derry." The same authority states that the first of the name came from Woolwich, and that the above James Spaight resided at Coleraine after the relief.

The Gartside Tipping Spaights of Derry Castle, Co. Tipperary, are the present representatives of this defender.[3]

---

[1] Mackenzie.
[2] "Londeriados."
[3] Burke's "Landed Gentry of Ireland," 1904.

In the Derry Cathedral window unveiled in 1913 in memory of the defenders of the city James Spaight is among the names so honoured, the descendant subscribers being Capt. W. F. Spaight, Lady Spaight, Miss G. Spaight, Richard F. Reeves, Mrs. John Adam Alexander and Major and Mrs. Maundrell.

834. **JOHN TORRENS**, defender. His signature (John Torrenes, *sic*) is attached to the Derry Corporation's 1690 Commission, indicating his presence during the siege, and standing in the city. In 1746 his grandson, the Rev. John Torrens, D.D., was appointed Headmaster of the Diocesan School, an institution which soon rose to fame under his management. Among the men of future distinction educated at this school were his four sons, afterwards so well known as—

1. The Very Rev. John Torrens, Archdeacon of Dublin.
2. Robert Torrens, a Judge of the High Court in Ireland.
3. General Sir Henry Torrens, K.C.B., military secretary to the Duke of Wellington in the Peninsular War, and afterwards Adjutant-General of the Forces.
4. Capt. Samuel Torrens, 52nd Regiment, killed at the Battle of Ferroe in the retreat on Corunna, the day before Sir John Moore's death at the latter place.

On General Sir Henry Torrens' death he was succeeded by his son, General Sir Arthur Wellesley Torrens, K.C.B., the 23rd Royal Welch Fusiliers (godson of the Duke of Wellington), who was mortally wounded at Inkermann in the Crimean War, dying a year later, when Military Secretary at Paris. It was he who founded the camp at Aldershot. He again was succeeded in a military career by his nephew, General Sir Henry D'Oyley Torrens, K.C.B., who died in 1889 while Governor and Commander-in-Chief of Malta.

Archdeacon Torrens was succeeded by his son, the Rev. Thomas Henry Torrens, who married Barbara Maria Richardson, one of the four daughters of the Rev. Thomas Rumbold Richardson, of Somerset, Co. Derry, on the death of whose son and grandson these four daughters became co-heiresses of the estate. By a family arrangement Mrs. Torrens eventually became sole owner, being succeeded on her death by her son, Major John Arthur Wellesley O'Neill Torrens, late Scots Greys, who, owing to the ever-increasing pressure of land legislation, sold the demesne of Somerset a few years ago.

The affection and regard in which the Torrens' name was held in Derry was shown by the almost unique compliment paid to three members of one family on the same occasion. On 1st September, 1818, the Rev. John Torrens, D.D.'s, three sons, the Archdeacon, the General and the Judge, were publicly admitted to the Freedom of the City at a meeting of the Corporation, while the same evening the three brothers so honoured were entertained at a great banquet given by their friends in the city and neighbouring counties. Among the large company of some 200 present there were Sir George Hill, Bart., in the chair, Sir Robert Ferguson, Bart., General Alexander,

M. S. Hill, Joseph Curry, Andrew Knox, Thomas Scott of Willsborough, Sir James Stewart, Bart., of Fort Stewart, the Dean of Derry, Sir James Galbraith, Bart., Lord John Beresford, Bishop of Raphoe, Arthur Chichester, M.P. for Belfast, &c. The chairman, in his opening speech, addressing Sir Henry, struck the right note. "The compliment paid you to-day is not, permit me to say, of a trivial nature, for it falls to the lot but of a very few public men to obtain such an unequivocal and ample testimony of esteem and approbation as is now conveyed to you." The usual speeches followed, among them the felicitous remarks of the Rev. Gardiner Young, speaking as senior clergyman of the Diocese, in which he alluded to the fact that he had known four generations of the family, that he had known them as eminent in literature and eminent in arms, but above all he had known them pre-eminent in the general virtues of a warm and benevolent heart."[1]

The Somerset estate was the original share of the Merchant Taylors' Company in the allocation of the county of Londonderry among the twelve city companies at the time of the Plantation. It was bought by the Richardson family in 1726 and continued in the family possession until sold as already stated. It should be added that the close relationship between the O'Neills and Torrens families, the Rev. William Chichester O'Neill, 1st Baron O'Neill, of Shane's Castle, having married two first cousins, viz.:—

1. Henrietta, daughter of Judge Torrens, who died in 1857,
2. Elizabeth Grace, daughter of the Ven. Archdeacon John Torrens, of Dublin,

has led to the most intimate association between these families. Consequently, when Major Torrens sold Somerset, it was not long before, under a family arrangement, Cleggan Lodge, on the O'Neill estate, was purchased by the Rt. Hon. Sir Hugh O'Neill, Bart., as it then stood, to be put in order by Major Torrens, and become the joint residence of himself and Sir Hugh and Lady O'Neill. Major Torrens, the representative of this old family, is the popular chairman of the Northern Counties Committee of the L.M.S. Railway Co., residing at Cleggan Lodge, Broughshane, Co. Antrim.

835. **JAMES CURRY**, of Derry, defender.

836. **EDWARD CURRY**, of Derry, defender. The importance of this family in the city is more than proved by these two signatures to the "Declaration of Union" of 21st March, 1689.

Graham, in his notes to the Catalogue, speaks of the high standing of this family for generations in civic affairs.

837. **JOHN BARRY**, defender. The only allusion to this name is the record of his being one of the officers present at a council of war on 13th April, 1689, when a strong resolution was passed protesting against Col. Lundy's inactivity.

---

[1] *Londonderry Journal* of that date.

838. **Robert Stevenson**, defender, an artillery officer during the siege:—

> "Robert Stevenson ne'er missed the enemy
> But furiously among the troops lets fly."[1]

839. Another **Robert Stevenson**. His signature is on the address from Enniskillen to King William. He was one of the captains who raised a company in the organisation of Enniskillen for defence.

840. **Capt. Michael Galland**, Vow, Co. Antrim.

841. **Benjamin Galland**, Vow, Co. Antrim. Both, described as above, were among the attainted in James' Dublin Parliament.

They were sons of Capt. John Galland, an officer in Cromwell's army, who obtained a grant of land at the Vow, near Ballymoney, at the time of the Cromwellian settlement. John Galland was High Sheriff of Co. Antrim in 1674 and Benjamin in 1702.

842. **Capt. Middleton**, of Co. Armagh, was one of the three members (the other two being Capt. Poyntz and Sir Nicholas Acheson) who represented Co. Armagh on the Hillsborough Consult, or standing committee of the Northern Counties Protestant Association in the beginning of the 1688 revolution.

843. **Capt. Charles Pointz** (or **Poyntz**), of Acton, Co. Armagh. Among the original grantees of lands in Co. Armagh at the Plantation was Charles Pointz, a younger son of Sir Charles Pointz, of Iron Acton, Gloucestershire. This Charles Pointz (knighted in 1630) added by purchase to his original grant, the whole being erected about 1618 into the manor of Acton. On his death he was succeeded by his son, Sir Tobias, who had died prior to the revolution, leaving a son, the Capt. Charles (above), in possession of the estate in 1688.

When the Northern Counties Associations were formed in the spring of 1689 in defence of Protestant interests, he was one of the most active in Co. Armagh, being nominated (with Sir Nicholas Acheson and Capt. Middleton) as a representative on the central committee sitting at Hillsborough.

When, in March 1689, Hamilton's success at Dromore had broken up the Northern coalition, enabling the Protestant troops to concentrate on Derry and Enniskillen, Capt. Charles Pointz with many other landlords was forced to retire across the Channel.

On Capt. Charles Pointz' demise, after the revolution, without male issue the estate devolved on his two sisters—co-heiresses:—

1. Sarah, who married Col. Charles Stewart, of Ballintoy, Co. Antrim.
2. Christian, who married Roger Hall, of Narrow-water, Co. Down, whose family now represent in the female line the Pointz family of Acton.[2]

---

[1] "Londeriados."
[2] See No. 928, Stewart, of Ballintoy.

The Skiptons of Derry.

Among the attainted in James' Dublin Parliament were three of the name, viz.:—

844. **Capt. Alexander Skipton**, of Donegal or Londonderry.

845. **Capt. George Skipton**, of Donegal or Londonderry.

846. **Capt. George Skipton**, of Donegal or Londonderry. Their army rank and attainture are indications of good service somewhere on King William's side.

The family were of considerable importance in the city of Derry, owning Ballysharkey (Bush Hall), near Prehen, John Skipton being Mayor in 1670 and Edward Skipton in 1735.

The Maxwells of Derry mentioned in siege records.

847. **William Maxwell**, defender, contributed to funds raised for the defence of the city prior to the investment[1] and was one of the signatories of the Corporation's 1690 Commission. An entry of 11th May, 1692, in the Corporation's minutes records that upon William Maxwell's petition "he was acquitted in the sum of £2. 5. 5. in regard to his public contribution for the preservation of the city."[2]

848. **Thomas Maxwell**, defender.[3] "On the 4th June, Thomas Maxwell, a youth of the city was killed by cannon."

849. **Capt. Maxwell**, defender. On 4th June, the second Windmill Hill sortie, Capt. Maxwell was badly wounded,[4] which is confirmed by the following lines:—

> "Of ours brave Maxwell fell upon the spot
> For he was wounded with a cannon shot."[5]

The Maxwells, Baron Farnham, of Farnham, Co. Cavan.

The only direct connection of this family with the siege is in Sir George Maxwell, of Killyleagh Castle, Co. Down, where he was then in residence as the husband of the last Countess of Clanbrazil. He was present at Derry in the engagements prior to the investment, and was one of the attainted in James' Dublin Parliament.[6] There was, however, another and interesting link:

---

[1] Mackenzie.
[2] Hampton's "Derry."
[3] Ash's "Diary."
[4] Walker and Mackenzie.
[5] "Londeriados."
[6] See No. 39, Sir George Maxwell.

850. The sister of the Rev. George Walker, the Governor and defender of Derry, was **ANNE MAXWELL**, who married William Maxwell, of Falkland, Co. Monaghan. The number of the attainted of the name in James' Dublin Parliament is sufficient evidence of the strong part they played on King William's side. I give the attaintures in full as described.

851. **JAMES MAXWELL**, of Londonderry or Donegal.

852. **ROBERT MAXWELL**, of Farnham, Co. Cavan.

853. **JOHN MAXWELL**, of Farnham, Co. Cavan.

854. **ARTHUR MAXWELL**, of Drumbridge, Co. Down.

855. **GEORGE MAXWELL**, of Derryboy, Co. Down.

856. **HUGH MAXWELL**, of Ballyquintan, Co. Down.

857. **HENRY MAXWELL**, of Glenarb, Co. Tyrone.

858. **JAMES MAXWELL**, of Glenarb, Co. Tyrone.

859. **THOMAS MAXWELL**, of Strabane, Co. Tyrone.

860. **REV. JAMES MAXWELL**, of Co. Leitrim.

861. **WILLIAM MAXWELL**, of Falkland, Co. Monaghan.

862. **JAMES MAXWELL**, of Co. Armagh.

The first of the family in Ulster was the Rev. Robert Maxwell, son of Sir Robert Maxwell, of Calderwood, N.B., who came over late in Queen Elizabeth's reign. He became Dean of Armagh and acquired large estate. He left, among other issue,

1. Robert, who became Bishop of Kilmore, from whom descend the Lords Farnham.
2. Henry, from whom descends the Finnebrogue line.

Of the Farnham line it is only necessary to say that the head of the family was raised to the peerage in 1756 as Baron Farnham of Farnham, and that the present representative of that old house is Sir Arthur, 11th Baron Farnham. He served with distinction in the Great War, was taken prisoner and made a most wonderful escape just before the Armistice.

The male line of Finnebrogue came to an end with the death of John Waring Maxwell, but by the marriage of his daughter and heiress, Anne, in 1809 with the Rev. William Perceval, of Kilmore Hill, Co. Waterford, has been continued as Perceval

Maxwell ever since, the present representative of this old stock being the late Rt. Hon. Robert Perceval Maxwell, P.C., D.S.O., &c., of Finnebrogue, Co. Down.

These two families of Farnham and Finnebrogue have for some three centuries taken a prominent part in their several counties and in Ulster as a whole in public affairs, and in everything tending to the welfare of the community at large.

The Galbraiths of Clonabogan, Omagh, Co. Tyrone.

Of this family there were two signers of the Corporation of Derry's 1690 Commission, a clear indication of their presence there during the siege, viz.:—

863. **ROBERT GALBRAITH.**

864. **ELIZABETH GALBRAITH**, and among the attainted in James' Dublin Parliament the following of the name, described as under:—

865. **JOHN GALBRAITH**, of Co. Leitrim.

866. **ROBERT GALBRAITH**, of Co. Leitrim.

867. **ROBERT GALBRAITH**, of Co. Fermanagh, but the following played a more important part in the actions of the Enniskillen men[1] when

868. **HUGH GALBRAITH** held a commission as captain in Col. Wynne's Regiment of Foot, and was a signatory of the Enniskillen address to King William, and

869. **JOHN GALBRAITH** was also a signatory of the Enniskillen address to King William.

The family, of Scottish extraction, settled early in the 17th century in Co. Tyrone, where they soon acquired considerable estate. In 1634 Col. James Galbraith was M.P. for Killibegs, and about 1700 a lady of the family married Robert Lowry, M.P., from whom descend the Earls of Belmore.[2] Capt. James Galbraith, who had succeeded to the family estates in 1668, married the widow of Capt. James Gledstanes, of Fardross, a defender of Derry. The family has been prominent in the county for over two centuries, and is still in residence at Clonabogan, Omagh, Co. Tyrone.[3]

870. **EDWARD WOOD**, defender, is the first signature to the Corporation of Derry's 1690 Commission, indicating his presence in the city.

871. **CAPT. EDWARD WOODS (WOOD?)** was one of the officers of Lord Kingston's Regiment operating round Ballyshannon until their disbandment a few days before the investment of Derry.

---

[1] See Trimble's "History of Enniskillen."
[2] See Lord Belmore's family histories.
[3] See Burke's "Landed Gentry of Ireland," 1904.

Among the attainted in James' Dublin Parliament were:—

872. **Archibald Wood**, of Co. Armagh.

873. **Alexander Woods (Wood?)**, of Co. Tyrone.

874. **William Woods (Wood?)**, of Co. Cavan.
Among the signatures to the Enniskillen address to King William is that of

875. **Edward Wood.** On this name Trimble in his "History of Enniskillen," p. 402, Vol. II., comments as follows: "It is likely that the ancestor of the Enniskillen Wood family, long identified with Enniskillen until recent years, came from Sligo at this time, in the person of Mr. Edward Wood, of Court, Co. Sligo."

876. **Capt. David Ross**, defender. On 23rd July a special Board of Court Martial was appointed to rectify misdemeanours in the garrison, Capt. David Ross being one of the officers selected for this duty.[1] A few days later Capt. Ross in prosecution of his duties went to the room in which Col. Adam Murray was lying seriously wounded in search of some missing saddlery. A fracas took place between the captain and Trooper Lindsay of Murray's Horse, who in the excitement of the moment seized a carbine and shot Ross dead.[1]
There were two of the name among the signatories to the Corporation's 1690 Commission, viz.:—

877. **Andrew Ross**,

878. **James Ross**, and the following were among the attainted in James' Dublin Parliament, viz.:—

879. **Francis Ross**, of Co. Monaghan.

880. **Robert Ross**, of Co. Down.

881. **James Ross**, of Co. Down.

882. **Hugh Ross**, of Rossgagh, Co. Tyrone.

883. **Rev. Robert Ross**, of Co. Leitrim.
Graham, in the notes to his Catalogue published in 1841, writes of the Ross family: "The ancient and highly respectable family of Ross has been long settled in the county of Londonderry, chiefly at Newtown Limavady," and describes them as "true as the dial to the sun."

884. **Capt. Thomas Lane**, defender. His name has special mention for good service

---

[1] Ash's "Diary."

in the second Windmill Hill sortie of 4th June, viz.:—

"Brave Capt. Lane encouraged our men."[1]

He served all through the siege, and was one of the signatories of the address to King William after the relief.

885. **HENRY LANE** was another of the signatories of the address to King William, while

886. **ANNE LANE** was among those signing the Corporation's 1690 Commission.

In the notes to his Catalogue, published in 1841, Graham thus alludes to the Lane family: "This family has been long, and respectably settled in the county of Londonderry; they held the Fishmongers' proportion for sixty years, and one of them, William Lane, of Coleraine, who died in 1725, was agent of the Irish Society." The native freehold of Ballycarton in the Haberdashers' proportion, forfeited by McGilligan in 1641, is now the property of Benjamin Lane, Esq., of Ballycarton.

887. **EDWARD DAVYS** was a signatory of the Derry address to King William after the relief.

888. **HUGH DAVEYS (DAVYS?),**

889. **NATHANIEL DAVIS (DAVYS?)** and

890. **JEAN DAVIS (DAVYS?).** These three names are among the signatures to the Corporation of Derry's 1690 Commission.

Among the attainted in James' Dublin Parliament are the following of the name, described as under:—

891. **JANE DAVIS (DAVYS?),** of Co. Fermanagh.

892. **CAPT. EDWARD DAVIS (DAVYS?),** of Co. Fermanagh.

893. **JAMES DAVIS (DAVYS?),** of Carrickfergus, Co. Antrim.

894. **HERCULES DAVIS (DAVYS?),** of Co. Antrim.

895. His son, **CAPT. HERCULES DAVIS (DAVYS?),** of Co. Antrim.
The Davys family were long and honourably connected with Carrickfergus, two at least serving as Sheriffs of Co. Antrim, and one as M.P. for the borough.[2]
A Cromwellian officer of the name, probably of the Carrickfergus family, settled

---

[1] "Londeriados."
[2] See Appendix, McSkimmin's "Carrickfergus," 1909 edition.

near Cullybackey, on a property called after him Mount Davys, afterwards passing by purchase to the Macmanus family and through them to the Rowans.

896. **Rev. — Cooke**, D.D., so described, of Co. Donegal, figures among the attainted in James' Dublin Parliament.

897. **George Cooke** is one of the signatories of the Corporation of Derry's 1690 Commission.

898. **Ralph Mansfield**, of Killygordon, Co. Donegal, was among the attainted in James' Dublin Parliament.

His ancestor, probably grandfather, Ralph Mansfield, had been a grantee at the Plantation of the 1000 acres afterwards erected into the manor of Killygordon, near Stranorlar. In 1639 his son Francis, who married a daughter of William Montgomery, of Rosemount, Co. Down, was in possession of the estate.[1]

899. **Alexander Irwin**, defender, was one of the gallant apprentices who made history by the shutting of the gates on 7th December. A few days later he was appointed ensign to one of the companies being raised for the defence of the city, with which he served through the siege.

900. **Edward Irwin.** His signature is attached to the Corporation's 1690 Commission.

The following of the name are among those attainted in James' Dublin Parliament, viz.:—

901. **Archibald Irwin**, of Timpain, Co. Tyrone.

902. **John Irwin**, of Mullinboy, Co. Londonderry.

903. **William Irwin**, of Ballydullagh, Co. Fermanagh.

904. His son, **Christopher Irwin**, of Ballydullagh, Co. Fermanagh.

905. **James Irwin**, of Co. Down. William Irvine was also a signatory of the Enniskillen address.[2]

906. **Capt. Erwin (Irvine?)**, defender. Thus spelt, he is mentioned by "Londeriados" as follows:—

> "Capt. Erwin acted above man's power
> But was disabled by a shot that hour.

---

[1] Graham's "Derriana."
[2] See No. 906, Capt. Erwin, or Irvine.

> He's son to Cornet Erwin of forty one
> Who gained great praise in that rebellion."

The Cornet Erwin was afterwards Sir Gerald Irvine (Erwin), Bart., who, on his demise in the Duke of Schomberg's camp in 1689, was succeeded by a nephew, as will be explained later, therefore the Capt. Erwin above was either killed or was some other member of the Castle Irvine family.

The Irvines were sprung from the ancient stock of Irvine, of Bonshaw, Co. Dumfries, N.B. Christopher, the original grantee of the Castle Irvine estate, Co. Fermanagh, died in 1666, leaving, among other issue:—

1. Gerard, his successor. He had an eventful life. As a cornet he fought on the Royalist side in the 1641 rebellion, earning considerable praise for escaping out of Cromwellian hands at Derry. He was afterwards a strong adherent of Charles II., being present with him at Worcester. After the Restoration he was, in 1677, created a baronet. In the 1688 revolution the Jacobite party counted on his support, and when the Duke of Schomberg with a force presented himself at Castle Irvine he was refused admission. Finally, Sir Gerard joined the Duke of Schomberg's camp, where he died in October 1689. He was succeeded at Castle Irvine by his next surviving brother,

2. William Irvine, of Ballydullagh, Co. Fermanagh, one of the attainted in James' Dublin Parliament,[1] probably served in King William's army. This William of Ballydullagh on his death in 1714 left two sons:—

   (i) Christopher, who succeeded his father at Castle Irvine (he was attainted as stated) and from whom descend the line of the D'Arcy Irvines, of Castle Irvine.

   (ii) John, from whom descend the line of Killadeas.

For some three hundred years these two families of the same stock have taken a prominent part in Fermanagh and neighbouring counties.

The Rowans of Mount Davys, Co. Antrim.

907. **REV. ANDREW ROWAN**, Incumbent of Old Stone (Donaghy), Clough, Co. Antrim, was of an old Scottish family. The first of his name in Ireland, he was inducted to Donaghy by Jeremy Taylor in 1661. He married a daughter of Capt. William McPhedris, of Carnglass, Co. Antrim.[2] He was one of the attainted in James' Dublin Parliament of 1689, as was also his son, styled of Londonderry.

908. **CAPT. WILLIAM ROWAN**, of whose services no trace is discoverable, although it

---

[1] See List of Irvines attainted Nos. 899–905.
[2] See McPhedris killed at siege of Derry, No. 329.

is certain he had a commission in King William's army. The only Rowan mentioned in siege annals is the Rev. John Rowan, Incumbent of Baltiagh, in the diocese of Derry.[1]

It is from Robert, grandson of the Rev. Andrew Rowan, that the Mount Davys line descends. This Robert was the owner of the estate of Mullans, and by his marriage with Letitia Stewart, daughter and heiress of a branch of the Ballintoy family, acquired the Garry property (held under a three hundred years' lease from the Antrim estate). His grandson, another John, by his marriage in 1809 with Eliza Honoria Macmanus, daughter and heiress of Macmanus of Mount Davys, added that property, the largest of all, to the family possessions.

The Macmanus family, whom the Rowans represented by this marriage, were an ancient Celtic sept. They had once been possessed of considerable territory in Co. Fermanagh, but for some generations had been settled on their estate of Ballybeg and Ahoghill, in Co. Antrim. Early in the 18th century Hercules Macmanus had by purchase acquired the lands of Mount Davys from the descendants of a Cromwellian settler (Davys), transferring his residence from Ballybeg to Mount Davys and retaining the name given by the Davys occupiers. On the death of the last male of the name, Col. Alexander Macmanus, who had served as High Sheriff and commanded the militia for many years, the property devolved through his daughter on the Rowans. An old memorial tablet (transferred from the old to the new church on its erection in 1870) calls attention to the fact that some seventy of the family are buried in the Macmanus vault in the churchyard.

Besides the marriage connections already mentioned, the Rowans and the Macmanuses were related to all the leading county families, viz. the O'Neills, of Flowerfield, the Macnaghtens, the Stewarts, of Ballintoy, the O'Rourkes, of Ballybolan, the O'Haras, of Crebilly, the Alexanders, of Portglenone, and the Magennisses, of Finvoy.

The last of this family to reside at Mount Davys, which passed many years ago into other hands, was the late Col. John Joshua Rowan, D.L. Popular with all classes of the community, he was as welcome at social meetings as at public gatherings. In short, he had few to surpass him, whether with a rod on a salmon river or after snipe in a bog. A good friend, no loss was more generally felt. The present representative of the family is Col. Rowan's nephew, the Rev. Robert Stack, the Rectory, Frome.

This account of the Rowan family cannot be ended without a reference to two great collaterals. Two brothers of the John of Mullans who had wedded the Mount Davys heiress got commissions in the 52nd Regiment of the Line, Charles Rowan and William Rowan. There were very few of the Napoleonic campaigns in which they did not take part with their regiment. One or both of them were present at all the battles of the Peninsula, Fuentes de Oñoro, storming of Badajoz, Salamanca and the forcing of the Pyrenees, and to crown all they were both present on the great day

---

[1] See No. 378.

of Waterloo. With nothing to live on but their army pay and no outside interest, these two Co. Antrim men won their way by sheer merit to the highest posts in the service, the younger, Sir William Rowan, dying a Field-Marshal of England, while his brother Sir Charles Rowan, K.C.B., almost as distinguished, eventually became Chief Commissioner of the London Metropolitan Police.

The Knoxes, Earls of Ranfurly, Dungannon.

The first of this family to settle in Ulster was

909. **THOMAS KNOX**, who was residing in Belfast for some years previous to the 1688 revolution. Although his name neither figures in Derry siege annals nor on the list of attainted in James' Dublin Parliament, one act of his is at least deserving of record. When early in December 1688 consternation was caused in Ulster by the finding in the street of Comber of an anonymous letter, addressed to the Earl of Mountalexander warning the Protestants of the North that on the 9th of the month an attempt would be made to repeat the massacre of 1641, steps were immediately taken to warn all centres of the peril. A letter signed by the local leaders, Sir William Franklin, Arthur Upton, William Cunningham, and by Thomas Knox, was immediately sent by express to their friends in Dublin with the information.[1] Mr. Thomas Knox's importance in the community is shown by his association with the three others mentioned.

When the revolution was over Thomas Knox purchased, in 1692, the Dungannon estate, of which his successors have been the popular landlords until quite recently. He became M.P. for Dungannon and was sworn a member of the Privy Council. In subsequent generations a member of the family or their nominee almost invariably sat for that borough. Meantime the head of the family had occupied many important positions in the Irish administration. Honours were quickly accumulated—a Barony in 1781, Viscountcy in 1791 and Earldom in 1832, all in the Irish peerage, with a Barony of the United Kingdom in 1826. The titles are Earl of Ranfurly and Viscount Northland.

The Knoxes are of an ancient Scottish house deriving the title of Ranfurly from Ranphorlie, an estate long in the family possession. Uchter (or Uchtred), the name of their original ancestor, is still a cherished Christian name. The present representative of the family is Uchter John Mark Knox, 5th Earl of Ranfurly, Dungannon, Co. Tyrone. His lordship married in 1880 the Hon. Constance Elizabeth Caulfeild, only daughter of the 7th Viscount Charlemont. Universal sympathy was felt for Lord and Lady Ranfurly on the death of their son, Viscount Northland, in action during the Great War. Lord Ranfurly has always played a prominent part in Ulster affairs, and has filled the high post of Governor-General of New Zealand. General regret is felt

[1] Mackenzie.

that circumstances obliged him to part with an estate with which so many generations of his family have been closely and honourably connected.

The following were those of the name of Knox figuring among the attainted in James' Dublin Parliament, described as under:—Rev. John Knox, Glasslough, Co. Monaghan.[1]

910. **JOHN KNOX**, Glasslough, Co. Monaghan.

911. **JOHN KNOX**, of Raphoe, Donegal or Londonderry.

912. **WILLIAM KNOX**, of Raphoe, Donegal or Londonderry.

913. **ANDREW KNOX**, of Donegal or Londonderry. Of the three latter sketches, Andrew Knox was the descendant representative of Andrew Knox, translated from the bishopric of the Isles in Scotland to that of Raphoe, which he filled from 1611 until his death in 1632. The Bishop was a cadet of the Knox of Ranfurly (Ranphorlie), N.B.[2] From this Andrew Knox descend the Knox family of Prehen, Co. Derry.[3]

914. **ALEXANDER KNOX.** His signature is attached to the address to King William after the relief.

915. **JAMES KNOX**, defender. Graham in his Catalogue mentions his name among the defenders of the city. He is, however, in error in including him among the signatories of the address to King William. There are two others of the name figuring among the defenders of the city, viz.:—

916. **JAMES KNOX**, defender, was the tenant of a farm of some 100 acres in the townland of Ballyvennox (the town of the Knoxes) near Newtown Limavady. He served in Sir Tristram Beresford's Regiment and was at the Boyne.

917. **ROBERT KNOX**, defender, was the owner of a mountain farm, on the side of the road between Coleraine and Limavady, popularly known as the murder hole. With the greatest difficulty he succeeded in getting his cattle across the Foyle and into Derry just before the investment was complete. He and his family were in the city all through the siege.

I am indebted for the family tradition of the above to the late Mr. Samuel Kyle Knox, of the Northern Banking Co., Belfast, whose family have for generations taken a prominent position in Coleraine and district.

918. **THOMAS COLE**, defender. He is probably the Thomas Cole described as of Co.

---

[1] See No. 368.
[2] See Burke's Peerage, under Earl of Ranfurly.
[3] See Burke's "Landed Gentry of Ireland," 1904.

Monaghan whose name figures among the attainted in James' Dublin Parliament. As Mr. Cole had come into Derry from a Jacobite camp, where he had been a prisoner for some time, doubts were at first entertained as to his motives. These were soon assuaged.[1] He was a signatory of the "Declaration of Union," serving in the defence all through the siege.

In the Cathedral memorial window unveiled in 1913 to commemorate the gallant defenders, his name is among those so honoured, the descendant subscribers being Col. Willoughby Cole Verner and Rudolph Cole Verner.

He was probably a member of the family of Florence Court.

The others of the name figuring among the attainted in James' Dublin Parliament were:—

919. **Lieut. Francis Cole**, Ballyleck, Co. Monaghan.

920. **Col. Richard Cole**, Ballyleck, Co. Monaghan.

921. **William Cole**, Colehill, Co. Fermanagh, and

922. **Sir Arthur Cole**, Bart., Co. Tyrone, who was the representative of the Coles of Florence Court during the 1688–89 revolution. This is best explained by a short account of the family.

The Cole progenitor, Capt. William (afterwards Sir William), had at the Plantation received large grants of land in the neighbourhood of, and had been appointed Constable of, Enniskillen Castle with the onerous duty of the building of the town. These duties had been satisfactorily performed, and it was owing to his care that Enniskillen had been saved in the 1641 rebellion. Dying in 1653, he had left two sons:—

1. Michael, his successor, who on his death in 1663 left another Michael to succeed. This Michael was absent in England during the revolution, but was afterwards M.P. for Enniskillen. His son John was created in 1760 Baron Mount Florence, of Florence Court, and in the next few decades the head of the family was advanced to a viscountcy (1776) and the Earldom of Enniskillen (1789). The present representative of the family is the 5th Earl of Enniskillen, who served with the North Irish Horse all through the Great War.
2. To return to John, the second son of Sir William Cole. He was created a baronet in 1666, being succeeded on his death by his son Sir Arthur Cole, Bart., the subject of this sketch, who took a prominent part on the side of King William, and was attainted as already stated. Sir Arthur was raised to the peerage as Lord Ranelagh in 1714, a title which on his death in 1754, without male issue, became extinct.

---

[1] Walker and Mackenzie.

923. **Capt. Stephen Miller**, defender. Held a commission as ensign in Lord Mountjoy's Regiment in 1684, and was a captain in Col. Mitchelburn's Regiment during the siege.

His name appears among the officers of the garrison on the commission of 11th July authorising the Governors to open the abortive negotiations with the investors for surrender on terms, and he was one of those selected to form the special court-martial appointed in the end of July.[1]

Described as Capt. Miller of Donegal or Londonderry, he is among the attainted in James' Dublin Parliament.

Capt. Miller lived at Kilrea, his will being proved in 1729. His son, Rev. Stephen Miller, born in 1708, was rector of Kilrea in 1731, dying in 1736, and a grandson of the latter, Rev. George Miller, of Armagh, died in 1849, leaving descendants.[2]

924. **Margaret Miller.** Her signature is on the Corporation of Derry's 1690 Commission.

The Stuarts of Castlestewart, Earls of Castlestewart.

Although none of this family was connected with the siege of Derry, so many relatives of the house were among the attainted in James' Dublin Parliament that they must find a place. Besides, there is a romance connected with their peerages which is more than deserving of mention.

The first of the family in Co. Tyrone was Andrew Stuart, 2nd Baron of Ochiltree, N.B., descended from the Duke of Albany, third son of King Robert II. of Scotland. He was a near kinsman of James I. of England, and was a Lord of his Bedchamber. At the time of the Plantation he was one of the favourites in the King's entourage who received a considerable grant of lands in Co. Tyrone. There Stuart Hall, still in occupation of his descendants, was erected. In order to stock his newly-acquired lands Lord Ochiltree was obliged to part with his heavily mortgaged estate of Ochiltree, and, as the barony was held by tenure, he lost his title, which went to the purchaser. To obviate this difficulty, in 1619 the King created him Baron Castlestewart in the Irish peerage. On the death of the 3rd Lord Castlestewart in 1650, without male issue, his estate devolved on his only daughter Mary, who by her marriage with Henry Howard, afterwards Earl of Suffolk, brought the property into that family. About 1672 the property was sold, William Houston of Craigs, Co. Antrim, being the purchaser.[3]

At the time of the revolution of 1688, a member of the family was 7th *de jure* holder of the title. This 7th Baron was summoned to attend James' Dublin Parliament, but was conspicuous by his absence. For a considerable period this peerage seems to have

---

[1] Ash's "Diary."
[2] Facts from Mr. Hugh Lecky of Beardiville.
[3] See No. 942, Houston of Craigs, Co. Antrim.

been dormant.[1] In 1793 a descendant of the 3rd son (Robert of Irry) of the first Baron Castlestewart was acknowledged as the 9th Baron Castlestewart, and created Viscount, and in 1860 the head of the family was raised to the Earldom of Castlestewart.

The present representative of this old family is the 7th Earl of Castlestewart, Stuart Hall, Co. Tyrone.

According to Hill's "Ulster Plantation," two of Lord Ochiltree's brothers accompanied him to Ulster, and acquired land in Co. Tyrone, viz. Capt. Andrew Stewart (the elder), who settled at Gortgall. His son or grandson was the attainted.

925. **Hugh Stuart** of Gortgall, Co. Tyrone, of 1689. From him descend the Stewarts, Baronets of Athenree, Co. Tyrone (creation in 1803), now represented by the 4th Baronet, Sir Hugh Houghton Stewart, Bart.,[2] and

James Stewart, who settled at Ballymenagh, and later at Killymoon, Co. Tyrone, two of whose sons or grandsons were among the attainted in James' Dublin Parliament, viz.:—

926. **William Stewart**, of Killymoon, Co. Tyrone.

927. **James Stewart**, of Killymoon, Co. Tyrone.

The William Stewart above was closely associated with the Rev. George Walker in holding Dungannon and marching their men to Derry before the investment.[3] "Londeriados" has the following couplet:

> "Lieutenant Colonel Stewart from Maghera
> Did to the city a party draw."

On the death of the last direct male of the Killymoon family, William Stewart, M.P., in 1850, the line became extinct, the old place being put on the market, and the representation passing to the Ballymenagh line, of whom the late Rev. Henry William Stewart, Rector of Knockbreda, Co. Down, was the head.

928. **William Stewart**, described as of Co. Tyrone, was another of the attainted in James' Dublin Parliament, probably of the Killymoon or Ballymenagh family.

There were several other Stewarts, cadets of the family, or close connections, in whom the first Lord Castlestewart was enough interested to figure as their cautioner, or guarantor, that they would carry out the conditions of Plantation, notably among these:—

William Stewart, Laird of Dundaff, Ayrshire, who received land in Co. Donegal. His son or grandson,

---

[1] See Burke's Peerage, where several peers of the name are put down as *de jure*.
[2] Burke's Peerage, 1904 edition.
[3] See Mackenzie.

929. **John Stewart**, of Dundaff, Co. Donegal, was attainted in James' Dublin Parliament.

Robert Stewart, who had a grant of land in Co. Tyrone, as also had Robert Stewart, of Hilton, N.B.[1]

In addition, of the name of Stewart, there were three others among the attainted in James' Dublin Parliament whose family connection I have failed to trace, viz.:—

930. **Alexander Stewart**, of Co. Down.

931. **Alexander Stewart**, of Co. Down.

932. **Patrick Stewart**, of Drumskeeny, Co. Tyrone.

The Stewarts of Ballintoy, Co. Antrim.

933. **Col. Charles Stewart**, of Ballintoy, Co. Antrim.

934. **Capt. William Stewart**, of Ballintoy, Co. Antrim. Both these names figure on the list of attainted in James' Dublin Parliament, while Col. Charles Stewart, the then head of the family, took a prominent part in organising King William's supporters in the county in the few months preceding the revolution. He was one of the twenty-three leaders issuing the manifesto to the Protestants of the county and raising regiments for self-defence. Until Richard Hamilton with his army overran Antrim, the struggle had been maintained. After that most of the leaders had to leave the country, as we presume he also had to do.

935. **James Stewart**, of Ballylusk, Co. Antrim, a cadet of Ballintoy, was another of the attainted in James' Dublin Parliament.

The Stewarts of Ballintoy were sprung from an illicit amour of Robert Stewart, afterwards Robert II. of Scotland, with Christian Leitch, of the island of Bute. From their son John Stewart descend the long line of Hereditary Sheriffs of Bute, now represented by the Marquess of Bute. The fifth Sheriff of the Island, Archibald, had among other issue two sons, who settled on the territory of the Macdonnells of the Glens, near Ballintoy on the Antrim coast, about 1560. Of these two sons Ninian left with other issue a son, Archibald, who, when the Macdonnells were given a grant of their vast territory and created Earls of Antrim by James I., received a sub-grant of the estate of Ballintoy. His appointment in 1630 as the Earl of Antrim's agent made him of the greatest importance on the Antrim coast.

In the course of a few generations the castle of Ballintoy with a fine oak staircase and rich panelling was erected, while a deer-park was enclosed in the vicinity. At

---

[1] See Hill's "Ulster Plantation."

the time of the revolution, Col. Charles Stewart, the subject of this sketch, was the owner of the estate. Dying without issue, he was succeeded by his brother Alexander, who was appointed Lord Antrim's agent in 1720. The rest of the story of this family is sorry reading. Serious dissension ensued between the agent and Lord Antrim, and affairs went badly. On his death in 1742 he was succeeded by a son and grandson, two Alexanders, who in a few years so dissipated the property that it had to be sold in 1760. Purchased by a Mr. Cupples, of Belfast, for £20,000, it was resold almost immediately to Mr. George Fullerton, in whose family it has since remained.[1]

Hill, in his graphic and interesting "Stewarts of Ballintoy," asserts that "few families have sent out from the main stem a greater number of collateral branches," or are connected in affinity with more families through the female line in Co. Antrim. I will give two instances of general interest:—

(1) The Rowans of Mount Davys.[2]

By the marriage of their ancestor the Rev. Robert Rowan with Letitia, great-granddaughter of Ninian Stewart, of Ballintoy, about 1760, they are representatives in the female line of this old stock.

(2) The MacNeills of Cushendun (now represented by the Lord Cushendun) by the marriage in 1760 of their ancestor Neill MacNeill, of Cushendun, with Rose (sister of the above Letitia) Stewart, are representatives in the female line of this house. *Note.*—After the sale of Ballintoy the last Stewart of the male line resided on his Acton estate, Co. Armagh, until his death in 1799.

The Stuarts of Ballyhivistock, Co. Antrim.

This family has consistently adhered to the ancient spelling of the name indicating their connection with the Royal blood of Scotland. From the pedigree and history of the family given by Thomas Camac in his "History of the Parish of Derry Keighan" it is to be gathered that Robert Stuart, a kinsman of James I. of England, received a considerable grant of lands in Co. Cavan, where he settled at the time of the Plantation. This Robert was sent by his sovereign on an embassy to the King of Sardinia, but on his return journey was drowned in the English Channel.

936. His grandson **WILLIAM STUART** was in possession of the Cavan estate at the time of the revolution.

He is stated to have eventually raised the 9th Regiment of Foot, which he commanded at the Boyne, and through the subsequent campaign down to the capitulation of Limerick, rising to the rank of Brigadier-General. According to family tradition (for which I am indebted to the late Mrs. William Stuart of Ballymena),

[1] For further particulars, see No. 515, Col. Downing, Nos. 620–21, Downing Fullerton.
[2] See under that name.

937. **HENRY STUART**, a nephew of the General, then in his teens, held a commission in his uncle's regiment, being present at the siege of Derry, where, it is stated, he was allowed to take a trial shot with one of the big guns on the ramparts, and blew the head off a French engineer officer who was emplacing a gun on the other side of the river. So impoverished was General Stuart by the raising and equipping of the regiment, for which he received no payment, that the estate had to be sold after the campaign, being incorporated with the Farnham property. His grandson, the Rev. Irwin Stuart, for many years curate of Derry Keighan, was in 1773 appointed incumbent of Ardclinis. From him descend the well-known family of Ballyhivistock.

Graham in his notes to the Catalogue attributes the Ballyhivistock ancestry to the Stewarts of Ballintoy, but as both these descents are from the Royal Stuarts it is immaterial.

938. **JAMES STEWARD**, Apprentice, defender, was one of the thirteen gallant apprentices whose names are immortalised by the shutting of the gates on 7th December. His name, thus spelt by Mackenzie, makes family identification all the more difficult.

939. **MARMION STEWART.** This name is among the signatures to the Derry address to King William.

940. **JENNET STEWART.** This signature is attached to the Corporation of Derry's 1690 Commission.

941. **COL. ROBERT HOUSTON**, of Craigs, Co. Antrim.

942. **FRANCIS HOUSTON**, of Craigs, Co. Antrim. Both these names were among the attainted in James' Dublin Parliament.

Lieut.-Col. Houston held a commission as such in the Skeffington Regiment and took part in all the operations prior to the investment of Derry. He is particularly mentioned for good service in the neighbourhood of Toome, where he commanded a section of his regiment.[1]

The Houstons were an old Scottish family settling in Co. Antrim early in the 17th century, and acquiring by purchase the estate of Craigs, where they erected the castle of that name. They were connected by affinity and association with several of the other Scottish settlers in the county, notably the Adairs, of Ballymena, the Colvilles, of Mount Colville (Galgorm) and the Edmunstons, of Duntreath (Red Hall). William Houston of Craigs Castle was High Sheriff of the county in 1628, and William Houston, the younger, was in 1636 one of the trustees to the settlement made by Sir Robert Adair on his marriage with Miss Gordon of Lochinvar, N.B. About 1672 another William Houston acquired, by purchase from the Earl and Countess of Suffolk, the manor of Castlestewart, Co. Tyrone. (The Countess had inherited the estate as only child

---

[1] Mackenzie.

and heiress of her father, the 3rd Baron, who died in 1650.) After this purchase he was styled of Craigs Castle and Castlestewart. He died in 1685, being succeeded by his son John, who was Sheriff of Co. Antrim in 1735 and of Tyrone in 1736. On his death in 1737 his Co. Antrim estate devolved on his two surviving sisters, viz.:—

1. Alice, who in 1728 had married Hon. and Rev. Charles Caulfeild, second son of the 2nd Viscount Charlemont. In the course of time their descendants succeeded to the viscountcy and are now represented by the present and 8th Viscount Charlemont, Drumcairne, Co. Tyrone, and by the Countess of Ranfurly, the only child and heiress of the 7th Viscount Charlemont.
2. Grace, who married in 1736 the Rev. Thomas Staples, third son of Sir Robert Staples, 4th Baronet, of Lissan, Co. Tyrone, whose descendants are now represented by the holder of the baronetcy and present family of Lissan.

The estate of Craigs was held jointly by these two families until purchased about 1820 by Mr. John McNeile, of Parkmount, in whose family it remained until sold to the occupying tenants towards the end of the century. During the McNeile ownership, their cousin and agent, Mr. Edmund McNeill, D.L., of Cushendun, emparked some 200 acres round the ruins of Craigs Castle and built the modern castellated mansion of Craigdunn, which was sold a few years ago to Mr. J. Percy Stott, who now resides there.

943. **Sir Robert Staples**, 4th Baronet, of Lissan, Co. Tyrone.

944. **Mathew Staples**, of Lissan, Co. Tyrone, were both on the list of attainted in James' Dublin Parliament.

Thomas, the first of the name in Ulster, received a grant of the Lissan estate, Co. Tyrone, at the time of the Plantation. He was created a baronet in 1628, and was High Sheriff in 1640. Sir Robert, the 4th Baronet (above), was the owner of Lissan at the time of the revolution and was M.P. for Dungannon in 1692 and for Clogher in 1695. The descendants of the Rev. Thomas Staples, third son of Sir Robert Staples, 4th Baronet, eventually succeeded to the baronetcy, in whose line it is to-day represented in the person of the 11th Baronet, Sir John Molesworth Staples, Bart., Lissan, Co. Tyrone.[1]

945. **John Donaldson** (*sic*) of Glenarm, Co. Antrim, was one of the attainted in James' Dublin Parliament. He was also one of the twenty-three leading men of the county issuing the manifesto of 1688 urging Protestants to resort to arms to meet the threatened dictation from Dublin. He had been High Sheriff of Co. Antrim in 1665.

The Donaldsons, Donelsons, or Donellsons, as the name was variously spelt, were illegitimate connections of the Antrim family, by whom they had been liberally treated

---

[1] For Rev. Thomas Staples' marriage with Grace, one of the co-heiresses of the Craigs Castle estate, Co. Antrim, see Nos. 941, 942, Houston of Craigs.

in regard to grants of land.[1] In 1626 a John Donellson, evidently the father of the subject of this sketch, held lands as follows on the Antrim estate, viz.:—

> 40 acres at Oynaloghaig,
> 40 acres at Ballytober and
> Tenements at Glenarm and Larne.

He died in 1634, leaving his son, aged some twenty years, to succeed him.

In 1715 there were several of this name on the Antrim estate with annual incomes reckoned from £60 to £250 each. The name is now practically extinct.

The Creightons of Crom Castle, Earls of Erne.

The first of the name in Co. Fermanagh was a member of the old house of Frindraught, Aberdeenshire. Abraham Creighton, who settled at the time of the Plantation on the small proportion of Dromdoory in that county. Dying about 1631, he left with other issue (of whom later)

946. **ABRAHAM**, his successor, who by his marriage with Elizabeth Spottiswoode, daughter and heiress of the Bishop of Clogher, acquired the Crom Castle estate in her right. Living there at the commencement of the revolution in 1689 the castle was the scene of two sieges. Hearing of the advance in March 1689 of a Jacobite army under Lord Galmoy to summon Enniskillen to surrender, Col. Abraham Creighton, then an aged man, determined to resist at all costs. With his sons and all the able-bodied men they could collect he refused admission to Lord Galmoy. The latter immediately laid siege to the place, but, not being able to bring his big guns over the boggy approach, resorted to the following stratagem. Two immense "tin guns" were dragged before the castle and the garrison was threatened. Seeing through the trickery, Col. Abraham sallied out, took and blew up "the guns" to Lord Galmoy's annoyance; an action ensued in which the Jacobites had the worst of it. Meanwhile Galmoy had sent an emissary demanding the surrender of Enniskillen, while the garrison had asked for succour from the same place. The upshot of it was that, some twenty-four hours later, a night attack by land and water was made by 200 of the Enniskillen boys on Lord Galmoy's investing force, and the place relieved. Three months later the attack was repeated by another Jacobite contingent, but again repulsed owing to the gallantry of Col. Abraham's son David. Not content with the two successful defences of his castle, Col. Abraham commanded his regiment on the field of Aughrim in 1691.

Besides his laurels in war, Col. Abraham took that leading position in his county since held by his family. He was Sheriff in 1673 and M.P. in 1692. His name, of course, figures among the attainted in James' Dublin Parliament. He died in 1705. His eldest son,

---

[1] Hill's "Macdonnells of Antrim."

947. **JAMES CREIGHTON**, a captain in his father's regiment, had greatly distinguished himself at Aughrim (1691) and the ensuing campaign. His name also figures among the attainted in James' Dublin Parliament. Dying in 1701, on his father's death in 1705 the succession went to James' son,

948. **JOHN CREIGHTON**, a third member of the family on the list of attainted in James' Dublin Parliament. He was High Sheriff in 1715, and dying in the same year without issue the Crom estate passed to his father's last surviving brother,

949. **DAVID CREIGHTON.** This David, as already mentioned, had been conspicuous in the second successful defence of Crom Castle.

He served with distinction as an officer in King William's army down to the capitulation of Limerick, rising to the rank of Brigadier-General. Dying in 1728, he was succeeded at Crom by his eldest surviving son, Abraham, who in 1768 was created Baron Erne of Crom. From that date further honours accumulated, the head of the family being created Viscount Crichton in 1781, and Earl of Erne in 1789.

The present representative of this old stock is the 5th Earl of Erne, Crom Castle, Co. Fermanagh. His father, Viscount Crichton, was killed in action in the beginning of the Great War, so that the present Earl succeeded to the title on his grandfather's death.

Among the attainted in James' Dublin Parliament there was another Creighton, whose family connection I have been unable to ascertain, viz.:—

950. **ALEXANDER CREIGHTON**, of Lissancara, Co. Fermanagh.

951. **COL. CHICHESTER FORTESCUE**, of Donoughmore, Co. Down, defender. At the time of the revolution he was resident on his Donoughmore estate. Sending his wife and children for safety to the Isle of Man, he raised, at his own charge in his neighbourhood, a troop of horse, with which he hurried to take part in the defence of Derry. He took part in all the operations prior to the investment, and his signature was attached to the "Declaration of Union" of March 1689.

He was one of the colonels to whom Lundy refused admission to the momentous Council of War on 18th April, when he and his associates were secretly plotting the surrender of the city.[1] A few weeks later, at the end of June, when Col. Baker, the Governor, lay dying, Col. Fortescue and Col. Lance, of Coleraine, were the deputation appointed by a conclave of officers to interview him regarding the nomination of his successor. The result was the selection of Col. Mitchelburn, than whom a better could not have been found.[2] To the great regret of the garrison he died of dysentery on 22nd July, just before the relief. According to contemporaries he was reputed one of the best swordsmen in the army.

---

[1] Harris.
[2] Mackenzie.

The following short history of the Fortescue family will be of interest. John Fortescue, of Buckland Filleigh, Devonshire, had by his wife, Susannah, daughter of Sir John Chichester, of Raleigh in that county (and sister of Sir Arthur Chichester, afterwards the famous Irish Lord Deputy), among other issue, Sir Faithful Fortescue, born in 1581, who joined his uncle, Sir Arthur Chichester, in Ireland in 1604. He occupied several important posts under his uncle, among others being for many years Constable of Carrickfergus Castle, besides acquiring considerable landed estate, Dromisken, Co. Louth, Donoughmore, Co. Down, and Fortescue Manor (Galgorm Castle), Co. Antrim, where he commenced the building of the castle, afterwards completed by the Rev. Alexander Colville, D.D., ancestor of the Earls Mountcashell.

In an "Account of Sir Arthur Chichester," written by Sir Faithful and still extant, he attributes his good fortune in Ireland to his uncle in the following words: "With him I had, from coming young (about twenty-three years old) from school, my education, and by him the foundation of any advancement and fortune I acquired in Ireland."

At the time of the rebellion of 1641 in Ireland and the Civil War in England, he was sent over as a warm supporter of Charles I. to collect supplies and recruit men, whom he was to bring back to Ireland for the suppression of the rebellion. His feelings may be imagined when, intercepted by a stronger Parliamentary party, he and his troop of horse were compelled to join the cavalry under Oliver Cromwell on the eve of the Battle of Edgehill, 1642. What took place is best quoted from Clarendon's "History of the Civil War": "detesting the force that was put upon him … as the right wing of the King's horse advanced to charge the left wing, which was the gross of the enemy's horse, Sir Faithful Fortescue, who having his fortune and his interest in Ireland was come out of that Kingdom to hasten supplies thither, and had a troop of horse raised for that service … He (Sir Faithful) and his whole troop advanced from their horse, and discharging their pistols into the ground presented themselves to Prince Rupert, and immediately charged with His Royal Highness." This disconcerting action materially assisted in the success of Prince Rupert's charge.

Sir Faithful shared in all the vicissitudes of his royal master during the Civil War. After Charles I.'s death he accompanied Charles II. in exile, returning with him to the fatal field of Worcester. Coming back with his Sovereign at the Restoration he was reinstated in offices and estates, being sworn of the Privy Council. Dying 1669–70, he was succeeded by his eldest surviving son, Sir Thomas Fortescue, who had held many important posts, among others the Governorship of Carrickfergus in Ulster.

In 1689 Sir Thomas, an ardent supporter of King William, had been turned out of office and imprisoned by the Jacobite Government in Dublin until released by the Boyne victory. He died in 1710, leaving two sons: Col. Chichester Fortescue, the subject of this sketch and William Fortescue, also serving in King William's army, from whom descended the Fortescues, Barons and Earls of Clermont (peerages now extinct), who are represented by the Fortescue family of Stephenstown, Co. Louth.

952. **Capt. Hercules Burleigh**, defender, was the son of William Burleigh, of Carrickfergus, his mother being a daughter of Sir Roger Langford, from which connection came the Christian name of Hercules.[1]

He served all through the siege of Derry, and is mentioned[2] as prominent in the last sortie of the garrison. His name is recorded as one of the signatories to the commission of the 11th July authorising the Governors of Derry to open the abortive negotiations with the enemy for surrender on terms. He died in 1744.

The family was one of old standing and consideration in Carrickfergus.[3]

953. **Popham Conway (Seymour)**, described as of Co. Antrim, thus figures among the attainted in James' Dublin Parliament as the owner of the large estate (since known as the Hertford estate), lying on the southeast of Lough Neagh and embracing the town of Lisburn and many villages in the Killultagh district.

The original grantee of this property had been an Elizabethan officer, Sir Foulke Conway, serving under Sir Arthur Chichester in the garrison of Carrickfergus. The last representative of the male line of this family, the Earl of Conway, who d.s.p. in 1683, left his estates under will to his cousin, Popham Seymour, on condition of his assuming the name of Conway. Popham was the eldest son of Sir Edward Seymour, by Letitia, daughter of Alexander Popham, of Littlecote, Wilts. Killed in a duel in 1693, his estates went to his brother, Francis Seymour, who was created Baron Conway of Raglan 1703 (English peerage) and Baron Conway of Killultagh 1712 (Irish peerage). With such large properties in England as well as in Ireland, few families were of greater territorial influence. Honours accumulated— a viscountcy in 1730, an earldom in 1750 and a marquessate in 1793 as Earl and Marquess of Hertford.

On the death, in 1870, of the 4th Marquess without legitimate issue, although the settled estates in England went with the titles to his cousin and successor, the 5th Marquess, the large Killultagh estate passed under his will to the late Sir Richard Wallace, Bart. During the Hertford tenure of the Killultagh estate, the family had exercised great political influence in Co. Antrim, and at the time of the 4th Marquess' death in 1870 the son of his successor, the 5th Marquess, known by the courtesy title of Earl of Yarmouth, was one of the county members. This seat he retained until the general election of 1874, when he retired and was returned as M.P. for a South Warwickshire constituency, where the Hertford name had influence. Lord Yarmouth succeeded his father as 6th Marquess and died in 1912. The present representative of the family is the 7th Marquess of Hertford, residing in England.

Besides Popham Conway or Seymour, the owner of the Killultagh estate attainted in 1689, there were, among others already mentioned, residing in Lisburn and district on the list of attainted in James' Dublin Parliament:—

[1] See Langford.
[2] Ash's "Diary."
[3] See McSkimmin's "History of Carrickfergus."

954. **Capt. Edward Harrison**, Killultagh, Co. Antrim. He had been High Sheriff of the county in 1678 and sat as M.P. for Lisburn from 1692 till his death in 1703, when his son,

955. **Michael Harrison**, was elected in his place, being member for that constituency till his death in 1709. He had also filled the office of Sheriff in 1697.

Both these men have a better right to recognition by their services to the county in the few months prior to the 1689 revolution in Ireland. The signatures of both father and son are among those of the twenty-three nobility and gentry of Co. Antrim signing the manifesto appealing to Protestants to rise in arms for mutual protection and defence of their religion.

The first of this old family in Ireland was Sir Michael Harrison, of Ballydargan, Master of the Staple in Charles II.'s time, who died in 1664. His son, Capt. Edward Harrison, according to family tradition lived in Old Maghraleave House, near Lisburn, marrying a daughter of the celebrated Jeremy Taylor, Bishop of Down, by whom, among others, there was the following issue:—

(1) Michael, subject of this sketch, d.s.p. in 1709.
(2) Jeremiah Taylor Harrison, of Brookhill, Lisburn, who left no issue.
(3) Hugh, in Holy Orders, Domestic Chaplain to the Rt. Rev. Edward Smith, Bishop of Down, whose daughter he married. He acquired the estate of Churchfield (Magherintemple), near Ballycastle, Co. Antrim. He was succeeded by their only son, the Rev. Michael Harrison, Vicar of Ramoan and Culfrughtrin, Ballycastle, who died in 1765, being succeeded by his son, Hugh Harrison, who married Miss Mary Casement, of Balinderry. Shortly after his death in 1786 his widow, Mrs. Harrison, sold the Churchfield (now Magherintemple) estate to her brother, Mr. Roger Casement, in whose family it still remains, the present owner being Capt. John Casement, R.N., D.L., Magherintemple, Ballycastle, Co. Antrim.

The Rev. Michael Harrison left several sons, of whom the second, Robert, of Raceview, near Ballymena, left a son, Michael, afterwards a Judge of the High Court of Justice in Ireland, who died in 1895. He left two sons, among other issue, the elder of whom, Robert Francis Harrison, K.C., of 17 Fitzwilliam Square, Dublin, died only a few years ago, leaving a considerable family, among them Michael, born 1888, Robert, born 1902, and Frances Mabel, who continued the family tradition by her marriage with Major Francis Casement, R.A.M.C., brother of the present owner of Magherintemple.

956. **Sir James Caldwell**, Bart., Castle Rossbeg, Enniskillen. His father, John, a member of the old Ayrshire family of Stratton, near Prestwick, had come to Fermanagh

early in the 17th century. His son James had been a successful merchant in Enniskillen. In 1662 he acquired by purchase from the Blennerhasset owners, the original grantees, the estate and castle of Hasset, the name of which he altered to Castle Rossbeg, that of the townland.[1] He was created a baronet in 1683, and was resident at Castle Rossbeg at the time of the revolution.

From the beginning of the revolution Sir James was one of the most prominent of the county gentry in aiding and assisting the Enniskilleners in their preparations for resolute resistance. He raised a regiment of foot, which he commanded in person, and two troops of horse commanded by his two sons, Capts. Hugh and John. With this force he operated from Ballyshannon to Donegal town during the siege of Derry. Before the investment of Derry he had interested himself to some purpose in procuring supplies of powder and ball for the Northern garrisons, the greater part of which was purchased from Mr. Mathew French, of Dublin.[2] In this dangerous work Sir James' daughter,

957. **ELIZABETH CALDWELL**, is said to have ridden on several occasions from Dublin to Enniskillen or Ballyshannon in charge of considerable quantities of powder. When General Kirke with the Fleet and supplies arrived in Lough Foyle in June 1689 and lay inactive there, Sir James was the first from the Enniskillen side to get in touch with and inform him of the position. This he managed by going round the Innishowen promontory from Donegal town to Lough Foyle in a small open rowing boat. The first result of this plucky venture was the dispatch of a vessel with powder for the Enniskillen garrison. In after years Sir James complained that he was kept for twenty-eight days idling at the General's headquarters before Kirke could make up his mind to send back with him, as he eventually did, Col. Wolseley, Major Tiffin, Capt. Wynne and other officers who so materially aided the men of Enniskillen in the coming campaign. From General Kirke he at the same time received King William's commission to command the regiment he had raised and led in the field. This kindly act was forgotten after the relief of Derry, when Kirke ordered its disbandment.

In a claim to the Government made in 1694 for compensation for his losses during the revolution, stressing his unfair treatment regarding his regiment, Sir James says: "I had four sons in the King's service all the war, and my eldest is lately dead in his service, another of my sons was a close prisoner in Dublin fourteen months, till relieved by the King after the battle of the Boyne. My other two sons were Captains in Col. Wolseley's Regiment till the war broke, and then they took up arms in the Dragoon regiment of the late Brigadier Wynne, and are now in the same regiment in Flanders."[3]

Of these sons three, described as of Co. Fermanagh, are among the attainted in James' Dublin Parliament, viz.:—

---

[1] It was not until 1792 that it became Castle Caldwell.
[2] See No. 962, under that name.
[3] Trimble's "History of Enniskillen," Vol. II. p. 413.

958. CAPT. HUGH CALDWELL,

959. CAPT. JOHN CALDWELL, both commanding troops of horse raised by Sir James, with which they did good service, especially Capt. John, who repulsed the Duke of Berwick's attack on Donegal Castle, and

960. CHARLES CALDWELL, who served in his father's foot regiment.

For many generations the family held a foremost position in their county. With, however, the death of Sir John the 5th Baronet, in 1830 the direct male line became extinct, the estate passing to his only daughter, Frances Arabella, who married John Colpoys Bloomfield, of Redwood, Co. Tipperary. Their second son, John Caldwell Bloomfield, inherited the Castle Caldwell estate, which in course of time devolved on his daughter, Blanche, who married the Rev. Charles Grierson (now the Lord Bishop of Down, Connor and Dromore). On her death the representation of this old family passed to their only daughter, Mrs. Kinahan.

When Sir John, the 5th Baronet, died in 1830, the baronetcy went to a distant cousin, becoming extinct in 1862.

961. DANIEL FRENCH, of Belturbet, Co. Cavan, and

962. MATHEW FRENCH, of Belturbet, Co. Cavan, so described, were among the attainted in James' Dublin Parliament.

These two brothers, sons of Mathew French, of Belturbet, seem to have been most useful in their assistance to the men of Enniskillen; not only in the field of action, but also in procuring arms and ammunition which Mathew, a merchant in Dublin, was able to have conveyed to Daniel in Belturbet.[1]

In proceedings taken by Mathew French's widow in the Chancery Court, Dublin, in 1710, and extant until the burning of such records in the Four Courts, she states in her evidence that having become obnoxious to the authorities for having supplied the garrisons of Londonderry and Enniskillen with powder and ball against the Irish, she, her husband and family were forced to fly for England; that he was attainted *in absentia*, that they remained in England until the end of the Revolution, and that her husband died in Chester on their return journey to Dublin. She adds that she found the most of her property burned or otherwise destroyed in their absence.

The importance of the family in Co. Cavan is shown by the fact that Mathew French served as High Sheriff of the county in 1677.

The Daniel French of No. 961 was one of the signatories of the Enniskillen address to King William.

In Trimble's "History of Enniskillen," Vol. II. p. 424, are the following interesting particulars of the French family: Mathew French's wife was Mary Meade, whose pres-

---

[1] In No. 957 it has already been told how Elizabeth Caldwell participated in this dangerous traffic.

ent descendants are represented in the line of the Nixons, late of Nixon Lodge, Co. Monaghan, and the Swanzys, of Avelreagh, Co. Monaghan. Daniel French's wife was Isabella, granddaughter of Bishop Bedell, celebrated for the humanity he displayed to all in distress regardless of creed or party during the 1641 rebellion. Their descendants are represented in the line of the Stanfords of Carn, Co. Cavan, and the Richardsons, of Summerhill, Co. Fermanagh.

963. **AMBROSE BEDELL**, Co. Cavan, a brother of Mrs. Daniel French (above) and grandson representative of the famous Bishop Bedell.

His name figures among the attainted in James' Dublin Parliament, and also on the Enniskillen address to King William.

964. **COLONEL WILLIAM WOLSELEY**, of Enniskillen fame. In No. 956, Sir James Caldwell, mention has already been made of how this officer (Capt. James Wynne, see No. 965, and Major Tiffin, see No. 957) accompanied Sir James back to Enniskillen from General Kirke's headquarters. His services with the men of Enniskillen at Newtownbutler and the Boyne are matters of history.[1] His name will ever be associated with the regiment of Enniskillen Horse which he led to victory on so many occasions, since so distinguished in the British Service as the VIIIth Royal Irish Hussars.

The above Col. William was the fifth son of Sir Robert Wolseley, 2nd Baronet (creation 1628), of the ancient Saxon family of Wolseley, Staffordshire, to-day represented by Sir Charles Michael Wolseley, 9th Baronet. From the third son of the second Baronet, Sir Robert Wolseley, are descended the Wolseleys of Mount Wolseley, Co. Carlow, on whose head another baronetcy was conferred in 1744, the present representative being Sir Reginald Beatty Wolseley, 10th Baronet, of Mount Wolseley, Co. Carlow. The late distinguished Field-Marshal Viscount Wolseley was a member of this old family.[2]

965. **CAPT. JAMES WYNNE**, of Hazlewood, Co. Sligo. This is the Capt. James Wynne mentioned in No. 957 as accompanying Sir James Caldwell from General Kirke's headquarters on Lough Erne to Enniskillen. He brought with him from General Kirke King William's commission as Colonel, and was placed in command of one of the Dragoon regiments raised or being raised by the men of Enniskillen (July 1689). In the actions round that town, at the Boyne and in the subsequent campaign, while he rose to the rank of Brigadier-General, his regiment did such good service as to be incorporated in the British army as the Fifth Royal Irish Lancers.[3]

As James Wynne, of Co. Leitrim, his name figures among the attainted in James' Dublin Parliament (May 1689).

---

[1] For particulars see Trimble's "History of Enniskillen."
[2] Burke's Peerage.
[3] See Trimble's "History of Enniskillen."

The first of the family in Ireland was Owen Wynne, of an ancient Welsh family, who settled in Co. Sligo in Queen Elizabeth's reign, where in a few generations the estate of Hazlewood, of which the demesne is still in possession of the family, was acquired. For three hundred years the family have held a prominent position in their county.

966. **Col. Thomas Lloyd**, of Croghan, Co. Roscommon, was the eldest son of Capt. Owen Lloyd, M.P. for Boyle in 1661, the first possessor of that estate (his father Thomas, of an ancient Welsh family, having settled in Co. Leitrim early in the 17th century).

From the beginning of the revolution he was one of the most prominent leaders of the men of Enniskillen.[1] Captain William McCormack, in his "Further Impartial Account of the Enniskillen Men," pithily summarises his usefulness to the garrison as follows: "Under whose conduct, we never failed accomplishing what we designed, and without him could not, nor ever did anything." His luck in his enterprises earned him the name of "the little Cromwell."

He and the Governor, Gustavus Hamilton, were mainly responsible for the raising of the Enniskillen regiments, and when General Kirke from his headquarters on Lough Foyle was organising the Ulster forces (July 1689) he received a colonel's commission to command one of these regiments, with which he was present in all the actions round Enniskillen and at the Boyne. Dying without issue (will proved in 1699), he was succeeded in the command of his regiment by Lord George Hamilton (Douglas), afterwards created Earl of Orkney. This regiment is to-day famous in the British army as the Royal Inniskilling Fusiliers.[2]

Descendants of his brother Richard are still in possession of the demesne, of which the present representative is John Merrick Lloyd, Croghan House, Co. Roscommon.

967. **Robert King**, defender, was a signatory of the Derry address to King William after the relief. He is mentioned as a defender.[3]

968. **Capt. Francis King** was an officer in Lord Kingston's Regiment[4] and later in Sir Albert Conyngham's. A signatory of Enniskillen address.

969. **Lieut. Toby Mulloy** was an officer in Sir Albert Conyngham's Regiment. In the spring of 1689 these two officers were sent to "observe and guard" a fort at the entrance to Lough Erne.[5]

Lieut. Toby Mulloy's signature is among those on the Enniskillen address to King William. He was on the list of attainted. Both these officers were in London in the

---

[1] For particulars of his services, see Trimble's "History of Enniskillen."
[2] See Trimble's "History of Enniskillen" and Dalton's "Army List," Vol. III. 1689–1714.
[3] See Graham's notes to Catalogue.
[4] See No. 32, Lord Kingston.
[5] Mackenzie.

spring of 1690, and their names are recorded in the War Office as among the officers lately of the Derry garrison and Enniskillen then in town who received three months' pay to enable them to return and report in the Duke of Schomberg's camp in Ireland.[1]

970. **Lieut. Henry Griffin** and

971. **Gunner Quartermaster Scimin** (Simond) were also officers lately of Derry and Enniskillen at the time in London who received, early in 1690, three months' pay to enable them to return and report in the Duke of Schomberg's camp in Ireland.[2]

972. **Charles Balfour**, of Castle Balfour, Co. Fermanagh, and his son,

973. **William Balfour**, of Castle Balfour, Co. Fermanagh, were both on the list of attainted in James' Dublin Parliament.

At the time of the Plantation two members of an ancient but impoverished Scottish house had been grantees of large estates in Co. Fermanagh, afterwards known as Castle Balfour, viz. Michael, Lord Balfour of Burleigh, and his son Michael, generally styled the "Laird of Mawhanney." On Lord Balfour's death his son and successor, afterwards created Baron Glenrawley, was owner of the Castle Balfour estate. After the latter's death without male issue the estates were sold in Charles I.'s reign to a nephew, Sir William Balfour, of Pitcullo, N.B. At the time of the revolution Sir William's son, Charles, was the owner of the estate. It was this son Charles and his son William (the subjects of sketches above) who were attainted in James' Parliament.

As nothing else except their attainture is to be traced, it may be concluded that they were in Scotland during the troubles. On Charles' death in 1713 he was succeeded by his son William, on whose death in 1738 the property devolved on his sister Lucy, who married Blayney Townley, of Piedmont, Co. Louth. Their son and heir, Henry Townley, adopted the surname of Balfour. Their descendants, the Townley Balfours, of Townley Hall, Co. Louth, are the representatives in the female line of the Balfours of Castle Balfour.[3]

974. **Oliver Stephens**, sen., Co. Cavan,

975. **Oliver Stephens**, jun., Co. Cavan,

976. **Thomas Stephens**, Co. Cavan, and

977. **William Stephens**, Co. Cavan, all so described, were among the attainted in James' Dublin Parliament. They were probably of the family of that name long settled at Ballynacargy in that county, of whom two, William and John, held commissions in the Co. Fermanagh Militia in 1725.

---

[1] Dalton's "Army List," Vol. III. 1689–1714, p. 168.
[2] Dalton's "Army List," Vol. III. 1689–1714.
[3] Burke's "Landed Gentry of Ireland," 1904 edition.

978. **Capt. John Lyndon**, of Carrickfergus, Co. Antrim, whose name figures on the list of attainted in James' Dublin Parliament, was the son of Sir John Lyndon of that town, whose family occupied an important position in the public affairs of Carrickfergus from early in the 17th century.[1]

Capt. Lyndon held a commission (1689) in Col. William Stuart's Regiment, and was killed before Limerick.[2]

979. **Rev. Lemuel Mathews**, Archdeacon of Down, described as of Hillsborough or Annahilt, was one of the attainted in James' Dublin Parliament. He was a pluralist. He was deprived of his livings and dignities in 1693.[3] His Christian name has been perpetuated by Dean Swift in his Lemuel Gulliver.

980. **Alexander Hogg**, Lough Eske, Co. Donegal.

981. **William Hogg**, Co. Down.

982. **Capt. James Huey**, Muff, Londonderry.

983. **Robert Hogg** (address) were all on James' Dublin Parliament's attainted list, but no other particulars are available.

984. **Jeremy Mussenden**, of Hillsborough, Co. Down, so described, was among the attainted in James' Dublin Parliament. Previous to the revolution he had acquired the estate of Larchfield near Hillsborough, which remained in his family until sold in 1865 by his descendant, General Mussenden, to Mr. Ogilvie Blair Graham, D.L. General Mussenden commenced his military career as an officer in the VIIIth Royal Irish Hussars, being present with them in the memorable charge at Balaclava, all through the Crimean campaign and in the Indian Mutiny. His son, Col. Mussenden, was an officer in the same regiment, having the honour of commanding it during the Great War.

985. **Patrick Agnew**, Kilwaughter Castle, Co. Antrim, was one of the attainted in James' Dublin Parliament.

The Agnews of Kilwaughter, who were settled on that estate long prior to the Plantation, were of the same stock as the Agnews of Lochnaw, near Stranraer, Wigtownshire, on the opposite side of the Irish Channel. Whether the Agnews came through Scotland to Ireland or *vice versa* is a matter of doubt that even the chief of the Scottish house, Sir Andrew Noel Agnew, Bart., of Lochnaw, Hereditary Sheriff of Galloway, is unable to solve. (See "The Hereditary Sheriffs of Galloway," by Agnew.) According to this authority the first Agnew or Agneau in the British Isles was a Norman

---

[1] McSkimmin's "History of Carrickfergus."
[2] Dalton's "Army List," Vol. III. 1689–1714, p. 108.
[3] Reid, Vol. II. p. 441.

knight of that name in the train of William the Conqueror.

The family is still represented in the female line by the owner of Kilwaughter Castle, Larne, Co. Antrim.

986. **James Auchinleck**, of Ballaghinleck, Co. Fermanagh, so described, was among the attainted in James' Dublin Parliament. He was the eldest son of the Rev. James Auchinleck, who died in 1680. He is now represented by the Auchinlecks of Creevenagh, Co. Tyrone.

987. **George Buchanan**, of Enniskillen, Co. Fermanagh, so described, was one of the attainted in James' Dublin Parliament. Of the Scottish house of Buchanan, of Carbeth, a cadet of Buchanan of that ilk.

He was the first of the family in Ireland, settling at Omagh in 1674. His grandson, John, acquired the estate of Lisnamallard near Omagh. The present owner and representative is Col. John Blacker Buchanan, R.A.M.C., a distinguished officer of many campaigns, who resides at Lisnamallard, Omagh, Co. Tyrone.

988. **Marc Buchanan**, of Enniskillen, of the same family as the above, was one of the signatories of the Enniskillen address, and afterwards an ensign in Col. Creighton's Regiment.

989. **John Blackwood**, of Bangor, Co. Down, and

990. **John Blackwood**, of Bangor, Co. Down, both so described, father and son, were among the attainted in James' Dublin Parliament.

The son, John Blackwood, jun., married Ursula, daughter of Robert Hamilton, of Killyleagh Castle. Their son, Robert Blackwood, created a Baronet in 1694, was of Ballyleidy, Co. Down, and from him descend the line of the Blackwoods of Clandeboye, Viscounts of Clandeboye and Earls and Marquesses of Dufferin and Ava.[1]

The first Marquess, great as a diplomatist, statesman, and Governor of our overseas Dominions, was honoured by his Sovereign in the higher titles linking Dufferin with Ava in recognition of services to the Empire of which his family have reason to be proud. His eldest son, the Earl of Ava, fell fighting for the flag at Ladysmith. The present representative of the house is the 4th Marquess of Dufferin and Ava, Clandeboye, Co. Down. The first Speaker of the Senate of Northern Ireland, the 3rd Marquess, was killed in the disastrous aeroplane crash of July 1930.

991. **Lieut. William Newtoun (Newton?)**, of Londonderry, so described, was among the attainted in James' Dublin Parliament. Probably the William Newton who

---

[1] See Burke's Peerage for particulars of the many other honours and dignities held by the head and members of the family, of which the present Marquess is senior heir general of the Hamiltons, Earls of Clanbrassil.

was Sheriff of Derry in 1686 and 1687. Francis Newton, of the same family, held that office in 1672, and Charles in 1677.

992. **N. W. NEWTON.** His signature is attached to the Corporation of Derry's 1690 Commission.

993. **JOHN SCOT**, Co. Donegal.

994. **MATHEW SCOT**, Kinore, Co. Donegal or Londonderry.

995. **ROBERT SCOT**, Co. Monaghan.

996. **ROBERT SCOT**, Co. Monaghan.

997. **WILLIAM SCOT**, Co. Monaghan.

998. **GEORGE SCOT**, Co. Monaghan. Spelt and described as above, all figure among the attainted in James' Dublin Parliament.

999. **JEAN SCOTT.** Her signature is attached to the Corporation of Derry's 1690 Commission.

1000. **THE REV. GIDEON SCOTT** was chaplain to one of King William's regiments in the 1690–1692 Boyne to Limavady campaign. In 1696 he purchased the estate of Willsborough, where his descendants have since resided, taking a prominent position in Co. Derry.

The most distinguished member of this family was the late Rt. Hon. Sir Charles Stewart Scott, P.C., G.C.B., G.C.M.G., &c., our Ambassador at Berne 1888–1892, at Copenhagen 1893–1898 and later at St. Petersburg. The family is now represented by his son, Charles Edward Stewart Scott, of Willsborough, Co. Derry.[1]

1001. **THOMAS ATKINSON**, of Ballyshannon, Co. Donegal.

1002. **THOMAS ATKINSON**, jun., of Ballyshannon, Co. Donegal, and

1003. **JOHN ATKINSON**, of Co. Monaghan. The first two were father and son. All three were among the attainted in James' Dublin Parliament.

A Capt. William Atkinson had settled in the North of Ireland in Elizabeth's reign; the two Thomases above were respectively his grandson and great-grandson (the latter of whom died in 1738), living at the time of the revolution on their Donegal estate, and being ardent supporters of King William. They are lineally represented by the owners of their old estate, the Atkinsons, of Cavan Garden, Co. Donegal.

John Atkinson (No. 1003 above) was a member of an old Cumberland family which

[1] See Burke's Peerage and "Landed Gentry of Ireland," 1904 edition.

settled in Co. Monaghan at the end of the 16th century. He was an ardent supporter of King William. His family acquired considerable estate in Co. Fermanagh, residing for many generations at Skea House, near Enniskillen, but now at Glenwilliam Castle, Co. Limerick. The present representatives of this family are the Atkinsons of Glenwilliam Castle, Co. Limerick, and the Atkinsons of Skea House, Co. Fermanagh. The most distinguished member of this family was the late Lord Atkinson of Glenwilliam, a Lord of Appeal. Before he was created (1905) a Lord of Appeal he was a leading K.C. at the Irish Bar, where he was known as the Rt. Hon. John Atkinson, P.C., K.C., M.P. He was Solicitor-General for Ireland 1889–1892, Attorney-General for Ireland 1892–1905 and Unionist Member of Parliament for North Derry 1895–1905.[1]

1004. The Rev. **EDWARD DIXIE**, Dean of Kilmore, Co. Cavan.

1005. **LIEUT. EDWARD DIXIE**, of Co. Monaghan. Father and son were both on the list of attainted in James' Dublin Parliament, while this Lieut. Edward was one of the defenders of Enniskillen, and a signatory of the Enniskillen address to King William.

1006. **CAPT. WOOLSTAN DIXIE**, the Dean's eldest son and an officer of the Enniskillen Horse, was brutally executed with his lieutenant, Edward Carleton by orders of Lord Galmoy after having received parole. The circumstances were as follows. After a gallant defence of his father's deanery near Belturbet, Capt. Dixie and his lieutenant fled in disguise from the burning house, but were taken prisoners and brought before Lord Galmoy. While they were in captivity negotiations had been opened by Lord Galmoy for an exchange of prisoners with the Enniskillen garrison. In answer to this, Enniskillen actually sent back a Capt. Maguire, for whose release Lord Galmoy was most anxious, on condition of the restoration of the two men in question. Notwithstanding this, and in spite of Capt. Maguire's vehement protests, Lord Galmoy had the two officers hanged before his own door. So furious was Capt. Maguire at this brutal act and disregard of honour that he threw up his commission in the Jacobite army a few days later.[2]

1007. **JOHN CROZIER**, of Co. Fermanagh, and

1008. **JOHN CROZIER**, of Co. Fermanagh, so described, were on the list of attainted in James' Dublin Parliament.

The Croziers were of an old stock, settled for many generations at Gortra, Co. Fermanagh, and at Rockview, Co. Cavan. Of the Rockview line the most distinguished owner was the late Most Rev. John Baptist Crozier, consecrated Lord Bishop of Ossery in 1897, subsequently Lord Bishop of Down, Connor and Dromore, who died Archbishop of Armagh and Primate of Ireland. His death was a great loss to all

---

[1] See Burke's Peerage and "Landed Gentry of Ireland," 1904 edition.
[2] See Trimble's "History of Enniskillen," Vol. II. pp. 466–67.

parties and creeds in Ulster, where his genial qualities and great personality had made him so popular.

1009. **DOWNHAM COPE** (Drumilly, Co. Armagh), Co. Donegal or Londonderry, and

1010. **HENRY COPE** (Loughgall), Co. Armagh, so described, are among the attainted in James' Dublin Parliament.

The first of the family in Ireland was Sir Anthony Cope, eldest son of Richard, the second son of Sir Anthony Cope, 1st Baronet of Hanwell, Berks. He got considerable grants of land in Co. Armagh, including the estates of Drumilly and Loughgall, on which the family have lived ever since, viz. the senior branch, the Copes of Drumilly, Co. Armagh, the junior branch, the Copes of Loughgall, Co. Armagh, always taking a prominent position in their county.[1]

1011. **SIR WILLIAM GORE**, 3rd Baronet, of Manor Gore. By his marriage with the daughter and heiress of Sir James Hamilton, of Manor Hamilton, Co. Tyrone, he had acquired the larger property of that name.

1012. His son **RALPH**, afterwards 4th Baronet, of Manor Gore and Manor Hamilton. Both these latter names were among the attainted in James' Dublin Parliament, being described as Sir William Gore, Bart., of Manor Hamilton, Co. Tyrone, and Ralph Gore, of Co. Leitrim. From this line descend the Baronets of Manor Gore, Co. Donegal, now represented by Sir Ralph St. George Claude Gore, 10th Baronet.[2] The 6th Baronet of this line was raised to the peerage in 1764 as Baron Gore, being created Viscount Belleisle 1768, and Earl of Ross 1771.

1013. (3) **FRANCIS**, later **SIR FRANCIS GORE**, who was an officer in Lord Kingston's Regiment.[3] His name is among the attainted in James' Dublin Parliament. He afterwards served with the men of Enniskillen in their gallant actions for the defence of the town and in the subsequent campaign. His grandson, Nathaniel Gore, married in 1711 Letitia, the Booth heiress, and assumed that name in addition to Gore. Their eldest son, Booth Gore Booth, of Lissadell, Co. Sligo, was created a Baronet in 1760. The family is now represented by the 6th Baronet, of Lissadell, Co. Sligo.[4] Arthur, afterwards 1st Baronet (1662 creation), of Newtown Gore, Co. Mayo, grandfather of the 3rd Baronet, Sir Arthur Gore, was in 1758 created a Baron and Viscount, and in 1762 Earl of Arran of the Arran Isles. The present representative of this branch of the family is the 6th Earl of Arran (and 8th Baronet), Castle Gore, Co. Mayo.[4]

---

[1] See Burke's "Landed Gentry of Ireland," 1904 edition, also Hill's "Plantation of Ulster."
[2] See Burke's Peerage.
[3] See Nos. 32, 33, under that name.
[4] See Burke's Peerage.

1014. **Capt. John Ryder**, of Co. Monaghan, so described, was among the attainted in James' Dublin Parliament. Probably one of the Protestant officers cashiered by Tyrconnell in his reorganisation of the army.

He was in Enniskillen early in 1689, and as an old army officer materially assisted the authorities in their preparations for defence.[1] He was one of the signatories of the Enniskillen address to King William, and in 1691 received a commission as Major in Col. Lloyd's Enniskillen Regiment (at that date commanded by the Earl of Orkney).[2]

1015. **Samuel Waring**, of Waringstown, Co. Down, who was Sheriff of the county in 1690, and M.P. for Hillsborough 1703–1715, was among the attainted in James' Dublin Parliament.

His grandfather, William, of an old Lancashire family, had settled in Co. Down early in the 17th century, and his father, John, had acquired the Waringstown estate by purchase in 1656, serving as Sheriff in 1669.

The family have been resident at Waringstown for nearly three centuries, taking a prominent position in county affairs. Among the best known of the family was the late Col. Thomas Waring, for so many years the popular Unionist M.P. for North Down, and Sheriff of the county in 1868. His son and successor, Major Holt Waring, fell at the head of his county regiment in the Great War, and universal sympathy was felt for his widow, Mrs. Waring, of Waringstown, who to the great delight of her friends and neighbours occupies the old family home. Her popularity was shown at the last General Election for the Northern Parliament, when she was returned to represent the division in which she lives.

1016. **Col. John Hawkins**, Co. Down, so described, was among the attainted in James' Dublin Parliament. He was one of the leaders of the Co. Down Association formed by the nobility and gentry for mutual protection and defence of Protestant interests. So conspicuous was he in the efforts at resisting General Hamilton's advance, that, after the Break of Dromore, when Tyrconnell's Proclamation was issued in March 1689, he was one of the few prominent men exempted from all hope of pardon.

1017. **Hirom Hawkins**, of Co. Armagh, so described, was among the attainted in James' Dublin Parliament.

1018. **Jason Hassart (Hassard)**, of Co. Fermanagh, and

1019. **Jason Hassart (Hassard)**, jun., of Co. Fermanagh. Both, so described, are among the attainted in James' Dublin Parliament.

1020. **Jason Hassart**, probably one of the above, was a signatory of the Enniskillen

---

[1] Trimble's "History of Enniskillen."
[2] Dalton's "Army List," Vol. III. 1689–1714.

address to King William.

The family were of Mullymesker, near Enniskillen, occupying an important position in the county, of which several had been Sheriffs. The large landed estate held by members of the family can best be realised from the fact that, between 1852 and 1876, 18,281 acres in Co. Fermanagh belonging to various members of the family were sold in the Encumbered Estates Court.[1]

1021. **HUMPHREY WRAY**, of Co. Armagh, and

1022. **WILLIAM WRAY**, of Castleroe, Donegal or Londonderry, so described, were among the attainted in James' Dublin Parliament.

The first of the name in Co. Donegal was John Wray, who in 1620 acquired by purchase from Sir John Vaughan the lands of Carnegill (some 1000 acres) near Castleroe. The William Wray above mentioned was the possessor at the time of the revolution.

The Wrays were for generations people of importance in Co. Donegal.[2] The family also held considerable estate in Co. Antrim at the end of the 18th and beginning of the 19th century, serving regularly on the Grand Jury of that county until the property was sold. The late Lord Macnaghten built his house of Runkerry between the Causeway and the long Port Ballintrae strand on the site of what had once been the Wray residence.

1023. **DOWAGER VISCOUNTESS LANESBOROUGH**, widow of 1st Viscount and mother of

1024. **2ND VISCOUNT LANESBOROUGH**. Both these names figure on the list of attainted in James' Dublin Parliament.

The first of the name in Ireland was Sir George Lane, Secretary for Ireland, who acquired the estate of Tulske, Co. Roscommon, and was created Viscount Lanesborough in 1676. On his death he was succeeded by his son, the attainted Viscount of James' Parliament. The second Viscount died in 1724, when the title became extinct, but the estate devolved on his sister, the Hon. Frances Lane, who married Mr. Henry Fox, of Grete, Worcestershire. Their son Henry assumed the additional surname of Lane. The present representative of this ancient family is Mr. George Lane-Fox, of Bramham Park, Yorkshire.

This viscountcy, creation 1676, extinct 1724, is not to be confused with the existing viscountcy and earldom of Lanesborough, conferred in 1728 and 1756 on the Butler family. (See next Nos. 1025 and 1026, Butler Earls of Lanesborough.)

1025. **FRANCIS BUTLER**, described as of Co. Cavan.

---

[1] Trimble's "History of Enniskillen," Vol. II. pp. 318–21.
[2] For this, and their marriage connections with leading families, see "Three Hundred Years in Innishowen," by Mrs. Robin Young.

1026. Francis Butler, described as of Co. Fermanagh.

1027. Sir James Butler, Kt., described as of Co. Down, figures among the attainted in James' Dublin Parliament.

The Francis of both attaintures, 1025 and 1026, may have been intended to include the same man for estate in each county.

The first of this name in Ireland was not an Irish Butler but of an old Huntingdonshire stock, viz. Stephen Butler, who acquired a considerable grant of land near Newtownbutler at the Plantation. So energetic was he in the work of the Plantation that he was knighted, and became later better known as Sir Stephen Butler, of Clonose, Co. Cavan. He left two sons, Stephen (the eldest), M.P. for Belturbet, who d.s.p. in 1662, when the succession went to his brother Francis, M.P. for Belturbet 1662 and 1692. This was the Francis (above) attainted in James' Parliament. Francis died in 1702, leaving three sons:

(1) Theophilus, the eldest, M.P. for Cavan, a member of the Privy Council and created Baron Newtownbutler in 1715, with special remainder to his brothers in succession. He died in 1728.

(2) Brinsley, who succeeded to his brother's estate and barony. He was created Viscount Lanesborough in 1728.

(3) James, afterwards Sir James, Kt. He is probably the Sir James Butler, described as of Co. Down, among the attainted in James' Parliament.

On the death of Brinsley, first Viscount, he was succeeded by his son Humphrey in the family estate and titles. This Humphrey was created Earl of Lanesborough in 1756.

The present representative of the family is Charles John Brinsley Butler, 7th Earl of Lanesborough, Lanesborough Lodge, Belturbet, Co. Cavan.

1028. The **Viscount Chaworth**, of Armagh, who figures on the list of the attainted in James' Dublin Parliament, was Patrick Chaworth, second Viscount.

His father, the first of the title, had been so created in 1637. On the second Viscount's death without male issue the title became extinct, but the property devolved on his only daughter and heiress, Juliana, who by her marriage in 1684 with the Hon. Charles Brabazon, third son of the second Earl of Meath, eventually brought the estate into the Meath family, as her husband succeeded as fifth Earl of Meath in 1715. It is interesting to note the importance attached to the Chaworth Viscountcy by the Meath family in the fact that when the tenth Earl of Meath was, in 1831, created a Baron of the United Kingdom he selected Chaworth, of Eaton Hall, Hereford, for his baronial title.[1]

The Chaworths of Annesley and Wiverton, Notts., were an old county family. The

---

[1] See Burke's Peerage.

first Viscount Chaworth was a younger son of the then head of the family, whose direct male line died out with the death of George Chaworth in 1805, and who left an only daughter, the "Mary Chaworth" referred to by Lord Byron in the well-known lines:—

> "Herself the solitary scion left
> Of a time honoured race."

She married Mr. John Musters, when the name of Chaworth Musters was adopted. Their descendants are still in possession of the Annesley and Wiverton estates, the present representative being Mr. John Patricius Chaworth Musters, Annesley, Notts.

1029. **EDWARD BRABAZON, 4TH EARL OF MEATH,** was one of the peers attainted in James' Dublin Parliament.

He raised a regiment in support of King William, was present at the Boyne, and through the subsequent campaign down to the fall of Limerick, where he was wounded.

1030. **JAMES BRABAZON,** probably a cadet of this family, was an officer of the Derry garrison or county contingents operating there previous to the investment.

His name figures among the signatories of the "Declaration of Union" made by the officers of the Derry garrison March–April 1689.

The first of the name in Ireland, Sir William Brabazon, was appointed Vice-Treasurer in 1534. His son and successor was created Baron Ardee in 1616, and his grandson Earl of Meath in 1627.

The present representative of this old family is the thirteenth Earl of Meath, Kilruddery House, Bray.[1]

1031. **WILLIAM FITZWILLIAM,** second Baron of Lifford, so described, was attainted in James' Dublin Parliament.

The first Baron's grandfather, Sir William Fitzwilliam, of Milton, Yorkshire, the head of an ancient Anglo-Norman family, was appointed Lord Deputy of Ireland in 1584, holding that office through the troublous times of the Spanish Armada. His son, another William, was created Baron of Lifford in 1620, his son and successor being the second Baron above, who was advanced in 1716 to the higher dignities in the Irish peerage of Viscount Milton, Co. Meath, and Earl Fitzwilliam, Co. Tyrone, the same titles in the peerage of the United Kingdom being conferred on the head of the family in 1748.

The present representative of this old family is the seventh Earl Fitzwilliam, Wentworth Woodhouse, Yorkshire, and Coolattin Park, Co. Wicklow.

1032. **HENRY ROBINSON,** Ballyclegan, Co. Monaghan.

---

[1] For the Brabazon connection with the Chaworth family see Burke's Peerage, also No. 1028, Viscount Chaworth.

1033. **George Robinson**, sen., Co. Monaghan.

1034. **George Robinson**, jun., Co. Monaghan.

1035. **William Robinson**, Co. Monaghan.

1036. **William Robinson**, Co. Monaghan.

1037. **George Robinson**, Co. Fermanagh.

1038. **Henry Robinson**, Co. Fermanagh.

1039. **George Robinson**, Co. Down.

1040. **John Robinson**, Co. Tyrone.

1041. **Mark Robinson**, Co. Cavan.

1042. **Joseph Robinson**, Co. Cavan.

The following of the name, spelt as given below, are among the signatories of the Enniskillen address to King William indicating their participation in the gallant actions:—

1043. **Robert Robison**, of whom Trimble in a note to the name states: "Probably a member of the old family of Robinsons, which held freehold for centuries in Mulleghy near Enniskillen."[1]

1044. **James Robinson**.

1045. **Richard Robinson**. His signature is attached to the Derry address to King William after the relief.

The following, as spelt, are among the signatories of the Corporation of Derry's 1690 Commission:—

1046. **James Robison**.

1047. **Robert Robison**.

1048. **Margaret Robertson**.

1049. **Paul Dane**, Provost of Enniskillen, 1688–89, and his son,

1050. **John Dane**, an officer in the Enniskillen Horse and Provost of Enniskillen in 1690. Both of these men took a prominent part in the preparations of Enniskillen

---

[1] See Trimble's "History of Enniskillen."

to resist the coming attack and in the subsequent action of the men of Enniskillen, and both their signatures are on the Enniskillen address to King William.

Trimble in his interesting "History of Enniskillen" says, "Seven generations of this family have been intimately connected with Enniskillen and Co. Fermanagh during the last 280 years," and gives details of the family and representatives.[1]

The first of the family in Enniskillen was Paul Dane's father, John, of an old Devonshire family, who settled there in 1647 and died in 1678.

1051. **ADAM BETTY**, of Carne, Co. Fermanagh.

1052. **JOHN BETTY**, of Ardverney, Co. Fermanagh.

1053. **ROWLAND BETTY**, of Ardverney, Co. Fermanagh. All three, so described, figure among the attainted in James' Dublin Parliament.

Trimble, in his "History of Enniskillen" Vol. II. p. 514, says the family were long connected with the townland of Ballymillen, Ballinamallard, and that they are now represented by two brothers, Mr. Rowland Betty, of Aughnacloy, and the Very Rev. W. A. Betty, Rector of Clough and Dean of Clogher.

Among the attainted in James' Dublin Parliament of 1689 were three of the name of Bingham, described as below:—

1054. **JOHN BINGHAM**, sen., of Co. Mayo.

1055. **CHARLES BINGHAM**, of Co. Mayo.

1056. **CHARLES BINGHAM**, of Co. Fermanagh.

This John was probably Sir George's second son, of Foxford. Who the second Charles was is not traceable, unless the name is repeated to cover estates in both counties. The first of the two families of Bingham in Ireland was Sir Richard Bingham, second son of the then owner of the family estate of Sutton Bingham, Somersetshire. He was a distinguished officer in Queen Elizabeth's service, holding an important command in Connaught, where he acquired considerable estate. On his death without male issue he was succeeded by his brother, Sir George, as Governor of Sligo. Sir George left two sons, viz.:—

(1) Sir Henry, created a Baronet in 1634, of Castlebar, from whom descend the senior line, Earls of Lucan. (See below.)

(2) John, of Newbrook House, Foxford, Co. Mayo, from whom descend the Barons Clanmorris. (See below.)

---

[1] See Vol. II. pp. 300–306.

The Lucan line.

The seventh Baronet, Sir Charles, of Castlebar, was created Baron Lucan of Castlebar in 1776 and Earl of Lucan in 1795. It is interesting to note that the Lucan title originally conferred by James II. on Patrick Sarsfield, which died with him on the field of Landen, was revived in the Bingham family, who through the marriage of Sir John, the fifth Baronet, with the granddaughter and heiress of William Sarsfield of Lucan (eldest brother of the famous Patrick, Earl of Lucan) became representatives of the Sarsfields of Lucan in the female line.

The third Earl of Lucan was the famous Field-Marshal whose name will ever be connected with the Crimean campaign and the charge of the Light Cavalry Brigade led by his brother-in-law the Earl of Cardigan. A mistake may have been made, but the episode in itself ranks as one of the most glorious in the annals of the British army.

The present holder of the title is the fifth Earl of Lucan and eleventh Baronet of Castlebar House, Co. Mayo.[1]

The Clanmorris line.

The descendant of John of Foxford, mentioned above, was in 1800 created Baron Clanmorris, the 5th Baron in 1878 marrying Matilda Catherine (now the Dowager Lady Clanmorris), daughter and heiress of Robert E. Ward, of Bangor Castle, Co. Down. Among the issue of this marriage are

(1) Arthur Maurice Robert, who succeeded his father in 1916 as 6th Baron Clanmorris, Newbrook House, Ballyglass, Co. Mayo.
(2) Capt. Edward Barry Stewart Bingham, R.N., V.C., who received the coveted cross for gallantry in the torpedo flotilla attack on the German Battle Fleet at Jutland.

The Ward family, Viscounts Bangor of Castleward, Co. Down, and the Ward family, of Bangor Castle, Co. Down.

Sir Thomas Ward, of an old Cheshire stock, the first of the family in Co. Down, was Surveyor-General of Ireland in 1570. He bought the Castleward estate (then Carrick-na-Shannagh) from the Earl of Kildare, where the main line has been in residence ever since. His great grandson,

1057. **BERNARD WARD**, who was among the attainted in James' Dublin Parliament, was the possessor of the estate at the time of the 1688 revolution. He was succeeded

---

[1] See Part II, No. 200, Patrick Sarsfield, Earl of Lucan, 1st creation by James II.

by his son Michael, who by his marriage with Anne, daughter and heiress of James Hamilton, of Bangor, brought that estate into the Ward family. Their son and successor, Bernard, of Castleward and Bangor, was created a Baron in 1770 and Viscount Bangor in 1781. He left three sons:—

(1) Nicholas, the second Viscount, d.s.p.
(2) Edward, whose son Edward Southwell succeeded as third Viscount on his uncle's death. (See main line of Viscounts Bangor below.)
(3) Col. the Rt. Hon. Robert Ward, who, under a family arrangement, became owner of the old Hamilton property of Bangor Castle.

Among the attainted in James' Dublin Parliament there were five other Wards, all probably of this family, described as below:—

1058. **John Ward**, of Castleward, Co. Down.

1059. **Charles Ward**, of Killyleagh, Co. Down.

1060. **Bernard Ward**, of Co. Fermanagh.

1061. **Capt. Bernard Ward**, of Carrick, Co. Monaghan.

1062. **Bryan Ward**, of Co. Monaghan.
The Wards of Castleward, Co. Down, are now represented by Maxwell Richard Crosbie, 6th Viscount Bangor, Castleward, Co. Down.

Among the attainted in James' Dublin Parliament were several Richardsons, described as below:—

1063. **William Richardson**, of Londonderry, who at the time of the revolution was the managing agent of the Merchant Taylors' estate near Coleraine, Co. Londonderry. In 1726 he purchased the estate of Summer Seat, afterwards called Somerset, of which his descendants were in possession until recently.[1]

1064. **Henry Richardson**, of Co. Monaghan, of an old Norfolk stock, whose family settled in that county in Elizabeth's reign, acquiring the Poplar Vale demesne and estate from Charles II. in 1667.

Henry Richardson served as High Sheriff of the county, as so many members of the family have done in subsequent generations.

1065. **Alexander Richardson**, of Co. Tyrone.

1066. **Archibald Richardson**, of Co. Tyrone.

---

[1] See No. 834, John Torrens.

1067. **WILLIAM RICHARDSON**, of Co. Tyrone. Whether these attainted individuals were members of the Poplar Vale family, the well-known family of Rossfad, Co. Tyrone, or of other connection, I have no means of ascertaining.

1068. **JOHN STEINSON**, described as of Co. Down, figures among the attainted in James' Dublin Parliament. He may be the same as

1069. **JOHN STINSOME** (*sic*), whose name is among the signatories of the Corporation of Derry's 1690 Commission, where he was probably a refugee.

1070. **WILLIAM BRETT**, described as of Co. Down, is among the attainted in James' Dublin Parliament,[1] and two of his sons (according to the generally accurate authority Hill in his notes to Montgomery Manuscripts) viz.:—

1071. **JASPER BRETT.**

1072. **BERNARD BRETT.** Both attainted.

An interesting paragraph in "The Roamer"[2] gives details of the family history to which the reader is referred. The Brett family were originally settled in Lecale, where William Brett (above) owned considerable property, being High Sheriff of the county in 1679. It was not until the latter part of the 18th century that the family came to Belfast, where for several generations they have taken an active part in public affairs, the most prominent being the late Sir Charles Brett.

The present representative of the family is Mr. Alfred Brett, Richmond Lodge.

1073. **REV. CHARLES LESLIE**, of Donegal or Londonderry, so described, was among the attainted in James' Dublin Parliament.

This remarkable man was Chancellor of Connor, the son of John Leslie, of the old house of Wardis, N.B., consecrated Bishop of Clogher in 1661. On the Bishop's death in 1672 he was succeeded in the Glasslough estate by his son, the Rev. Charles Leslie of the revolution. His name figures in the literature of that period as the champion of James' inalienable title to the Throne, the Divine Right of Kings, &c. On his refusal to take the oath of allegiance to King William and Mary he was deprived of all Church preferments and became a leader among the few Episcopalian non-jurors. So far did he carry out his principles that he is stated to have repaired to St. Germains on a mission to convert the Royal James to Protestantism. (His reception can be imagined.)[3] He died at Glasslough in 1722.

Since his time the succession has passed through several generations of Leslies, and a baronetcy was conferred in 1876, the present representative of the family being the second Baronet, Sir John Leslie, C.B.E., Glasslough, Co. Monaghan.

---

[1] Harris.
[2] *Belfast Newsletter*, March 1st, 1930.
[3] Hill's notes to the Montgomery Manuscripts, p. 275.

1074. **REV. DAVID HOUSTON.** Just as the Rev. Charles Leslie of the previous sketch was remarkable as an Episcopalian non-juror, so does David Houston figure as the typical non-juror of the old Covenanting spirit of Presbyterian Scotland.

He had come over to Ulster at the beginning of the revolution and soon made himself troublesome by his extreme views. He too refused to take the oath of allegiance to King William and Mary, on very different grounds, because, forsooth, they had placed themselves at the head of the Episcopal Church of England, which was little better than the Church of Rome.

The following additional Leslie names figure among the attainted in James' Dublin Parliament, all probably of the family of Henry Leslie, Bishop of Down in 1635, or connections through the Ballybay or Glasslough lines, as clerical preferment ran in these families:—

1075. **REV. DR. JOHN LESLIE**, of Co. Fermanagh.

1076. **REV. DR. JOHN LESLIE**, of Co. Leitrim. These two attaintures may be for the same man in order to include estates in each county.

1077. **JOHN LESLIE**, of Co. Tyrone. This must be the John Leslie, son of the rector of Urney, Co. Tyrone, who fell charging at the head of his father's troop of cavalry at the battle of Aughrim.[1]

1078. **WILLIAM LESLIE**, of Co. Monaghan.

Ulster Bishops of the Church of Ireland attainted in James' Dublin Parliament of 1689 were:—

1079. **WILLIAM SMITH**, Bishop of Raphoe.

1080. **CAPELL WISEMAN**, Bishop of Dromore.

EZEKIEL HOPKINS, Bishop of Derry, already referred to. (See No. 21.)

Regarding the occupants of the other sees, the Bishopric of Clogher was vacant. The Archbishopric of Armagh and Primacy of Ireland was occupied by the Rev. Dr. Michael Boyle, who, although summoned, does not seem to have attended the meeting of Parliament.

The see of Down and Connor was occupied by

1081. **RT. REV. THOMAS HACKETT**, who made himself so conspicuous by preferring Hammersmith as a residence to that of his diocese that he earned the sobriquet of Bishop of Hammersmith.

Although summoned he did not attend Parliament. He was not attainted. After the revolution he was deprived as an absentee.

---

[1] See Graham's notes to his Catalogue in "Ireland Preserved."

The Gardners or Gardiners.

Of this family, so prominent in Derry and in the neighbouring counties, of which Mr. William Gardner was Mayor of the city in 1662,[1] we have only the following siege and revolution mentions:—

1082. **HENRY GARDNER**, described as of Co. Antrim.

1083. **HENRY GARDNER**, described as of Co. Down, figure among the attainted in James' Dublin Parliament.

1084. **ALEX GARDNER** and

1085. **WILLIAM K. GARDINER** are both among the signatories of the Corporation of Derry's 1690 Commission.

In Ash's "Diary of the Siege" we have the following record under date May 27th, 1689, which would have been all the more interesting had names been given: "My sister Gardner got a pass to go to her husband from General Baker" (the Governor), and that he (Ash) conveyed her outside the lines.

Admiral Gardner was created Baron Gardner in 1800, the title becoming extinct in 1883.

In 1662 William Gardner was Mayor of Derry, in which the family were for many generations of considerable importance.

1086. **REV. EZEKIEL WEBB**, Incumbent of Enniskillen. His name figures among the attainted in James' Dublin Parliament.[2]

1087. **JONATHAN POWELL**, of Londonderry, so described, is among the attainted in James' Dublin Parliament.

1088. **MARGARET POWELL** is among the signatories of the Corporation of Derry's 1690 Commission.

The Conollys of Castletown.

1089. **PATRICK CONOLLY**, of Ballyshannon, Co. Donegal, was attainted in James' Dublin Parliament, 1689. This is the only mention of the name in records of the 1688–89 revolution, but the family figures so largely in Irish affairs of the 18th century as to deserve more than a passing notice.

His son William, so well known as the Rt. Hon. William Conolly, Speaker of the Irish House of Commons, commenced his successful career as attorney to the Duke

---

[1] See Mrs. Young's "Three Hundred Years in Innishowen."
[2] See Trimble's "History of Enniskillen."

of Ormonde, becoming Chief Commissioner of the Irish Revenue. He acquired a huge fortune, with estates in no fewer than thirteen Irish counties. By his marriage with Catherine, daughter of Sir Albert Conyngham (ancestor of the Marquesses Conyngham), he became owner of property in Co. Donegal, where his successors in future generations were among the largest landowners and exercised much political influence. In 1691 he bought from George Phillips the large manor of Limavady, Co. Derry, with its borough returning two members of Parliament. Of this borough, which adopted the Conolly coat of arms as their corporate seal, he served as both M.P. and Provost. During his Speakership the magnificent Parliament House in Dublin was begun, and there is reason to believe that he was responsible for the selection of Sir Edward Lovett Pearce as the architect, the more so as his own great mansion of Castletown, completed a few years earlier, is generally ascribed to the same genius. The Speaker died in 1729, his estate passing to his widow for life and then to his nephew William, son of his favourite brother Patrick.

This William, later another Rt. Hon. William Conolly, P.C., occupied nearly as commanding a position in Irish affairs as the Speaker had done. In fact for a few generations the Castletown family were a great force in Ireland. On the death of the Rt. Hon. Thomas Conolly, P.C., in 1808 the male line became extinct, the estates passing through the female line to a grand-nephew, Edward Michael Pakenham (of the Earl of Longford's family), who assumed the Conolly surname, becoming Edward Michael Conolly, of Castletown. He died in 1848, leaving among other issue:—

(1) Thomas, his successor at Castletown.
(2) Capt. Arthur Wellesly Conolly, killed at Inkermann.
(3) Col. John Augustus Conolly, V.C., Coldstream Guards, who was one of the first recipients of the Victoria Cross in the Crimea.

Thomas Conolly of Castletown, usually known as "Tom," found himself on his succession (1848) in possession of large estates, which he had to part with to meet his lavish expenditure. He was M.P. for Co. Donegal, where his reckless daring and love of adventure made him the idol of a sport-loving people. Many stories are still current of his remarkable doings, one of which is worth repeating, although I cannot vouch for every detail. At the time of the great American Civil War (1863–1866), pressed for money on his heavily mortgaged estates, he determined on a bold venture. Buying a large vessel and filling her with an expensive cargo, he attempted to run the blockade into the southern port of Charleston. Intercepted by cruisers of the Northern States and his ship sunk, he found himself cast adrift on an unknown coast and without resources. Nothing daunted, he served his passage home on a sailing vessel as an ordinary sailor before the mast. On the voyage to England the ship chanced to pass very close to the coast of Co. Donegal. Without hesitation Conolly plunged into the sea and swam ashore. A general election was in progress, he had himself nominated, and a few days later he was again returned M.P. for Co. Donegal by an admiring people. Of this Tom Conolly an interesting story has been told me by the present head of the family. He was an intimate friend of Napoleon III., who used to refer to him as "mon ami intime." About the year 1868 Tom Conolly was well known in Paris for both his coach and riding horses. In fact his coach and equipage were second to none. This resulted in a friendly competition between the Emperor and himself one summer day in the Bois de Boulogne. The judges, it is said, did not like to award the prize to Tom without ascertaining from both competitors that no detail had escaped their notice. Napoleon, having pointed out the plaiting of his horses' manes and the turn-out of his grooms, Tom merely drew their attention to the fact that his horses were shod in silver. "Tom" had the verdict of the judges. The chief of the Paris police subsequently called on him to reduce "the splendour of his equipage." On his death he was succeeded by his eldest son Thomas, Major Scots Greys, who was killed in South Africa in 1900, when the succession devolved on his next surviving brother, Major Edward Michael Conolly, of Castletown, the present representative.

The Hamiltons of Abercorn, Earls of Abercorn.

Cadets of their line, and others of the Hamilton name, associated with events of the 1688–89 revolution and the siege of Derry.

In the 1688–89 revolution, particularly in the struggle round Derry, no family was more prominent than the Hamiltons of Abercorn, their numerous cadets, and many of the name claiming connection with the same Scottish origin. Civil war is a great divider of families, and the Abercorn family were no exception. While the fourth Earl of Abercorn, from close attendance on James II. and hereditary attachment to the Stuart dynasty, was a staunch supporter of his legitimate Sovereign, the large majority of the house, cadets, connections and tenantry in Ulster, were as strong in support of William of Orange. In this course they saw the only hope of maintaining the Protestant succession to the Crown and saving their estates from the threatened restoration to the descendants of the old Celtic and Roman Catholic owners of the land.

In order to explain the position a short outline of the history of the Abercorn family and their establishment in Ulster is necessary. In the centuries that evolved from the day of Bannockburn (1313) when Sir Walter Hamilton had stood by Robert the Bruce's side, the family had ranked among the nobility of Scotland. Allied with the Blood Royal, they had become Earls of Arran and Dukes of Hamilton. The second Earl of Arran was Regent of Scotland during the long minority of Queen Mary, and was, as next in blood, declared by Act of Parliament heir to the Throne in case of the Queen's death without issue. This Earl of Arran was created Duke of Châterault by the French King in 1549, when Ambassador of Scotland at the Court of France. On his death in 1575 he was succeeded in turn by his two elder sons, the son and successor of the last being in 1643 created Duke of Hamilton, from whom through the female line (under special remainder) descends the present Duke.

Claude Hamilton, the fourth son of the second Earl of Arran (above) espoused the cause of the unhappy Mary Queen of Scots after her escape from Lochleven. He commanded a wing of her army at Langside, and, after the defeat, was one of the chivalrous few who accompanied Her Majesty in her flight to the English border. "Put to the horn" at the Cross of Edinburgh and his estates confiscated, Claude remained for some years an outlaw in exile. Although James VI. allowed his mother, Mary Queen of Scots, to go to the scaffold at Fotheringay, without raising every spear in Scotland, he took into favour and restored to his estates this Claude Hamilton, whom in 1583 he created Baron Paisley. His son the second Baron Paisley was in 1603 created Baron of Abercorn; and in 1606 Earl in the peerage of Scotland. When the Ulster Plantation took place (1608–11) this Earl of Abercorn was the recipient of large grants of land in Cos. Tyrone and Donegal. While the Earl spent most of his time on his Scottish estates, the Irish were managed by cadets of his family. Pynnar, in his survey (1618) of the Ulster Plantation, reports that the Earl of Abercorn had made good progress on his estates, having erected a castle at Strabane, and some 80 houses with many Scottish tenants thereon, and at Dunnalong some houses and Scottish tenants planted.

The second Earl of Abercorn died in 1638, but in 1634, with the sanction of the Crown, he had granted his Ulster estates and transferred the Barony of Strabane (Irish Peerage) conferred on him that year to his brother Claude. The third Earl of Abercorn, who lived on his Scottish estates or abroad, died at Padua in 1683, when his heir (the grandson of Claude, first Baron), fourth Baron Strabane, succeeded as fourth Earl of Abercorn, thus again uniting the estates in Scotland and Ireland.[1]

On the death of the fifth Earl in 1701 he was succeeded by his cousin, Capt. James Hamilton, as sixth Earl of Abercorn, the direct ancestor of the Duke of Abercorn. This Capt. James was the grandson and heir of Sir George Hamilton, Bart., of Dunnalong, the fourth son of the first Earl of Abercorn. Capt. James' father, Col. James Hamilton, had been killed in a naval action against the Dutch in 1673 and was buried in Westminster Abbey.

The sixth Earl, with his successors the seventh, eighth and ninth Earls of Abercorn, had comparatively quiet times to look after and consolidate their large estates. During this period the old castle of Strabane had gone to ruin, and the stately house of Baronscourt with its wide demesne had become the family home, as it is to-day.

The ninth Earl, who succeeded in 1789, was raised to a Marquessate in 1790. His son, the tenth Earl and second Marquess, was created in 1868 Duke of Abercorn. This first Duke of Abercorn was twice Lord-Lieutenant of Ireland (1866–68 and 1874–76), and no Viceroy by commanding presence and splendid hospitality has ever so enhanced

---

[1] For this fourth Earl of Abercorn, and his brother Charles, who succeeded as fifth Earl in 1690, see Part II, where sketches of the Hamiltons of Abercorn, supporters of the Jacobite cause, are given.

the dignity of the Viceregal Court. His son and successor, the eleventh Earl and second Duke, following his father's example, took a prominent part in the public affairs of the United Kingdom, particularly in Ulster, where his memorable words of 1892: "We will not have Home Rule," will never be forgotten. Of his son, the twelfth Earl and third Duke of Abercorn, now for the second time Governor of Northern Ireland, his actions, in accordance with the traditions of his house, have endeared him to the kindred people whom he governs, while his Duchess by her geniality and genuine interest in the welfare of the community at large has won all hearts, wherever she goes. Through the Duchess (*née* Lady Rosalind Cecilia Bingham, only daughter of the fourth Earl of Lucan) there is a link connecting her with Patrick Sarsfield, one of James II.'s most gallant Generals in the long campaign from the Boyne to the capitulation of Limerick, when he went into voluntary exile with a large section of the Irish troops he had commanded. He had been created Earl of Lucan by James II., and under that name had acquired still greater renown in command of troops in the Irish Brigade in the service of France. Falling at the bloody Battle of Landen in Flanders a few years later, his death was mourned by friend and foe, everyone recognising his gallant and chivalrous qualities. On Patrick Sarsfield's death the Lucan property (from which he took the title) remained in a brother's hands. A few generations later a Sarsfield daughter and heiress intermarried with the head of the Bingham family, and when ennobled the Binghams of the day not unnaturally revived a title of such romance and lustre, in the Barony (1776) and Earldom (1795) of Lucan. The present holder of the title is the Duchess' brother, the fifth Earl of Lucan.

There is no better index to the number of the Hamilton name prominent in support of William of Orange than the list of attainted in James' Dublin Parliament of May 1689. In this there are thirty-eight Ulster Hamiltons. In the following Nos. 1090 to 1132, all these names, besides many others who were not on the attainted list but served in the defence of Derry, are given, while, where obtainable, their family origin, &c., is appended.

1090. **JAMES HAMILTON**, defender, attainted. He was the eldest son of Col. James Hamilton, killed in a naval action against the Dutch in 1673, who was eldest son and heir of Sir George Hamilton, of Dunnalong. On Sir George's death in 1679, for some reason he did not assume the baronetcy. In 1701 he succeeded to the family honours as sixth Earl of Abercorn (see preceding family history and peerage).

Capt. James Hamilton arrived in Derry on 21st March, 1689, on a special mission from King William, bringing with him the much-needed supply of arms, powder and money, a commission for Col. Lundy, approval of what had been done and promises of further support. He threw himself with ardour into all the city's preparations for defence, and no man rendered more efficient service during the long siege.

1091. **GEORGE HAMILTON**, younger brother of the above, was present in all the actions preliminary to the investment. He was attainted. He served all through the subsequent campaign, and afterwards in Flanders, where he was killed at the battle of Steinkirk (1692).

1092. **Col. Gustavus Hamilton**, of Monea Castle, was the grandson of Archibald Hamilton, of Cuchonaught, N.B., a distinguished branch of the family. He had earned military experience in the service of Gustavus of Sweden.

He was the Governor of Enniskillen in its historic defence, and took a prominent part in the subsequent actions round the town in command of the Enniskilleners. He died in 1690, leaving a widow in poor circumstances. He was attainted and a signatory of the Enniskillen address to King William.

1093. **Col. Gustavus Hamilton**, son of Sir Frederick Hamilton, of Manor Hamilton, Co. Leitrim (a son of the first Baron Paisley and brother of the first Earl of Abercorn).

He took part in all the actions round Derry preliminary to the investment, when he retired to Enniskillen. There he did splendid service culminating in Newtownbutler. He served at the head of his Enniskilleners at the Boyne and down to the fall of Limerick. He was created a viscount in 1717, selecting for his title the famous river Boyne. His descendant and representative is the ninth Viscount Boyne. His name figures among those attainted.

1094. **Rev. James Hamilton**, Archdeacon of Raphoe, of Mongivlen Castle, near Derry. On King James' approach to the city, the Archdeacon (probably at the instance of his relative the Earl of Abercorn) offered His Majesty the hospitality of his castle. Being a Hamilton and having relations in both camps, he was induced by His Majesty to visit the beleaguered town with the object of inducing surrender. Although the negotiations failed in their object, they have given his name a place in history. His name is on the list of attainted.

1095. **Rev. Andrew Hamilton**, Rector of Kilskerrie, was one of the most prominent of the Enniskillen fighting men, whose actions he so graphically describes in the standard authority, "The Actions of the Inniskilling Men." His name is among the attainted, and he was a signatory of the Enniskillen address to King William.

1096. **Sir Frederick (Francis) Hamilton**, 3rd Baronet (of Enderwick, N.B.), of Castle Hamilton, Co. Cavan, where his family were Plantation grantees, and his son,

1097. **Francis Hamilton**, raised a regiment which they brought to the assistance of Derry.

Both were attainted, taking part in actions preliminary to the investment, while the son with most of the men remained in the city throughout the defence.

1098. John Hamilton, of Murvagh, who removed to Brown Hall, Co. Donegal, in 1697, where his descendants still reside, took a conspicuous part in the defence of Derry, and was attainted.

His family have since held a prominent position in the county, their present representative being Capt. John Hamilton, of Brown Hall, Ballintra, Co. Donegal.

1099. James Hamilton, a leading merchant of Strabane, who played a leading part in the preliminary actions round Derry and in the actual defence. Before the investment he was sent by the Derry authorities to Scotland to get powder and supplies, a mission he executed satisfactorily.

He is probably the James Hamilton who signed the "Declaration of Union" on 21st March. He was one of the attainted, and a signatory of the Derry address. On the minutes of the Irish Society, after the relief, there is a resolution absolving him of all arrears as a small recognition of the services he had rendered during the siege.

1100. William Hamilton, of Ballyfatton, Co. Tyrone, defender, in preliminaries and all through the siege, holding a commission in Col. Monro's Regiment. "Londeriados" has the following reference in his description of one of the sorties from the city:—

> "Brave Ballyfatton fell briskly on their flank
> And with his men overthrew both file and rank."

He was one of the attainted. His brothers James, Charles, Archibald and Patrick[1] are in all likelihood the following attainted in 1689, viz.:—

1101. Capt. James Hamilton, defender, of Derry, and described in list of attainted as James Hamilton, of Co. Tyrone.

1102. Patrick Hamilton, described as of Dergal, Co. Tyrone, was one of the attainted. Probably a Derry defender.

1103. Capt. Archibald Hamilton, defender, and attainted. His name is frequently mentioned by annalists of the siege for gallantry in the numerous sorties. He rose in the subsequent campaign to the rank of Lieut.-Colonel in Lord Mountjoy's Regiment. The first Hamilton of this family was the grandfather of William Hamilton of No. 1100. He, another William, of Priestfield, N.B., came to Ulster in 1617 and in 1634 obtained a lease of the lands of Ballyfatton from Lord Strabane. The present representatives of this old family are: (1) The mainline of Ballyfatton, now residing on their estate of Mossvill, Glenties, Co. Donegal, and (2) the Hamiltons of Castle Hamilton, Co. Cavan, who are descended from Galbraith, the sixth son of a Hamilton of Ballyfatton.[2]

---

[1] See Burke's "Landed Gentry of Ireland" (1904 edition).
[2] For further particulars of Hamiltons of Ballyfatton see under families of Hamilton of Mossvill and

1104. There remains the last brother of William Hamilton of Ballyfatton, viz. CHARLES HAMILTON, described in the list of attainted as of Co. Tyrone, of whom there is no other mention. It is presumed that he was a defender of Derry.

There are, in addition, the following of the name attainted in Co. Tyrone, of whom no further particulars are available, viz.:—

1105. **ROBERT HAMILTON**, of Co. Tyrone (Killeloony), attainted.

1106. **PATRICK HAMILTON**, of Co. Tyrone, attainted.

1107. **ROBERT HAMILTON**, of Co. Tyrone (Carrowbeg), attainted.

1108. **JOHN HAMILTON**, of Co. Tyrone (Caledon), attainted.

1109. **MARGARET HAMILTON** (widow), of Co. Tyrone, attainted.

There were three Hamiltons of Co. Antrim among the attainted, but their connection with the main line cannot be traced, viz.:—

1110. **JAMES HAMILTON**, Cloughmills, Co. Antrim.

1111. **WILLIAM HAMILTON**, Cloughmills, Co. Antrim.

1112. **CAPT. JOHN HAMILTON**, Cloughmills, Co. Antrim.

The Hamiltons of Co. Down on list of attainted 1689.

Before giving the names a few words are necessary as to their origin, their coming to Ulster, and their prominence at the time of the 1688–89 revolution.

James Hamilton (subsequently created a Baronet and Viscount Clandeboy) was *persona grata* at the Court of King James I. of England. He was the son of the Rev. Hans Hamilton, minister of Dunlop, N.B., of the same stock as the Hamiltons of Abercorn. With his friend Montgomery (afterwards Viscount Montgomery of Ards) he managed to secure from O'Neill of South Clannaboy three-quarters of his territory. The transaction was sanctioned by the Crown.[1] Hamilton's possession was the large estate centring round the Castle of Killyleagh, which became the family residence.

On the first Viscount's death he was succeeded by his son, raised to the higher honour of Earl of Clanbrassil. This Earl died a few years previous to the revolution, leaving his widowed Countess and children in possession of the estate, the titles becoming extinct.

At the time of the revolution the Hamiltons were all prominent members of the

---

Castle Hamilton in Burke's "Landed Gentry of Ireland" (1904 edition).

[1] See Hamilton and Montgomery Manuscripts.

Co. Down Association, and raised their tenantry to meet the Jacobite troops on their way to Derry. After the Break of Dromore they had to retire across the Channel.

The four brothers mentioned above were the progenitors of the following on the attainted list:—

1113. **James Hamilton**, of Bangor, attainted, a grand-nephew of the first Viscount Clandeboy. He is represented through the female line by the present Viscount Bangor, of Castle Ward.

1114. **James Hamilton**, of Tullymore, Co. Down, attainted, also a grand-nephew of the first Viscount Clandeboye. Represented in the female line by the present Earl of Roden.

1115. **Gawen Hamilton**, of Lisivine, Co. Down, ancestor of the Hamiltons of Killyleagh Castle and the Marquess of Dufferin, of whom presently.

1116. **William Hamilton**, of Co. Down.

1117. **Patrick Hamilton**, of Granskeogh, Co. Down.

1118. **John Hamilton**, of Erinagh, Co. Down.

1119. **James Hamilton**, of Carricknasure, Co. Down.

1120. **Robert Hamilton**, of Co. Down.

1121. **Robert Hamilton**, of Co. Down.

The Hamiltons of Killyleagh Castle, and the Marquesses of Dufferin and Ava.

According to Burke's Peerage the Hamiltons of Killyleagh Castle, represented by the late Col. Gawen Rowan Hamilton, were the senior male representatives of this old family, while the Marquess of Dufferin and Ava was the senior heir-general of the Hamiltons Earls of Clanbrassil. The close relationship and friendship between these two houses is well known, Harriet, the Dowager Marchioness, widow of the first Marquess of Dufferin, being a sister of the late Col. Rowan Hamilton.

The old Castle of Killyleagh with its picturesque courtyard and ancient walls was still further beautified by a barbican gate standing at the head of Killyleagh Street, erected and presented by the first Marquess of Dufferin to his brother-in-law as a wedding gift.

The present owner of Killyleagh Castle and representative of the family is the late Col. Rowan Hamilton's granddaughter, Miss Hamilton of Killyleagh Castle. Her father, Archibald, was killed in the Great War.

In Co. Fermanagh the following of the name were attainted:—

1122. **Archibald Hamilton**, Co. Fermanagh.

1123. **James Hamilton**, Co. Fermanagh.

In Co. Cavan there were the following, also attainted:—

1124. **Henry Hamilton**, Co. Cavan.

1125. **James Hamilton**, Co. Cavan.

In the city of Derry itself two of the most prominent Burgesses were among the gallant defenders, viz.:—

1126. **Andrew Hamilton** of Londonderry.

1127. **Charles Hamilton.** Both were on the list of attainted.

On the address to King William from the city there were five signatories of the name, viz.: Andrew, of No. 1126, and

1128. **William Hamilton**, of Londonderry.

1129. **John Hamilton.**

1130. **John Hamilton.**

1131. **Arthur Hamilton**, of Londonderry.

No family occupied a more important position in the city at the time of the revolution or in the 18th century, John Hamilton being one of the Sheriffs 1742–43, William Hamilton one of the Sheriffs 1745, 1750–51, and Mayor in 1758.

It may interest Northern Ireland to know that Ronald McNeill, Lord Cushendun of Cushendun, had a double connection with the defenders of Derry, his great great-grandfather, Neill McNeill, of Cushendun, having married Christian Hamilton, of Londonderry, while his great-grandfather, Edmund, married his first cousin Elizabeth, daughter of John Hamilton, of Londonderry.

In the above Nos. 1090 to 1131 I have given all the Hamilton names attainted in 1689 or connected with the defence of Derry. There remains one other name, prominent at the Boyne and subsequent campaign down to the fall of Limerick, viz.:—

1132. **Lord George Hamilton** (or Douglas), fifth son of Lord William Douglas (created Duke of Hamilton for life) by his wife Anne, Duchess of Hamilton, through whom under special patent the honours of the ducal house of Hamilton descend.[1]

---

[1] See Burke's Peerage.

[It should be noted in this connection, that through the passing of the Hamilton dukedom to the Douglas Hamilton line the lineal male representation of that ancient stock with the French dukedom (1549) of Châterault became vested in the Hamiltons of Abercorn.]

Appointed colonel of one of the famous Enniskillen regiments in 1691, and serving with distinction in the subsequent campaign and in Flanders, he was in 1697 created Earl of Orkney, a title still borne by his descendant the seventh Earl of Orkney.

1133. CAPT. the HON. CHIDLEY COOTE, son of the Earl of Mountrath.[1]

When the Protestants of Sligo appointed Lord Kingston in the spring of 1689 to command their levies, Captain Coote was nominated second in command. After the disbandment of this force in March of the same year, Capt. Coote was most useful to the Enniskilleners in their preparations for defence.[2]

His name is on the list of attainted as of Co. Carlow. There were two others of the name, probably of the same family, on the list of the attainted, viz.:—

1134. CAPT. THOMAS COOTE, of Co. Monaghan.

1135. THOMAS COOTE, of Co. Cavan.

In the following Nos. 1136 to 1256 will be found the rest of the names on the list of attainted not already dealt with in previous sketches in the counties of Donegal or Londonderry, Tyrone, Antrim and Down, who, it is presumed, if not refugees across the Channel, had taken refuge before the investment in Derry, where they had shared in the defence. Where any other information is available it is appended.

1136. EDWARD CLIFFORD, Co. Donegal.

1137. THOMAS COACH, Co. Donegal.

1138. JOHN CRAWFORD, Donegal, Londonderry.

1139. WILLIAM CRAWFORD, Donegal, Londonderry.

1140. WILLIAM DENNY, Londonderry.

1141. FRANCIS EARLS, Ballyshannon, Londonderry.

1142. CAPT. NICHOLAS EDWARDS, Kilrea, Co. Derry. Probably a member of the old Ulster Plantation family of that name.

1143. WILLIAM FARRARD, Donegal, Londonderry.

---

[1] See *ibid.*
[2] See Trimble's "History of Enniskillen."

1144. **Rev. John Forker**, Co. Donegal.

1145. **John Gage**, Magilligan, Londonderry. The then representative of that family of Magilligan or Bellarena, Co. Derry, still in the possession of their descendant in the female line, Sir Frederick Heygate, Bart., D.L., Bellarena, Co. Derry.

1146. **James Gillespie**, Londonderry.

1147. **Thomas Glascow**, Donegal.

1148. **William Heardman**, Londonderry.

1149. **John Hueson**, Ballyshannon, Donegal.

1150. **Michael Hueson**, Ballyshannon, Donegal. The family name to-day is spelt Hewson, and is still represented by that well-known name.

1151. **Patrick Jordan**, Castleroe, Donegal.

1152. **John Kingsmill**, Donegal.

1153. **Capt. William Leathem**, Donegal, Londonderry. Grandson of William Leathem, a former Recorder of Derry.

1154. **Capt. Mathew McLornane**, Donegal or Derry.

1155. **Daniel Madden**, Londonderry.

1156. **Randall Moore**, Donegal or Derry.

1157. **John Orr**, Letterkenny, Donegal.

1158. **James Orr**, Letterkenny, Donegal.

1159. **Nicholas Parmetter**, Killygordon, Donegal.

1160. **Henry Paton**, Ramelton, Donegal.

1161. **Capt. John Quelsh (Welsh)**, Donegal.

1162. **Capt. James Rea (Wray?)**, Donegal.

1163. **Capt. Hugh Reney (Rainey?)**, Londonderry.

1164. **David Rossal**, Londonderry.

1165. **Patrick Spence**, Donegal or Londonderry.

1166. **Tristram Sweetman**, Burt, Donegal or Londonderry.

1167. **George Sweetman**, Burt, Donegal or Londonderry.

1168. **Ralph Trueman**, Londonderry.

1169. **Meredith Workman**, Londonderry.

1170. **Mathew Baldington**, Donegal or Londonderry.

1171. **Basil Benson**, Donegal or Londonderry. The family were small landed proprietors in the neighbourhood of Culdaff, Co. Donegal.[1]

1172. **Quartermaster Blackwell**, Donegal or Londonderry.

1173. **William Brice**, Letterkenny, Donegal.

1174. **George Byers**, Londonderry or Donegal.

1175. **John Ayerly**, Manor Rod, Tyrone.

1176. **John Burley (Burleigh)**, Tyrone.

1177. **John Burney (Byrney?)**, Tyrone.

1178. **Robert Carton**, Tyrone.

1179. **John Christall**, Tyrone.

1180. **Thomas Colson**, Tyrone.

1181. **John Cornwall**, Tyrone.

1182. **Andrew Darragh**, Tyrone.

1183. **Adam Evans**, Tyrone.

1184. **William Garvan**, Tyrone.

1185. **William Goodlet**, Tyrone.

1186. **John Grayson**, Tyrone.

1187. **Henry Grayson**, Tyrone.

1188. **John Hallow**, Tyrone.

---

[1] See Mrs. Robin Young's "Innishowen."

1189. **Simon Harrington**, Tyrone.

1190. **John Hinderton**, Tyrone.

1191. **Samuel Lee**, Tyrone.

1192. **Thomas Leech**, Ballore, Tyrone.

1193. **William Leech**, Ballore, Tyrone.

1194. **Andrew McClenaghan**, Tyrone.

1195. **David McClenaghan**, Tyrone. Probably a relation of the Rev. Michael McClenaghan, Incumbent of Derry (see No. 365) was of this family.

1196. **Rev. John Morris**, Tyrone. Clerk in Holy Orders.

1197. **Joseph Mounteith**, Tyrone.

1198. **Rev. Richard Moss**, Tyrone. Clerk in Holy Orders.

1199. **John Spence**, Tyrone.

1200. **John Speere**, Tyrone.

1201. **John Speere**, Tyrone. Probably father and son.

1202. **William Swan**, Turlough, Tyrone.

1203. **Adam Tate**, Ballygawley, Tyrone.

1204. **John Williams**, Tyrone.

1205. **William Williams** was a signatory of the Derry 1690 Commission indicating participation in the defence.

1206. **Nicolas Bagnall (Bagenal?)**, Newry, Down. This family is represented by the Earl of Kilmorey.

1207. **Thomas Bagnall (Bagenal?)**, Co. Cavan. With the death of the above Nicolas in 1712 the Co. Down family became extinct in the male line. Their ancestor, a distinguished officer in the Elizabethan army, acquired considerable estate in Newry and district during the Tyrone wars.

1208. **Mathew Bates**, Down.

1209. **John Braton**, Co. Tyrone.

1210. **JOHN BROWN**, Co. Down.

1211. **ALEXANDER BROWN**, Co. Down.

1212. **JOHN BOYSE**, Co. Down.

1213. **CHARLES COSSLETT**, Co. Down. One of this family was Charles Cosslett, a Judge in North Carolina.

1214. **HUGH FACELY**, Co. Down.

1215. **CAPT. JOHN FARRER**, Co. Down.

1216. **REV. MICHAEL GIBSON**, Co. Down. Clerk in Holy Orders.

1217. **JOHN GRIFFITH**, Co. Down.

1218. **JOHN HADDOCK**, Co. Down.

1219. **WILLIAM HALBRIDGE**, Co. Down.

1220. **ROGER HALL**, Co. Down. Ancestor of the Halls of Narrow Water, Co. Down, represented by Major Hall, of Narrow Water. (For marriage connection with the old family of Pointz, of Acton Manor, Co. Armagh, see No. 843, Capt. Charles Pointz.)

1221. **THOMAS HARRINGTON**, Co. Down.

1222. **WILLIAM HARRINGTON**, Co. Down.

1223. **MARK HODGES**, Co. Down.

1224. **CORNET JOHN LAW**, Co. Down. An officer in the Earl of Mountalexander's Horse.

1225. **ANTHONY LOCK**, Co. Down.

1226. **JOHN MCNAB**, Co. Down.

1227. **JAMES MOORE**, sen., Co. Down.

1228. **JAMES MOORE**, jun., Co. Down.

1229. **JOHN NORRIS**, Co. Down.

1230. **WILLIAM PALMER**, Co. Down.

1231. **JAMES PALLENT**, Co. Down.

1232. **WILLIAM PRINGLE**, Co. Down.

1233. **WILLIAM REDMOND**, Co. Down.

1234. **JOHN RINGLAND**, Co. Down.

1235. **JOHN SANDERS**, Co. Down.

1236. **JOHN SMART**, Co. Down.

1237. **ROBERT SWIFT**, Co. Down.

1238. **RICHARD TURK**, Co. Down.

1239. **JAMES WADDLE**, Co. Down.

1240. **REV. MUNGO WALKINGHAM**, Down.

1241. **THOMAS WARDLOW**, Down.

1242. **JEAN WARDLAW**, signatory of the Derry 1690 Commission, indicating her presence as refugee during siege.

1243. **RICHARD WARREN**, Co. Down.

1244. **THOMAS WARREN**, Co. Down.

1245. **HENRY WEST**, Co. Down.

1246. **PETER BEAGHAN**, Co. Antrim.

1247. **JOHN BLACK**, Belfast, Co. Antrim.

1248. **ALEXANDER BOYLE**, Co. Antrim.

1249. **HENRY CHADES**, Belfast, Co. Antrim.

1250. **ROBERT CLEYSTON**, Belfast, Co. Antrim.

1251. **QUARTERMASTER THOMAS CRAWFORD**, Belfast, Co. Antrim.

1252. **WILLIAM CRAGG**, Glenarm, Co. Antrim.

1253. **CAPT. WILLIAM EATON**, Dunfane, Co. Antrim.

1254. **ROBERT GIBSON**, Co. Down.

1255. **JAMES MACLURE**, Co. Antrim.

1256. **ROGER WARING**, D.D., Belfast, Co. Antrim.

The following Nos. 1257 to 1507 give the remainder of the names of the attainted in the counties of Fermanagh, Armagh, Monaghan, Cavan and Leitrim not already dealt with in previous sketches. It is presumed that all the attainted of these counties who did not fly across the Channel became refugees in Enniskillen, sharing in the glories of the defence.

For further particulars of the doings of the Enniskillen men and the battles round the town I would refer to Trimble's graphic "History of Enniskillen," from which I have taken much of the information noted in these sketches, especially the townland mentioned with each attainted, the county only being given in Harris' list of attainted.

1257. **JOHN ABERCROMBY**, Drumcroe, Co. Fermanagh. Of an old Plantation family, associated with all the doings of the Enniskillen men.[1]

1258. **REV. JOHN ANDREWS**, Kinohir, Co. Fermanagh, Clerk in Holy Orders, whose signature to the Enniskillen address to King William is in itself proof of association with the defence.

1259. **WILLIAM BARTON,** Roe Island, Co. Fermanagh. Of an old Plantation family.[1]

1260. **WILLIAM BALL**, signatory of Enniskillen address to King William. Of an old Enniskillen Fermanagh family. His father, Henry, was Provost in 1668.

1261. **JOHN BALL**, Co. Armagh, was probably of the same family.

1262. **PATRICK BRIADON**, Derryboy, Co. Fermanagh.

1263. **WILLIAM BRIADON** was a signatory of the Derry 1690 Commission. Probably of the same family.

1264. **THOMAS BIRD (BRID)**, Lissaneskea, Co. Fermanagh. Of an old Plantation stock, active with defenders of Enniskillen.[1]

1265. **JOHN BOARDMAN (BOEREMAN, or BOURMAN)**, Coolebey, Co. Fermanagh. Of an old Enniskillen (Co. Fermanagh) family.[1]

1266. **WILLIAM BYRNEY (BURNEY?)**, signatory of the Enniskillen address to King William. Of an old Enniskillen, Co. Fermanagh, family.[1] See No. 1177, John Burney, Co. Tyrone.

1267. **LIEUT. GEORGE CASHELL**, Co. Fermanagh, an officer in Creighton's Horse, one of the gallant Enniskillen boys and a signatory of the Enniskillen address to King William.

[1] See Trimble.

1268. **William Catlington**, Enniskillen, Co. Fermanagh.

1269. **Alexander Charters**, Co. Fermanagh.

1270. **Thomas Chittie (Chittoge)**, Enniskillen, Co. Fermanagh.

1271. **Capt. Cooper**, Co. Monaghan, is probably the same as

1272. **George Cooper**. Captain in the local Enniskillen forces, and signatory of the Enniskillen address to King William.

1273. **Alexander Cooper**, Co. Monaghan.

1274. **James Cooper**, Co. Monaghan. The family was one of considerable standing in Enniskillen and bordering counties. A William Cooper had been Provost of the town in 1674 and 1677, and many members of the family did their devoir in the revolution.[1]

1275. **Capt. Arnold Cosby**, officer of local horse, Co. Cavan.
He was a member of the family of Lismore, Co. Cavan, and prominent among the Enniskillen men. He was a signatory of the Enniskillen address to King William as was also his relative,

1276. **Edward Cosby**.[1]

1277. **Laurence Crawford**, Cravencarry, Co. Fermanagh.

1278. **James Dundas**, Enniskillen, Co. Fermanagh, a member of a landed family prominent in the town and neighbouring counties.[1]

1279. **Charles Eccles**, Fintona, Co. Tyrone.

1280. **Capt. Samuel Eccles**, Co. Monaghan.

1281. **Samuel Eccles**, Co. Tyrone. These were all members of the same family as

1282. **Daniel Eccles**, who rendered most important service in bringing in express information from Clones at a critical juncture in the preparations of the Enniskillen men.
This Daniel was the son of a Mr. Gilbert Eccles, who, settling in Fermanagh in Charles I.'s reign, had acquired the manors of Shannon and Rathmoran, near Clones, and of Castlelee, near Fintona.
The two other Eccles mentioned, evidently of the same stock, were associated with the actions of the Enniskillen men.[2]

---

[1] See Trimble.
[2] See *ibid.*, Vol. II. pp. 362–365, 495.

1283. **GEORGE ELLIT (ELLIOT?)**, Tully, Co. Fermanagh.

1284. **THOMAS ELLIT (ELLIOTT?)**, Galoone, Co. Fermanagh.

1285. **THOMAS ELLIOTT**, Galoone, Co. Fermanagh. Probably the same as No. 1284.

1286. **ROBERT ELLIOTT**, Storchin, Co. Fermanagh.

1287. **JAMES ELLIOTT**, Storchin, Co. Fermanagh.

1288. **WILLIAM ELLIOTT**, Storaghin, Co. Leitrim.

1289. **THOMAS ELLIS**, Co. Monaghan.

1290. **EDWARD ELLIS**, Enniskillen, Co. Fermanagh.

1291. **AUGUSTUS ELLIS**, Enniskillen, Co. Fermanagh.

1292. **FRANCIS ELLIS**, Enniskillen, Co. Fermanagh, and

1293. **HERCULES ELLIS**, Enniskillen, Co. Fermanagh, signatories of the Enniskillen address to King William. Five signatures of one name prove the importance of that family in the community and vouch for their efficiency in the past crisis.[1]

1294. **RICHARD EVETT**, Magherastephenagh, Co. Fermanagh.

1295. **ALEXANDER FARQUHAR**, Co. Fermanagh.

1296. **JOHN FORSTER**, Carnemackasker, Co. Fermanagh.

1297. **REV. JOHN FORSTER**, Co. Monaghan, Clerk in Holy Orders.

1298. **CAPT. FRANCIS FORSTER**, Co. Monaghan.

1299. **ANDREW FORSTER**, Drumgorme, Co. Fermanagh.

1300. **GEORGE FRIZELL**, Co. Monaghan.

1301. **JO. FRIZELL**, Enniskillen, Co. Fermanagh, signatory of the Enniskillen address to King William.

1302. **JOHN HALL**, Enniskillen, Co. Fermanagh, attainted. Signer of Enniskillen address to King William.

1303. **GEORGE HAMMERSLEY**, Co. Monaghan, signatory of Enniskillen address to King William.

---

[1] See Trimble, Vol. II. pp. 362–365, 495.

1304. **THOMAS HINISTON (HINSTON? FINISTON?)**, Killiny, Co. Fermanagh, attainted.

1305. **DANIEL HUDSON**, Co. Cavan, came as a refugee in the spring of 1689 to Enniskillen, where he rendered useful assistance during the operations. He was a signatory of the address to King William, subsequently settling in the town.

1306. **ROBERT HUDSON**, Co. Tyrone, was probably of the same family. He was also a signatory of the Enniskillen address to King William.

1307. **JOHN LEONARD**, Maguiresbridge, Co. Fermanagh.

1308. **WILLIAM LITTLE**, Drumenagh, Co. Fermanagh.

1309. **ROBERT MCCREERY**, Co. Tyrone.

1310. **CHARLES MCFADDEN**, Cavan. Probably a signatory of the Enniskillen address to King William.

1311. **LIEUT. EDWARD MADDSON**, Arny, Co. Monaghan.

1312. **CORNET JOHN MADDSON**, Arny, Co. Monaghan.

1313. **JOHN MADDSON**, Clonegally, Co. Fermanagh.

1314. **EDWARD MORTON**, Mullinagough, Co. Fermanagh.

1315. **JOHN MEANS**, Stranaragh, Co. Fermanagh.

1316. **RICHARD MERRICK**, Magherastephenagh, Co. Fermanagh.

1317. **HUGH MERRICK**, Co. Armagh.

1318. **JOHN MOFFET**, Letterboy, Co. Fermanagh.

1319. **EDWARD POCKRIDGE**, Gortnachige, Co. Fermanagh.

1320. **RICHARD POCKRIDGE**, Co. Monaghan. A family long settled in Enniskillen and neighbourhood.[1]

1321. **THOMAS ROSGRAVE**, Toridonochie, Co. Fermanagh.

1322. **DAVID RYND (RYNE?)**, Dewsland, Co. Fermanagh, attainted. A family long settled in Enniskillen and district. This David had been Provost in 1682.[1]

1323. **GABRIEL SHORE**, Magheraghoy, Co. Fermanagh.

---

[1] See Trimble.

1324. **THOMAS SHORE**, Co. Fermanagh. The latter was also a signatory of the Enniskillen address to King William.[1]

1325. **JOHN SLACK**, Monaghan.

1326. **WILLIAM SLACK**, Enniskillen, Co. Fermanagh, was a signatory of the Enniskillen address to King William. He was a son or grandson of the former incumbent of the parish.

1327. **JOHN WEBSTER**, Co. Monaghan.

1328. **MATHEW WEBSTER**, Enniskillen, Co. Fermanagh. The latter was also a signatory of the Enniskillen address to King William.[1]

1329. **ALEXANDER WEAR (WYRE)**, Mumaghan, Co. Fermanagh.

1330. **ROBERT WEAR (WYRE)**, Enniskillen, Co. Fermanagh, a signatory of the Enniskillen address to King William.[1]

1331. **CAPT. WILLIAM WISHARD**, Clontivern, Co. Monaghan.

1332. **WILLIAM WISHART**, Co. Fermanagh. These two names as spelt and described both figure on the list of attainted, and William Wishart is a signatory of the Enniskillen address to King William.

Sir John Wishardt, Laird of Pettaro, N.B., had at the time of the Plantation been granted the middle portion of Leitrim or Laytrim, Co. Donegal. This had been disposed of to Sir Stephen Butler, and the son, Capt. William Wishart, had his residence at Clontivern. He raised and maintained a troop of horse at his own expense, with which he did good service in co-operation with the Enniskilleners.[2]

1333. **WILLIAM ALLEN**, Co. Monaghan.

1334. **MATHEW ADDRINGTON**, Co. Armagh.

1335. **ARTHUR ANSLOW**, Co. Armagh.

1336. **REV. THOMAS ASSINGTON**, Loughgall, Co. Armagh. Clerk in Holy Orders.

1337. **WILLIAM BARKER**, Co. Armagh.

1338. **BROOK BRIDGES**, Co. Armagh.

1339. **JOHN BRIGHT**, Co. Armagh.

[1] See Trimble.
[2] See *ibid.*, Vol. II. p. 527.

1340. **Loftus Brightwell**, Co. Armagh.

1341. **Robert Boyle**, Co. Armagh.

1342. **Henry Byne**, Co. Armagh.

1343. **John Castle**, Co. Armagh.

1344. **Thomas Chaplain**, Co. Armagh.

1345. **Thomas Chemmick**, Co. Armagh.

1346. **Thomas Chiney**, Co. Armagh.

1347. **Thomas Cleegston**, Co. Armagh.

1348. **Richard Clutterbuck**, Co. Armagh.

1349. **Edward Crofton**, Co. Armagh.

1350. — **Daniel**, Co. Armagh.

1351. **Achilles Daunt**, Co. Armagh.

1352. **Robert Dixon**, Co. Armagh. Probably the Capt. Dixon, defender of Derry of No. 795.

1353. **John Evelyn**, Co. Armagh.

1354. **Alexander Frazer**, Co. Armagh.

1355. **John Gaffikin**, Co. Armagh.

1356. **William Gibbs**, Co. Armagh.

1357. **John Gills**, Co. Armagh.

1358. **John Huelt**, Co. Armagh.

1359. **Nathaniel Huelt**, Co. Armagh.

1360. **John Jones**, Co. Armagh.

1361. **Thomas Jones** and

1362. **Mary Jones**, signatories of the Corporation of Derry's 1690 Commission. It is not improbable that they were refugees in Derry during the siege.

1363. **John Lovell**, Co. Armagh.

1364. **CHARLES LOYD**, Co. Armagh.

1365. **JOHN McCAUL (McCALL)**, Co. Armagh.

1366. **JAMES MOORE**, Co. Armagh.

1367. **RICHARD MAY**, Co. Armagh.

1368. **ALGERNON MAYO**, Co. Armagh.

1369. **WILLIAM MEREDITH**, Co. Armagh.

1370. **EDWARD NELTHORPE**, Co. Armagh.

1371. **ANTHONY OBINS**, Co. Armagh.

1372. **HANSLETT OBINS**, Co. Armagh.

1373. — **PAGE**, Co. Armagh.

1374. **HUGH RADCLIFF**, Co. Armagh.

1375. **ALICK RADCLIFF'S** signature is on the Derry address to King William.

1376. **JOSEPH RUTTHORNE**, Co. Armagh.

1377. **OLIVER ST. JOHN**, Co. Armagh.

1378. — **SKIPWORTH**, Co. Armagh.

1379. **GILBERT THACKER**, Co. Armagh.

1380. **WILLIAM TRENCHARD**, Co. Armagh.

1381. **WILLIAM TRENCHARD**, Co. Armagh. Son of above.

1382. **THOMAS VALENTINE**, Co. Armagh.

1383. **WILLIAM WARWICK**, Co. Armagh.

1384. **PUREFOY WARWICK**, Co. Armagh.

1385. **WILLIAM WATTS**, Co. Armagh.

1386. **JOSEPH WILLIAMSON**, Co. Armagh.

1387. **REV. RALPH BARLOW**, Co. Monaghan. Clerk in Holy Orders.

1388. **DACRE BARRET**, Co. Monaghan.

1389. **John Brawshaw**, Co. Monaghan.

1390. **William Brown**, Co. Monaghan.

1391. **Edward Briaghan**, Co. Monaghan.

1392. **Thomas Burgess**, Co. Monaghan.

1393. **James Bunden**, Co. Monaghan.

1394. **Charles Carson**, Co. Monaghan.

1395. **John Corners**, sen., Co. Monaghan.

1396. **John Corners**, jun., Co. Monaghan.

1397. **John Cozens**, Co. Monaghan.

1398. **Ensign Christopher Cron**, Co. Monaghan.

1399. **David Ferguson**, Co. Monaghan.

1400. **Richard Fish**, Co. Monaghan.

1401. **Rev. Thomas Fitzsimons**, Co. Monaghan. Clerk in Holy Orders.

1402. **Sergeant William Fox**, Co. Monaghan.

1403. **Fulke Flinton**, Co. Monaghan.

1404. **George Gibb**, Co. Monaghan.

1405. **Gilmore John**, Co. Monaghan.

1406. **John Gun**, Co. Monaghan.

1407. **William Gun**, Co. Cavan.

1408. **James Holland**, Co. Monaghan.

1409. **John Holland**, Co. Monaghan.

1410. **Henry James**, Co. Monaghan.

1411. **David Karnoghan**, Co. Monaghan.

1412. **William Keyran**, Co. Monaghan.

1413. **John Knelson**, Co. Monaghan.

1414. **George Knight**, Co. Monaghan.

1415. **Abraham Knight**, Co. Monaghan.

1416. **Patrick Legate**, Co. Monaghan.

1417. **John Logher**, Co. Monaghan.

1418. **Alexander Lundsell**, Co. Monaghan.

1419. **James McGirby**, Co. Monaghan.

1420. **Andrew McNab,** Co. Monaghan.

1421. **William Moorecroft**, Co. Monaghan.

1422. **David Mead**, Co. Monaghan.

1423. **John Mills**, Co. Monaghan.

1424. **Thomas Ostler**, Co. Monaghan.

1425. **Blayney Owens**, Co. Monaghan.

1426. **Edward Owens**, Co. Monaghan.

1427. **Sergeant John Oyster**, Co. Monaghan.

1428. **Sergeant John Oyster**, Co. Cavan.

1429. **James Parr**, Co. Monaghan.

1430. **Richard Parry**, Co. Monaghan.

1431. **Thomas Ports**, Co. Monaghan.

1432. **John Scouts**, Co. Monaghan.

1433. **John Sharpe**, Co. Monaghan.

1434. **John Sparks**, Co. Monaghan.

1435. **William Springland**, Co. Monaghan.

1436. **Robert Thomas**, Co. Monaghan.

1437. **Christopher Thomas**, Derry 1690 Commission.

1438. **George Thornton**, Co. Monaghan.

1439. **JOSEPH THORNTON**, Co. Monaghan.

1440. **THOMAS THORNTON**, Co. Monaghan.

1441. **WILLIAM TORREN**, Co. Monaghan.

1442. **JOSEPH WALSH**, Co. Monaghan.

1443. **SERGEANT THOMAS WALSH**, Co. Monaghan.

1444. **HENRY WALTON**, Leghlenagalgrene, Co. Monaghan.

1445. **WILLIAM WALTON**, Leghlenalgrene, Co. Monaghan.

1446. **ROGER WATSON**, Enniskillen, Co. Fermanagh.

1447. **REV. WILLIAM WARREN**, Co. Monaghan. Clerk in Holy Orders.

1448. **JOHN WEST**, Co. Monaghan.

1449. **WILLIAM WILCOCKS**, Co. Monaghan.

1450. **JOHN WILDMAN**, Skeogh, Co. Monaghan.

1451. **THOMAS WILDMAN**, Skeogh, Co. Monaghan.

1452. **THOMAS WINSLOW**, Gerrygore, Co. Monaghan.

1453. **ABRAHAM D'ARCY**, Co. Monaghan.

1454. **PATRICK D'ARCY**, Co. Monaghan. See D'Arcy Irvine family, No. 906.

1455. **BARTHOLOMEW DROPE**, Carrowaskey, Co. Monaghan.

1456. **JOHN LACKEN** (yeoman), Co. Monaghan.

1457. **JOHN LOUGHEY** (yeoman), Co. Monaghan.

1458. **PATRICK LOUGHEY** (yeoman), Co. Monaghan.

1459. **THOMAS NETTERS** (yeoman), Co. Cavan.

1460. **JOHN RICHARDS** (yeoman), Co. Cavan.

1461. **JOSEPH TATE** (yeoman), Co. Cavan.

1462. **BRYAN VOSS** (yeoman), Co. Cavan.

1463. **WILLIAM WARDELL** (yeoman), Co. Cavan.

1464. **ROBERT BOOTH** (yeoman), Co. Cavan.

1465. **WILLIAM COPLIN** (yeoman), Co. Cavan.

1466. **WILLIAM COPLIN**, jun., his son, Co. Cavan.

1467. **ABRAHAM COTNAM** (yeoman), Co. Cavan.

1468. **ROBERT CRIGG** (yeoman), Co. Cavan.

1469. **PETER ECHENBY** (yeoman), Co. Cavan.

1470. **THOMAS HENNEY** (yeoman), Co. Cavan.

1471. **RICHARD HENNEY** (yeoman), Co. Cavan.

1472. **ROGER HOLLAND** (yeoman), Co. Cavan.

1473. **RICHARD KEEP** (yeoman), Co. Cavan.

1474. **REV. JOHN AUNGER**, Co. Cavan. Clerk in Holy Orders.

1475. **JOHN BALLARD**, Co. Cavan. A signatory of the Enniskillen address to King William.

1476. **WILLIAM BRODY**, Co. Cavan.

1477. **THOMAS COACH**, Co. Cavan.

1478. **ARTHUR CULME**, Co. Cavan.

1479. **HENRY EDGEWORTH**, Co. Cavan.

1480. **RICHARD GIBSON**, Co. Cavan.

1481. **BAR. GIBSON**, Enniskillen, Co. Fermanagh, signed the Enniskillen address.

1482. **HENRY GROYLINS**, Co. Cavan.

1483. **CAPT. MEREDITH GWYLIM**, Co. Cavan.

1484. **CHRISTOPHER HARMAN**, Co. Cavan.

1485. **GRACE KEMPSON**, Co. Cavan.

1486. **RICHARD LEWIS**, Co. Cavan.

1487. **MICHAEL LEODS**, Co. Cavan.

1488. **THOMAS MCVISE**, Co. Cavan.

1489. **CHARLES MORTIMER**, Co. Cavan.

1490. **JAMES MORTIMER**, Co. Cavan.

1491. **JOHN MEE**, Co. Cavan.

1492. **BROGHILL NEWBOROUGH**, Co. Cavan.

1493. **THOMAS NEWBOROUGH**, Co. Cavan.

1494. **JOHN PERROT**, Co. Cavan.

1495. **BERRY PRATT**, Co. Cavan.

1496. **JOSEPH PRATT**, Co. Cavan.

1497. **GEORGE RUSSELL**, Co. Cavan, attainted. Also a signatory of the Enniskillen address to King William.

1498. **JOHN TERMAN**, Co. Cavan.

1499. **SAMUEL TOWNLEY**, Co. Cavan.

1500. **HENRY WALDRON**, Co. Cavan.

1501. **CAPT. MANSLY**, Co. Leitrim.

1502. **GUSTAVUS NICHOLLS**, Co. Leitrim.

1503. **WILLIAM NICHOLLS**, Co. Leitrim.

1504. **CAPT. EDWARD NICHOLSON**, Co. Leitrim.

1505. **REV. JAMES PALMER**, Co. Leitrim. Clerk in Holy Orders.

1506. **THOMAS VERNLOE**, Co. Leitrim.

1507. —**WAAGLE**, Co. Leitrim.

In the foregoing 1507 sketches the full list of Ulster's attainted in King James' May 1689 Parliament, some 950 names in all, is exhausted in the individual or family sketch. The same has been done in regard to the signatories of the Derry and Enniskillen address to King William and Mary, but in the case of Derry there remains a balance of some nineteen names, and in the case of Enniskillen of forty-five names, not otherwise mentioned. The mere fact that they were honoured by their fellow citizens in being asked to sign such an address proves that they had co-operated satisfactorily in the critical struggle.

Nineteen signatories of the Derry address to King William and Mary not already mentioned:—

1508. RICHARD CORMAC.

1509. ROBERT DENNISTON.

1510. ANDREW GREGSON.

1511. RICHARD FANE.

1512. RICHARD ROYSE.

1513. RICHARD ISLEN.

1514. JAMES STILES.

1515. THOMAS GUTHRIDGE.

1516. JOHN HALSTON.

1517. BENJAMIN WILKINS.

1518. THOMAS BURNETT.

1519. GEORGE CROSLAND.

1520. DAN McCUSTION.

1521. JOHN FULLER.

1522. JOHN HERRING.

1523. JAMES BARRINGTON.

1524. HENRY EVERETT.

1525. THOMAS CONLAY.

1526. MICHAEL RULLOCK.

Forty-five signatories of the Enniskillen address to King William and Mary not already mentioned:—

1527. ROBERT McCONNELL.

1528. **John Roberts.**

1529. **Robert Ward.**

1530. **Hugh Blair.**

1531. **Edward Davenport.**

1532. **Thomas Davenport.** The Davenports were a Co. Donegal Plantation family. Probably refugees in Enniskillen.[1]

1533. **Oylett Summes.**

1534. **James Mitchell.**

1535. **John Fulton.** Captain in local forces.

1536. **Andrew Fulton.** Lieutenant in local Forces.

1537. **James Ewart.** Provost of Enniskillen in 1684.

1538. **James Lucy.**

1539. **Edward Gubin.**

1540. **Thomas Letournel.** A Huguenot settler in Enniskillen. Prominent in defence. Provost in 1694 and 1702.

1541. **Jo Neper.**

1542. **John Sheriffe.**

1543. **Cor Donellan.**

1544. **Theo. Bury.**

1545. **James King**, Cornet of horse.

1546. **Charles King.**

1547. **Samuel Forth.** A lieutenant, afterwards captain in Wolseley's Horse; he was wounded at the Boyne and Aughrim.

1548. **Isaac Collyer.**

1549. **Richard Skelton.**

---

[1] See Mrs. Robin Young's "Innishowen."

1550. **ICHABOD SKELTON.**

1551. **THOMAS SCOT.**

1552. **NINIAN SCOT.**

1553. **THOS. ROSECROW**, member of an old Enniskillen family, whose grandfather William had been Provost in 1618.

1554. **WILLIAM KILTE.**

1555. **JAMES DEVITT.**

1556. **HENRY HOWELL.**

1557. **CHRISTOPHER CARLETON.** See Nos. 318–322 on members of same family, Carleton and Charlton.

1558. **POVEY HOOKES.**

1559. **RICHARD NEWSTEAD.**

1560. **ROBERT STERLING**, a lieutenant in local force.

1561. **JAMES GOLDEN.** Probably a refugee from Screen, Co. Sligo.

1562. **LAURENCE CROWE.**

1563. **FRANCIS ALDRICH.** Quartermaster in Wolseley's Horse.

1564. **WILLIAM PARSONS.**

1565. **EDWARD HUGHS**, lieutenant in local force.

1566. **THOMAS HUGHS.**

1567. **JAMES MATHEWS.**

1568. **CLAUD BEATTY.**

1569. **GEORGE DRURY**, a lieutenant in local force.

1570. **ROBERT DRURY.** Probably refugees from the family of that name of Callow, Co. Roscommon.

1571. **WILLIAM FRITH.**

For most of the above information and many additional particulars of the Enniskillen men see Trimble's "History of Enniskillen."

Of the lists of names to be dealt with, taken from all available records of the 1689 revolution, including the list of Ulster attainted, and signatories of Derry and Enniskillen addresses to King William and Mary, there only remains to give the balance of the names (not already given in previous Nos. 1 to 1571) of those signing the Derry Corporation 1690 Commission empowering them to appoint agents to repair to London and press the Government for compensation for the heavy expenses and losses incurred during the siege. It is obvious that the said signatories had endured all the perils and privations of the siege of the previous year and are entitled to mention. The Very Rev. Richard King, Dean of Derry, has kindly sent me a copy of these signatures—216 in all. Of these some 142 have been already mentioned in the foregoing individual and family sketches, leaving seventy-four names to enumerate in the following list.

Seventy-five signatures to the Derry Corporation's 1690 Commission not previously noted in individual or family sketches.

1572. **MARY AIRDS.**

1573. **JONATHAN AUSTIN.**

1574. **ROBERT ALLEN.**

1575. **JOHN BONNER.**

1576. **ROBERT BONER.**

1577. **WILLIAM BALDRICK.**

1578. **JAMES BIGLAND.**

1579. **CHARLES CARRIGAN.**

1580. **JAMES CARBWODE.**

1581. **THOMAS CRANE.**

1582. **HEN. CUTHBERT.**

1583. **THOMAS CUMING.**

1584. **WILLIAM DUN.**

1585. **WILLIAM DAVIDSON.**

1586. **WALTER DAVISON.**

1587. **Neeve Derring.**

1588. **John Daglish.**

1589. **William Evory.**

1590. **Helenor Freear.**

1591. **John Gilling.**

1592. **John Grier.**

1593. **William Grigg.**

1594. **James Getty.**

1595. **Chris. Gifford.**

1596. **William Gamble.**

1597. **Wm. Hamond.**

1598. **Jemmet Hay.**

1599. **Margaret Hibbitts.**

1600. **Sam. Harris.**

1601. **Helinor Jenkins.**

1602. **Jennett Jack.**

1603. **Jean Knobbs.**

1604. **David Lithgorn.**

1605. **Robert Lithgoe.**

1606. **John Latey.**

1607. **Kath. Letey.**

1608. **Pat. Linegar.**

1609. **Mary McGee.**

1610. **An. McDowell.**

1611. **John McCutcheon.**

1612. **Joshea McKain.**

1613. **David McKerragh.**

1614. **John McLaughlin.**

1615. **Ann McCrea.**

1616. **Kath. McCaffer.**

1617. **Jean McCamus.**

1618. **John Man.**

1619. **Peter Mercer.**

1620. **John Marshall.**

1621. **Andrew Nutt.**

1622. **William Nivine.**

1623. **Robert Nivine.**

1624. **Samuel Nivine.**

1625. **Roger O'Brien.**

1626. **Thomas Price.**

1627. **Humphrey Price.**

1628. **Mary Pitts.**

1629. **William Poore.**

1630. **Elizabeth Roe.**

1631. **Ann Robin.**

1632. **Mathew Ripley.**

1633. **John Stinsome.**

1634. **Robert Stinnie.**

1635. **Kath. Slater.**

1636. **Jean Shenles.**

1637. **Enery Stott.**

1638. **Enery Stott.**

1639. **Thomas Sankey for Jeremima Sankey.**

1640. **Thomas Thorn.**

1641. **John Vaile.**

1642. **John Westgate.**

1643. **William Welsh.**

1644. **Robert Whyt.**

1645. **Mary Whyt.**

1646. **Capt. Hugh Savage**, son of John Savage of Ardkeen, The Ards, Co. Down, an officer in King William's army.

Present at the Boyne and Aughrim, he was wounded, according to family tradition, in both actions.

For particulars of the Savages of the Ards, and sketches of Savages serving in the Jacobite army, see Part II, Nos. 160–179.

The Butlers of Kilkenny and Ormonde.

1647. **James, 12th Earl of Ormonde.**

The founder of the great house of Ormonde was Theobald Fitzwalter, one of the Anglo-Norman Barons who came to Ireland with Strongbow. He was nominated Chief Butler of the Island by Henry II. From this office the family patronymic was assumed.

The head of the house was created Earl of Ormonde in 1328, followed in a few centuries by further titles and honours. James, 12th Earl of Ormonde, was Charles I.'s Lord-Lieutenant of Ireland during the English Civil War and the 1641 rebellion. He was a skilful administrator, and in recognition of his services was raised to the Dukedom of Ormonde by Charles II. after the Restoration. He was succeeded in 1688 by his grandson, another

1648. **James, 13th Earl**, and **2nd Duke of Ormonde.** The times were critical. England was being driven to revolution and William of Orange was preparing for a landing. The Duke must have been aware that the majority of his house and family in its many branches were staunch supporters of the Stuart dynasty.[1] He never hesitated; presenting himself in King William's camp a few months later in Ireland, where he was

---

[1] For supporters of the Stuart side, see Part II.

with him at the Boyne, and after that victory magnificently entertained his Sovereign at Kilkenny. Not content with this evidence of his loyalty to the new dynasty, two years later he accompanied King William to Flanders. On the hard-fought field of Landen in 1693 he had a horse shot under him, was severely wounded and taken prisoner. He was, however, exchanged two days later for the Duke of Berwick.

After King William's death he was a prime favourite of Queen Anne. He was appointed by Her Majesty to command a military expedition on the continent. After George I.'s accession he was impeached by the House for his failure, deprived of honours and estates and obliged to fly to Avignon in France, where he eventually died. He left no male issue, the succession passing in estates and earldom to a cousin John, the 14th Earl of Ormonde, through whose line it descended to James, 19th Earl and 1st Marquess of Ormonde and through him and descendants to the present representative, the 22nd Earl and 4th Marquess of Ormonde, 28th Chief Hereditary Butler of Ireland, Kilkenny Castle, Co. Kilkenny.

1649. WILLIAM O'BRIEN, 7TH BARON and 2ND EARL OF INCHIQUIN,[1] unlike the other peers of his family, was a strong supporter of William of Orange. He had been summoned and was attainted in King James' Dublin Parliament of 1689. In 1691 he was appointed by King William's administration Governor of Jamaica. In direct descent of this line, owing to the extinction of the titles of Thomond and Clare, Donough Edward Foster, 16th Baron Inchiquin, is the present representative of the great house of Thomond, Clare and Inchiquin, residing at Dromoland, Co. Clare.[2] It may be added that the holders of the Barony of Inchiquin in the course of their fifteen baronial descents were several times in possession of the higher dignities of the Earldoms of Inchiquin and Thomond, and Marquessate of Thomond, of which the Barony has alone survived.

It would be impossible to close Part I. without some reference to the Generals on King William's side who played a conspicuous part in the Irish campaign down to the fall of Limerick, and afterwards in the Flanders campaign. Most prominent of these is

1650. THE DUKE OF MARLBOROUGH, who owed much of his advancement to his famous Duchess, Sarah Jennings, the intimate friend of Queen Anne, whom he had married in 1678.

John Churchill was created in 1685 Baron Churchill by James II. A General in that monarch's army, his defection soon after William's landing at Torbay to that side secured him an earldom in 1689. Dispatched a few months later to command the English army in Flanders, he earned a reputation for gallantry in the allied army under

---

[1] For particulars of the great houses of O'Brien of Thomond, Inchiquin and Clare, see Part II under O'Briens, Earls of Thomond and Viscounts Clare.

[2] See Burke's Peerage.

Prince Waldeck. When William left for his Boyne campaign in 1690, Marlborough remained to command in England, and in the autumn of the same year, at his own suggestion, was ordered to land in the south of Ireland with 5000 men, whom he used so adroitly as to capture in a few weeks the Irish strongholds of Cork and Kinsale. This was Marlborough's contribution to the Irish campaign.

A prime favourite with the King and honoured with his confidence, it was not until 1692 that the discovery of his secret correspondence with the Court of St. Germains led to his dismissal from all his posts and an order never again to enter the King's presence. Shortly, however, before King William's death in 1702 a reconciliation was effected, and the King, recognising his great ability, took him again into his confidence and appointed him to command the English troops operating in the allied army on the continent. On William's death he was confirmed in this appointment and raised to a dukedom by his old friend, Queen Anne. No more signal vindication of King William's selection of a General to continue his European struggle against Louis XIV. of France could be conceived than the Duke's brilliant continental campaigns, in which, with never a defeat, the great victories of Blenheim (1704), Ramillies (1706), Oudenarde (1708) and Malplaquet (1709), added reputation to the arms of England, and names still emblazoned with honour on many a regimental flag. Although disgraced and dismissed from his command and offices in 1712, he had done his work, and in 1713 Louis XIV. was forced to sign the humiliating Treaty of Utrecht.

The present representative of the family is the 9th Duke of Marlborough, Blenheim, Oxford, while the Rt. Hon. Winston Churchill, M.P., son of the late Lord Randolph Churchill, upholds the prestige of his line in the political world.

1651. GENERAL ANDREW MACKAY, a Scotchman, described by Macaulay as "a soldier of fortune," had gained experience and reputation in continental warfare. In 1689 he was appointed by the Scottish convention to command the army to operate in the Highlands against the Jacobites under Viscount Dundee (Claverhouse). At Killiecrankie (1689), although Dundee fell in the moment of victory, Mackay suffered an overwhelming defeat. A few months later, however, he was master of the Highlands, and Fort William still remains to mark the submission he forced on the clans.

In 1690, appointed to various commands in King William's Irish army, he won distinction and reputation at Athlone, Aughrim and the Siege of Limerick. It was at Steinkirk, in William's Flanders campaign, that his death brought him undying renown. Leading the English division of the allied army, his furious onslaught had wedged him deep in the French lines, where he fought gallantly to the last. It was generally supposed in the English rank and file that the Dutch General Solmes failed in his duty in not advancing to his aid. Too late in the day King William made every effort to extricate him, but Mackay had fallen, and with him several other Generals, viz.:—

1652. GENERAL SIR JOHN LANIER, an English officer experienced in continental war. He commanded what is now the 1st Dragoon Guards at the Boyne and served through the ensuing campaign. He was killed at Steinkirk in 1692.

1653. **General James Douglas** commanded the Scots Guards at the Boyne and served with distinction through the subsequent campaign. He was killed at Steinkirk in 1692.

1654. **General Talmash**, an English General of some experience in continental war. He served with distinction at Athlone and Aughrim. At Steinkirk in 1692 he made himself conspicuous by his gallantry in assisting King William to cover the retreat of his beaten army. Later he was appointed to command an expedition to capture Brest, but was mortally wounded in the attack.

Among the Dutch Generals were:—

1655. **Count Solmes**, a distinguished officer, who commanded the Dutch forces at the Battle of the Boyne and served in the campaign down to the fall of Limerick. Never popular with the English army, he made himself hated by his failure to go to the assistance of General Mackay at the Battle of Steinkirk in 1692. He was mortally wounded at the Battle of Landen in the following year.

1656. **General Ginkell**, better known by his title of Earl of Athlone, conferred by William in recognition of his services.

He was present at the Boyne and through the subsequent campaign, particularly distinguishing himself at Athlone (hence his title) and Aughrim.

After the return of William to England he was left in command of the army, and to him fell the honour of the reduction of Limerick (1691). He was a reliable General and a trusty friend of King William, with whom he served afterwards in his Flanders campaign.

1657. **General Ouverquerke**, a distinguished Dutch officer, of noble family, connected with the house of Nassau, and a personal friend of the King, who appointed him Master of the Horse on coming to England.

He had a great reputation for bravery, having saved the King's life in one of his earlier campaigns. He accompanied the King in Ireland and Flanders.

1658. **The Marquis de Ruvigny**, a Huguenot who was present at the Boyne and through the Irish campaign down to the fall of Limerick, being created Earl of Galway for his services.

He was afterwards with King William in his Flanders campaigns, being wounded and taken prisoner at the Battle of Landen (1693), but his magnanimous captors, knowing the fate that awaited any Huguenot falling into Louis XIV.'s hands, allowed him to escape.

1659. **GENERAL CUTTS.** Of all officers taking part on King William's side in the Irish and Flanders campaigns no one bore such a reputation for personal gallantry. At the Boyne he was in command of an English regiment long in the Dutch service, with which he had made his name in continental war. Macaulay, mentioning him at the Boyne, writes that he was admitted by the whole army to be the bravest of the brave. This character was borne out by his actions at the taking of Athlone, the Battle of Aughrim and the Siege of Limerick. But it was at the assault on the Castle of Namur in 1695 that, in the presence of King William, he led a forlorn hope against the citadel, earning for himself the name of "The Salamander." So withering was the fire that he was wounded in the head and his men were driven back. After having his wound roughly dressed he returned to the battle line, rallied his men and won an entrance, causing the capitulation of the fortress. His name still lives in the records of the British army.

1660. **LIEUT.-COL. WILLIAM BERRY** was an officer in Sir George St. George's Regiment accompanying General Kirke's forces for the relief of Derry (June 1689). Sent by Kirke to Enniskillen, he was appointed Lieut.-Col. of the Enniskillen Horse, which he commanded at Lisnaskea, Newtownbutler, the Boyne and through the campaign.

He was a son of James Berry, of Cromwell's Ironsides, and afterwards a Major-General in the Cromwellian service, greatly distinguished at the Battles of Naseby and Preston. Major-General James Berry held subsequently many high posts under Cromwell, while his son William Berry (then Major) got a good appointment in Ireland. Some time about 1659 he married Anne, daughter of Sir Phelim O'Neill, and as marriage with a Roman Catholic was a grave offence in the model army he lost his commission.

In the revolution of 1688–89 his commission was restored in the service of William of Orange. On his march with the Enniskillen Horse to join the Duke of Schomberg's army at Dundalk they encamped for a night at Richhill Castle, then in the possession of the Sacheverell family, when a fight took place between Col. Berry and a French spy—in which Mrs. Berry intervening was wounded—and a few days later at some popular demonstration to celebrate her recovery was burnt to death. The Richhill Castle and estate subsequently came into the possession of the Berry family, whose representative Col. Robert Berry disposed of it in 1918.

The Berrys are of the ancient stock of Berry Nerbor, Devonshire, where they were the feudal lords for many centuries. The present representative of this family, the lineal descendant of Lieut.-Col. William Berry and his wife (Anne O'Neill) is Col. R. G. Berry, Ardilaun, New Castle, Co. Down.

ILLUSTRATIONS

David Cairnes from a copy of the portrait by Sir Godfrey Kneller

Memorial tablet to David Cairnes in the vestibule of St Columb's Cathedral, Londonderry

The memorial tablet to Colonel Henry Baker and Captain Michael Browning who are buried in the north aisle of St Columb's Cathedral

Section of the stained glass siege window, St Columb's Cathedral

Jacobite cannon ball on display in the vestibule of St Columb's Cathedral

View of the Guild Hall from the walls of Derry

View of St Columb's Cathedral

Portrait of King William III by Sir Godfrey Kneller

King James II from an engraving of the portrait by Sir Godfrey Kneller

Rev. George Walker from an engraving of the portrait by Sir Godfrey Kneller

Walker's Pillar, Walls of Derry, an engraving from a drawing by W. H. Bartlett

Bishop's Gate, Derry, rebuilt as a triumphal arch in 1789 to mark the centenary of the siege

PART II

INVESTMENT OF DERRY AND CAMPAIGN

JACOBITE ARMY

Individual sketches of officers of the Jacobite army at or associated with the Siege of Derry in 1689, the struggle round Enniskillen, and subsequent campaign down to the fall of Limerick in 1691, with details of family history, the present-day representative and, in some cases, particulars of their services in the Irish Brigades of France and Spain.

The Preface and Introductory Chapter to Part I. generally explain the scope of this work and the position in Ulster in 1688–89, prior to the investment of Derry. The Introductory Chapter to Part II. goes more fully into the Jacobites' position, their difficulties, and the reasons which forced the Irish of Ulster and the whole kingdom to espouse the cause of their legitimate and Roman Catholic Sovereign.

INTRODUCTORY CHAPTER

TYRCONNELL'S promises—restoration of lands and of their ancient religion under a legitimate Sovereign of their own Faith—had made his task comparatively easy of preparing Ireland for the reception of his Royal master. All Celtic Ireland had rallied to the Jacobite standard. The Dublin Exchequer was empty, and even the lavish gold which James brought, with 6000 troops, from Louis XIV. of France, was insufficient for the requirements of the Irish forces. The badly-equipped army which invested Derry was up to the end of the siege in free communication with Dublin, in spite of the threat of Enniskillen. Supplies and reinforcements, to supply losses by disease or battle, were constantly arriving in camp. Officers came and went. In this way most of the officers on the Jacobite army list served in the investing army for some period during the siege. In my selection of names I have relied on those mentioned by the leading historians of the day and on "King James' Army List of 1689," published by John D'Alton in 1855. As D'Alton states, in this list are the names of the representatives of at least 500 of the ancient Celtic septs and Anglo-Norman families of the kingdom.

After the fall of Limerick in 1691 and the ruin of the Jacobite cause, except for the favoured few who took advantage of the special clauses of the Treaty there was nothing but loss of title, attainder with confiscation of estate and exile to the continent, where service in the Irish Brigades was the only career open. The loss of such fighting material then and the flights of "Wild Geese" in the subsequent century cannot be too strongly deplored. Many of the old aristocracy of Ireland are to-day represented by former grandees of Spain and Portugal, and by nobles resident in France and Austria, who bear honoured names in their adopted countries, all descendants of those who left their home to serve in the Irish Brigades.

INVESTMENT OF DERRY AND CAMPAIGN

JACOBITE ARMY

1. **RICHARD TALBOT, EARL** (1685) and **DUKE OF TYRCONNELL** (1689), James II.'s Lord-Lieutenant of Ireland 1687–1691.

He was a member of the Anglo-Norman family of Malahide, Co. Dublin, sprung from the same stock as the Earls of Shrewsbury. Well known in his earlier days at the Court of Versailles, he was still better known at Whitehall, where his ability, versatility and unscrupulous methods of pushing Roman Catholic propaganda had won him the favour of James II., then Duke of York, continued after his accession to the Crown. Even at Court his debauched habits and uncontrollable temper had made him a marked man. His reputation had earned him the sobriquet of "Lying Dick." A sentence from Macaulay[1] not inappropriately summarises his character: "The intemperance of his bigotry was thought amply to atone for the intemperance of all his other passions." Such was the man that James II. sent over to Dublin in 1685 to command the Irish army. So well did he carry out his Sovereign's mission that when in 1687 the Protestant Lord-Lieutenant, the Earl of Clarendon, perforce resigned, Dick Talbot was appointed in his stead and created Earl of Tyrconnell. As uncontrolled Commander-in-Chief and Viceroy Tyrconnell soon had the Executive and Army Roman Catholicised and Ireland ready to bow to James' wishes.

In 1688 came the revolution, William of Orange's landing at Torbay and James' flight to France. Meantime the Protestants of Ulster, warned by events in England, had been preparing to meet the storm. Protestants were already concentrating in Derry and Enniskillen, and county associations for mutual protection and defence of their religious interests had been formed.

Keeping in close touch with St. Germains, Tyrconnell was now in a position to apprise James that the Kingdom of Ireland was armed and prepared for his reception. The shutting of the gates of Derry (8th December, 1688) had been the first blow to Tyrconnell's schemes, forcing his hand before he was prepared to act with overwhelming force.[2] Early in March Richard Hamilton was dispatched from Dublin in command of 5000 men to take and punish Derry.[3] On 13th March, 1689, King James landed at Kinsale, where he was met by Tyrconnell and escorted to his capital, in which he remained a few days. The next step was his march to Derry at the head of one of Tyrconnell's new armies.[4]

---

[1] Vol. II. p. 193.
[2] For particulars see the Introductory Chapter, Part I.
[3] See No. 11, General Richard Hamilton.
[4] For what followed, see Introductory Chapter, Part I.

Tyrconnell was with his Royal master at the Boyne, and after the defeat, when the latter fled to France, was again left to repair the Jacobite fortunes in the shattered kingdom. History is full of those disastrous days down to the capitulation of Limerick in 1691, where he had died a few months before.

No man played a more tragic part in the Irish Revolution. His ideas were grandiose, and might have been successful but for Derry and Enniskillen. One of his dreams was the transporting of an Irish army to Scotland, a juncture with Dundee and a combined march on London to restore James to the throne.

Tyrconnell's second marriage with Frances, "la Belle Jennings," sister of the more famous Sarah, Duchess of Marlborough, lady-in-waiting to Princess Anne, afterwards Queen Anne, had contributed much to his influence at Court. His Duchess was permitted to reside in Dublin, where she died in 1732 at the age of ninety-two.

The Duke of Tyrconnell left no legitimate male descendants, but the main family is still represented by the sixth Baron Talbot de Malahide, Malahide Castle, Co. Dublin. The Dukedom died with him, but his earldom, in default of male issue, went by special patent of 1685 to his nephew,

2. **WILLIAM TALBOT**, of Haggardstown, second (titular) Earl of Tyrconnell. He was attainted after the fall of Limerick, and retiring to France was so recognised at the Courts of St. Germains and Versailles.

His son, who succeeded him as the third Earl, served in the Irish Brigade of France, rising to the rank of Lieutenant-General. On his death in 1752 the earldom became extinct.[1]

There were many of the name (Talbot) on the list of attainders after Limerick, 1691.[2]

There were two presumed illegitimate sons of the Duke of Tyrconnell prominent in the 1688–89 revolution, viz.:—

3. **LIEUT.-COL. WILLIAM TALBOT**, holding commission as such in one of Lord Antrim's regiments, which he commanded in the investment of Derry.

Mortally wounded and taken prisoner by the besieged in their successful attack of 6th May on Windmill Hill, he was most kindly treated, every effort being made to preserve his life. His wife was permitted to join him, while surgeons and food were supplied from the enemy's camp. Negotiations took place for his release, £500 being offered as ransom, which the garrison refused, demanding as a condition the right to free communication with the English Fleet by that time lying in the Foyle.[3] He died in Derry on 28th June, 1689. His body was courteously placed at the disposal of his wife and removed with due honours to the camp of the investing army for interment.

---

[1] D'Alton's "Jacobite Army List." O'Callaghan's "Irish Brigade," pp. 499, 500.
[2] D'Alton.
[3] Walker's "Siege."

4. **LIEUT.-COL. MARK TALBOT.** He held his commission in one of Lord Antrim's regiments. Whether he was present with the investing army at Derry is uncertain, but he was one of the Lieut.-Colonels commanding the Carrickfergus Castle garrison which repulsed the attacks of the Cos. Down and Antrim Associations in February of 1689, and again he was a commanding officer in Carrickfergus when, after a few days' bombardment, that castle yielded later in the same year to the Duke of Schomberg. Under the conditions of surrender the garrison were allowed to march to Dublin with full honours and under protection. Such, however, was the feeling of the people that the victors had considerable difficulty in securing their safety *en route*.

5. **LIEUT. TALBOT**, a Jacobite officer, probably of the same family, is mentioned as having lost an arm at Culmore on 28th July, 1689, when, at the time of the Breaking of the Boom, that fort was bombarded by H.M.S. "Dartmouth."[1]

6. ALEXANDER MCDONNELL, 3RD EARL OF ANTRIM.

In the 1688–89 revolution there is nothing more remarkable than, in the general dissatisfaction of Ulster, the unwavering attachment of the two great Earls of Antrim and Abercorn to the Stuart dynasty. The fundamental reason for this loyalty may have had its origin in the long connection between these noble houses and the long line of Scottish kings, to whom they owed titles and estates.

The third Earl of Antrim, a comparatively old man, had succeeded his brother Randal, the second Earl, and Marquess of Antrim in 1682. No man had been a more faithful adherent of the unfortunate Charles I. than the great Marquess. The Cromwellian period almost ruined the Marquess, but the Restoration of 1660 brought him back his estate, and his marriage with Rose O'Neill, his Marchioness, the owner of the great O'Neill estate,[2] had replaced him in a position of commanding power in the province. Although the O'Neill estate had passed from the Antrim title at the Marquess' death, the third Earl's close connection with the widowed lady gave him a provincial influence little inferior to that of his dead brother.

Previous to the revolution, Tyrconnell, who appreciated not only the Earl's Antrim influence but also his Mull of Cantire connection, had appointed him H.M.L. for Co. Antrim. When Derry at the end of 1688 began to show disaffection, the Viceroy ordered the Earl of Antrim to raise a regiment and occupy the refractory city for the King. The result of his obedience to these instructions was the first overt act of rebellion, the shutting of the gates.[3]

In the few days that James was in the investing camp before Derry the Earl was in

---

[1] Walker's "Siege."

[2] See Part II, No. 44, Rose O'Neill, Marchioness of Antrim.

[3] For particulars, see Introductory Chapter, Part I. The original instructions of Tyrconnell ordering his occupation of Derry are now among the valuable documents lodged in the archives of Derry Cathedral.

attendance upon his Royal master. The Lieut.-Colonel of one of his regiments, William Talbot,[1] was killed at the head of his men in one of the sorties of the garrison. From the commencement of the regular investment of the city down to the Boyne campaign Lord Antrim held Coleraine and its vicinity with one of his regiments, while another under his Lieut.-Col. Cormac O'Neill was quartered at Carrickfergus Castle. The Earl commanded a regiment at the Boyne and through the subsequent campaign down to Limerick, where he was lucky enough to be one of the favoured few in the special clauses of the Treaty to retain his estates.

The Earl died in 1699, being succeeded by his son Randal as fourth Earl, who is the ancestor of the present representative of the family in the female line, Randal Mark Kerr, seventh Earl of Antrim of the later creation and twelfth of the first.

Nothing can be more indicative of the clan spirit, and the ties of the old alliances with neighbouring Celtic septs still existing in 1688, than the names of the commissioned officers of one of Lord Antrim's regiments, viz.:—

The Earl of Antrim. Colonel.

Lieut.-Col. Mark Talbot.[2]

Major James Wogan.

Captain	Lord Enniskillen (Maguire)		
,,	Daniel McDonnell	Captain	Ulick Burke
,,	Charles McDonnell	,,	Henry Vaughan
,,	Hugh O'Neill	,,	Arthur Magill
,,	Terence O'Neill	,,	Edmond O'Reilly
,,	Bryan Maginnis		
Lieut.	Archibald McDonnell	Lieut.	George Moore
,,	Randall McDonnell	,,	Francis Moore
,,	John McDonnell	,,	Manus McManus
,,	Eneas McDonnell	,,	Denis O'Callaghan
,,	John O'Neill	,,	Randolph Sexton
,,	John O'Neill	,,	Terence McSweeny
,,	Bryan O'Neill	,,	Bryan McGrath
,,	Bryan O'Neill		
Ensign	Randall McDonnell	Ensign.	— Vaughan
,,	Eneas McDonnell	,,	Francis O'Reilly
,,	Augustus McDonnell	,,	John O'Cahan (O'Kane)
,,	Augustus McDonnell	,,	Constantine O'Rorke
,,	Turlough O'Neill	,,	George Sexton
,,	Francis O'Neill	,,	John McManus
,,	Hugh Mackey	,,	— McMahon

[1] See No. 3.
[2] See No. 4.

Adjutant, Capt. Alexander McDonnell
Chaplain, Hubert Dolphin of Co. Galway.[1]

Of these names, forty-four in all, twelve were of his own clan, eight were O'Neills, fifteen others of Irish septs or Anglo-Norman family. Reference to most of these names will be made in subsequent sketches, as in the case of the officers of Col. Cormac O'Neill's, of Kilmacevet, Clannaboy Regiment.[2] In these necessarily short sketches there is not space for more than the merest outline of the history of the family. Sprung from the same great Celtic stock as the O'Neills of Ulster, their forbears had selected the Western Islands of Scotland and the Mull of Cantire for their scene of operations. Thereafter some generations their great ancestor Somerled (Sorley) founded the Kingdom or Lordship of the Isles. After his death this kingdom passed away, being now vested in the Crown of the United Kingdom. For the succession to the titular Lordship there are many claimants among his descendants, chiefs of ancient Highland clans, of whom the Earl of Antrim is one. Always at home on the sea, their galleys were not infrequent visitors to the Antrim coast in the 13th and 14th centuries, but it was not until the middle of the latter century that the marriage of John Macdonnell Mor with the Bisset heiress gave the family legal tenure of the large estate of Glenarm, in whose glen the Earl of Antrim still resides. In a few generations, with sword and galley, they had established themselves among the great Celtic tribes or clans of Ulster. Sometimes at variance with The O'Neill of Tyrone, or of Clannaboy, or The O'Donnell, they were dexterous enough in counter alliance, or with the sword, to gain their point; failing which there remained their galleys, useful in bringing men from Cantire or removing them to the Western Isles till the danger was over. Their fight with the Macquillans was long and stubborn, and it was not until near the end of the 16th century that the bloody Battle of Aura put them in full possession of the Macquillans' territory of the Route, with Dunluce Castle.

Sorley Boy Macdonnell was the greatest of the name. He had beaten the Macquillans, and for years waged perpetual war with Elizabeth and her Lord Deputies. The Queen said that Sorley was a Scot, and should live in Cantire. Back sailed Sorley and his galleys to the Mull, but once the Lord Deputy had retired Sorley was at his old games. At last, in 1585, the Queen could stand it no longer and accepted Sorley as the recognised possessor of the Route and sea coast of Antrim from the Curran of Larne to Portrush. In the great struggle of Elizabeth *versus* Tyrone, Sorley's successor Randall, afterwards the first Earl of Antrim, was for some time a supporter of the Earl of Tyrone, but made his submission in good time. The accession to the throne in 1603 of his kinsman, friend and ally, James VI. of Scotland, was a happy change from Elizabeth. One of James' first acts was the grant of the vast territory (360,000 acres)

---

[1] D'Alton's "Jacobite Army List," 1689.
[2] See Part II, No. 46.

stretching along the Antrim coast from Larne to Portrush, and including the Route, to Randall McDonnell, who a few years later was created Viscount Dunluce and Earl of Antrim. What "the sword" and "the galley" had begun was consummated by James.

The dates of the peerage creations are as follows: First creation, Viscount Dunluce 1618, Earl of Antrim 1620. Second creation, same titles, in 1785. At the latter date the sixth Earl of Antrim, having no male issue, surrendered the original patent, receiving from his Sovereign the fresh patent, securing to his daughters primogeniture and to their male issue the right of succession to the family honours.

7. CLAUD HAMILTON, BARON STRABANE AND 4TH EARL OF ABERCORN.[1]

This fourth Earl of Abercorn accompanied his Sovereign James II. to Ireland in March 1689. In Dublin he was sworn in of the Privy Council. He attended His Majesty to Derry, where he was horrified to find so many of his relations, connections and tenantry fighting in support of William of Orange. On the ground of his relationship with Capt. James Hamilton and acquaintance with other prominent defenders, he was sent into the city to negotiate surrender. His mission was a failure. In one of the first sorties of the Derry garrison he was wounded, having his horse shot under him and losing his cloak. He was one of the nobles in attendance on his Royal master at the Battle of the Boyne. After the defeat he sailed for France but was drowned on the voyage (1690). He was succeeded by his brother,

8. CHARLES, as 5TH EARL OF ABERCORN, a title which he retained (being a peerage of Scotland), while owing to his being attainted in Ireland he lost the Barony of Strabane. He died in 1701, when he was succeeded by his cousin, Capt. James Hamilton, as sixth Earl of Abercorn.[2]

The death of the fifth Earl of Abercorn in 1701 had brought the family honours to the line of Sir George Hamilton, Bart., of Dunalong, who died in 1672. His eldest son James was killed in a naval action in 1673, so that the latter's eldest son, Capt. James (as already stated), became the sixth Earl. But Sir George of Dunalong left among other issue at least four sons, all more or less prominent in the Jacobite cause. Taking these in their order of seniority, there are:—

9. GEORGE HAMILTON, a Count of France, and prominent at the Court of Louis XIV. He married Frances Jennings, whose sister Sarah, afterwards Duchess of Marlborough, was the famous lady-in-waiting to Queen Anne. After George Hamilton's early death in 1667 his widow became the second wife of the Duke of Tyrconnell. She died in Dublin in 1732 at a ripe old age.

---

[1] A sketch history of the house of Abercorn with names of members of the family, of cadets and other Hamilton supporters of King William of Orange will be found in Part I, Nos. 1090 to 1132. In sketches immediately following this, Nos. 7–12, Part II, will be found the names of the other Hamiltons of the Abercorn house on the Jacobite side.

[2] See Part I, No. 1090.

10. **ANTHONY HAMILTON** was also conspicuous at the Court of Versailles. He was a Count of France and a Lieutenant-General in the French service. His famous "Memoires de Grammont" give a vivid picture of life at the Court of Charles II.

At the commencement of the revolution, returning to Ireland he raised a regiment for the Jacobite service on his estates near Roscrea in Co. Tipperary. He was present with his regiment at the investment of Derry, and is thus referred to in the "Londeriados" poem:

> "Anthony Hamilton in the King's County
> Raised a noble regiment near Roscrea."

Serving through the subsequent campaign, he was severely wounded at the Battle of Newtownbutler, which probably necessitated his return to France, where he died in 1720.

11. **RICHARD HAMILTON.** No man of the Jacobite side stood out more prominently in Ireland in the 1688 revolution than he did. He had won considerable reputation as an officer in the French service, and was a favourite at the Court of Versailles until an amour with one of the monarch's illegitimate daughters drew down on him the ire of Louis XIV. Obliged to leave France, he served in several continental armies, among others, it is said, William of Orange's in Flanders. Later he was at the Stuart Court of Whitehall, where he was noted for wit and gallantry.

At the beginning of the 1688 revolution he was with James II.'s army in England, commanding one of the Irish regiments sent over by Tyrconnell to the assistance of his Royal master. With James II. a fugitive at the Court of France and William of Orange the constitutional King, he found himself "a sort of prisoner of war in the Isle of Wight."[1] Meantime, the Duke of Tyrconnell was showing signs of wavering in his allegiance to James II. and at the instigation of King William's old friends Sir William and his son, Sir John Temple, Richard Hamilton was sent over to Ireland to arrange a peaceful settlement. Once in Dublin he deserted the side of William, co-operating whole-heartedly with Tyrconnell in the preparing of Ireland for the reception of James. Heart-broken at the behaviour of the emissary he had recommended with such confidence, Sir John Temple drowned himself in the Thames.[2]

Raised to the rank of Brigadier-General, Richard was dispatched early in March 1689, at the head of 5000 men, to march on Derry and punish the refractory city.[3] While this was in progress King James had landed on 13th March at Kinsale and, after a week in Dublin, marched at the head of another army via Omagh to join Hamilton's camp before the city.[4] When on 18th April, thoroughly disgusted with

[1] Burnet.
[2] Macaulay.
[3] For his successful progress north see Part I, Introductory Chapter.
[4] For the events immediately following see *ibid.*

the "No Surrender" determination of the besieged, James left for Dublin, it was one of the French Generals brought in his train, de Maimont, who was appointed to the chief command of the investing army, while Hamilton commanded the Irish troops. The fall of de Maimont put another French General, Pusignan, to the front, but his death restored Hamilton to his original command, which he held through most of the siege, except for a short period when the French General Rosen was in command.

There was nothing in the conduct of the siege to distinguish Richard as a great General, but the same may be said of all the leading officers, English, Irish and French alike, in the investing army. Hamilton experienced the greatest difficulties. Constant dissension and bickerings in his camp, bad equipment of his men, poor, if any, commissariat arrangement, lack of powder, and above all inadequate train of guns for the bombardment. A day or two prior to the relief of Derry, in a letter dispatched on 23rd July, 1689, to King James in Dublin, seeing the hopelessness of their task, the following officers of the investing army advised His Majesty to raise the siege and withdraw his army: Generals Richard Hamilton, Waucop, Buchan and Sheldon, the Duke of Berwick and the French officers Girardin and the Chevalier Carney. It must be remembered to Hamilton's credit that when the brutal French General Rosen placed some thousands of old men, women and children drawn from the surrounding districts before the city walls in order to force the besieged to surrender, the Irish, headed by Hamilton, protested most vehemently against such inhuman conduct.[1] To Hamilton after the relief was left the invidious task of withdrawing the beaten army to Dublin.

At the Boyne he gallantly led the last cavalry charge of the day against the Enniskilleners, with whom was William of Orange. Severely wounded and a prisoner, he was brought before William, who inquired, "Will your cavalry make more fight?"

To which Hamilton replied: "On my honour, I believe they will."

"Your honour," muttered the monarch, and no more passed between them.

Hamilton remained a prisoner in England until 1692, when, through the intervention of friends, his exchange was arranged for that of Viscount Mountjoy.[2] Returning to France, he again took service in the French army, rising to the rank of Lieutenant-General. He died in France.

12. **JOHN HAMILTON**, a Colonel in the Jacobite army in Ireland. He was killed at the Battle of Aughrim 1691.

When Duke of York, James II. had by a *liaison* with Arabella, sister of John Churchill, afterwards the famous Duke of Marlborough, become the father of two boys, whom, still in their early teens, he brought in his suite to Ireland, viz.:—

13. **JAMES FITZJAMES, DUKE OF BERWICK**, born in 1671, and only in his seventeenth year. He was on arrival in Dublin appointed to command the 2nd troop of the Irish Guards.

---

[1] See General Rosen, Part II, No. 23.
[2] See Part I, No. 18.

Accompanying his father to Derry he remained with the army of investment, or operating an independent command in the province all through the siege. It was to the Duke of Berwick's Horse that the Fort of Culmore, commanding the river approach to the city, surrendered a few days after the commencement of the investment. He was wounded in one of the early sorties of the besieged, and played a prominent part not only in the siege itself but also in cavalry operations at Inch and in the province.[1] Towards the end of the siege (23rd July) he was one of the investing Generals to advise his Royal father to order the raising of the siege and withdrawal of the army.

He was present at the Boyne, where he had a horse shot under him, and served with the Jacobite forces down to Limerick. He afterwards joined James II. at St. Germains. Taking service in the French army, he greatly distinguished himself, rising to the rank of Field-Marshal. At the Battle of Landen in 1693 he was taken prisoner, and, being recognised by George Churchill, his mother's brother, was conducted to the presence of the victor, King William. The interview was embarrassing for both. The King courteously uncovered, the Duke solemnly bowed, and the interview ended. He was exchanged a few days later for the Duke of Ormonde, who had been captured in the same action.[2]

The Duke of Berwick was killed in 1734 at the Battle of Phillipsburgh. He has been succeeded by a long line of ducal descendants, bearing his title, grandees of Spain, and is now represented by the Duke of Alba.

14. **Col. Henry Fitzjames**, the younger brother of the above. Born in 1673, he could not have been very old when given command of a Jacobite regiment in Ireland. Present at the Boyne, he returned to France with his father after the loss of the day. In Paris he was better known as "The Lord Grand Prior," an ecclesiastical preferment gained for him by James' influence with the Vatican.

Nos. 15–23.

French Generals and officers, lent for the campaign by his ally Louis XIV. of France, whom King James brought in his train to Derry, and who took a leading part in the siege.

These officers, accustomed to regular continental campaigns on the scale of the Grand Monarch, disciplined troops, and siege guns with proper equipment for the assault of fortified towns, looked with disdain on the Irish preparations for the attempt, and James' marked preference for these soldiers of experience did not tend to allay the friction, which from the very beginning prevented proper co-operation between the two nations. The French officers, looking down on the quality of the besieged, openly stated that Derry could be taken by a determined *coup de main*. The Irish,

---

[1] Witherow's "Derry" and "Londeriados."
[2] Macaulay.

knowing their opponents, thought differently. King James left the camp on 18th April for Dublin, leaving the French General de Maimont in supreme command.

15. **GENERAL DE MAIMONT.** A few days later, on 21st April, de Maimont put his *coup de main* proposal in operation. At the head of his French and Irish cavalry he gallantly encountered Derry's troopers, as gallantly led by Col. Adam Murray. How these two bodies met on the field, riding through and through each other, is most graphically described in the "Londeriados" poem.[1] The day was stubbornly contested, the French engaged being wounded or killed to a man, among the killed being General de Maimont, who fell in a Homeric encounter with Col. Adam Murray. Historians of that day, and local tradition are certain on this point, but Macaulay discredits it, on the authority of Count D'Avaux, Louis XIV.'s Ambassador to King James' Court, then in Dublin, who could only have had second-hand information from the Irish camp. So perished de Maimont. He was of noble family and had so distinguished himself in many campaigns that he had risen to be Marechal de Camp in Louis XIV.'s army.

He is thus mentioned by "Londeriados":—

> "Maimont, whose early valour on the Rhine
> 'Bove all the Gallic officers did shine."

He was succeeded by his colleague,

16. **GENERAL DE PUSIGNAN**, a Brigadier in the French army. So severely wounded was he when de Maimont was killed that he only survived a few days, leaving Hamilton again in command. His death[2] was entirely due to scarcity of qualified surgeons and lack of proper treatment.

17. **MONTMEGAN**, aide-de-camp to General de Maimont, fighting at his General's side, was severely wounded in the same action, but escaped with his life.[3]

18. **QUARTERMASTER CASSORE** is another of the French officers killed in the action of 21st April.[4]

19. **PONTEE.** French engineer officer, was wounded in one of the Derry sorties at the same time as the Duke of Berwick. "Londeriados" has the following mention:—

> "Berwick and Pontee likewise wounded were
> By valiant Murray and the bold Dunbar."

20. **CHEVALIER CHARLES DE VAUDREY**, another French officer at the Derry investment. General Rosen mentions his name to King James in a dispatch of 27th June.

---

[1] For this description in full, see Part I, No. 411, Col. Adam Murray.
[2] See Count D'Avaux' "Letters to Louis XIV."
[3] Witherow's "Derry."
[4] Walker's "Siege."

He was one of the commissioners appointed by Hamilton to treat with the commissioners appointed by the besieged for surrender of the city on 12th July, 1689. These negotiations were abortive.

Mackenzie in his "Siege" speaks of this officer as a Sir Edward Vaudry, an evident mistake.

21. CHEVALIER DE CARNEY.

22. GENERAL GUAROLIN. Two other of these French officers, whose signatures were appended to the letter from the Irish camp to King James in Dublin dated 23rd July, advising the raising of the siege and withdrawal of the investing army.

23. GENERAL CONRADE ROSEN was a man of very different stamp from the Chevalier de Maimont and de Pusignan.

He was by birth a Livonian, of mean extraction, who managed to get a commission in Louis XIV. 's army, where his gallantry in action, coupled with his brutality in the devastation of the Palatinate and in the dragooning of Huguenots, had advanced him to the rank of Marechale de Camp. He is described by contemporaries as savage in manner and overbearing.

He had come to Derry with James II., but returned with His Majesty, after his repulse at the gates of the city, to Dublin, where he was busied for some months in organising and preparing Tyrconnell's levies for the coming campaign. Disgusted with the slow progress of the siege, James II. sent Rosen back to Derry on 20th June to supersede Richard Hamilton in the supreme command and to capture the city at all costs. It was not long before Rosen's brutality and disregard of the amenities of civilised war brought him into variance with Hamilton and the other Irish officers. On 20th June Rosen officially notified the Derry garrison that, unless they made submission and surrendered before 6 of the clock of the afternoon of 1st July, measures would be taken to place thousands of non-combatants of their faction, old and young, women in every condition and babies in arms, before the walls of the city, to die of hunger, cold or the missiles of both sides, if not admitted inside the walls. The garrison's reply was an immediate and scornful refusal.

Meantime some 3000 unfortunates, collected by Rosen's instructions at Coleraine, Antrim, Carrickfergus, Belfast, Dungannon, Charlemont, Belturbet and Ballyshannon, were conveyed to the Irish camp, and placed below the walls on 1st or 2nd July. But Derry was not yet beaten. There were some thirty Jacobite officers of distinction, captured by the garrison in their various sorties, prisoners in their hands. The Governors immediately erected a gallows on the walls, and notified Rosen that unless the unfortunate captives were at once returned in safety to their homes, these thirty prisoners would be executed.[1] Richard Hamilton's vehement protest, and the sympathy of the

---

[1] For names of these prisoners and some correspondence see No. 25, Lord Netterville, who was one of them.

Irish troops, who are stated to have fed the unfortunates, carried the day. The unfortunates were restored to their homes and the thirty prisoners reprieved.

Talking of Rosen's fury at his failure to capture the obstinate city, Walker's "Siege" has the following paragraph: "Rosen was not many days in supreme command before he expressed himself with great fury against us, and swore by the belly of God that he would demolish our town, and bury us in its ashes, putting all to the sword, without consideration of age or sex."

It is greatly to King James' credit that on hearing of Rosen's infamous proposal, not indeed until 3rd July, when the incident was already ended, he wrote to Rosen: "It is positively our will that you do not put your project into execution, but on the contrary that you send them (the captives) back to their habitations, without any injury to their persons." Indeed so angry was James II. with General Rosen that he is stated to have asked Louis XIV. for the General's recall.

Before the relief of Derry Rosen had rejoined His Majesty in Dublin. He continued through the Irish preparations for the coming campaign as a Lieut.-General and chief military adviser. He was present at the Boyne, but, having advised the King against the policy of leaving his fate to the arbitrament of one great battle, his influence was without much weight.

After James' return to France he remained with Tyrconnell in Ireland, but their frequent dissension on military strategy led to the withdrawal of Rosen to France shortly before the first attack on Limerick in 1691.

He was an able General, but so unpopular with his fellow officers, that, although appointed a Marshal of France in 1703, he never, as a Marshal, had a command in the field. He lived to the ripe age of eighty-seven, dying in 1713 on his property in Alsace.

24. **Count D'Avaux**, Louis XIV.'s Ambassador to King James' Court in Ireland.

Landing in Ireland with King James II. he was with him more or less down to the Boyne, remaining after that Sovereign's departure up to the investment of Limerick.

During his embassy in Ireland his regular letters to his Royal master in France apprising him of military and political matters are among the most valuable historical documents regarding the 1689 revolution in Ireland. His criticisms on the military equipment of Tyrconnell's forces are of particular interest.

He and General Rosen were closely associated in attendance on James II., and generally were of the same opinions. Macaulay, in reference to these notable men, has the following pithy sentence: "Immoral and hard-hearted as Rosen and D'Avaux, Rosen was a skilful General, and D'Avaux was a skilful politician."

Sketches Nos. 25–29. Jacobite Prisoners of the Derry Garrison under sentence of execution, unless Rosen sent home in safety the captives placed under the walls.

25. **The 3rd Viscount Netterville**, of Dowth, Co. Dublin, the representative

of the old Anglo-Norman family of that name of the Pale. The viscountcy had been conferred in 1622.

He held a commission as Captain in Lord Dongan's Regiment of Foot, with which he was serving in defence of the Windmill Hill when attacked by the garrison's sortie of 6th May. He was severely wounded and among the prisoners taken and incarcerated with some thirty others in Derry when the events described[1] took place. In the uncertainty as to their fate, some five of these prisoners, representing all in the same danger, signed the following pathetic appeal asking for the intercession of General Richard Hamilton with General Rosen:—

> "We are willing to die (with our swords in our hands) for His Majesty, but to suffer like malefactors is hard, nor can we lay our blood to the charge of the garrison, the Governor and the rest having used and treated us with all civility imaginable,
> "Your most dutiful and dying friends.

> "(Signed)   NETTERVILLE.   Writ by another hand, he himself has lost the fingers of his right.
> „   E. BUTLER
> „   SIR G. AYLMER
> „   MACDONNELL
> „   D'ARCY
> "In the name of all the rest."

Hamilton's reply, which was a sympathetic refusal, ended in the following sentence:—"And if you must die it cannot be helped, but shall be revenged on many thousands of the people (as well innocent as others) within and without the city." A poor satisfaction to the condemned men! But the action of the garrison, coupled with General Richard Hamilton's protest, had the desired result. Rosen gave in. The helpless captives were removed from before the city walls and returned in safety to their homes, while the garrison were relieved of the gruesome necessity of hanging their defenceless prisoners.

After the relief of Derry Lord Netterville was exchanged but died in a few months' time, probably owing to his wounds.

On the death of the eighth Viscount in 1882 the title became extinct and the family without a male representative. The daughter and heiress of the last Viscount married J. J. McEvoy, who assumed the additional surname of Netterville.

26. **CAPT. EDMOND BUTLER**, son of the fifth Viscount Mountgarret, and his successor as sixth Viscount in 1706, was the E. Butler, prisoner in the hands of the Derry garrison, and signatory of the prisoners' appeal to General Richard Hamilton.[2]

---

[1]   See General Rosen, No. 23.
[2]   See previous sketch, Viscount Netterville.

He was serving in his kinsman Lord Galmoy's regiment as Lieut.-Colonel during the investment. On 4th June he led a fierce cavalry attack on the garrison's position outside the city. Driven off by the garrison with considerable loss, this Capt. Butler was among the officers captured. After the relief he was one of the prisoners exchanged and afterwards served in the Jacobite army at the Boyne and down to Limerick. Coming under the favoured clauses of the Treaty of Limerick, the family retained their title and estates. The viscountcy dates from 1550, the present representative being the fourteenth Viscount Mountgarret, Nidd Hall, Ripley, Yorkshire.

27. **Richard, 5th Viscount Mountgarret**, sat in James' Parliament of 1689.

28. **Sir George Aylmer, 2nd Bart.**, of Balrath, Co. Meath, was another of the prisoners in the hands of the Derry garrison signing the letter to Richard Hamilton.[1]

He was a captain in Lord Abercorn's Jacobite Regiment at the investment and was among the prisoners captured by the garrison in their attack of 4th May on Windmill Hill. He was exchanged in 1691. Coming under the favoured Treaty clause, he retained his title and estates.

After his death he was succeeded in the baronetcy by his brother Mathew, a distinguished admiral, raised to the peerage in 1718 as Baron Aylmer.

The Aylmers settled in Ireland in the end of the 13th century. The baronetcy was a 1662 creation. The present representatives of the family are the ninth Baron Aylmer, Queen's Bay, Kootenay, B.C., Canada, and Lieut.-Gen. Sir Fenton Aylmer, Bart., V.C.

29. **Capt. D'Arcy** was another of the Jacobite prisoners in the hands of the Derry garrison signing the appeal to General Richard Hamilton.[1]

Of this Capt. D'Arcy we know nothing more than what we are told by Mackenzie, viz. that when Capt. James Hamilton came to the city with arms and munitions early in April, he brought with him, as a prisoner, a Capt. D'Arcy, "who on the 27th of the same month was given a pass by our Governors to go with horse and arms, which he accordingly did."

It would therefore appear that Capt. D'Arcy had joined the investing army, and had been captured by the garrison in one of their sorties.

30. **Capt. Archibald Macdonnell**, a kinsman of Lord Antrim, was adjutant of his regiment serving in the investment of Derry. In the gathering of the Jacobite forces before Derry he is mentioned in the "Londeriados" poem as

"Capt. Macdonnell, Colkitto's famous son."

He was indeed the son of Sir Alastair McColl Kittagh (Kitto) Macdonnell, who won such renown as the commander of the Irish contingent in Montrose's campaign

---

[1] See No. 25, Viscount Netterville.

in the West of Scotland. He was the representative descendant of Colla, the elder brother of the more famous Sorley Boy.

Capt. Archibald Macdonnell was taken prisoner by the garrison in the Windmill Hill sortie of 6th May. After the relief of Derry he was exchanged with other prisoners, rejoining the Jacobite army, in which he rose to the rank of Lieut.-Colonel, and served up to the fall of Limerick. Returning to Co. Antrim at the end of hostilities he settled down on a small property belonging to the family, that of Glassmullan, near Cushendall. There he died at the age of seventy-four, and was buried in the ancient graveyard of Layde, where so many of his relations of Murlough, Kilmore, and Monivert, all descendants of Colla, rest in peace.

Nos. 31–36. Distinguished English or Scottish officers serving in the investing army at Derry.

31. BRIGADIER-GENERAL RAMSEY. Of the English officers serving in the investing army no one had a greater reputation than this General, to whom even the Irish commanders, so jealous of interference, seemed to have paid due deference.

At dawn of 6th May the garrison awoke to discover that during the night some 5000 men under the command of General Ramsey had entrenched themselves on Windmill Hill, where big guns were being emplaced which would dominate and render the city almost untenable. "Londeriados" thus describes the situation:—

> "Then General Ramsey, with five thousand strong
> By break of day entrenched himself upon
> The Windmill Hill. Our liberty was gone.
> They from their trenches could kill ev'ry one
> That issued forth, or entered Bishop's Gate.
> This sudden motion did much hurt create."

Immediate action on the part of the garrison was imperative. Led by Col. Adam Murray, a vigorous assault was delivered, and after a fierce hand-to-hand struggle by 12 o'clock the Jacobite force was driven out and the danger averted. In this bloody engagement General Ramsey and some 200 of his men were killed, and 500 wounded with loss of many prisoners. The garrison's loss was slight.

The next day under a flag of truce the enemy were allowed to come and bury their dead, while the General was interred with full military honours in the Cathedral church. Ash in his "Diary of the Siege" writes as follows: "Brigadier Ramsey was interred in the Long Tower, and much lamented by all that knew him, for he was reckoned the best soldier in the army, next to Col. Richard Hamilton."

32. BRIGADIER-GENERAL DOMINICK SHELDON was a member of an old Warwickshire family. It was a Ralph Sheldon who, after Worcester, assisted Charles II. into the oak of Boscobel and ensured his safe hiding.

In the beginning of the revolution he was appointed Lieut.-Colonel of Tyrconnell's own regiment of horse, and soon rose to the rank of Brigadier-General.[1] He served in a leading capacity with the investing army all through the siege, while he was one of the Irish commissioners appointed by Hamilton to negotiate with the garrison for surrender on terms on 12th July.

He was one of the Jacobite Generals signing the letter of 23rd July to King James advising the raising of the siege and withdrawal of the investing army. He had two horses shot under him at the Boyne, and fought with distinction down to Limerick. He was one of the Irish commissioners signing the Treaty of Limerick, and was afterwards employed in the arrangements for the embarkation of the Irish troops who selected the French service.

He eventually rejoined his exiled Sovereign at the Court of St. Germains, where he obtained a high command in the Irish Brigade, with which he served with distinction in many campaigns.[1]

33. **WILLIAM ERSKINE, 8TH EARL OF BUCHAN**, a Scottish peer in the entourage of James II. in Ireland. He served in the campaign down to the fall of Limerick.

He died unmarried in 1695. The present representative of the family is the fourteenth Earl of Buchan.[2]

34. **GENERAL THOMAS BUCHAN.** He was in command of a regiment at the investment of Derry. He was among the Generals signing the letter of 23rd July from the camp before Derry to King James advising the raising of the siege and withdrawal of the investing army.

35. **BRIGADIER-GENERAL JOHN WAUCHOPE**, served in the investing army before Derry, and his signature is attached with other Generals' to the letter of 23rd July addressed to King James in Dublin advising His Majesty to raise the siege and withdraw the investing army.

He served through the Boyne campaign and down to the fall of Limerick, and his name is frequently mentioned in regard to the Treaty, particularly in association with General Patrick Sarsfield in the embarkation of the Irish troops who had elected to serve in the Irish Brigade in France.[1]

36. **LIEUT.-COL. FRANCIS WAUCHOPE** held a commission as such in Lord Iveagh's Regiment (the Magennis Regiment), with which he was present before Derry, at the Boyne and in the campaign down to Limerick.[1]

Referring to the names Wauchop and Buchan as present at the siege the "Londeriados" poem has this allusion:—

[1] D'Alton's "Jacobite Army List."
[2] Burke's Peerage.

"Wauchop and Buchan, two Scots gentlemen
From Tyrconnell two regiments obtain."

In 1899 the head of the Scottish house, Major-General Andrew Wauchope, C.B., C.M.G., when leading the Highland Brigade, was killed at the Modder River.

37. LIEUT.-COL. SKELTON, an English officer who commanded a regiment in the investing army before Derry.

He was one of the commissioners appointed by General Richard Hamilton to treat with the garrison for the surrender of the city on terms in the abortive negotiations of 12th July.

He served with distinction in the Jacobite army in the campaign down to the fall of Limerick.

38. CAPTAIN TROY, an English officer in attendance on King James. He was with him when he advanced on 18th April to demand the surrender of the city, and was killed near his Royal person by fire from the city walls.

39. COL. CHARLES O'KELLY, of Castle Kelly (Manor Screen), Co. Galway.

As the author of "Macariæ Excidium" he has left us one of the best accounts of the war in Ireland, 1689–1692, from the Irish and Jacobite point of view. This is so often quoted by Macaulay and other historians of that period that no excuse is required for a short account of his life.

The O'Kellys were of ancient Celtic origin, possessing from about the 5th century considerable territory in the vicinity of Galway, long designated "The O'Kelly country." About the beginning of the 17th century, when the Plantation of Ulster took place, the O'Kelly family had been confirmed in the possession of a portion of their ancient territory as the Manor of Screen.

Born in 1621, he was the eldest son of the eighth Lord of the Manor of Manor Screen (Castle Kelly). He was educated at the College of St. Omer in Flanders, which accounts for an erudition remarkable, as unusual, in an Irish layman of that time. Returning in 1641, he served with the Royalist party against the rebels. In later years he gained both experience and distinction as an officer in the French and Spanish services. The Restoration of 1660 found him again in London, where his ability and learning ensured him a cordial reception.

When the 1689 troubles broke out in Ireland he was in residence at Castle Kelly. A warm supporter of James II., he raised, among his own people in Co. Galway, a regiment which he commanded all through the campaign down to Limerick, earning distinction and credit. His regiment does not appear to have served at the investment of Derry, but was employed under General Lord Mountcashell in the operations round Enniskillen. After the fall of Limerick he came under the special clauses of the Treaty, and was allowed to return to his family estate, where he occupied his remaining years in writing the book in question.

He died in 1695, being succeeded in the estate by his brother,

40. **Lieut.-Col. John O'Kelly**, who had been Lieut.-Col. of his regiment during the war. In 1740 this brother's line became extinct. The old race of the O'Kellys is, however, still represented by the O'Kellys of Gurtray, Co. Galway.[1]

(The above particulars are taken from a memoir on Col. Charles O'Kelly, by the editor of "Macariæ Excidium," prefacing the edition published by the Irish Archaeological Society in 1850.)

Nos. 41–95.

This series gives the names of the principal members of the family of O'Neills of Tyrone, of the family of the O'Neills of Clannaboy and "The Feevagh" and of their great feudatories, such as the Maguires, the Macmahons, the O'Kanes, the O'Hagans, etc., who held commissions in the Jacobite army at the siege of Derry, and for the subsequent campaign down to the fall of Limerick.

Nothing shows more clearly the thoroughness of the Ulster Plantation and the rigorous suppression of the 1641 rebellion than the comparative paucity of officers from families which barely a century before had officered armies dominating the Province, and held their own for years with the Generals of Queen Elizabeth. The people joined the Jacobite colours in their thousands, but officers of experience were hard to find. In these individual sketches the members of each sept, clan, or family are grouped together, with their origin, history, present-day representatives.

The O'Neills as Kings or Princes of their Provincial Kingdom of Ulster had maintained a semi-independence in spite of the continual encroachment of the English. During this latter period they had divided into the two great houses of Tyrone (Ulster) and Clannaboy, Tyrone embracing most of the ancient Provincial Kingdom of Ulster, while Clannaboy, comprising the present counties of Antrim and Down, had been carved out of the Ulster Palatinate, after the ruinous years of Edward Bruce's invasion, by a Prince of the Tyrone House, viz. Hugh Buidh O'Neill. Hence the name, the Principality of Clannaboy, the territory or clan of Hugh Buidh. For the next few centuries these two families, the O'Neills of Tyrone and Clannaboy, and their feudatories, with the O'Donnells, Princes of Tyrconnell[2] and the McDonnells of the Glens[3] dominated Ulster, in continual fight with each other, or in half-hearted alliance resisting the never-remitting encroachment of England. The end came in the long and desperate struggle between Elizabeth and Tyrone, backed by these others as allies. Deserted at last by his allies, who made their own terms as a favourable opportunity arose, Tyrone was forced to make submission at Mellifont in 1603. The Ulster chiefs

[1] Burke's "Landed Gentry of Ireland."
[2] See No. 96.
[3] See No. 6.

were broken, their independence was gone.

There followed in 1607 the flight of the Earls first to Brussels and then to Rome, the O'Neill, Earl of Tyrone, the O'Donnell, Earl of Tyrconnell, and the confiscation of their vast territories with those of their feudatories and the Plantation of Ulster, which involved the importation of English and Scottish families to replace the old Celtic chiefs and clans.

The O'Neills of Clannaboy had fared slightly better. By a fiction of English law, the territory of Clannaboy (the Ulster Palatinate) was vested in the Crown. That territory was disposed of, during and after the Elizabethan War, by grants either direct from the Crown or under the management of the Lord Deputy, Sir Arthur Chichester, Shane O'Neill, the ancestor of the Shane's Castle main line, being confirmed in an estate of some 60,000 acres.

The O'Neills of Tyrone.

The flight of Hugh, Earl of Tyrone, in 1607 had left his people without a leader. He died in Rome in 1616, leaving sons who succeeded to his titular honours, none living to return to Ireland, and all dying without leaving legitimate heirs.

The fate of the family is tragic, and that of the near relatives and kindred left in Ireland is nearly as bad. His brother Cormac, who had remained as custodian of the Earl's estate, was consigned to the Tower of London, where he died after a long captivity. To another brother, Art O'Neill, was granted for life an estate in Orior. He was the father of the famous General Owen Roe O'Neill, of whom presently; while to Catharine, widow of Tirlough O'Neill, and their son Phelim, a minor, was granted the manor of Kinnaird in Tyrone. (Tirlough and his father Sir Henry Oge O'Neill, princes of the house, had deserted the cause of their kinsman the Earl, and eventually lost their lives fighting on the English side in the suppression of Sir Cahir O'Dogherty's uprising in 1607.)

There being no direct descendant of Hugh, Earl of Tyrone, to lead the Irish of Ulster at the time of the 1641 rebellion, it fell to the lot of General Owen Roe and Phelim O'Neill, the rival claimants for the chiefship, honours, and titles of Tyrone, to raise his standard. Sir Phelim O'Neill took the lead at the very beginning, and he had most of Ulster at his feet when General Owen Roe O'Neill made his meteoric appearance in the North. An officer in the French army, already a Major-General, he had won distinction as the defender of Arras. His experience in war led to his being employed at the head of an army, recruited among his own people in Tyrone. By patience, discipline, and organisation he was soon at the head of an independent army. After many minor successes he won an overwhelming victory over General Monro at Benburb in 1646. To the great chagrin of his rival, Sir Phelim O'Neill, the Pope immediately acknowledged him as the great Earl of Tyrone's successor, "The O'Neill of Ulster," and sent him the Earl's sword with His Holiness' blessing.

Thwarted by the incompetence of other Generals and worn out by useless operations, he died of a lingering fever at Cloughouter Castle in 1649. His death left Sir Phelim O'Neill the unrivalled representative of the family in the Irish ranks. It is said that at the height of his domination of the province he had himself inaugurated as "The O'Neill," with all the ancient ceremonial, at Tullaghogue.

Although Sir Phelim failed after a long investment to capture Derry, he took Strabane Castle and in it the widowed Lady Strabane (before her first marriage Lady Jane Gordon, a daughter of the Marquess of Huntley). She became the third wife of Sir Phelim. By this union there was one son, Gordon O'Neill, of whom presently.

In the last dying flickers of the great rebellion Sir Phelim was captured, hiding in a wood, and taken to Dublin, where, after a historic trial, he was hanged, drawn, and quartered in 1652.

Having now dealt with the two great O'Neill chiefs of the Tyrone family an account will be given of Sir Phelim's son.

41. **Col. Gordon O'Neill**, after his father's execution, whose Kinnaird estate was confiscated, was brought up with his mother, Lady Strabane, who was reconciled to her former husband's Abercorn family. It was probably through the Hamilton influence that young Gordon obtained a commission in one of the regiments on the Irish Establishment.

Tyrconnell, who missed no opportunity, early saw in Gordon the representative of the old O'Neill stock, and prior to the revolution had placed him at Charlemont Fort, Co. Tyrone, in command of a regiment he had raised, and other troops. From this position of vantage he gave material assistance to General Richard Hamilton in his passage of the Bann and advance on Derry. He was present with his regiment all through the investment, being thus mentioned by "Londeriados":—

> "Gordon O'Neale came next, with heart and hand
> To fight for's King, against his native land
> Most of his foot, he raised in Tyrone,
> O'Kane, his nephew joined some of his own.
> Gordon O'Neale is that great traitor's son
> Who raised a great rebellion in Tyrone."

Towards the end of the siege, in the abortive negotiations of the 12th July for surrender of the city on terms, he was one of the commissioners representing the investing force.

He fought at the Boyne, and later at Aughrim, where he was so severely wounded that he had to retire to France to recuperate. Returning to Ireland, he fought down to the fall of Limerick. After Limerick he elected for French service, and under his command his own old regiment, "The Charlemont," became a famous unit in the Irish Brigade of France.

In 1703, having received permission to raise a regiment for the Spanish service, he went to Spain, where he died the following year. He left one son, Charles, who died a year later.

42. **Col. Conn O'Neill.** What branch of the O'Neill family this member belonged to I am unable to ascertain, although probably to the Feevagh cadets of Clannaboy.

He was an officer of the investing army at Derry, and was killed in one of the garrison's sorties.

43. **Don Juan O'Neill** of Palma, Majorca. Perhaps in dealing with the fortunes of descendants of the house of Tyrone who established themselves in the armies of continental monarchs, the following experience of the author may be of sufficient interest to excuse insertion. When in Spain in 1877 the author paid a visit to the British Consul at Palma in the island of Majorca. He had hardly landed ere the Consul insisted on formally presenting him, as coming from Ulster, to a compatriot, "The O'Neill," Prince of Tyrone and Clannaboy, etc. Before the presentation the author had admitted a distant connection with a branch of the great house. Presented to "The O'Neill" as a *pariente* or cousin, he was immediately welcomed as a relation by a most charming middle-aged caballero, Don Juan O'Neill, a grandee of Spain, and hereditary Knight of Calatrava, as proud as could be of his Tyrone lineage. During a fortnight's stay on the island nothing could have exceeded Don Juan's attention. I was introduced to a charming se&ñra and family, to all the notables of the island, and finally entertained at a banquet, given in "The O'Neills" old Moorish Palace, at which his family and some twenty grandees were present. Grand as was the hospitality, it was eclipsed by the uniqueness of the ancient table-cloth which his ancestor had brought from Ireland. At both ends of this cloth were displayed the family coat of arms, with the supporters of the Earl of Tyrone, while the sides and centre of the fabric were replete with crest, emblems, and devices of the princely house. Historic in itself, it was the only remaining relic of their Ulster past.

Don Juan gave me many interesting papers, copied from original documents lodged in the Heralds' College at Madrid, proving his descent, which at his request I handed to Lord O'Neill of Shane's Castle. I have unfortunately forgotten much of this family story, but what follows is the general purport. His ancestor, one of the minor chiefs of the princely house, remained in Tyrone for some decades after the departure of the Earl, but early in the 17th century arrived in Spain armed with a letter of introduction from the Catholic Hierarchy of Ireland, recommending the bearer to the Most Christian Monarch as the representative of a family who in centuries of struggle with the power of England had killed so many thousands of heretics and defeated them in so many battles. With such a letter his ancestor was cordially received at the Court of Madrid, given a commission, and made speedy advancement in the service. He died in considerable affluence and a Captain-General of Spain. His son, a grandee of Spain, followed with like success in his father's footsteps. The Napoleonic era in Spain had nearly put an end to their prosperity. What was left of the estate was dissipated by Don Juan's grandfather in Paris. Don Juan, on his succession to the family honours, found himself in possession of nothing but the name and the old palace in Palma, granted by a monarch of Spain to an ancestor.

The O'Neills of Clannaboy, Edenduffcarrick or Shane's Castle, etc.

It is a matter of history how the Earl of Essex, Queen Elizabeth's favourite, when President of Ulster in 1575, at a great banquet given in his honour by Sir Brian McPhelim O'Neill, Chief of Clannaboy (Shane's Castle), in his castle of Belfast, turned on his entertainers, killing all present except Sir Brian, Lady O'Neill, and her brother, Rory Macquillan, who were reserved for Carrickfergus Castle, where they were hanged, drawn, and quartered.

Some two and a half years later, when Sir Arthur Chichester was resettling Cos. Down and Antrim, Shane O'Neill, Sir Brian's son, was restored to the chiefship of northern Clannaboy and some 60,000 acres comprising the Shane's Castle estate with its ancient castle of Edenduffcarrick. (At the same time Conn O'Neill, another Prince of the Clannaboy, was confirmed in the possession of the Castlerea territory of southern Clannaboy. Into the doings of this unfortunate branch there is no reason to enter, as long before the 1688–89 revolution the estate had passed out of their hands.)

On Shane O'Neill's death he was succeeded by his eldest son, Sir Henry, who, after his marriage with Martha, daughter of Sir Francis Stafford, President of Ulster, took up his residence in London. They were frequenters of the Court of Charles I., becoming so popular at Whitehall that when the Court were seeking a girl of the same age to accompany Princess Mary, Charles I.'s daughter, to The Hague as the affianced bride of the Stadtholder, their choice fell upon Rose, the only surviving child of Sir Henry and Lady O'Neill and heiress of Shane's Castle.

44. This **ROSE O'NEILL**, afterwards **MARCHIONESS OF ANTRIM**, is the subject of this sketch.

During her many years' absence as lady-in-waiting to her Royal mistress many changes had taken place in her life and surroundings. Her father had died, leaving her the owner of Shane's Castle. Charles I. had lost his head on the scaffold, and Oliver Cromwell commanded the destinies of the three kingdoms. It was not until the death of the Stadtholder and the birth of William of Orange a few months later that Rose left the service of Princess Mary. Returning to London, she took up her residence with her mother, Lady O'Neill, subsisting, it would appear, on a small subsidy granted by Cromwell out of the estate. There she met the Marquess of Antrim, an old family connection and an acquaintance at the Court of Whitehall in Charles I.'s palmy days.

Like herself, he was a landless exile depending on the bounty of Cromwell. His first wife, the Duchess of Buckingham, was dead. So naturally enough these two old friends who were not permitted to visit their Co. Antrim estates were married, thus linking together the great Celtic families of O'Neill and McDonnell.

When the Restoration (1660) came, both thought their difficulties over, but on the Marquess, the old and steadfast supporter of Charles I., presenting himself at the son's Court, he was sent with contumely to the Tower. Months of weary waiting ensued, the Marchioness exercising every possible influence on his behalf. At length the "Declaration of Innocence" was obtained, thanks to the efforts of such men as the Earl of Clarendon, and their estates were restored. Returning to Co. Antrim, their time was divided between the two estates, residing part of the year at Shane's Castle and part at Ballymagarry (a house near Dunluce Castle now in ruins), which had been lent by the Macnaghtens.

Until the Marquess's death in 1686 they had as much as they could manage in repairing their several estates. The Marquess was buried in Bunnamairgie Abbey. The Marquessate became extinct, but his brother Alexander succeeded to the Earldom.[1] The widowed Marchioness returned to her own estate of Shane's Castle, where she died in 1695, being buried close to her father and mother, Sir Henry and Lady O'Neill, in the ancient church of Carrickfergus.

Whatever her own sentiments in the difficult years of the revolution, all the males of the Clannaboy clan were fighting on the Jacobite side, while her brother-in-law, the Earl of Antrim, who was His Majesty's Lieutenant and held Co. Antrim with regiments under his command up to the Battle of the Boyne, was one of their foremost leaders. The Marchioness's difficulties were great, but it can be gathered from the fact of no O'Neill of Clannaboy figuring on the list of attaintures of James II.'s Dublin Parliament (May 1689) that the Jacobites counted on the Marchioness as one of their faction. After her death her cousin (see following sketch) Col. Cormac O'Neill, the next in succession under Sir Henry O'Neill's will, was allowed to inherit the estate. By this fact the secret influence of William of Orange can well be felt. He was adverse to the driving of the old Celtic nobility from the soil, and, probably reminded by the Marchioness of her service to his Stuart mother, had helped in thus continuing the O'Neill succession.

45. **Lieut.-Col. Cormac O'Neill**, of Broughshane, Clannaboy, Shane's Castle. He was the heir, under his uncle Sir Henry O'Neill's will, to the O'Neill estate as the son of his next brother, Art.

Owing to the Marchioness's influence with her brother-in-law the Earl of Antrim he occupied many prominent positions during the revolution period. He was His Majesty's Lieutenant of Co. Derry, High Sheriff of Co. Antrim, and appointed by

---

[1] See Part II, No. 6, the 3rd Earl of Antrim.

Tyrconnell in the new charter granted to that city in 1688 to be Mayor of Derry. "Londeriados" thus alludes to this appointment

> "Yet in spite of reason and the English laws
> Talbot[1] the charter from the city draws.
> Turns out the English corporation
> And chose all popish members of his own
> Cormac O'Neill of Broughshane chosen Mayor."

Before the troubles resulting in the shutting of the gates and after-events, Cormac O'Neill had named a Deputy-Mayor and left the city to rejoin one of Lord Antrim's regiments, of which he was Lieut.-Col., at Carrickfergus Castle. With this regiment he served at the Boyne and in the subsequent campaign down to the fall of Limerick. He seems to have been among the favoured few who came under the special clauses of the Treaty of Limerick, as he was permitted, on the Marchioness's death in 1695, to succeed to the Shane's Castle estate. This is all the more curious as in the list of attaintures and confiscations after the collapse at Limerick we find Cormac O'Neill's name, described as of Broughshane, figuring among the confiscated land-owners for ten townlands in the Braid district, Co. Antrim, and forty houses in Broughshane, all held under the Marchioness of Antrim.

Cormac O'Neill died about 1705, and was buried in the old church of Skerry, near Broughshane, where so many of his kindred lie.

It is just possible that, in some matters above, his name may have been mixed up with that of another prominent member of the Clannaboy family,

46. **Col. Cormac O'Neill**, of Kilmacevet. In Chichester's settlement of Co. Antrim his grandfather, Hugh O'Neill, a leading cadet of the house of Clannaboy, had been confirmed in the possession of fifteen townlands near Crumlin. What happened to the estate is not clear, but his representative at the revolution, the above Col. Cormac, raised among his own people and those of the allies and feudatories of Clannaboy a Jacobite regiment which he commanded in person at the Boyne and in the subsequent campaign down to Limerick. Coming under the special clauses of the Treaty, he was permitted to return to Broughshane, where, dying in 1706, he was interred in the family burial ground of Skerry church.

The names of the officers of this regiment, as being of so much local interest, are given, viz.:—

Colonel-Commanding, Cormac O'Neill.
Lieut.-Col., Felix (Phelim) O'Neill, of the Feevagh.

---

[1] Tyrconnell.

Captains.

James O'Neill

Henry O'Neill

Brian O'Neill

Conn O'Neill

Conn O'Neill

Dan Hegarty

Hugh O'Gribbon

Art O'Harane

Robert Butler

Thomas Macnaghten

Henry Courtney

Peter Dobbin

Cormac O'Hagan

Art O'Hagan

Dan O'Hagan

Cormac O'Hara

Ross McQuillan

Thomas O'Kane

Roger O'Kane

Thomas Magill

William Stewart

John Clements

Christopher Russell

Lieutenants.

James O'Neill

Henry O'Neill

Oliver O'Hagan

John O'Hagan

Arthur O'Hara

Hugh Magennis

Bryan McCann

Edmund McIlderry

Cormac Magill

Christopher Fleming

Daniel McKay

John Gernon

Cormac McQuillan

Bryan O'Kane

Daniel O'Donnell

Conn O'Dogherty

Patrick O'Shiel

Donaghey McGunshennan

Bryan MacManus

Thomas Dobbin

Edmund Savage

Alexander Stewart

Henry Smith

Edward McConway

Ensigns.

Art O'Neill

Manus O'Hara

Theodore McQuillan

Patrick O'Harane

Donaghey O'Kane

Darby O'Kane

Darby O'Kane

Bryan O'Connor

Cormac O'Hagan

James O'Hagan

Maurice O'Heggarty

John O'Dogherty

Cormac McCann

Terence McConway

James O'Crilly

Myles McNamee[1]

Most of these officers will be referred to again in special family groups (O'Neills, O'Hagans, O'Kanes, etc.).

---

[1] D'Alton's "Jacobite Army List."

47. Col. Sir Niall O'Neill, 2nd Bart., of Killelagh, Co. Antrim.

At the time of the Chichester settlement Niall Oge (a brother of Hugh O'Neill, to whom had been granted the fifteen townlands of Kilmacevet[1] had received a grant of the fifteen townlands of Killelagh, near Crumlin. Henry, his son, was created a baronet in 1666. He was succeeded by his son, the 2nd Baronet, who, in possession of Killelagh at the time of the revolution, raised a regiment of dragoons in the Jacobite service, thus referred to in "Londeriados":—

> "To Antrim and Lough Neagh Sir Neal O'Neal
> Did for his regiment of Dragoons appeal."

Commanding this regiment at the Boyne, he was mortally wounded, but was carried off the field by his troopers, who conveyed him to Waterford. He died a few days after arrival and was buried under a monument still to be seen. His only son, afterwards General Carlos Felix O'Neill, a distinguished officer in the Spanish service, died at Madrid in 1791.[2]

48. Sir Brian O'Neill, 2nd Bart., of Clannaboy, was the son of Sir Brian O'Neill, created a Baronet by Charles I. for gallantry in defence of the Royal person at the Battle of Edgehill in 1642.

He was the landless chief of a well-known branch of the O'Neills of southern Clannaboy. Sir Bryan (the son) commanded a regiment at the investment of Derry and through the subsequent campaign. After the fall of Limerick he was among the attainted.[3]

O'Neills of "The Feevagh," etc., of Clannaboy.

49. Phelim (Felix) O'Neill, of "The Feevagh."

"The Feevagh" (wooded district) was a wide territory running along the Northern end of Lough Neagh, from the River Maine to the Bann and extending almost to Portglenone, practically the parishes of Cranfield, Duneane, and the Grange.[4] It had been included in Chichester's settlement in the estate granted to Shane O'Neill, and was now vested in Rose O'Neill, Marchioness of Antrim. The occupiers of "The Feevagh," nearly all O'Neills, more or less closely connected by blood, looked upon

[1] For this line, see Part II, No. 46, Col. Cormac O'Neill, of Kilmacevet.
[2] "The O'Neills of Ulster," by Mathews.
[3] For his descendant representatives, and their misfortunes, see Burke's "Vicissitudes of Great Families." Please note that D'Alton says that Sir Niall died leaving no male issue and that his brother, Daniel, succeeded as 3rd titular Baronet, on whose death the baronetcy became extinct. According to the same authority, Rose, a sister of Sir Niall's, married Conn Modera O'Neill, of the Feevagh, ancestor of Charles H. O'Neill, the present chief of Clannaboy. (D'Alton, Vol. I., 2nd edition, published in 1860.)
[4] See Reeve's "Ecclesiastical Antiquities."

her, not so much as the landlady, but as the hereditary chieftainess of the O'Neills of Clannaboy. Their instinct was the sword, inherited from generations of fighting men, and, as the following sketches will show, "The Feevagh" furnished more than its quota to the service of James II.

The above Phelim (Felix) O'Neill, of "The Feevagh," was the great-great-grandson of Murcertae O'Neill, representative descendant of Brian Ballagh, second son of Niall Mor, Prince of Clannaboy. Murcertae was himself Prince of Clannaboy, but being deposed in 1552 took up his residence in the Feevagh. At the commencement of the revolution Phelim obtained a lieutenant's commission in his cousin, Col. Gordon O'Neill's, regiment, then occupying Charlemont Fort. With this regiment he was present at the investment of Derry, the Boyne, and subsequent campaign down to the fall of Limerick. Going with Col. Gordon O'Neill's Charlemont Regiment to France, he distinguished himself as an officer of the Irish Brigade until the Battle of Malplaquet (1709), where he fell with 93 brother officers of that brigade. For his long service in the Irish Brigade (1691–1709) his widow was granted a small pension by Louis XIV. of France. (No children of this marriage left issue.) Through a former marriage he left issue in Ireland, among whom was Conn O'Neill, whose son, Shane O'Neill, emigrated to Portugal in 1740, where he bought a small estate near Lisbon. In 1756 Shane O'Neill drew up an elaborate pedigree of his descent, proving him to be the senior representative of the O'Neills of Clannaboy, and of the extinct line of Tyrone, and claiming to be "The O'Neill," Prince of Clannaboy, Earl of Tyrone, etc.[1]

The late George O'Neill, of Lisbon, "The O'Neill," hereditary Prince of Ulster and Tyrone and Clannaboy, Knight Grand Cross of the Order of St. Gregory the Great, Chevalier of the Order of Malta, Comte de Tyrone, direct descendant of the Shane O'Neill above, was the representative of the family residing in Lisbon until his death two years ago, when he was succeeded by his son.

50. **LIEUT.-COL. PHELIM O'NEILL**, of "The Feevagh," held a commission as such in his cousin, Col. Cormac O'Neill of Kilmacevet's, regiment.[2] He fell at the Battle of Aughrim. In his pocket was found a letter addressed to the Countess of Antrim, interesting because of the statement that the Irish of the Jacobite army were not entering the coming battle in any despondency, attributing the loss of Athlone entirely to the incompetency of the French engineers with the army.[3]

The following officers of Col. Cormac O'Neill of Kilmacevet's Regiment[4] had their interest in leases held under the Marchioness of Antrim on the O'Neill estate confiscated after the fall of Limerick, viz.:—

---

[1] For a copy of this pedigree, etc., see Mathews' "O'Neills of Ulster," appendix to Vol. III. pp. 323–56.
[2] D'Alton's "Jacobite Army List."
[3] See copy of letter in Rawdon Papers.
[4] For full list, see Part II, No. 46.

51. **Capt. Henry O'Neill**, of "The Feevagh." His lease was valued at a profit of £40 per annum.

52. **Capt. James O'Neill**, probably of "The Feevagh."

53. **Capt. Brian O'Neill**, of Aghalogan, one townland so designated. He died in the Jacobite service.

54. **Capt. Conn O'Neill**, of the Braid, in possession of two townlands near Broughshane.

55. A second **Capt. Conn O'Neill**, probably from the same part of the O'Neill estate.

56. **Lieut. James O'Neill**, probably of "The Feevagh."

57. **Lieut. Henry O'Neill**.

58. **Ensign Art O'Neill**. Both probably of "The Feevagh."

The following officers of the O'Neill name, serving in the Earl of Antrim's regiment, had their estates (the profit rent on leases held on the Marchioness of Antrim's estate) confiscated after the fall of Limerick, viz.:—

59. **Capt. Hugh O'Neill**, of "The Feevagh," where he held the townland of Tobrin.

60. **Capt. Terence O'Neill**, probably of "The Feevagh."

61. **Lieut. John O'Neill**.

62. **Lieut. John O'Neill**. Probably near relations of John O'Neill, of Ballybolan, in "The Feevagh," of whom presently.

63. **Ensign Turlogh O'Neill, and**

64. **Ensign Francis O'Neill**, probably both from "The Feevagh."

65. **Lieut. Brian O'Neill**, of "The Feevagh," four townlands at Cashell.

66. **Lieut. Brian Boy Ardagh O'Neill**, of "The Feevagh," one townland.

There were three others of the Clannaboy family who, although they do not appear to have borne arms in James II.'s service, were prominent enough on the Jacobite side to have their estates confiscated, viz.:—

67. **Shane O'Neill**, a near relative of Col. Sir Neal O'Neill, Bart., of Killelagh, Crumlin, who lost his leasehold of one townland on that estate.

68. **CORMAC** or **JOHN O'NEILL** who lost his lease of half a townland of Glenkean on the Marchioness's estate.

In addition to the foregoing sketches (No. 49 to No. 68) there were the following officers of the name in Sir Niall O'Neill's Dragoons[1] whose names may possibly be identical with some of those already given, viz.: Capt. Shane O'Neill, sen., Capt. Henry O'Neill, Lieut. Henry O'Neill, and Cornet Phelim O'Neill.

69. **JOHN O'NEILL**, of Ballybolan, in "The Feevagh." He was the great-grandson of Shane Oge O'Neill, of Shane's Castle, and inherited two townlands on the estate, living in his residence at Ballybolan.

He was the Jacobite High Sheriff of Co. Antrim in the few months prior to the Boyne, which accounts for his confiscation. How it was managed is not known, but the estate remained in the family, John O'Neill's daughter marrying an O'Rourke, of Brefny, in whose line, the O'Rourkes of Ballybolan, the place has remained until recent years.

The O'Rourkes of Brefny, of which the Ballybolan family are the leading representatives, was one of the most prominent Celtic septs in Ulster. Their chief had been hanged at his own door in the Elizabethan wars, and the tribe lands confiscated. The Ballybolan family adhered to their ancient faith and occupied an important position among the smaller landowners of Co. Antrim.

Ambrose O'Rourke was High Sheriff of the county in the latter half of last century.

70. **ENSIGN CON O'ROURKE**, probably of this connection, held his commission in Lord Antrim's Regiment, which served at Derry, the Boyne, and subsequent campaigns down to the Treaty of Limerick, and a Constantine O'Rourke was one of the new Burgesses appointed on the Derry Corporation under Tyrconnell's new Charter of 1688.

The O'Hagans, of Tullaghogue, Co. Tyrone.

One of the most important of the septs feudatory to the O'Neills of Tyrone. At Tullaghogue was the ancient Coronation chair, and to the O'Hagans fell the duty at the inauguration ceremony of putting his sandals on the Prince of the house. Dispossessed of their lands after the flight of the Earls their glory was a thing of the past.

In the muster of the Jacobite forces before Derry "Londeriados" has the following mention:—

> From Glenwood the O'Hagans came apace,"

probably referring to some gathering of the sept from the neighbourhood of Tullaghogue.

---

[1] D'Alton, Vol. I.

They were ancient allies, both in the field and in matrimony, of the Clannaboy O'Neills. In Col. Cormac O'Neill of Kilmacevet's Regiment there were no fewer than six officers of the name:—

71. **Capt. Cormac O'Hagan.**

72. **Capt. Daniel O'Hagan.**

73. **Lieut. Oliver O'Hagan.**

74. **Lieut. John O'Hagan.**

75. **Ensign Arthur O'Hagan.**

76. **Capt. Arthur O'Hagan.** The latter had married Martha, sister of "French" John O'Neill, of Shane's Castle. They resided on the O'Neill estate in "The Feevagh." The wife died in 1704, the husband in 1717, both being interred in the old church of Cranfield, where a stone marks their grave.

A great lawyer of this family, Sir Thomas O'Hagan, was twice Lord Chancellor of Ireland. On his elevation to the peerage in 1870 he took the title of Baron O'Hagan of Tullaghogue. The present representative of the family is the 3rd Baron O'Hagan of Tullaghogue.

The O'Haras of Lissanoure, Crebilly and O'Harabrook.

This family, of the same stock as that of Sligo, is said to have been brought to Co. Antrim by Richard de Burgho,[1] who was Earl of Ulster and of Connaught in the early part of the 14th century. Acquiring considerable estate they were prominent landlords for many generations.

The Lissanoure estate was sold to the Macartneys, the present owners, in 1733. Crebilly remained in the family down to the end of last century, and the Cramsies became owners of O'Harabrook by purchase some fifty years ago.

The family is extinct in the male line. The late Right Rev. Henry Stewart O'Hara, Bishop of Cashel, Emly, Waterford, and Lismore, who had so many friends in his native country, was the last of this ancient family.

At the time of the 1688 revolution the following of the name held commissions in Col. Cormac O'Neill of Kilmacevet's Jacobite Regiment, which served down to the fall of Limerick, viz.:—

77. **Capt. Cormac O'Hara** had his townland of Sharvogues on the O'Neill estate confiscated.

---

[1] Burke.

78. **Lieut. Arthur O'Hara.**

79. **Ensign Manus O'Hara.**

The following O'Haras figure in the list of confiscations after the Treaty of Limerick:—

80. **Lieut. Conn O'Hara**[1] had two townlands held under Sir Robert Colville in Glenwherry confiscated. He was killed in the Jacobite service.

81. **Conn Oge O'Hara.** His two townlands in the Kurt were confiscated.

The O'Cahans (O'Kanes), of Keenaght.

This family was among the greatest of the feudatories or allies of the O'Neill of Tyrone. Owners of most of the present Co. Derry, with their castles of Limavady and Dungiven, they were all-powerful. The last great chief of the house, who had married a daughter of Hugh, Earl of Tyrone, Sir Donnell Ballagh O'Cahan, was a staunch supporter of the Earl until almost the close of the Elizabethan War, when his defection to the English side practically ended the struggle. In spite of his great services his territory after the flight of the Earls was included in the general confiscation. Room had to be found for the City of London Companies, who turned it into the present county of Londonderry.

The fate of the family is sorry reading. Sir Donnell Ballagh ended his life a few years later as a prisoner in the Tower of London. To his wife and some of his sons small grants of land were allotted on which to eke out a miserable existence. Many cadets of the house went to the Continent, and many more lost their lives in the 1641 rebellion. At the time of the 1688 revolution there were still some of the name left in the country, among whom the following held commissions in the Jacobite army, all being near relations of the last chief, Sir Donnell Ballagh O'Cahan.

82. **Capt. Manus O'Kane**, probably an officer in Col. Gordon O'Neill's Regiment (the latter being, according to "Londeriados," his uncle).

At the muster of the Jacobite army before Derry Capt. Manus O'Kane joined his relative, Col. Gordon O'Neill:—

"O'Kane, his nephew, joined some of his own"[2]

83. **Ensign John O'Kane** held a commission in Lord Antrim's Regiment, while the following held commissions in Col. Cormac O'Neill of Kilmacevet's Regiment:

---

[1] I have not ascertained his regiment.
[2] "Londeriados."

84. Captain Thomas O'Kane.

85. Captain Roger O'Kane, who was also appointed an Alderman of Derry under Tyrconnell's new Charter of 1688.

86. Lieut. Bryan O'Kane.

87. Ensign Donaghy O'Kane.

88. Ensign Darby O'Kane.

89. Ensign Darby O'Kane, there being two of this name.

There were two burgesses of the name appointed to the Corporation of Derry under Tyrconnell's new Charter of 1688, Francis O'Kane and Maurice O'Kane.

It is curious to note that a daughter of Florence O'Kane, of Limavady, had in 1683 married John King, brother of the 2nd Baron Kingston, whom he eventually succeeded as third Baron.[1] Through the O'Kane influence John King became a Roman Catholic and a strong supporter of James.[2]

The Maguires of Fermanagh.

Another of the great feudatories of the O'Neills of Tyrone. For centuries dominating that territory and the surrounding districts, their chief residence was the Castle of Enniskillen.

Faithful allies and strong supporters of the Earl of Tyrone in the Elizabethan wars, it was not until the desertion of Connor Roe Maguire, a claimant for the chieftainship, to the English side, that the castle of Enniskillen was taken and the clan power diminished. The Chief, Sir Hugh Maguire, was killed in battle in 1599, and his brother and successor, Cuconnaught, was one of the Ulster chiefs accompanying the Earls of Tyrone and Tyrconnell in their flight (1607) to the Continent. Cuconnaught died at Genoa in 1608. The flight of the Earls entailed the confiscation of their territories, and that of their tributaries, including the Maguires. Only a few of the Maguires received small grants of land. To Connor Roe Maguire, now the Chief, was granted some 7000 acres. Dying in 1625, he was succeeded by his son, Sir Brian Maguire, raised to the peerage (1627) as Baron Maguire of Enniskillen. His son, the second Baron, Connor Maguire, a prominent leader in the 1641 rebellion, was taken prisoner and executed at Tyburn in 1644. The estates were confiscated.

90. Connor Maguire, a grandson of the second Baron, was acknowledged by James II. as fifth Baron, and sat in his Dublin Parliament of 1689.

---

[1] See Part I, Nos. 32 and 33.

[2] In Part I, No. 287, will be found an account of Brigadier-General Richard Kane (or O'Kane), who served on King William's side.

This fifth Baron Maguire of Enniskillen held a commission as captain in his kinsman the Earl of Antrim's Regiment, with which he served all through the campaign. Attainted with fresh confiscation, he fled to France, and died at St. Germains in 1708.

Some three of his family, serving in the Irish Brigade in France, seem to have borne the titular honour until about 1750, when it became extinct with the death of the seventh Baron.

91. **COLONEL CUCONNAUGHT MAGUIRE** raised a regiment in Fermanagh with which he served at the investment of Derry, the Boyne, and at Aughrim, where he fell in 1691.
There were two others of the family in his regiment, viz.:—

92. **LIEUT.-COL. ALEXANDER MAGUIRE.**

93. **MAJOR CORNELIUS MAGUIRE.**

Descendants of Col. Cuconnaught Maguire were in possession of the Tempo estate, Co. Fermanagh, for several generations in the 18th century, Hugh Maguire, of Tempo, being High Sheriff in 1780. His successor, Constantine,[1] sold the property to Mr. Tennent, a banker of Belfast, father-in-law of the well-known politician Sir James Emerson-Tennent, Bart., of Tempo Manor.

The MacMahons of Monaghan.

This was another of the great Celtic tribes or clans of Ulster, generally among the feudatories of The O'Neill of Tyrone. The long Elizabethan wars had broken them, and the general confiscation after the flight of the Earls in 1607 left them landless.

At the revolution of 1688 there were still many of the name to rally to the call of any members of the family of their hereditary chiefs. Such were found in

94. **COL. ARTHUR MACMAHON**, who raised a regiment in his old county, and commanded it in the investment of Derry, at the Boyne, and down to the fall of Limerick. His second in command was

95. **LIEUT.-COL. OWEN MACMAHON.**[2] "Londeriados" in mentioning the muster of the Jacobite forces before Derry has the following

> "From Carrickmacross, and from Monaghan
> A regiment was raised by Macmahon."

Many of the name took service in the army of France, and it may be assumed

---

[1] For the story of their passing away, see Burke's "Vicissitudes of Great Families." For most of the particulars in the foregoing Nos. 90 to 93, I am indebted to Trimble's "History of Enniskillen," Vol. I. and D'Alton's "Jacobite Army List" with its full notes.
[2] D'Alton's "Jacobite Army List."

that the great soldier, Marshal Macmahon, Duke of Magenta, of the French army, and President of the French Republic, was descended from one of these. Hill, in his "Ulster Plantation," referring to the McMahons and Maguires, makes the following sympathetic comment:—

"They had indeed a long and distinguished history. Will any of the families, planted by James I. in Ulster, be found, if sought for, after a lapse of fourteen hundred years?"

The O'Donnells of Tyrconnell (Donegal).

Sprung from the same stock as the O'Neills of Tyrone. In fact, two brothers, Owen the elder and Donnell, of whom Owen held the territory of Tir-owen (Tyrone) and Donnell the territory of Tyr-Donnell (Tyrconnell). United they made Ulster impregnable to the aggression of the Anglo-Norman, but unfortunately for themselves they frittered away their man power in centuries of internecine wars, and, what was even worse, each was at any time ready to combine with the Dublin Lord Deputy in invading and devastating his rival's country.

The territory of Tyrconnell, lying along the Atlantic with its forests, fastnesses, and castles of Ballyshannon and Donegal, was practically impervious to English attack as long as it was allied to Tyrone to guard its southern border. Realising this, Henry VIII., through his Lord Deputies, tried to conciliate the Irish chiefs by offers of alliance and peerages. Conn, the grandfather of Hugh, accepted the Earldom of Tyrone, which his grandson, the great Hugh, afterwards held. The playing off of one chief against the other was also attempted with some success.

Queen Elizabeth was not long on the throne before she determined on bringing Ulster to its senses. Sterner measures, invasion of its territories, were adopted, but Shane the proud, "The O'Neill" of Tyrone, rose to the occasion. He defeated Elizabeth's armies in the field, and would have possibly succeeded had it not been for his inordinate ambition, which led him into an expedition against the Macdonnells of Co. Antrim, successful at the time, but which led to his eventual ruin. Not content with this, he turned on the O'Donnells, losing a large army and nearly his life in the wilds of Tyrconnell. To such despair was Shane now reduced that he rode with some fifty followers into the Macdonnell camp at Cushendun and was murdered the same night at a banquet given in his honour (1567).

To Elizabeth's chagrin, Shane's destruction did not bring peace to Ulster. For the next twenty-five years Turlough O'Neill and the Earl of Tyrone, rival claimants for the chiefship, coquetted with Her Majesty's Lord Deputies, and it was not until after the death of Turlough that, in 1593, the Earl threw off the cloak, declaring himself The O'Neill, and ruler of an independent Ulster. He did not make Shane O'Neill's mistake, but had meantime consolidated the closest alliance with the chieftain of

Tyrconnell, Hugh Roe O'Donnell, who had married his sister. There followed the eight years of struggle with England, successful in the beginning, as these two allies, with their tributary clans, held together; but at last, harassed on all sides, deserted by many of their tributaries, and with the defection of several of the leading cadets of their own families, they were on the verge of ruin.

At this juncture the long-promised assistance from the King of Spain arrived. A Spanish army of 5000 men landed at Kinsale, and messages were sent to the Earl and O'Donnell to join them there. Meantime Lord Mountjoy, the Queen's Lord Deputy, with a large army had invested that town. Gathering an army of some 6000 men the two chiefs marched down to the relief. A battle disastrous to the Irish hopes was the result (1601), and only a sorry remnant under the Earl succeeded in regaining Ulster, while Hugh Roe O'Donnell was dispatched to Spain to invoke further aid. Hugh Roe O'Donnell was cordially received at Madrid, but after obtaining the usual promises he fell ill and died a few weeks after arrival.

His brother Rory (Roderick) became chief of the O'Donnells. For two more years the struggle was maintained, until in 1603, with further disaffection of their own clans and tributaries, the end came. Rory made terms with the Government, and the Earl submitted at Mellifont. How the Earl and Rory O'Donnell (the latter being created Earl of Tyrconnell) were graciously received by James I. at the English Court and restored in name to their ancient possessions is well known.

So close and irritating was the Dublin Executive's interference with their every movement that, fearing that their doom was sealed, in 1607 the Earls with many of their family and chief adherents fled to the Continent. This flight of the Earls sealed the fate of their Ulster. Their territories were confiscated and James I.'s Ulster Plantation was ruthlessly carried into execution.

Among the greatest of the O'Donnell family traitors was Sir Niall Garve O'Donnell, who counted on receiving the clan chieftainship for useful service, but, like Sir Donnell Ballagh O'Cahan, he found himself in the Tower of London, where he died some twenty years later.

Many of the name went to the Continent, where in the armies of France and Spain they distinguished themselves in the career of arms, founding houses such as those now represented by the Duke of Tetuan, one of the grandees of Spain, and by Count O'Donnell.

Few of the O'Donnells figure in the 1688–89 revolution, but the arrival of

96. HUGH BULDEARG O'DONNELL from Spain in 1690 among the people of Tyrconnell had a stirring effect. In his person he carried all the marks and characteristics given in an old prophecy that an O'Donnell would one day save Ireland. He was a descendant of one of the cadets of the family who had accompanied the Earl of Tyrconnell to Spain. By a superstitious people he was acclaimed The O'Donnell and their saviour. He soon had a rabble of thousands of men at his back. Among the other Jacobite leaders there was considerable jealousy, Col. Gordon O'Neill, in particular, resenting his pretensions in Ulster, where he thought himself alone entitled to be supreme. With nothing but his name and the prophecy behind him, a few months saw his following dwindling away, and with it his aspirations.

He went over to the English towards the end of the war, taking the remnant of his rabble, of which he was given command, with him. After the fall of Limerick he disappeared from Ireland.[1] He went to Austria, becoming a Major-General in the Emperor's Army, and dying in 1704.[2]

Among the Aldermen appointed by Tyrconnell's new Charter to the Corporation of Derry figure Manus O'Donnell and Daniel O'Donnell, probably identical with

97. **Capt. Manus O'Donnell**, an officer in Lord Antrim's Regiment, probably the Major of that name who fell at Aughrim in 1691.[3]

98. **Lieut. Daniel O'Donnell**, an officer in Col. Cormac O'Neill of Kilmacevet's Regiment.

The O'Doghertys or O'Dohertys of Innishowen, Co. Donegal.

This ancient family, of the same stock as the O'Neills and the O'Donnells, were for centuries in possession of the peninsula of Innishowen, a wild district with its borders guarded on two sides by the Atlantic and on the other two by Loughs Foyle and Swilly. Like their neighbours, they were often at war, being frequently involved in the recurring struggle between the O'Neills and the O'Donnells, as they were always tributary to one or the other.

Their very inaccessibility left them immune from outside interference. They had the good fortune after Sir Henry Docwra had established the English garrison in Derry to be recognised by him as the possessors of Innishowen. In 1607 Sir Cahir O'Doherty in a fit of rage attacked the city of Derry, which he burnt to the ground. Retribution was rapid, the county was wasted, his people were slaughtered, and he himself starved to death in one of his castles; hence the skeleton added to Derry's coat of arms to commemorate the event. After the flight of the Earls in the same year the O'Dohertys suffered in the general confiscation, Innishowen being granted to Sir Arthur Chichester, then Lord Deputy of Ireland, the ancestor of the Marquess of Donegal, in whose descendant (female line) the Earl of Shaftesbury the feudal ownership still lies.

---

[1] D'Alton and Harris.
[2] "Irish Abroad," by Elliott O'Donnell.
[3] D'Alton's "Jacobite Army List."

Few of the family seem to have been left at the time of the 1688 revolution, for there is scarcely a mention of the name. Graham in his Catalogue ("Ireland Preserved") in referring to the Jacobite muster before the investment of Derry had the lines:

"From Aileach's throne on Innishowen
O'Doherty came shouting."

When in 1688 Tyrconnell granted the new Charter to the Corporation of Derry, the following of the name were appointed: Daniel O'Doherty, Constantine O'Doherty, and Roger O'Doherty, Aldermen, and Hugh Margrath O'Doherty, a Burgess, while the two undernoted had commissions in Col. Cormac O'Neill of Kilmacevet's Regiment with which they served at the investment of Derry, the Boyne, and subsequent campaign down to the capitulation of Limerick.

99. **LIEUT. CONN O'DOHERTY.**

100. **ENSIGN JOHN O'DOHERTY.**[1]

There is none of this family prominent to-day in Innishowen, though the name is common. The best known representatives of the family are the Dohertys (O'Dohertys), of Oatlands, Co. Cork,[2] who are descended from John, brother of Sir Cahir O'Doherty, the last chief.

The Macquillans of the Route and Dunluce Castle, Co. Antrim.

The origin of this clan, so long in doubt, has been happily solved by Mr. H. C. Lawlor,[3] who traces them to the Anglo-Norman Mandevilles, Barons of the Ulster Palatinate. There is no other way of accounting for their centuries of possession of that Anglo-Norman keep. Edward Bruce's invasion (1315) wiped out the Anglo-Norman Palatinate, its earl and barons, and in the chaos which ensued only a few, like the Savages of the Ards, escaped destruction by alliance with Celtic neighbours and adoption of Irish names and customs. Mr. Lawlor's assumption is confirmed by the fact that there is no mention of the Macquillans in the Irish annalists until the latter end of the 14th century, when they suddenly blossom out as an important clan, with large territory and fighting power. In the next two centuries the same annalists are full of their fights with the O'Cahans for the salmon of the Bann, of their struggle with the O'Neills of Clannaboy for supremacy in North Antrim, of their alliance with the Savages of the Ards to assist them against Clannaboy, and of their long feud with the McDonnells of the Glens, ending in the loss of Dunluce, and their final discomfiture

---

[1] D'Alton's "Jacobite Army List."
[2] Burke's "Irish Landed Gentry," 1904 edition. Mathews' "O'Neills of Ulster," Vol. III., p. 317.
[3] In his "Dunluce Castle and the Route."

at the battle of Aura (1580), where their clan was almost exterminated and the Route passed for ever to the victors.[1]

It was not until 1603, when James I. granted a tenure from the Crown to his kinsman Sir Randal McDonnell of the Glens, the large estates stretching from Larne to Portrush, and including the Route, that the Macquillans abandoned hope. Even then Chief Edward Macquillan, an old man in his 100th year, repaired to London. His sons had all fallen in battle against the Macdonnells, but he had the interests of a grandson, Rory Oge, to look after. Favourably received by his sovereign, he was promised future consideration. Edward died in 1605, but after the confiscation of Sir Cahir O'Doherty in 1608, the territory of Innishowen was granted to Rory Oge. What precisely led to the exchange will never be known, but the Lord Deputy, Sir Arthur Chichester, obtained Innishowen, while Rory Oge Macquillan got the 60,000 acres of Glenagherty, a wide district in Co. Antrim, with the Clough Water its northern, the Braid its southern, the Maine its western, and the heather mountains its eastern borders. On this estate Rory Oge took up his quarters, residing sometimes in an old Dun or fort two miles north of Ballymena, and sometimes in the present demesne of Galgorm. Rory Oge Macquillan by degrees sold this large property, part passing into the hands of Sir Robert Adair, of Ballymena,[2] part to Sir Faithful Fortescue,[3] and other portions much of which afterwards became the Colville (Mountcashel) estate.[4]

After Rory Oge's death (about 1635) the name practically disappeared from Co. Antrim.[5] In the revolution of 1688 there are three of the name holding commissions in Col. Cormac O'Neill of Kilmacevet's Regiment,[6] with which they served at the investment of Derry, and down to the capitulation of Limerick, viz.:—

101. **Capt. Ross Macquillan.** According to the Macquillan manuscript (mentioned above), two brother Macquillans served in the defence of Limerick, one being killed, while the other, the Captain Ross above, took service in the Irish Brigade in France, where he had a distinguished career.

102. **Lieut. Cormac Macquillan.**

103. **Ensign Theodore Macquillan.**

---

[1] It is worthy of note that a leading O'Neill of Clannaboy fell fighting for the Macquillans on the slopes of Aura, while it was a Macquillan lady, his wife, who was executed along with the unfortunate Sir Brian McPhelim O'Neill of Clannaboy in 1575.

[2] See Part I, Nos. 113–116.

[3] See Part I, No. 951.

[4] See Part I, No. 112.

[5] For further particulars of descendants, see an interesting article in "The Ulster Journal of Archæology," Vol. VIII. (1860) entitled "The Clan of the Macquillans of Antrim," in which a valuable family manuscript is quoted.

[6] D'Alton's "Jacobite Army List."

The O'Reillys of Cavan.

This great Celtic clan, sprung from a brother of "Nial of the Nine Hostages," had for centuries been dominant in the Cos. Cavan and Leitrim. For generations they had struggled against the encroachments of England. The flight of the Earls put an end to their tribal power and their territory was included in the general confiscation to make way for the colonists of the Ulster Plantation. Many leading members of the family were placated with small grants of land.

At the time of the 1688 revolution many of the name rallied to the Jacobite standard. Among them

104. **Edmond O'Reilly** raised and commanded a regiment of his own people through the whole campaign down to the fall of Limerick.

105. **Philip O'Reilly** was Lieut.-Col. of Col. Arthur MacMahon's Regiment,[1] and the following were officers in Lord Antrim's Regiment[2]:—

106. **Capt. Edmond O'Reilly.**

107. **Ensign Francis O'Reilly.**[3]

After the Treaty of Limerick many of the family went to the Continent, serving in the Irish Brigades of France or Spain. From one there sprung the family of the Marquis of Buena Vista, high among the grandees of Spain.

The O'Reilly clan are now represented by "The O'Reilly," The Heath House, Co. Leitrim, the O'Reillys, Knockabbey, Co. Louth, and the O'Reillys, Baltrasna, Co. Meath.[4]

We cannot leave the O'Reilly family without an allusion to the so-called "Battle of Scarva," which was inaugurated when an O'Reilly was lord of that demesne. Here annually in the picturesque garb of that period King William of Orange on his white horse, with a large force, is to be seen chasing King James with his army across the country. Miss Eleanor Alexander, in her fascinating book, "Lady Ann's Walk," devotes a charming chapter, "The Battle of Scarva," to this annual event, for which we have to thank an O'Reilly.

The Magennis' of Iveagh, Co. Down.

This old Celtic clan, for centuries prominent in the north of Ireland, rose to power in the 12th century. They were Lords of Iveagh and much of the surrounding

---

[1] See Part II, No. 94.
[2] See Part II, No. 6.
[3] D'Alton's "Jacobite Army List."
[4] Burke's "Landed Gentry of Ireland," 1904 edition.

districts. They were bitter opponents of the encroaching power of England. They were often at variance with their Celtic neighbours, with many of whom they were closely allied by matrimonial ties, particularly the O'Neills of Tyrone and Clannaboy. In the re-settlement of north-east Ulster after the flight of the Earls some twelve of the family obtained confirmation of estates of from eight to fifty-seven townlands each, their chief, Sir Arthur Magennis, securing the larger.

In the 1641 rebellion most of the descendants of these grantees, joining with the rebels, lost their lands in the subsequent confiscations.

In 1623 the chief, Sir Arthur Magennis, who resided at his castle of Rathfriland, was raised to the peerage as Viscount Iveagh.

108. In the revolution of 1688 his grandson **Brian**, the **3rd Viscount Iveagh**, was chief of the clan. An ardent Jacobite, he raised the Magennis Regiment in his own county, and was one of the peers attending James' Dublin Parliament. With his regiment he was present at the Boyne, and in the subsequent campaign down to the fall of Limerick, where he was one of the Irish negotiators of the Treaty, and also one of the hostages sent to the English camp as a pledge for the due execution of its clauses. Lady Iveagh and his daughter, who were in Limerick during the siege, are said to have been put under special protection by their captors.[1] Half of his regiment elected for foreign service and accompanied Lord Iveagh to the Continent where they entered the service of Austria.[2] Lord Iveagh died in 1693, when the title became extinct.

Besides many of the name who officered Lord Iveagh's Regiment there were:—

109. **Capt. Brian Magennis**, an officer in Lord Antrim's Regiment.

110. **Lieut. Hugh Magennis**, an officer in Col. Cormac O'Neill of Kilmacevet's Regiment.

The attaintures and confiscations which ensued after the Treaty of Limerick practically obliterated the name among the landlords of Co. Down.

Among the present representatives of this old stock are the Earl of Roden, of Tullamore Park, who inherits the Bryansford portion of his estate by the marriage of an ancestor with the heiress of Bryan McAgholy Magennis, of Bryansford.[3] The Magennis family, of Finvoy Lodge, Co. Antrim, "are descendants of this ancient family, of which the Viscount Iveagh was chief."[4]

---

[1] Note in D'Alton's "Jacobite Army List."
[2] Harris.
[3] Montgomery manuscript, p. 319, note.
[4] Burke's "Landed Gentry."

The Macmanus' of Ballybeg and Mount Davys, Co. Antrim.[1]

111. **BRYAN MACMANUS**, of Ballybeg, the head of the family at the time of the revolution, held a commission as lieutenant in Col. Cormac O'Neill of Kilmacevet's Regiment. He is probably the Bryan Macmanus who, after the Treaty of Limerick, forfeited his leasehold of twenty-one townlands held under the O'Neill estate. The accusations against him were the killing and wounding of Protestants and the hanging of King William's picture, maliciously and disgracefully, to the tail of a horse.[2]

112. **LIEUT. MANUS MACMANUS**,

113. **ENSIGN JOHN MACMANUS**, two officers holding commissions in Lord Antrim's Regiment.

There were two others of the name, who forfeited their holdings for being on the Jacobite side, viz.:—

114. **HENRY MACMANUS**,

115. **THOMAS MACMANUS**, who held the lease of the townland of Cardonaghey on the O'Neill estate.

Names of several officers of the minor clans who had been subject to The O'Neill of Clannaboy or the McDonnells of the Glens in past times.

116. **CAPT. DANIEL HEGARTY**.

117. **LIEUT. MAURICE O'HEGARTY**.

118. **CAPT. ART O'HARRANE**.

119. **ENSIGN PATRICK O'HARRANE**.

120. **LIEUT. PATRICK O'SHIEL**.

121. **LIEUT. DANIEL MACGUNSHENNAN**.

122. **ENSIGN BRIAN O'CONNOR**.

123. **ENSIGN JAMES O'CRILLY**.

124. **ENSIGN MYLES MCNAMEE**.

All the above held commissions in Col. Cormac O'Neill of Kilmacevet's Regiment,

---

[1] For particulars of this family, see Rowan, Part I, No. 908.
[2] Massereene manuscript.

as also did the following:—

125. **Capt. Hugh O'Gribbon**, of Clough, Co. Antrim, whose estate of one and a half townlands held under the Earl of Antrim was forfeited after the fall of Limerick.

126. **Lieut. Brian McCann.**

127. **Ensign Cormac McCann.**

128. **Lieut. Edmund McElderry.**

These four surnames are still well known in Co. Antrim.

129. **Lieut. Edward McConway.**

130. **Ensign Terence McConway.**

There were two McKays holding land under the Earl of Antrim at Ballyteerim, viz.:—

131. **Lieut. Daniel McKay**, an officer in Col. Cormac O'Neill of Kilmacevet's Regiment, and

132. **Ensign Hugh McKay**, an officer in Lord Antrim's Regiment. Other officers in Lord Antrim's Regiment were:—

133. **Lieut. Denis O'Callaghan.**

134. **Lieut. Brian McGrath.**

135. **Lieut. Terence McSweeney**, Co. Donegal, a member of the clan of that name who supplied so many fighting men to their overlord, The O'Donnell of Tyrconnell, in times past.

The Dobbin Family.

The Dobbin family, of Drumseugh and Aghoghill, Co. Antrim, were divided in the sides taken in the 1688–89 revolution.[1] The following were officers in Col. Cormac O'Neill of Kilmacevet's Regiment:—

136. **Capt. Peter Dobbin**, of Drumseugh. Fighting all through the campaign he was taken prisoner at the capture of Athlone, but soon exchanged. After the fall of Limerick he went to France. His two townlands, held under lease on the O'Neill estate, were forfeited.

---

[1] For particulars of family and those supporting King William's side, see Part I, Nos. 606–609.

137. **LIEUT. THOMAS DOBBIN**, of Drumseugh. His lease of the townland of Moneyrod on the O'Neill estate was forfeited after the fall of Limerick.

There was another of the name serving as adjutant in Sir Niall O'Neill's Regiment of Dragoons, viz.:—

138. **LIEUT. WILLIAM DOBBIN**, who, at the end of the revolution, forfeited his Culnagoogan townland held under lease from The O'Neill, and also

139. **LIEUT. HENRY DOBBIN**, of Drumseugh, probably an officer in the same regiment, who after the revolution forfeited his leasehold of three townlands on the O'Neill estate.

140. **LIEUT. JOHN GERNON**, an officer in Col. Cormac O'Neill of Kilmacevet's Regiment.

Two of this family forfeited their leasehold estate for being on the losing side in the revolution, viz.:—

141. **CAPT. MARTIN GERNON**, two townlands held under Sir Niall O'Neill, Bart., and one townland held under Lord Antrim.

142. **CAPT. NICHOLAS GERNON** of Clough, some £300 property on the O'Neill estate and two townlands on Lord Antrim's estate.

The undernoted McLorinans for their Jacobite tendencies had their leaseholds on the O'Neill estate confiscated, viz.:—

143. **LIEUT. DAVID McLORINAN**, of Cranfield,

144. **HUGH CARRAGH McLORINAN**, of Ballylummin, and

145. **THOMAS McLORINAN**, of Magheraleave, one townland each.

Officers of his own clan, Macdonnell kinsmen, holding commissions in Lord Antrim's Regiment. Nothing shows the survival of the old clan feeling more than that there were ten such, viz.:—**CAPT. ARCHIBALD MACDONNELL.**[1]

146. **CAPT. DANIEL MACDONNELL**, a natural son of the third Earl, who held a considerable property near Cushendall on a twelve years' lease from the Antrim estate. This was forfeited after the revolution.[2] Of the other eight, the exact relationship is to-day not traceable. Their names are:—

[1] See Part II, No. 30.
[2] "Macdonnells of Antrim," p. 361.

147. **Capt. Charles Macdonnell.**

148. **Lieut. Archibald Macdonnell.**

149. **Lieut. Randal Macdonnell.**

150. **Lieut. John Macdonnell.**

151. **Lieut. Eneas Macdonnell.**

152. **Ensign Randal Macdonnell.**

153. **Ensign Eneas Macdonnell.**

154. **Ensign Augustus Macdonnell.**[1]

155. **Sir James Macdonnell**, of the Crosse, Ballymoney, a leading cadet of the Macdonnell clan (the son of Sir Alexander, of Kilconway, who was grandson of Sir James, of Dunluce, at one time chief of the clan). He held considerable estate at the Crosse near Ballymoney under the Earl of Antrim.

For his complicity in the 1641 rebellion this property had been confiscated, but partly restored in 1662. At the time of the revolution he was again attainted with forfeiture.

Of the two Randalls in above list of officers in Lord Antrim's Regiment one is probably his son.

Officers of old Anglo-Norman families, descendants of the Barons of De Courcy's Ulster Palatinate, who held commissions in Lord Antrim's or in Cormac O'Neill of Kilmacevet's Regiment.

156. **Lieut. Christopher Fleming.** An officer in Col. Cormac O'Neill of Kilmacevet's Regiment.

He was the 22nd Baron of Slane, Co. Louth, one of the oldest of the Anglo-Norman baronies, and sat as such in King James' Dublin Parliament of 1689. The estates of Slane Castle had been confiscated for the complicity of the nineteenth Baron in the 1641 rebellion, but the title had been restored at the Restoration (1660).[2]

The history of the vicissitudes of this family have a tragic interest. William, the nineteenth Baron of Slane, had only succeeded to the estates early in 1641, when an elder brother, on becoming a Dominican friar, had renounced the world. This nineteenth Baron had married Lady Anne Macdonnell, a daughter of the first Earl of Antrim. He lost his estates and title for complicity in the 1641 rebellion, dying in the same year. After the Restoration, in 1660, their eldest son was restored to the title as

---

[1] D'Alton's "Jacobite Army List."
[2] Harris.

twentieth Baron, who died unmarried, being succeeded by their second son Randal, as twenty-first Baron, on whose death in 1676 the title passed to his son, Christopher, the twenty-second Baron of Slane, the subject of this sketch.

Christopher, having espoused the Jacobite side, again lost his title and estate. He seems, however, to have regained the royal favour, as he was created Viscount Longford by Queen Anne in 1713. He died in 1726, and was interred in Bunnamairge Abbey, the burying place of his Antrim relatives, when the title passed to his first cousin, the son of Thomas Fleming of Gillanstown, Co. Meath, William, the titular twenty-third Baron of Slane, who resided at Anticur, near Finvoy, on a small property on the Antrim estate, kindly placed at his disposal. He left one son, Christopher, twenty-fourth titular Baron, on whose death in 1772 the direct male line became extinct.[1]

In the "Londeriados" poem the lines, referring to his presence with the army investing Derry:—

> "Lord Slane his men near to Ardee he chose
> Brave valiant youths fit to oppose the foes,"

seem to imply his commanding a regiment of his own as well as holding a commission in Lord Antrim's Regiment.

157. A **Captain Fleming.** Probably of this family. Serving with the investing army, he was among the enemy officers slain in the garrison's Windmill Hill sortie of 6th May.[2]

158. **Hon. Henry Fleming**, brother of Christopher, Lord Slane (No. 156), a captain in Lord Galmoy's Horse.

159. **Capt. Christopher Russell**, an officer in Col. Cormac O'Neill of Kilmacevet's Regiment.

The first Russell in Co. Down had come with De Courcy in 1178, and the family had resided on their territory round Killough for nearly five centuries. The name is still remembered in a wide district in Co. Down. Lord Russell of Killowen, Lord Chief Justice of England, so famous as an advocate, was a member of this family.

The Savages of the Ards, Co. Down.

This ancient Anglo-Norman family is descended from Sir William Le Sauvage, one of the knights accompanying John de Courcy in his invasion of north-east Ulster in 1177, when the Palatinate Earldom of Ulster was created, of which Sir William was the first of the family hereditary barons. To him was allotted as a fief the Peninsula of the Ards. Here were erected his castles of Portaferry and Ardkeen.

---

[1] "Macdonnells of Antrim," p. 24. For particulars of descendants in female line, see same.
[2] Walker's "Siege."

In the terrible chaos resulting from the Bruce invasion of 1315 to 1317, when the Palatinate was overrun, the Savages were among the few baronial families that survived, and by the end of that century they were even more powerful, having added to their possessions the lordship of Lecale, Co. Down, and the lands of Lissanoure and Moylinny, Co. Antrim.

In the next two centuries (15th and 16th) their Anglo-Norman origin was almost lost in the name of MacSeneschal, by which the Savages of Ardkeen were designated (from their office of Seneschal of Ulster under the Crown). The Savages ranked in the records of the times with the O'Neills of Clannaboy, the Macdonnells of the Glens, the Magennis of Iveagh and the Macquillans of the Route as an independent clan. They had their own petty wars, either in alliance with the Lord Deputy or one of their neighbours, against some other clan combination. During this time the Savages had divided into the two main lines of Portaferry and Ardkeen, the seniority of which is doubtful, but at all events the line of Portaferry has the advantage of being still in possession of that castle and estate, a direct ownership of 753 years (1177–1930). All this time the English, with occasional setbacks, were steadily encroaching on Ulster, but it was not until Queen Elizabeth, at enormous cost to her Treasury, took the matter sternly in hand that the end came. Her Majesty certainly made expensive failures in attempts under Mr. Smith and her favourite, the Earl of Essex, to plant the Clannaboy with English.

In Cos. Down and Antrim, which, as the old Ulster Palatinate, were considered Crown property, a new settlement was effected. The Savages of Portaferry and Ardkeen were confirmed in their possessions in the Ards, while several cadets of the family received minor grants. Until the rebellion of 1641 the Savages loyally accommodated themselves to the habits of country squires, though some of the name lost their estates in that struggle. So things progressed up to the 1688 revolution.

The family or clan, having no cause to be grateful to the ruling dynasty for their treatment at the Settlement, and no ingrained love of Protestantism, remained neutral, so far as concerned the main lines of Portaferry and Ardkeen, of whom only one fought on King William's side, while many members of the cadet branches were attainted with loss of estates in the Jacobite service.

Serving in King William's Army.

Part I. No. 1646. **Capt. Hugh Savage** of Ardkeen.[1]

Serving in Jacobite Army, attainted, etc.

160. **Major John Savage**, of Ballyvarley, held a commission in Tyrconnell's Regiment commanded by Brigadier Mark Talbot.

---

[1] See Part I.

Officers in Sir Niall O'Neill's Dragoons.

161. **Capt. Roland Savage.**

162. **Lieut. John Savage.**

163. **Cornet Henry Savage.**[1]

Officers in Col. Cormac O'Neill's Regiment.

164. **Lieut. Edmond Savage.**

165. **Ensign Henry Savage.**[1]

Officers in Lord Iveagh's (Magennis) Regiment.

166. **Capt. Patrick Savage**, of Ballygalget.

There were five others of the name holding commissions in this regiment. The Christian names not being in D'Alton's "Army List," we may assume them to have been among the following on list of attainted, viz.:—

167. **Lucas Savage**, of Dunturk.

168. **Henry Savage**, of Ballygalget.

169. **Thomas Savage**, of Drumaroad.

170. **Hugh Savage**, of Drumaroad.

171. **Hugh Savage**, of Ballydawes.

172. **James Savage**, of Rock Savage.

173. **John Savage**, of Rock Savage and Ballyspurge.

The following were officers in General Maxwell's Dragoons.[1] Only in one case is the Christian name given, so that some of them may be among the attainted above.

174. **Capt. Savage.**

175. **Lieut. Savage.**

---

[1] D'Alton.

176. **Lieut. Robert Savage.**

177. **Cornet Savage.**

178. **Cornet Savage.**

179. **Quartermaster Savage.**

The present-day representatives of this old family are:—

(1) Edmond H. S. (Savage) Nugent, D.L., Baron Savage, of Portaferry, Co. Down, whose residence lies in full view of the ancient castle of that name, erected by his ancestor over 750 years ago. The name of Nugent was only adopted by the family in 1912. He is a Savage in direct male descent.

(2) The Savages of Ardkeen, now only a ruin, which passed out of the family a century ago, are represented by Col. Henry Charles Savage, late 1st Batt. South Staffordshire Regiment.

(3) The Savages of Glastry and Ardkeen now represented by Major John Raymond Savage-Armstrong, Strangford, Co. Down. Major Savage-Armstrong served with distinction in the Great War, being severely wounded.

(4) Col. William H. Savage, C.M.G., residing at Rarkmoyle, Cushendall, Co. Antrim, is the representative of the Prospect branch of the family. After commanding his Gurkha battalion in India, the age limit compelled his unemployment, but on the outbreak of the Great War he had the honour of being selected to train and command the Co. Down battalion 13th Royal Irish Rifles, which he took out to France, being present at the terrible battle of 1st July, 1916. Afterwards retired to make way for younger men, he served in various posts, receiving for his services the C.M.G. at the end of the war.

(Most of this information is taken from the late Mr. George F. Savage Armstrong of Glastry's painstaking and admirable publications, "The Savages of the Ards" and "The Savage Family in Ulster." The family owe Mr. Savage Armstrong an immense debt of gratitude for the preservation of their past history.)

Other officers serving in the Jacobite regiments of the Earl of Antrim and Col. Cormac O'Neill.

180. **Capt. Ulick Burke**, Lord Antrim's Regiment. He was a connection of the third Earl of Antrim through his second Countess, a daughter of Sir John Burke, of Derrymaclaghny, Co. Galway.

181. **Capt. John Clements**, Col. Cormac O'Neill's Regiment, a member of the old Carrickfergus family of that name.[1]

---

[1] See Part I, Nos. 588–92, same family.

182. **Capt. Henry Vaughan**, Lord Antrim's Regiment, and

183. **Ensign Vaughan**, Lord Antrim's Regiment. Probably of the Buncrana, Co. Donegal, family of that name.[1]

184. **Capt. Henry Courtney**, Col. Cormac O'Neill's Regiment. Probably a member of the old Devonshire family settled for generations near Portglenone.

185. **Capt. William Stewart**, Col. Cormac O'Neill's Regiment, and

186. **Lieut. Alexander Stewart**, Col. Cormac O'Neill's Regiment, cadets of the family of Stewart of Ballintoy.[2]

187. **Capt. Robert Butler**, Col. Cormac O'Neill's Regiment. Probably one of the numerous Butlers of the south of Ireland.[3]

188. **Lieut. George Moore**, Lord Antrim's Regiment.

189. **Lieut. Francis Moore**, Lord Antrim's Regiment.

190. **Lieut. Randolph Sexton**, Lord Antrim's Regiment.

191. **Ensign George Sexton**, Lord Antrim's Regiment.

192. **Lieut. Henry Smith**, Col. Cormac O'Neill's Regiment.

193. **Capt. Arthur Magill**, Lord Antrim's Regiment.

194. **Capt. Thomas Magill**, Col. Cormac O'Neill's Regiment.

195. **Lieut. Cormac Magill**, Col. Cormac O'Neill's Regiment.

The fact that the widowed Countess of the fourth Earl of Antrim (who died in 1721) married the head of the Gilhall family, Robert Hawkins Magill, in 1728, points to a long family intimacy and accounts for some of the family being on the Jacobite side. The head of the family in 1688 and his sons were staunch supporters of King William.[4]

196. **Capt. Thomas Macnaghten**, of Kiltemurry, an officer in Col. Cormac O'Neill's Regiment, who was attainted with confiscation of lands held under the Antrim estate at the end of the 1688 revolution.

---

[1] See Part I, Vaughans, Nos. 299–303.
[2] See Stewarts of Ballintoy, Part I, Nos. 933–35.
[3] See Part II, No. 26.
[4] See Part I, Nos. 46–52, Sir John Magill, of Gilhall, and family.

He was the son of John Macnaghten, a younger son of Shane Dhu Macnaghten.[1] His father, the above John, had been one of the 1641 rebellion. Refusing to submit to General Monro, Col. Duncan Campbell, of Auchinleck, N.B., was sent to take a castle he had improvised, and John and his garrison of some eighty of his tenants and followers were exterminated.[2] It is interesting to know that this Duncan Campbell, of Auchinleck, afterwards met his fate at the hands of Sir Alastair Colkitto Macdonnell in the Montrose campaign. Thomas of this sketch was evidently permitted by his kinsman the Earl to continue in occupation.

197. **O'GALLAGHER**, a trooper in the Duke of Berwick's Horse, served in the investment of Derry, at the Boyne and down to the fall of Limerick.

His career was so remarkable, and varied with so many incidents, that I give the chief events.[3] Born at Walshestown, Co. Donegal, he was barely eighteen when he joined the Duke of Berwick's Horse before Derry. He had the excitement of seeing the surrender of Culmore, of opposing the famous Col. Murray's troopers in many of the garrison's sorties (in one of which the Duke was severely wounded), and of following him in his wild cavalry raids through the north-west of the Province. When the relief took place, and the investing army retreated, Graham pays him a compliment in a couplet:—

> "And Gallagher tall from fair Donegal
> Was the last of the men that retreated."

At the Boyne in the furious charges and counter-charges of the cavalry of both sides the Duke had his horse shot under him, and in the *mêlée* that ensued Gallagher was overridden and wounded. At the end of the war in Ireland he took service in the English army, being present at Blenheim and Malplaquet, and afterwards went to Italy, where he served in the raising of the siege of Turin in 1715. In the subsequent campaign he was incapacitated for further service by a wound in the leg. Returning to Ireland, he settled down in his native village of Walshestown, Co. Donegal, where he died in 1778 aged 107.

The O'Gallaghers were one of the minor Celtic clans of Co. Donegal.

198. **THE MCKENNAS**, of Trough, Co. Monaghan, and of Braeface, Maghera, Co. Derry. They are mentioned as being present in some force in the muster of the Jacobite army at the investment of Derry.[4] As late as 1823 the name was by no means uncommon round Maghera.

---

[1] See Macnaghten, Part I, Nos. 103–4.
[2] See "Macdonnells of Antrim," p. 443, note, with quotation from Morris' "Historical Sketch of Persecutions Suffered by the Catholics of Ireland," p. 169.
[3] Graham, in his notes to his Catalogue in "Ireland Preserved."
[4] "Londeriados."

A few of the principal officers (outside Ulster) in the Jacobite army, with some particulars of family, and to-day's representatives, etc.

199. **COL. O'FARRELL**, of Co. Longford, raised and commanded a regiment in the investment of Derry. His death on the 4th June in the attack on the Windmill Hill is thus recorded:—

> "Then brave O'Farrell
>   Upon his right with two Battalions
>   Came fiercely up, and fought like lions
>   Till he was slain."[1]

This is probably the Col. Farrell mentioned as one of the enemy officers killed in the garrison's sortie of that date.[2]

This ancient clan, divided into the O'Farrell Ban and O'Farrell Boy, had for centuries been lords of Anally, Co. Longford. After their participation in the 1641 rebellion they suffered confiscation.

Early in the last century a member of this family, dining as a guest of The Apprentice Boys Club of Derry in Dublin, asked to be admitted a member. This was refused on the ground that he did not possess the qualification of descent from a defender—to which he humorously replied that that was no reason for exclusion, as no one had worked harder than his ancestor to gain admission to the city.[3]

The present representatives of the clan are the O'Farrells, of Dalyston, Co. Galway.[4]

200. **LIEUT.-GENERAL PATRICK SARSFIELD**, of Lucan, **EARL OF LUCAN**, so created by James II. after his return to France.

Among the Generals of the Jacobite army in Ireland none bore such a reputation for humanity, chivalry and gallantry as this Irish Bayard. Sprung of an Anglo-Norman stock which had settled in Ireland in Henry II.'s reign, acquiring considerable landed property, Patrick Sarsfield was a man of estate, position and influence when the 1688 revolution broke out. Early training and association with the ruling dynasty had made him a staunch supporter of James II. He had held a commission in the unfortunate Duke of Monmouth's Regiment when serving in Flanders, but on the latter's defection he had accepted service in the King's Guards, becoming a favourite of that monarch at the Court of Whitehall. So great was his loyalty that he fought against his old commanding officer, the Duke of Monmouth, at Sedgemoor.

Such a man found immediate employment in the Irish Jacobite service. He was given the command of a flying column in Connaught to watch the borders of Ulster

---

[1] "Londeriados."
[2] Walker's "Siege."
[3] Graham's Catalogue.
[4] Burke's "Landed Gentry."

and check the doings of the men of Enniskillen. When James arrived in Dublin, March 1689, he was one of the council of war held in the capital to discuss an advance against Derry. According to the "Londeriados" poem Sarsfield made the following protest in reply to the advocates of such action with a force of some 10,000 men:—

> "My liege, ten thousand thrice will scarce suffice
> To grapple with such stubborn enemies
> ·
> Where's a just number to push on a siege?
> Derry will certainly hold out, my liege
> ·
> Lets to the North a puissant army send
> If we that city to obtain intend."

No one knew the Protestant stubbornness of Ulster better than Sarsfield, but his warning was not heeded. James II. presented himself before Derry and was rebuffed at the gates, April 1689. The Dublin Parliament sat in May, and the sweeping Act of Attainder was passed, with its confiscation of Protestant estates. The only vehement protesters against this infamous policy were the Earl of Granard and the Bishop of Meath in the Lords, and Sarsfield, himself a Catholic, in the House of Commons.

Into his soldierly conduct of his Connaught command there is not space to enter, but the relief of Derry (July 28th) more than vindicated his advice. At the Boyne, much to his disgust, he had little chance of showing his brilliant qualities, being held in reserve for the sorry task of escorting His Majesty off the field of battle and in safety to Dublin.

In the ensuing campaign he was one of the most successful of the Jacobite leaders, but at King William's attack on Limerick he performed a feat which still lives in the history of the war. On the 11th of August, 1690, King William lay with his army along the Co. Limerick side of that town, daily expecting the arrival from Dublin of his heavy siege guns, which would enable effective bombardment and immediate surrender of Limerick. The way was considered safe, and no effort made to guard the guns *en route* further than the escort of 60 men in charge. Determined to intercept and destroy them, Sarsfield two days earlier had with his cavalry crossed at night to the Clare side of the town, marched some twelve miles up the Shannon, after which, recrossing at a ford, he concealed his men on Keeper Hill, some miles in rear of the English camp. Here, informed by his scouts that the convoy would encamp that night near Cullen, he waited until dark, when he swooped down, killing the whole escort and taking the guns. Filling the guns with powder to the muzzles, they, with all their equipment, were placed in a large pile, a train of powder was laid, and a match applied. The explosion was heard in Limerick. King William was furious and the siege was abandoned at the end of August, while Sarsfield became a hero to his compatriots.

The following year General Ginkell, in command of the English army, again laid siege to Limerick, of whose defenders Sarsfield was the life and soul. At last even Sarsfield despaired, and on the 1st of October, 1691, the capitulation and the Treaty of Limerick were arranged, of which Sarsfield, with Lords Westmeath, Dillon and Galmoy, General Sheldon and the Archbishop of Armagh, was one of the negotiators. He was one of the hostages sent to the English camp as pledges of the Irish completion of the Treaty and was appointed one of the commissioners for superintending the embarkation of the Irish troops for service abroad. He was allowed to retire to France, where he had a short but distinguished career, falling in 1693 on the bloody field of Landen, when Luxemburg won a Pyrrhic victory over King William, who withdrew with his beaten army in safety, while the French army lost some 10,000 dead. Sarsfield was carried off the field, but never rose from the pallet on which he was placed.

201. His only son, the **2ND EARL OF LUCAN**, served with distinction in the Irish Brigade, under his stepfather, the Duke of Berwick, and died at St. Omers in 1716, when the title became extinct.[1]

His widowed Countess (*née* Lady Honora de Burgh, daughter of the Earl of Clanricarde) afterwards married the Duke of Berwick.

Present-day representatives of the family are the Sarsfields of Doughcloyne, Co. Cork, and the Binghams, Earls of Lucan. Anne Sarsfield, granddaughter and heiress of the last Sarsfield of Lucan, married the fifth Baronet of Castlebar. Their second son and eventual successor as seventh Baronet, when raised to the peerage, took the title of Baron Lucan of Castlebar in 1776, and Earl of Lucan in 1796, thus reviving a name of such lustre.[2]

202. **DOMINICK SARSFIELD, 4TH VISCOUNT KILMALLOCK** (creation 1625), was a brother of Patrick Sarsfield, and sat as a peer in James II.'s Dublin Parliament. He was attainted with confiscation of estates. He afterwards served in the Irish Brigade of France, where he died in 1709. His brother David, fifth Viscount, fell at the battle of Villavicosia (1711) in the service of Spain.[1]

(For officers in Sarsfield's Regiment of Horse, see D'Alton's "Jacobite Army List," Vol. I. p. 145.)

203. **COL. THOMAS NUGENT, 4TH EARL OF WESTMEATH** and **18TH BARON DELVIN**, was Colonel-Commanding a Jacobite regiment, raised by himself, all through the campaign, at the Boyne and down to the fall of Limerick (1691), where he was one of the negotiators of the Treaty. Although attainted with consequent confiscation, claiming advantage of the special clauses of the Treaty, which he had himself assisted to draw up, he was shortly restored to titles and estates. His regiment, officered in

---

[1] O'Callaghan.
[2] Burke's Peerage.

great part by members of his own family, elected for foreign service, and none bore a more distinguished name in the Irish Brigade of France than the Nugent Regiment, while many of its officers founded families of distinction whose names are still well known on the Continent.[1]

He died in France in 1752, being succeeded by

204. His brother, **JOHN, 5TH EARL OF WESTMEATH**, who served with distinction in command of his regiment at Ramillies, Oudenarde and Malplaquet. He died at Nivelles in 1754, aged eighty-two.

205. **LIEUT.-COL. HON. WILLIAM NUGENT**, a son of the second Earl of Westmeath and M.P. for Co. Meath, sat in James' Dublin Parliament of 1689.

He served as Lieut.-Col. in General Richard Hamilton's Regiment of Foot. He it was who, in that General's advance on Derry, was the first to get over the Bann near Portglenone, and held the position till the main army effected a crossing.

According to "Londeriados," in one of the many sorties of the Derry garrison early in the siege

"Col. Nugent had made a solemn vow
That he would Col. Murray overthrow."

It was not, however, the redoubtable Murray who was routed, but Nugent.

On 4th June Col. Nugent was one of the leaders in an attack on the entrenched position of Windmill Hill, but was wounded and compelled to retire.[2] He was killed a few months later at Cavan.

206. **CAPT. NUGENT**, presumably of this family, was wounded and taken prisoner by Capt. Frank Wilson in a sortie made by the garrison of Derry on 25th July.[3]

The present representative of the house is the eleventh Earl of Westmeath and twenty-third Baron Delvin, Pallas, Co. Galway.

The Nugents of Farren Connell, Mount Nugent, Co. Cavan, are descended from Oliver, the third son of the thirteenth Baron Delvin (the Earldom of Westmeath was conferred on the fifteenth Baron). This Oliver inherited a large section of the original Nugent estate round Farren Connell, where they have resided for generations. The late head of this house was General Sir Oliver Nugent, K.C.B., D.S.O., D.L. This gallant soldier had the distinction, as an Ulster officer of considerable war experience, to be selected by the War Office (September 1915) to take over the command of the Ulster 36th Division.[4] Sir Oliver took the Division out to France early in October 1915, and

[1] D'Alton's "Jacobite Army List."
[2] Walker and Mackenzie.
[3] Mackenzie.
[4] This Division had been recruited, organised and trained by Major-General Charles H. Powell, C.B.,

commanded it with honour, not only to himself but also to the splendid force he led, until May 1918, when he was transferred to the command of a Division in India. For the services rendered by the Ulster Division under his command, see "History of the 36th (Ulster) Division." It is a curious commentary in Ulster history that the man who led the men of Ulster so often to the old Derry cry of "No Surrender" should be of the same blood as the Westmeath Nugents, who were in the Jacobite army investing Derry. Regret was universal in Ulster at the death of this gallant gentleman, which occurred two years ago.

Mr. Edmund Savage Nugent, of Portaferry, Co. Down, although actually a Savage in lineal line, represents, through a marriage of one of his ancestors with an heiress of that family, his branch of the Nugents of Delvin and Westmeath.

The McCarthys or McCarties of Desmond and Cork.

Early in the 17th century the head of this house, Cormac Oge McCartie, had accepted the Viscountcy of Muskerry from the Crown and, dying in 1634, was succeeded by his eldest son, Donough, 2nd Viscount Muskerry, raised later to the Earldom of Clancarty. This Earl left several sons, of whom the third, Callaghan, eventually succeeded as third Earl of Clancarty. A younger son, Justin, was afterwards the celebrated General Viscount Mountcashel.[1]

Callaghan was succeeded by his eldest son, Donough, as fourth Earl of Clancarty.

207. **DONOUGH, 4TH EARL OF CLANCARTY.** This Earl was a frequenter of the Court of Whitehall, and in 1684 his influential position and large estates were sufficient inducement for the King's Minister, the Earl of Sunderland, to give him the hand of his daughter, Lady Eleanora Spencer, in marriage. The bridegroom was only fifteen and the bride eleven years of age.

When the 1688 revolution broke out, he, like the rest of his name, was an ardent supporter of the legitimate monarch. Returning to Ireland he raised a regiment of foot among his own people. A great favourite with James II., he was one of the Irish nobility to welcome the monarch on landing at Kinsale (1689), where he loyally entertained him. His close attendance on his Royal master, and taking his seat as a peer in the Dublin Parliament (May 1689), probably account for his not being present at Derry at an earlier date. His arrival there on 30th June with his regiment was signalised by an extraordinary act of daring. There was an old Irish prophecy current in his country that "The McCarthy" should knock at the gates of Derry. Calling immediately for volunteers, he led an impetuous assault on the Butcher's Gate, and so surprised were

who, in recognition of his valuable services in the creation of this Division, was decorated with the K.C.B. a few months later.
[1] See No. 208.

the garrison that he nearly got in. But a strong counter-attack soon drove the assaulters back with considerable loss. The prophecy had said nothing about gaining admittance.[1]

Of this Earl "Londeriados" makes the following mention:

> "Near Cork, Clancarty raised his regiment
> Who skipped and danced all the way they went
> In ancient times his ancestors were Kings
> O'er all that country which his praises sings."

He was later on in the campaign one of the prisoners taken by Churchill (afterwards Duke of Marlborough) when he captured Cork in 1690. Consigned to the Tower of London, he was not released until 1694 under condition of leaving England for ever. He went to France, where he obtained a commission in King James' Guards at St. Germains. Meantime his estate had been confiscated (1691) but a small annuity was granted to his wife. Returning secretly and in disguise (1698), he succeeded in getting access to his wife's room in her father, the Earl of Sunderland's, house in London. Discovered by an irate brother-in-law, he was denounced and again consigned to the Tower. The incident caused considerable excitement, but thanks to the good offices of Lady Russell, the widow of the martyred Lord, who intervened with the King on his behalf, the Earl and Countess were permitted to leave the country and a small annuity out of the estate was granted to them.[2] They settled at Altona, where the Countess died in 1704. The Earl, who had been granted a reversal of attainder, but not of estate, in 1721, died in 1734. The titular honours passed to his son, on whose death in 1769 the title became extinct.[3]

This Earldom of Clancarty is not to be confounded with the title granted to the Trench family in 1803.

208. JUSTIN McCARTIE (McCARTHY), 1ST VISCOUNT MOUNTCASHEL. He was an uncle of Donough, fourth Earl of Clancarty.[4]

He too raised a regiment of foot, which he commanded in person. Having risen to the rank of Lieut.-General in the Jacobite army, he was summoned to Dublin to confer with his sovereign, and, created Viscount Mountcashel, sat in James' House of Parliament (May 1689). He was later appointed to command the army sent to subdue Enniskillen.

On July 31st, 1689, a few hours after the relief of Derry, Lord Mountcashel encountered the Enniskilleners at Newtownbutler. The result was disastrous to the Jacobites; thousands were left dead on the field or prisoners in the victors' hands. Among the latter was the Viscount himself, so severely wounded that his case seemed

---

[1] Walker and Mackenzie.
[2] Macaulay.
[3] D'Alton.
[4] See No. 207.

hopeless. Seeing the day lost, and determined not to outlive his disgrace, Mountcashel threw himself almost alone on the advancing troops, and would have been killed outright but for the intervention of an Enniskillen officer who recognised him as the man who had some months before rescued Col. Creighton from the hands of the inhuman Lord Galmoy, who was ordering his execution after quarter had been given. The Mountcashel Regiment was almost annihilated while twelve of its officers were among the prisoners. Lord Mountcashel made his escape from captivity in the following December. There seems to have been some delicate question about breaking parole, but the French military authorities, so punctilious in such matters, honourably acquitted him when tried by court-martial on his arrival in France.

The following year (1690) Mountcashel was given the command of some 6000 Irish troops, whom he took out to France, in exchange for an equal number of trained French soldiers whom Louis XIV. was sending to Limerick.[1] The 6000 men comprised among others his own Mountcashel Regiment, Viscount Clare's Regiment and that of Arthur Dillon, regiments that won such renown in the Irish Brigade in France.[2] On arrival in France he was graciously received at St. Germains, and confirmed by Louis XIV. in his command of the Irish troops, whom he led with great honour in a campaign in Italy.[1]

After the fall of Limerick and the arrival of the Irish troops who had elected for the French service, he was given command of the Irish Brigade so distinguished in Louis XIV.'s campaigns, and earned a reputation second to none.

He died at Bareye in 1694 from effects of wounds received some months before in Savoy. He had married Lady Arabella Wentworth, a daughter of the ill-fated Earl of Strafford, but there being no issue the title became extinct.[1] He had been attainted and his estates confiscated in 1691 after the fall of Limerick.

(This Viscountcy of Mountcashel is not to be confounded with the Viscountcy of Mountcashel, 1766, and Earldom of Mountcashel, 1781, conferred on the Moore family, of Moore Park, Co. Cork.)

209. "The McCarthy More," Col. Owen McCartie. He had raised a regiment

of his own.[1] With this regiment and two others under his command he had been appointed Governor of Carrickfergus, which he had to defend against the Duke of Schomberg's attack after the landing of his army in August 1690. Short of supplies and powder, he held out for several days of bombardment, only surrendering when reduced to his last barrel of powder, and on condition of being allowed to retire with his men and all the honours of war to the nearest Jacobite garrison.[3] Harris further states that after the surrender "The McCarthy More" was found in the Duke of

---

[1] D'Alton.
[2] See No. 279, Viscount Clare, No. 285, Arthur Dillon, and No. 344, The Irish Brigade of France.
[3] Harris and D'Alton.

Schomberg's kitchen camp, which made the Duke smile, and forbear inviting him to dinner, saying, "If he had stayed with his men like a soldier, he would have sent for him, but if he would go and eat with servants in a kitchen, let him be doing."

He probably served through the rest of the campaign.

210. **CAPT. DONOUGH MCCARTHY** was among the prisoners taken by the Derry garrison on 30th June, 1689, in repulsing Lord Clancarty's attack on the Butcher's Gate. He was an officer in the Clancarty regiment.[1]

The family figures largely among the commissioned officers in the Clancarty, and Mountcashel and other Jacobite regiments. There were no fewer than seventy-eight of the name on the list of attainders and confiscations after the fall of Limerick in 1691.

The present-day representative of this ancient house is Lieut.-Col. Frederick Fitzgerald McCartie, of Carrignavar, Co. Cork. He is descended from Donald, second son of the first Viscount Muskerry.[2] This Donald was the builder of Carrignavar Castle, where the family have resided for generations.

211. **RICHARD DE LA POER, 1ST EARL OF TYRONE, 8TH BARON LA POER (POWER)** of Curraghmore, Co. Waterford.

He raised a regiment of foot in the Jacobite service. With this regiment he formed part of the garrison of Cork, which surrendered to Churchill (afterwards Duke of Marlborough), and was one of the negotiators of the terms of capitulation in 1690.[3] He died shortly afterwards, being succeeded by his brother John as second Earl of Tyrone, on whose death in 1693 another brother, James, succeeded as third Earl. This third Earl died in 1704, leaving an only daughter and heiress, Lady Catherine Poer, who by her marriage with Sir Marcus Beresford, fourth Baronet of Coleraine, in 1717, brought the Curraghmore estate into the Beresford family.[4] In right of his wife Sir Marcus Beresford was created Baron Beresford of Beresford and Viscount Tyrone in 1720, and Earl of Tyrone and Marquess of Waterford in 1746.

The first Earl of Tyrone (subject of this sketch) was attainted in 1691, but as mentioned above the daughter of the third Earl was eventually allowed to succeed to the estates. It is doubtful whether Lord Tyrone's Regiment was with the investing army at Derry, but the "Londeriados" poem has this reference to their presence at the muster of the Jacobite forces:—

> "From Waterford my Lord Tyrone collects
> A Regiment which the name of Power affects."

212. **JOHN DE LA POER (POWER)**, of Kilvogan, sat in James' House of Commons in Dublin, 1689.

---

[1] D'Alton, Walker and Mackenzie.
[2] See No. 207.
[3] D'Alton.
[4] See Part I, No. 45 in the Beresfords, Marquesses of Waterford.

He held a commission in a Jacobite regiment. After the fall of Limerick in 1691 he served in the Irish Brigade in France,[1] being attainted. After the death of the third Earl of Tyrone (1704), whose earldom died with him, he claimed and assumed the titular Lordship of de la Poer (Power) of Curraghmore, an assumption continued by his son, who died in 1742. It was not until 1747 that the Beresford family laid claim to this 1375 barony, which was admitted by the Irish House of Lords in that year.

There were many others of the name figuring among the commissioned officers in the Jacobite army and on the list of attainted after the fall of Limerick in 1691.

213. RICHARD DE BURGH (BURKE), 8TH EARL OF CLANRICARDE, Connaught.

When the revolution of 1688 broke out, among James' supporters none were stauncher than this eighth Earl of Clanricarde, his family and clan. The Earl met his sovereign on his arrival in Dublin, and sat in the Dublin Parliament (May 1689). Raising a regiment of foot he commanded them throughout the campaign down to the fall of Limerick in 1691. He was attainted, with confiscation of estates.

214. His brother, the **HON. JOHN BURKE**, created **BARON BOPHIN** in 1689 by James II., sat in the Dublin Parliament. He too raised a regiment of foot in that King's service, with which he served until taken prisoner at Aughrim in 1690.[1]

He succeeded, on the death of his brother, as ninth Earl of Clanricarde. He was attainted in 1691, and it was not until Queen Anne's accession to the throne that he was restored by Act of Parliament to titles and estates.

215. **THE HON. ULICK BURKE**, another brother of the Earl, created Viscount Galway in 1689, sat in James II.'s Dublin Parliament. He also raised a regiment which he commanded at the Battle of Aughrim, when he was killed, it is stated, after quarter had been given. With his death the title became extinct.[1]

Besides those already mentioned, the following members of the family also raised regiments.

216. **COL. WALTER BURKE,**

217. **COL. PATRICK BURKE**, and

218. **COL. MICHAEL BURKE**, who all fell at Aughrim.[1] In the Aughrim Battle there were also killed

219. **LIEUT.-COL. DAVID BURKE**, and

220. **LIEUT.-COL. ULICK BURKE**,[1] while among the prisoners taken was

221. **BARON BURKE**, of Brittas, a peer created by James II. who sat in the Dublin

---

[1] D'Alton.

Parliament. He held a commission in the army.

This Baron Burke was the son of the Hon. William Burke, executed, by Cromwell's orders, at Cork in 1653. After the fall of Limerick he retired to France, his son and grandson who succeeded him, both serving in the French army, bearing the title in turn until the latter's death, when it became extinct.[1]

Besides the Earl of Clanricarde, Viscount Galway and Barons Burke and Bophin already mentioned there were two other members of the Burke family sitting as peers in James' Dublin Parliament of 1689, viz:—

222. **THEOBALD BOURKE VISCOUNT MAYO** and

223. **WILLIAM BURKE BARON CASTLECONNELL**.[2]

The only Burke named in connection with the investing army before Derry is a

224. **LIEUT. BURKE**, killed in one of the fierce fights for Windmill Hill, outside the walls of Derry.[3]

In addition to the above sketches the Burke name is recorded as commissioned officers in thirty of the Jacobite regiments serving through the campaign, and they figure in number on the list of attainted with confiscation of estates after the fall of Limerick in 1691. The most prominent of them was

225. **LIEUT.-COL. SIR ULICK BURKE**, 3rd Bart., of Glinsk, Co. Galway. He served in the Jacobite army down to the fall of Limerick, but although attainted in 1691, coming under the special clauses of the Treaty, he was restored to titles and estates.[1]

The thirteenth and last Baronet of this long line, Sir Theobald Burke, Bart., of Glinsk, died quite recently, but the family is still represented by his sister, Miss Marianne Aline Alice Burke, 19 Bury Street, London.[4]

Many of the family distinguished themselves in the Irish Brigades of France and Spain, among them:[1]

226. **LIEUT.-COL. ULICK BURKE**, of the Irish Brigade in France, who died in 1762, leaving no issue.

227. **GENERAL EDWARD BURKE**, in the Spanish service, killed in the Battle of Campo Santo in 1743.

228. **WILLIAM BURKE**, in the Irish Brigade of France, killed at the battle of Fontenoy.

---

[1] D'Alton.
[2] For particulars of these see Burke's "Extinct Peerages."
[3] Walker's "Siege."
[4] Debrett's Peerage.

The representation of the Burkes, Earls of Clanricarde.

The fourteenth Earl was raised to the Marquessate of Clanricarde in 1825. On his death he was succeeded by his son, the second Marquess, who died some years ago, when the titles became extinct, the estates passing to his sister, Lady Elizabeth Joanna de Burgh. Lady Elizabeth by her marriage with the fourth Earl of Harewood conveyed the succession to the Lascelles family. Their grandson, the sixth and present Earl of Harewood, now representing the Clanricarde family in the female line, when Viscount Lascelles had the honour of marrying in 1922 H.R.H. Princess Mary, the Crown Princess. Their Irish residence is Portumna Castle, Co. Galway, and by the reception that they received *en route* and during their stay shortly after their marriage, they can feel assured of a warm welcome at any time.

The Plunketts of Louth and Meath.

229. **MATHEW PLUNKETT, 7TH BARON LOUTH.** He raised a regiment of foot, which he commanded at the investment of Derry and in the subsequent campaign down to the fall of Limerick. Walker's "Siege" tells how on 6th May, 1689, he, representing the garrison, attended an arranged parley with Lord Louth and Col. O'Neill outside the walls, how shots were fired at him and how he barely escaped with his life.

After a strenuous part in the defence of Limerick Lord Louth was one of the Irish commissioners appointed to negotiate the Treaty of Capitulation. He was attainted with confiscation in 1691, but on pleading the special clauses of the Treaty he was restored to title and estate. However, on attending the House of Lords to take his seat, he was not permitted to do so on the ground of a 1641 rebellion attainder which had never been reversed. It was not until 1798 that this outlawry was reversed, and the eleventh Baron was allowed to take his seat.[1]

The present representative of the family is the fourteenth Baron Louth, Louth Hall, Ardee.

230. **LUKE PLUNKETT, 4TH EARL OF FINGALL.** He sat, as did Lord Louth, as a peer in James' Dublin Parliament of 1689. He was attainted with confiscation in 1691, but restored to titles and estate in 1697.

Robert Plunkett, sixth Earl of Fingall, was a captain in the Berwick Regiment of the Irish Brigade. He died in Paris in 1728.

The present representative of the family is the eleventh Earl of Fingall, Killeen Castle, Dunsany, Meath.

231. **CHRISTOPHER PLUNKETT, 10TH BARON DUNSANY**, sat as a peer in James' Dublin Parliament, but dying in 1690 was succeeded by his brother,

---

[1] Burke and D'Alton.

232. RANDAL PLUNKETT, 11TH BARON DUNSANY. This Baron was a captain in Sir Henry Luttrell's Horse, with which he served all through the war down to the fall of Limerick.[1]

He was attainted in 1691, but under the special clauses of the Treaty of Limerick he was restored to titles and estates.

The present representative of the family is the 18th Baron Dunsany, Dunsany Castle, Meath.

233. QUARTERMASTER JAMES PLUNKETT, served in Sarsfield's Horse.

234. CAPT. OLIVER PLUNKETT, served in Lord Dongan's Regiment.

235. LIEUT. WALTER PLUNKETT, served in King's Own Regiment.

236. ENSIGN JOHN PLUNKETT, served in King's Own Regiment.

237. LIEUT. GARRETT PLUNKETT, served in Fitzjames' Regiment.

238. CAPT. PLUNKETT, served in Col. Richard Butler's Regiment.

239. ENSIGN PLUNKETT, served in Lord Gormanston's Regiment.

240. LIEUT. PLUNKETT, served in Lord Kenmare's Regiment.

241. LIEUT. GEORGE PLUNKETT, served in Sir Walter Creagh's Regiment.

242. LIEUT. WALTER PLUNKETT, served in Col. John Hamilton's Regiment. The two last-named were promoted captains and one of them was killed before Derry.[1]

243. COL. SIR MAURICE EUSTACE, of Castle Martin, Co. Kildare.

At the time of the revolution, 1688–89, Sir Maurice had raised a regiment of foot. He was severely wounded at Aughrim, and after the fall of Limerick retired to France, where he was in 1693 appointed to command a regiment of the Irish Brigade. He died in 1698.

He was, with many of his name, attainted in 1691 with confiscation of estates. Many of his family held commissions in his or other regiments, the most notable being

244. LIEUT.-COL. RICHARD EUSTACE, of Barretstown, Co. Kildare, who served in Lord Gormanston's Regiment. With his regiment he took part, being severely wounded, in the garrison's attack of 4th June, 1689, before the walls of Derry.[1]

245. LIEUT. CHRISTOPHER EUSTACE, an officer in Sir Niall O'Neill's Dragoons. He was wounded and taken prisoner in the same action of 4th June, 1689.[2]

---

[1] D'Alton.

[2] Walker's "Siege" and D'Alton.

246. **Capt. Nicolas Eustace,** an officer in Sir Niall O'Neill's Dragoons.[1] The three above were attainted in 1691, as were some fifteen to twenty other members of the family.[1]

247. **Col. Sir Michael Creagh,** Lord Mayor of Dublin, came of an old Co. Limerick stock, an ancestor being mayor of that town in 1216, an office filled by thirty members of the family in subsequent centuries.[1]

Sir Michael possessed considerable property in Dublin and was Lord Mayor at the time of the revolution. An ardent supporter of the Jacobite cause, he raised a regiment, which he commanded at the investment of Derry. To him and his regiment were given the task of guarding the Boom on the Foyle below Culmore. His failure to prevent the breaking of the Boom ensured the relief of Derry.[1]

In the "Londeriados" poem there are two references to the name:—

> "Sir Michael Creagh, Lord Mayor of Dublin
> Raised a regiment of valiant men.
> . . . .
> Sir Michael Creagh did the boom command
> To stop all succour from the neighb'ring land.
> The Boom was made of great long oaken beams
> Together joined with Iron athwart the streams."

He was present at the Boyne and Aughrim, serving down to the fall of Limerick. He and several of his family were attainted with confiscation of estates in 1691.

The Nagles or Nangles of Cos. Cork and Meath.

This old Anglo-Norman family (De Angulo) came over to Ireland with Strongbow, acquiring considerable estate in the counties indicated. The family at the time of the revolution were strong supporters of the Stuart dynasty.

248. **Sir Richard Nagle** was elected Speaker of the Dublin House of Commons of 1689, subsequently becoming King James' Secretary of State for Ireland, an office which he continued to hold under the exiled sovereign at St. Germains until his death.

249. **Major Nagle.** We are told by "Londeriados" how he met his death at Cladyford on the Finn when leading the van of General Richard Hamilton's army to invest Derry:—

> "Major Nagle, who led the Irish force,
> Dropt in the river, headlong from his horse,
> And many a valiant trooper floating lay
> Which the slow river scarce could bear away."

---

[1] D'Alton.

This account is confirmed by Walker's "Siege." In neither story is any Christian name given, but the Major in question is probably the Capt. Francis Nagle of Patrick Sarsfield's Horse, promoted to the rank of Major.

The following of the name held commissions in the Jacobite service:—

250. **Capt. Nagle**, in Richard Butler's Regiment.

251. **Lieut. Garrett Nagle**, in Lord Kenmare's Regiment.

252. **Lieut. Ignatius Nagle**, in Lord Slane's Regiment.

253. **Lieut. Arthur Nagle**, in Col. Gordon O'Neill's Regiment.

254. **Lieut. David Nagle**, in Sir John Barrett's Regiment.

255. **Capt. Walter Nagle**, in the King's Own Regiment.

256. **Capt. George Nagle**, in the King's Own Regiment.

257. **Lieut. Edward Nagle**, in the King's Own Regiment.

The present representative of this old family is Mr. Garrett Thomas Nagle, Clogher, Co. Cork. During many years' service as Resident Magistrate in Cos. Londonderry and Antrim and in the city of Belfast, Mr. Nagle made a reputation both on the Bench and on the banks of many an Ulster river.

The Fitzgeralds of Offaly and Leinster.

In the 1688 revolution the Fitzgeralds were still of predominating influence in Leinster and the south of the island. The eighteenth Earl of Kildare, though summoned to James' Dublin Parliament, does not appear to have attended, but, as will be shown later, the bulk of the name were strong supporters of the Stuart dynasty. When this eighteenth Earl died in 1707 he was succeeded by a cousin, Robert, a grandson of the sixteenth Earl, as nineteenth Earl of Kildare. This individual, when Capt. Robert Fitzgerald, played such an important part in the revolution as to deserve a sketch to himself.

258. **Capt. Robert Fitzgerald, 19th Earl of Kildare.** Having been in durance in Trinity College, on hearing from the uproar in the streets of James' defeat at the Boyne, he broke prison and induced the authorities of Dublin to make a quiet surrender, he himself having the honour of presenting the keys to King William on his arrival at the gates. For this timely service he was sworn of the Privy Council by the grateful monarch.[1] As already stated, he succeeded as nineteenth Earl in 1707.

---

[1] D'Alton.

259. **Col. Sir John Fitzgerald**, the representative of an important branch of the family, sprung from a younger son of the seventh Earl, raised a regiment of foot which he commanded all through the campaign.

Present at the investment of Derry, he took part in a serious engagement on 25th July, 1689. The Derry garrison, having seen some cows grazing behind an entrenched position held by the Fitzgerald Regiment, made a determined attack to seize the prey. Their onslaught was successful, the trenches being overrun and the Colonel severely wounded, but the garrison were obliged to retire without obtaining their objective.[1] After the fall of Limerick Sir John retired to France, where he obtained a command in the Irish Brigade. He fell at the Battle of Oudenarde in 1698. He was attainted with confiscation of his estates in 1691.

Two other officers of the name in Sir John's Regiment were present in the action of 25 th July described above, viz:—

260. **Lieut.-Col. Fitzgerald** was killed, as was also

261. **Capt. Fitzgerald.**[2]

The part played by the Fitzgerald family on the Jacobite side can be gathered from the fact that the name held commissions in Purcell's Horse, O'Neill and Clifford's Dragoons, and in Galmoy and Sarsfield's Cavalry, while no fewer than 115 suffered attainder with confiscation of their estates at the end of the war.[1]

The present representative of this ancient family is the seventh Duke of Leinster, Carton, Co. Kildare.

The Wogans.

262. **Major** or **Lieut.-Col. Wogan**, of Sir Maurice Eustace's Regiment, was killed in the Pennyburn sortie of the Derry garrison on 21st April, 1689.[2]

263. **Major James Wogan** was an officer in Lord Antrim's Infantry.

264. **Capt. John Wogan** was an officer in the Fitzjames Infantry.[3]

A Wogan rose to high rank in the Irish Brigade of Spain after Limerick.[4]

---

[1] Mackenzie.
[2] Walker's "Siege."
[3] D'Alton, Vol. II, p. 424.
[4] "The Irish Abroad," by Elliott O'Donnell.

Butlers of the house of Ormonde on the Jacobite side.[1]

When James' Parliament of May 1689 assembled in Dublin the following Butler cadets sat, as peers, in the Lords[2]:—Viscounts Mountgarret, Ikerrin and Galmoy, Barons Dunboyne and Cahir. The sketches below (No. 265 to No. 276) deal with these, with the exception of Viscount Mountgarrett (for whom see Part II, No. 26).

265. **PIERS BUTLER, 3RD VISCOUNT GALMOY.** A leading cadet of the house of Ormonde, he was the possessor of large estates in Kilkenny. He raised a regiment of horse at the commencement of the revolution, with which he operated in the neighbourhood of Enniskillen and in Connaught, earning a reputation for rapine, cruelty, and execution of prisoners after quarter had been given. Graham, in "Ireland Defended," quotes an observation of "Oldmixon," "That he was a monster whom no title could ennoble."

He was present with his regiment for a short time during the investment of Derry, taking part in the actions round the walls. He sat in James' Dublin Parliament of 1689.

After the relief of Derry and that of Enniskillen, he was present at the Boyne, and a few months later was severely wounded and taken prisoner at Aughrim. Exchanged, he fought through the two sieges of Limerick down to the capitulation in 1691, being one of the Irish Commissioners responsible for the drafting of the Treaty. Electing with his regiment for service in France, the Galmoy Regiment won a distinguished name in the Irish Brigade, until it was incorporated in the Dillon battalion. Lord Galmoy seems to have returned to this country in 1692, when he attempted to take his seat in the Irish Lords, but on his refusing the oath of supremacy, he was excluded. He was attainted with confiscation.[2]

The following were Butler officers of his regiment:—

266. **CAPT. EDWARD BUTLER,** his son and successor in the title as fourth Viscount. On this Viscount's death without issue the title became extinct.[3]

267. **CAPT. PIERS BUTLER.**

268. **LIEUT. JAMES BUTLER.**

269. **QUARTERMASTER JAMES BUTLER.**

270. **QUARTERMASTER PIERS BUTLER.**[4]

---

[1] For rough outlines of family history and the second Duke of Ormonde, head of the house at the revolution, see Part I, No. 1648.
[2] D'Alton.
[3] O'Callaghan.
[4] D'Alton. For reference to the Galmoy Regiment in France see No. 344, The Irish Brigade.

271. **JAMES BUTLER, 6TH BARON DUNBOYNE.** He was a captain in Col. Nicholas Purcell's Infantry Regiment, with which he took his share in the campaign down to the fall of Limerick in 1691. Coming under the special clauses of the Treaty, he retained title and estates.

The Dunboyne family are one of the main branches of the house of Ormonde. The title was by summons in 1274 and by patent in 1541.

The present representative of this family is Baron Dunboyne, twenty-sixth by summons and seventeenth by patent, Knoppogue Castle, Co. Clare.

272. **PIERS BUTLER, 5TH BARON DUNBOYNE,** the father of the sixth Baron (preceding sketch), sat in the Lords of James' Dublin Parliament in 1689. He died in 1690.

273. **PIERS BUTLER, 4TH VISCOUNT IKERRIN** (creation 1629). His father James, third Viscount, had died in London in the middle of the 1688 political crisis. This Viscount on arrival in Dublin in May of 1689 was sworn of James' Privy Council, and was summoned to sit in the Lords.[1]

His name does not figure among the officers of the Jacobite army. After the fall of Limerick he was attainted with confiscation of estates in 1691. In 1698, on the reversal of attainder, he took his seat in the Irish House of Lords.

The eighth Viscount Ikerrin was, in 1748, raised to the higher dignity of Earl of Carrick, in which the Viscountcy is now merged, being the courtesy title of the eldest son. The present representative of the family is the eighth Earl of Carrick.

274. **PIERS BUTLER, 7TH BARON CAHIR.** He sat in James' Dublin House of Lords. After the fall of Limerick he was attainted with confiscation of estates. In 1693 he was restored. The title became extinct in 1858.[2]

Butlers of various branches of the Ormonde family held commissions in nearly all the regiments of the Irish Jacobite Army, among others in Sarsfield's Horse, in Lord Dongan's, Sir Niall O'Neill's and Clifford's Dragoons and in Tyrone's, Clancarty's, Kilmallock's, Cormac O'Neill's, Creagh's and Boiselen's Infantry Regiments, while the following members of the family raised infantry regiments which served on the Jacobite side during the war:—

275. **COL. THOMAS BUTLER** and

276. **COL. EDWARD BUTLER.** They both served all through the campaign.[1]

There were some thirty-five of the Butler name on the list of attainted after the fall of Limerick in 1691.[1]

---

[1] D'Alton.
[2] Debrett.

The O'Briens of Thomond, Earls of Thomond, Viscounts Clare and Barons Inchiquin.

WILLIAM O'BRIEN, 7TH BARON and 2ND EARL OF INCHIQUIN, a strong supporter of William of Orange. He was among the peers attainted in James' Dublin Parliament of 1689.[1]

277. HENRY O'BRIEN, 5TH EARL OF THOMOND. A staunch supporter of King James. Although summoned to the Dublin Parliament of 1689 he does not appear to have attended, but any want of zeal on his part was more than atoned for by his near kinsman,

278. DANIEL O'BRIEN, 3RD VISCOUNT CLARE. This Viscountcy had been granted in 1662, after the Restoration by Charles II. to this peer's grandfather, Daniel, second son of the third Earl of Thomond, one of the monarch's faithful adherents and companions during his wanderings on the Continent.

This Viscount Clare was one of the peers who sat in the Dublin Parliament of 1689. He was responsible for the raising of two regiments of infantry and one of dragoons in the Jacobite service, in which many of the name held commissions.[2] At the battle of Newtownbutler (1689) two of these regiments had suffered severely at the hands of the men of Enniskillen.

He was present at the battle of the Boyne, and dying shortly afterwards was succeeded by his son,

279. DANIEL O'BRIEN, as 4TH VISCOUNT CLARE. This Daniel had been in command of one of the Clare regiments at Newtownbutler. Serving all through the campaign, he accompanied his regiment to France in 1690, where it became famous in the Irish Brigade as the Clare Regiment.

In 1693 he died at Pignerol of wounds received at the Battle of Marsaglia, where the Irish Brigade had won distinction. He was succeeded in 1693 by his brother,

280. CHARLES, as 5TH VISCOUNT CLARE. This Viscount had served on the Jacobite side all through the Irish campaign, and after the fall of Limerick had gone to France, where he was appointed to a commission in King James' Guards at St. Germains. In 1698 he was given the command of the family regiment of Clare.

Serving in many campaigns with the Irish Brigade, he was so severely wounded at Ramillies that he died a few weeks later (1706) at Brussels.

281. CHARLES, 6TH VISCOUNT CLARE, was a minor at the time of his father's death, and therefore ineligible to command, but by an act of graceful consideration

---

[1] See Inchiquin, Part I, No. 1649.
[2] D'Alton.

Louis XIV. appointed a cadet of the house to the temporary command, reserving the post for the young Viscount on coming of age. So in due time Charles, sixth Viscount, commanded the family regiment of Clare. Under his leadership the Clare Regiment and the Irish Brigade won still further renown, particularly at the Battle of Dettingen in 1743. Meantime the last Earl of Thomond[1] had died, leaving no issue, so that the representation of the great house of Thomond devolved on his kinsman, the sixth Viscount Clare, henceforward known in France as Viscount Clare and Earl of Thomond.[2] This sixth Viscount Clare and Earl of Thomond commanded the Irish Brigade on the great day of Fontenoy in 1745. The French troops under the command of Marshal de Saxe, with King Louis XV. present, held a position at Fontenoy (Flanders) covering a section of their army besieging Tournai. This siege the allies, English, Hanoverian and Dutch, under the command of the Duke of Cumberland were determined to raise. On the morning of the battle the allies had been so successful in their earlier attacks that the French had thought of raising the siege and retiring. The Irish Brigade had not so far been engaged. At last, when the attack was renewed, the Irish Brigade, the infantry being under the command of Viscount Clare, were given their chance. Three times were the allies repulsed with terrible losses on each side, and at length driven from the field. The glory of the day was with the Irish Brigade, on whom honours were showered, Viscount Clare being raised to the rank of Marshal of France shortly afterwards.

On his death in 1762 his son Charles succeeded to the titular honours as seventh Viscount Clare and Earl of Thomond, but he never commanded the Clare Regiment, graciously reserved for him by Louis XV., as he was still too young on his death in 1774, when the titular honours of Clare and Thomond became extinct, and the famous Regiment of Clare was merged in that of Berwick in the Irish Brigade.[3]

282. **CAPT. O'BRIEN**, of the Thomond family, was an officer taken prisoner in Lord Clancarty's attack on the Butcher's Gate, Derry, June 28th, 1689.[4]

283. **THEOBALD DILLON, 7TH VISCOUNT DILLON**, of Costello Gallen, Co. Mayo, was the head of this ancient Anglo-Norman family, which had settled in Ireland in Henry II.'s reign. At the time of the 1688 revolution he and his family were staunch supporters of the Stuart dynasty. The title dated from 1622.

This 7th Viscount sat in James' Dublin Parliament, while he was Lieut.-Col. of the Earl of Clanricarde's Infantry Regiment, with which he served all through the

---

[1] See No. 277.

[2] Under the will of the deceased Earl the Thomond estates were left to the Inchiquin line, while £20,000 were bequeathed to Viscount Clare.

[3] See No. 344, The Irish Brigade. All the above references to the O'Briens, Earls of Thomond and Viscount Clare, and to the Clare Regiment, are taken from O'Callaghan's "History of the Irish Brigade in the Service of France" and from D'Alton's "Jacobite Army List."

[4] Walker and Mackenzie's "Sieges." D'Alton says killed.

campaign down to the 12th July, 1691, when he was killed at Aughrim. A few weeks later his widow was killed by a shell at Limerick.

284. **Henry**, his eldest son and successor, as **8th Viscount Dillon**, raised an infantry regiment of his own in the Jacobite service of which he was Colonel-Commanding down to the fall of Limerick. He died in 1713, being succeeded by his son Richard as ninth Viscount Dillon. His only daughter and heiress had married in 1734 her cousin Charles, the Colonel Proprietor of the Dillon Regiment, who succeeded as tenth Viscount Dillon in 1737.

285. **Arthur**, second son of the seventh Viscount, also raised an infantry regiment in King James' army with which he served through the campaign. This regiment went as part of 6000 men to France in 1690, and under the leadership of this Col. Arthur Dillon became famous as the Dillon Regiment of the Irish Brigade in France. Commanded and officered by Dillons and their Irish connections, the Regiment, like the Clare and Berwick Regiments, was recognised by the monarchs of France as being proprietary to the Dillon family. On Col. Arthur's death in 1733 he was succeeded in the Colonelcy by his son, Col. Charles, in 1737 tenth Viscount Dillon. This tenth Viscount died in 1741, when he was succeeded by his brother Henry as eleventh Viscount and Colonel Proprietor of the Dillon Regiment, who died in 1787. This Viscount had a distinguished career with the Irish Brigade down to the Battle of Dettingen (1743), but in 1744, in view of contemplated legislation to prevent British subjects holding commissions in Continental armies, it is said, by the consent if not on the advice of Louis XV. he resigned his commission and returned to England.[1] So recognised, however, was the Dillon colonel proprietorship of the regiment that he was permitted to retain it, while two members of the family were allowed to deputise for him, viz.: Col. James Dillon, killed at Fontenoy, 1745, and Col. Edward Dillon, killed at Laffeldt, 1747.

For the next twenty years until 1767 other deputies held the command. Then the two sons of the eleventh Viscount, who was still alive, were of sufficient age to be considered for the colonel proprietorship of the regiment, and it was arranged by Louis XV. and the family that, while Charles, the elder son, remained in England to succeed eventually to his father as the twelfth Viscount Dillon, his brother Arthur, aged seventeen years, should succeed to the colonel proprietorship of the regiment. In the course of the French Revolution the Irish Brigade with the Dillon Regiment were disbanded, and in 1794 this Col. Arthur Dillon, last colonel proprietor, died by the guillotine in Paris on the charge of conspiring to restore the Bourbons, with the cry of "Vive le Roi!" on his lips.[1]

Few families furnish so much historic romance as the Viscounts Dillon of Costello Gallen, Co. Mayo, Counts of France and Colonel Proprietors of the Dillon Regiment,

---

[1] O'Callaghan.

Irish Brigade of France. They are to-day represented by the direct descendant of the twelfth Viscount Dillon, viz.: the eighteenth Viscount Dillon, Ditchley, Oxfordshire.

To go back to the 1688 revolution. Besides the names already mentioned there were no fewer than twenty-three of the family holding commissions in the Dillon and other Jacobite regiments.[1] The Dillon Regiment of the Irish Brigade in France was officered by their name and connections.[2] Among the attainted, with confiscation of estates in 1691, after the fall of Limerick, there were more than thirty Dillons.[3]

286. **WILLIAM DONGAN, VISCOUNT DONGAN** and **EARL OF LIMERICK**, created by James II. in 1685, was the representative of an old family in possession of a large estate at Celbridge, Co. Kildare.

He raised a regiment of dragoons in the Jacobite service, which shortly before the advance on Derry he transferred to the command of his son,

287. **WALTER DONGAN, VISCOUNT DONGAN**, who commanded the regiment at the siege of Derry.

While the father, the Earl, sat in James' Dublin Parliament the son is said to have been sent on a special mission by James to warn Richard Hamilton, in charge of the siege operations, of the preparations being made in England for the dispatch of the relieving force under General Kirke.[1]

The son, Walter, at the head of his dragoons, lost his life at the Battle of the Boyne, and his body was interred in the old church of Celbridge, near the family mansion. After the son's death the father, the Earl, followed the army to Limerick, and after the capitulation retired to France, where he was graciously received at St. Germains.[4]

The Earl of Limerick was attainted with confiscation of estates in 1691, and died in Paris a few years later, when the title became extinct. This is the 1685 Earldom of Limerick, and is not to be confounded with the Earldom of Limerick conferred on the Pery family, of Dromore Castle, Co. Limerick, in 1803.

288. **JOHN BELLEW, BARON BELLEW**, of Duleek, Co. Louth, so created by James II. in 1686, a man of considerable estate and influence, representing an old Anglo-Norman family.

He raised an infantry regiment, which he commanded in the field, in which three of the name held commissions, while twelve Bellews were among the officers of other regiments in the Stuart service. Whether the regiment was at Derry is doubtful, but his grandson,

---

[1] D'Alton.

[2] O'Callaghan.

[3] For further information regarding the family and regiment I would refer the inquirer to O'Callaghan's "Irish Brigades in the Service of France." See No. 344, The Irish Brigade.

[4] For details of the Dongan Dragoons in the Irish Brigade, where it was incorporated with others and known as "The King's Regiment of Dismounted Dragoons," see O'Callaghan's "Irish Brigades," p. 77.

289. Capt. Richard Bellew, who held a commission in the Dongan or Limerick Dragoons, was present with that regiment at the siege. We are told by "Story" that when the Duke of Schomberg made Dundalk his headquarters some 2000 sheep were raided from Lord Bellew's estate near Duleek for provisioning the army.

Lord Bellew fell at the head of his regiment at the battle of Aughrim in 1691, being succeeded by his eldest son,

290. Walter, 2nd Baron Bellew, who was attainted in 1691, but claiming to come under the special clauses of the Treaty of Limerick the attainture was reversed a few years later, and he took his seat in the Irish Lords in 1704. On the death of this Baron's grandson in 1776 the title became extinct. The Barony was, however, revived in 1848 by a second creation in favour of a branch of the family sprung from the same original stock, to-day represented by the fourth Baron Bellew, Barmeath Castle, Co. Louth.

291. Capt. Richard Fagan, of Feltrim, Co. Dublin, was the representative of an ancient Dublin family holding large estates in Co. Meath, acquired from the Lacy family in the 13th century.

He held his commission in King James' Own Regiment of Infantry. He fought all through the campaign down to the fall of Limerick, when he went to the Continent and took service in the Spanish army. With several members of his family, he was among the attainted after Limerick.[1]

The present representative of this old family is William Charles Fagan, of Feltrim, Co. Dublin.[2]

292. Col. Charles Macmurrough Kavanagh, of Carrickduff, Co. Carlow, second son of Morgan Macmurrough Kavanagh, of Borris, raised an infantry regiment for the Jacobite service at the commencement of the revolution.

Holding commissions in this regiment were the following of the name, all kinsmen:—

293. Capt. Ignatius Kavanagh, of Carrickduff.

294. Capt. Symon Kavanagh.[3]

295. Capt. Edward Kavanagh.

296. Lieut. Denis Kavanagh.

297. Ensign Kavanagh.

---

[1] D'Alton.
[2] Burke's "Landed Gentry of Ireland."
[3] D'Alton's "Jacobite Army List."

298. ENSIGN EDMOND KAVANAGH.[1]

This regiment was present at the investment of Derry, the position it occupied in the investing lines being marked in Capt. Neville's old map of the siege.[2] The regiment served through the subsequent campaign. After Limerick several Kavanaghs went to the Continent, one at least of the name holding high posts, military and civil, in Austria, viz. Charles Kavanagh, who was Governor of Prague in 1766.

The Kavanagh family had for generations been among the most prominent of the ancient Celtic landlords of Ireland, but it fell to the lot of Arthur McMurrough Kavanagh, of Borris, to rise superior to disabilities which would have daunted most men, and establish a name second to none in the politics of Ireland. Born in 1831, without arms or legs (attributed by popular superstition to the fulfilment of an old prophecy), the youngster not only with remarkable resolution and ability fought his way in life, but managed to get returned for an Irish seat in the House of Commons in 1868. Once in the House he remained there for eleven years (until 1880), earning the admiration, respect and affection of all with whom he came in contact. He was sworn in a member of the Privy Council in 1886, and died three years later. The author had the pleasure of meeting him when a guest in the smoking-room of the House, and being greatly impressed by his charm of manner, his simplicity and cleverness in expression. The present representative of this ancient stock is his grandson.

299. ROBERT BARNEWALL, 9TH BARON TRIMLESTOWN, of Trimlestown, Co. Meath, was at the revolution of 1688 the representative of one of the oldest Anglo-Norman families of the Pale, the barony dating from 1461.

Like nearly all the great houses of the Pale, he was a strong supporter of James II. Summoned to James' Dublin Parliament of May 1689, ill-health prevented his attendance. He died later in the same year, being succeeded by his son,

300. MATTHIAS BARNEWALL, 10TH BARON TRIMLESTOWN. This Baron was a captain in Viscount Galmoy's Horse, with which he served at the investment of Derry and through the subsequent campaign down to the fall of Limerick, where he was one of the negotiators of the Treaty. After Limerick he retired to the Continent, where he fell in the Austrian service in 1692. Three of his sons served in Irish Brigades abroad:—

301. **THOMAS BARNEWALL**, in France,

302. **JAMES BARNEWALL**, in Spain, and

303. **ANTHONY BARNEWALL**, in Austria.[3] The tenth Baron and many of the family

---

[1] D'Alton's "Jacobite Army List."
[2] See notes in Graham's "Ireland Defended."
[3] D'Alton.

were attainted with confiscation of estates in 1691, and it was not until 1797 that the attainder was reversed.

The present representative of this old family is Charles Aloysius Barnewall, eighteenth Baron Trimlestown.

304. **NICOLAS BARNEWALL, 3RD VISCOUNT KINGSLAND,** was another of this old house, representing a junior branch, who sat in James' Dublin Parliament. He was an ardent Jacobite, holding a commission as captain in the Earl of Limerick's (Dongan's) Dragoons, with whom he fought at the Boyne and down to the fall of Limerick,[1] and was among those attainted with confiscation of estates in 1691. The title was subsequently restored, the last peer dying in 1834, when the Viscountcy became extinct.[2]

305. A **CAPT. BARNEWALL** and an

306. **ENSIGN BARNEWALL,** probably in Lord Gormanston's Regiment,[1] two members of this family, are mentioned as officers of the Jacobite regiment investing Derry killed in the garrison's assault on Windmill Hill (May 6th, 1689).[3]

307. **LIEUT.-COL. ALEXANDER BARNEWALL,** served with distinction in France as a Lieut.-Colonel in the reformed regiment styled "Lord Clare's Dismounted Dragoons."[1]

308. **JENICO PRESTON, 7TH VISCOUNT GORMANSTON,** of Gormanston Castle, Co. Meath, the representative in the 1688 revolution of this ancient baronial house of the Pale, was a strong supporter of the Stuart dynasty.

The first of this ancient Anglo-Norman stock had settled in Ireland early in the 14th century. His son was Lord Chancellor of Ireland, and created a Baron *circa* 1370. A few generations later the successor to the family honours was, in 1478, raised to the Viscountcy of Gormanston.[4]

The seventh Viscount sat in James' Dublin Parliament 1689 and raised an infantry regiment in the Jacobite service, with which he served all through the campaign, being present at the Boyne, Aughrim and the siege of Limerick.

309. His son, **JENICO PRESTON,** his successor as 8th titular Viscount, was a lieutenant in the Earl of Tyrone's Horse, with which he served through the campaign.

There was one of the name in the seventh Viscount's own regiment, viz.:—

310. **LIEUT. PRESTON.** After Limerick in 1691 the Viscount, his son and many members of his family were among the attainted with confiscation of estates, and it was not until 1800 that the thirteenth Viscount got the attainder reversed and was restored to the family honours.

---

[1] D'Alton.
[2] Debrett.
[3] Walker's "Siege."
[4] Burke's Peerage.

The present representative of this old family is Jenico William Richard Preston, sixteenth Viscount Gormanston, Premier Viscount of Ireland and a Baron (United Kingdom, 1868).

311. **LIEUT.-COL. WILLIAM MAUNSELL BARKER,** an officer in the King's Own Infantry Regiment, with which he was at the investment of Derry.[1]

According to Walker's "Siege" he was one of the Jacobite officers killed in the garrison's sortie of July 6th or 7th, 1689, but D'Alton states that he fell at Aughrim in 1691.

The Barkers were a southern family holding property in Cos. Limerick and Tipperary,[1]

312. **CAPT. TERENCE MACDONOUGH,** a member of the powerful sept of that name in Co. Sligo.

He held his commission in Col. Henry Dillon's Infantry Regiment, with which he was present at the investment of Derry.[1] He is mentioned as one of the prisoners taken by the garrison in the sortie of 4th June, 1689.[2]

Several of the name figure in the list of attainted in 1691 after the capitulation of Limerick, and others were officers in the Irish Brigade of France.[3]

313. **LIEUT.-COL. SIR THOMAS NEWCOMEN,** 5th Bart., of Keenaght, Longford, a baronetcy created in 1625.

By his first wife he was brother-in-law of Tyrconnell and a strong supporter of the Stuarts. In the spring of 1689 he was in command of an infantry regiment holding Lisnagarvey (Lisburn) when the Protestant Associations of Cos. Antrim and Down made their abortive attempt to surprise and seize Carrickfergus and that town. He barricaded the streets, and by his energy the attack was repulsed. A few days later, some of his officers and men having deserted to the enemy, he retired with the rest of the regiment to Dublin.[4] He was afterwards killed at the head of his men in one of the actions round Enniskillen.

314. **LIEUT. NEWCOMEN,** probably one of the above Sir Thomas' six sons, was taken prisoner by the garrison of Derry in their sortie of May 6th, 1689.[5] The family were evidently divided in political beliefs, possibly accounted for by his father's first wife's relationship to Tyrconnell, while his second wife was of the St. George family closely related to many of the staunchest Ulster supporters of William.

[1] D'Alton.
[2] Walker.
[3] O'Callaghan.
[4] Montgomery MS., p. 277.
[5] In Part I, Nos. 594–597, will be found references to four of Sir Thomas Newcomen's sons serving on the side of William of Orange.

315. **Col. John Parker** raised a regiment of horse in the neighbourhood of Dublin, with which he served on the Jacobite side all through the campaign. No regiment suffered more severely than his at the Battle of the Boyne, many of the officers and men being killed or wounded. Among the severely wounded were himself and his lieut.-colonel.[1]

After the fall of Limerick he went to France and became a trusted emissary between the exiled James and the English Jacobites. In 1693 he was arrested in London and consigned to the Tower, from which he escaped in 1695. Returning to France, he resumed his role of conspirator.[1]

He is not to be confounded with Col. Parker of Coleraine.

316. **Brian Fitzpatrick, 7th Baron of Upper Ossory**, was at the time of the 1688 revolution the chief of the great sept "McGilla Phaedruig," who for centuries had been the possessors of the territory of Upper Ossory, lying between the rivers Nore and Suir. The title had been created in 1541.

This seventh Baron, an ardent supporter of the Stuarts, sat in James II.'s Dublin Parliament and, holding a captain's commission in the Earl of Clancarty's Infantry Regiment, fought throughout the campaign. He was present at the investment of Derry, and shared in the gallant attack of 30th June, 1689, on the Butcher's Gate. After the fall of Limerick he was among the attainted in 1691, but claiming advantage of the special clauses he was restored to his title and estates. He died in 1696. The title is extinct, but in 1869 Mr. John Wilson Fitzpatrick succeeded to the family estate, and was raised to the peerage as Baron Castletown of Upper Ossory. The present representative is the second Baron Castletown, of Upper Ossory.

317. A **Lieut. Fitzpatrick**, of this family, was killed on 23rd April, 1689, in an attack by the garrison of Derry on the Jacobite position.

Several other Fitzpatricks held commissions in Jacobite regiments, and many were among the 1691 attainted.

318. **Col. Nicholas Purcell** raised a regiment of horse in the Jacobite service, in which some six members of his family held commissions, viz.:—

319. **Lieut.-Col. Robert Purcell.**[1]

320. **Capt. John Purcell.**

321. **Lieut. Thomas Purcell.**

322. **Lieut. Theobald Purcell.**

323. **Cornet Anthony Purcell.**

---

[1] D'Alton.

324. **CORNET HUGH PURCELL,**[1] while another of the family,

325. **COL. JAMES PURCELL**, raised a regiment of infantry in the Stuart service.

326. **CORNET JAMES PURCELL** held a commission in Lord Galmoy's Horse and was wounded in one of the engagements outside the walls of Derry during the investment.[1]

Capt. Nicholas Purcell was head of an old family in Co. Tipperary whose ancestor in the 13th or 14th century had been denominated Baron of Loughmoe. He raised a regiment of horse in the Jacobite service, and was sworn a member of the Privy Council soon after King James' arrival in Ireland. He fought at the head of his regiment through the long campaign, being present at Derry, the Boyne, Aughrim and Limerick. After King William's raising of the first siege of Limerick and the Duke of Tyrconnell's departure for France to solicit further succour from the French Court (autumn 1690), Col. Purcell, the Bishop of Cork, and Cols. Simon and Henry Luttrell were sent as a deputation to St. Germains from the Irish army to protest against the misconduct of military matters by Tyrconnell. Both parties met at St. Germains, and although Tyrconnell returned in January 1691 as Viceroy of Ireland with full powers, there followed him early in May the French General St. Ruth, who had been appointed to command the Irish troops in the field. During the siege of Limerick, having risen to the rank of Lieut.-General, Purcell was most active in the defence. He was one of the Irish Commissioners who arranged the capitulation and Treaty. He was adverse to the Irish troops embarking for France, and was accused by his compatriots of playing into the hands of the English. Refusing to claim advantage of the special clauses of the Treaty, he suffered attainture and confiscation.[1] Going to France, he took service in the Irish Brigade and was killed in action. He left an only daughter, Anastasia, who was brought up at St. Germains under the care of the exiled Monarch and his Queen, owing to whose intervention she was eventually received by Queen Anne in London. Queen Anne so interested herself in her behalf that she was restored to a small portion of her father's large estates.[2] She married Col. O'Hehir, of Clare, and through the marriage of her granddaughter Susanna Mahon with an O'Gorman the line of Col. Nicholas Purcell is now represented by Col. Nicholas Purcell O'Gorman, Bellevue, Co. Clare.

The Purcells of Crumlin, Co. Dublin, now extinct, at the time of the revolution were an influential family on the Jacobite side, of whom

327. **MAJOR PURCELL**, according to Story's "History," was killed at Aughrim in 1691.[1]

---

[1] D'Alton.
[2] Graham's "Ireland Defended."

The Luttrells of Luttrellstown, Co. Dublin.

This old Anglo-Norman family, in possession of their Luttrellstown estate since King John's reign, were represented by two brothers at the time of the revolution, who, as will be seen in the following sketches, took a prominent part on the Jacobite side down to the fall of Limerick.

328. **COL. SIMON LUTTRELL**, the elder, was the owner of the family estate. He raised a regiment of dragoons which he commanded in the field. Sworn of the Privy Council, he was the Jacobite Governor of Dublin.

329. **COL. HENRY LUTTRELL**, the younger brother, also raised a regiment of horse. Both these brothers served with distinction down to the siege of Limerick. After the raising of the first siege by King William's withdrawal of his army, a strong party opposed to Tyrconnell's conduct of military affairs had risen in the Irish camp. Tyrconnell had taken advantage of the raising of the first siege to go in person to France to put the position before the Courts of Versailles and St. Germains and solicit further assistance in troops and supplies. A few weeks later the malcontents met and appointed the following deputation, Colonels Nicholas Purcell, Simon and Henry Luttrell and the Bishop of Cork, to go to France and voice their views to James II. and Louis XIV. The contesting parties met at Versailles and St. Germains, the result being that, while Tyrconnell, accompanied by the malcontent deputation, returned early in January 1691 to Limerick with his viceregal authority uncurtailed, he was followed on 8th May by the arrival of a French fleet and supplies under the French General St. Ruth, who was appointed Commander-in-Chief of Irish troops in the approaching campaign. This solution brought more harmony to the divided garrison.[1]

Both brothers were in Limerick during the terrible days of the second siege, and historians are unanimously agreed in the summing up of their characters as follows: Simon Luttrell was a conscientious man, devoted to the interests of his country and the Jacobite party. Henry Luttrell was a man who only thought of self-interest, and who would sacrifice King or party to gain his own ends. In the closing days of the siege he had been discovered in treasonable correspondence with the English camp. Court-martialled and sentenced to death, he would have been shot but for Ginkell's intervention.[2] These characters are more than substantiated by their subsequent careers. Both were attainted with confiscation of estates. Simon Luttrell went to France, and, given the command of the Queen's Own Infantry in the Irish Brigade, served with distinction in the Italian campaign of 1696. He died in 1698. A fine tablet in the Irish

---

[1] We all know how Tyrconnell died on 14th August, 1691, at Limerick before the second siege, and how St. Ruth had fallen at the Battle of Aughrim on July 12th.
[2] Macaulay, D'Alton and Callaghan.

College in Paris has an inscription bearing testimony to his character and worth.[1] He left no issue, so that the family estates devolved on his brother, Henry Luttrell, who, coming under the special clauses of the Treaty of Limerick, had been permitted in consequence of his services at the siege to occupy Luttrellstown *in custodiam.* He was given command of an English regiment and served in at least one campaign under King William in Flanders. Unpopular with all parties, there was little regret when he was assassinated in the streets of Dublin in 1717. He left two sons, who succeeded in turn to Luttrellstown, the youngest of whom was created Earl of Carhampton in 1785. His only son, who succeeded, died in 1829, when the title became extinct.

The mansion of Luttrellstown was entirely rebuilt early in the 19th century by the celebrated Luke White, father of the first Lord Annaly, and is now the residence of the Hon. Brinsley Plunket.[2]

330. **LIEUT.-GENERAL ST. RUTH,** of the French army, who commanded the Irish army at the Battle of Aughrim, where he was killed on 12th July, 1691.

He was an officer of "great conduct and experience" in the French army, where twenty years' service had earned him a considerable reputation. In 1690 he had been the leader of a successful French force in the reduction of Savoy. In this army he had commanded the Irish Brigade of Lord Mountcashel, the beginning of the famous Irish Brigade of France. This experience of Irish troops in action was probably the reason for his selection by Louis XIV. and James II. to command the Irish troops in Ireland, in answer to the deputation of the Limerick malcontents. Appointed to the command, he arrived in the Shannon on 8th May, 1690, bringing with him, not indeed the French troops required, but some 300 French officers and cadets, 24 cannon, 10,000 muskets and various needed supplies. St. Ruth immediately set about the re-organisation of the army for the approaching campaign. His difficulties were great, interference from Tyrconnell, dissension among the Irish Generals and want of supplies and munitions.

On 20th June, hearing that Ginkell was besieging Athlone, he advanced with his army and encamped within a few miles of the town. Here he lay inactive for some days, over-confident in the belief that the town was impregnable. To his chagrin, Athlone was taken by assault on 30th June. Fully aware of his disgrace, and determined to retrieve his reputation, he retired to Ballinasloe and took up a strong position on ground carefully prepared to await attack at Aughrim. Before this position Ginkell presented himself on 12th July, and immediately joined battle. For some hours the Irish held their ground and seemed to have the advantage, but at a crisis in the day St. Ruth's head was shot off by a cannon ball, and the Irish broke and fled. The carnage and disorder were terrible. Ginkell had won a decisive victory; a remnant of the beaten army fled to Limerick and another to Galway. As at Athlone, St. Ruth had made

[1] O'Callaghan.
[2] For Macaulay's appreciation of Henry Luttrell, see Macaulay's "History," Vol. IV., pp. 108, 109.

another great mistake. Patrick Sarsfield, in command of the Irish Reserve, had been ordered to remain out of sight of the battle until ordered to advance. No provision for his successor had been made by St. Ruth. All was confusion, no order was sent to the Reserve, so all Sarsfield could do was to cover as far as possible the Irish retreat.

Other French Generals connected with the Defence of Limerick.

331. **Lieut.-General D'Usson** was one of the French officers who came to Limerick in St. Ruth's train in 1690. Appointed to the command of Athlone garrison, its fall by assault was attributed to his carelessness and want of proper supervision. He was present at Aughrim, and afterwards commanded the garrison of Galway, which he yielded on terms to the English, retiring to Limerick. He was one of the Generals commanding in the defence of that city, and to his mistakes several Irish writers attribute its loss.[1]

332. **Chevalier de Tessè** was another French officer who arrived in Ireland with St. Ruth in 1690.

De Tessè commanded a wing of the Irish army at Aughrim, and was afterwards prominent in the defence of Limerick.

Both these officers were parties to the military articles of the Treaty of Limerick. The Chevalier was in 1704 raised to the rank of Brigadier-General and Maréchale de Camp in Louis XIV.'s army.[1]

333. **Antonine Lauzun, Comte de Lauzun**, French General, played a contemptible part at the Battle of the Boyne. Sent at the head of 6000 veteran French troops to show the Irish how to fight, after watching the Irish fight for some eighteen months he declared Limerick untenable and took his veterans back to France with scarcely the loss of a man.[2]

A lively and ambitious man, he was for some years a prime favourite with Louis XIV. at the Court of Versailles, but his pretensions to the hand of a Bourbon Princess, the Princess of Montpensier, led to his disgrace and imprisonment for some years in the castle of Pignerol, from which by the intercession of the lady, to whom he had been secretly married, he was eventually released.

Escaping to London, he became a favourite of James II., whom in 1688 he put under a debt of gratitude by securing a safe means of escape to Paris for the Queen and the Prince of Wales. When in 1689–90 an arrangement was made between Louis of France and James II. to send 6000 veteran troops to the latter's assistance in Ireland in exchange for an equal number of undisciplined Irish levies, de Lauzun, at the instance

---

[1] D'Alton.

[2] The following facts are gathered from Harris's "History of King William of Orange," D'Alton's "Jacobite Army List," and Macaulay's "History of England," Vol. III.

of the exiled monarch, was selected for the command in spite of Louis' personal dislike and Louvois, his Minister's, protests as to his incapacity. At the head of this French force de Lauzun, who took Rosen's place, arrived in Ireland before King William's landing.

Present at the Boyne, this veteran French Brigade remained inactive until called upon to cover the retreat to Dublin, which they did in an unbroken array. After James II.'s flight to France, which de Lauzun strongly advocated, he retired with Tyrconnell to Limerick. Once in Limerick, to the disgust of the Irish, he declared the place incapable of defence and withdrew his Brigade to Galway without waiting for King William's advance. Urgent appeals were meanwhile made for shipping his convoy of men back to France, but it was not until the Irish, without his assistance, had compelled King William to raise the siege, 30th August, 1690, that he transported his command back to their own country.[1]

The Taafes, Viscounts of Curren, Co. Sligo, and Earls of Carlingford.

334. **NICHOLAS, 2ND EARL OF CARLINGFORD,** who sat as the family representative in the Lords of James' Dublin Parliament. He fell while gallantly leading his regiment at the Boyne. Leaving no issue he was succeeded by his brother,

335. **FRANCIS, 3RD EARL OF CARLINGFORD.** This Francis had gone to Germany early in life, had been made a page in the Emperor's Court, and had risen to the highest posts in the German Empire. So great was his position and influence at Vienna that he was courted by all the Courts of Europe. King William in his negotiations with the Princes Electors and German Emperor for the coalition against France fully recognised that his favour must be won, and it was probably for this reason that he was exempted by special clause in the Act of Parliament of 1691 from attainder and confiscation.

On his death in 1704 he was succeeded by his son Theobald, 4th Earl of Carlingford, who also rendered great services on the field of battle and in diplomacy. On his death in 1738 the Earldom became extinct, but the Viscountcy devolved on his nephew descended from a brother of the 1st Viscount Taafe,[2] viz. Nicholas, 6th Viscount Taafe, from whom descend the line of the six later viscounts.

For the best part of three centuries no family has held a higher position at the Court of Vienna or among the proud nobility of Austria. Several of them rose to the rank of Field-Marshal, many occupied the highest offices in the Diplomatic Service, while it was a Taafe that captured Belgrade from the Turk.

The present representative of this old stock is Henry Taafe, Count of the Holy

[1] For an account of the doings of the 6000 Irish troops, exchanged for these veteran French soldiers, who afterwards became the nucleus of the famous Irish Brigade in France, see Part II., No. 208, under the name of Viscount Mountcashel.
[2] D'Alton.

Roman Empire, Ellischau Castle and Kolinetz Castle, Bohemia.[1] The claim to this peerage was established before a Committee of the House of Lords in 1860, but the title suffered attainder during the European War, 1914–19.

336. **Major John Taafe**, probably a younger son of the first Viscount Taafe, was killed in the Derry garrison's sortie of 21st April, 1689, at Pennyburn.[2]

Several of the name were among those attainted with confiscation of estates after the fall of Limerick. Many held commissions in the Jacobite army, among them being:—

337. **Lieut. Christopher Taafe**, and

338. **Ensign Mathew Taafe**, of the King's Own Regiment.[3]

339. **Almeric de Courcy, 23rd Baron Kingsale**, held a commission as Lieut.-Colonel in Col. Patrick Sarsfield's Horse, with which he served until the fall of Limerick.

He sat in James' House of Lords in the 1689 Parliament. He was attainted in 1691, but the attainder was reversed in 1692, when he took his seat in the Irish House of Lords. He died in 1719 and was buried in Westminster Abbey, being succeeded by his cousin,

340. **Myles de Courcy, 24th Baron**, who had held a commission in General Boiselen's Infantry Regiment, with which he served through the campaign down to Limerick.

The barony had been conferred on Myles de Courcy, a brother of John, Earl Palatine of Ulster in 1323, and King John had further granted the Baron and his successors the privilege of wearing their hats in the presence of the sovereign.

The present representative of the house is Michael William Robert Constantine de Courcy, thirty-fourth Baron Kingsale, Homefield, Coffinswell, South Devon, Premier Baron of Ireland.

341. **Henry Jermyn, Lord Dover** (creation 1685), an English peer and strong supporter of James II., whom he accompanied to St. Germains on leaving England. Returning with his sovereign to Ireland, he was sworn of the Irish Privy Council, and received a commission as Lieut.-Colonel in the King's Guards. He was present at the Boyne, and afterwards was solicitous for a pass from friends in King William's army to enable him and his family to go abroad. This King William eventually granted, but his action in protecting an English peer from the results of his Jacobite services was later the cause of friction between King William and his Parliament.[4] Returning

---

[1] Burke's Peerage.
[2] Walker's "Siege."
[3] D'Alton.
[4] Macaulay's "History of England" and D'Alton.

to England, he died in Cambridgeshire in 1708, when all his titles became extinct.

342. **Thomas Fitzwilliam, 4th Viscount Fitzwilliam of Merrion**, was sworn of the Irish Privy Council by James II. in 1689. He held several Government posts and saw some service during the campaign as Colonel of one of the Jacobite Regiments of Horse.

Attainted after the fall of Limerick, the attainder was reversed in 1692, and he died in 1704. The title is extinct.

343. **Major-General Boiselen**, of the French army, a distinguished and experienced officer among those lent by Louis XIV. for service in Ireland.

He commanded an infantry regiment through most of the campaign.[1] His most notable service was at the first siege of Limerick, where, placed from his experience in charge of the defence, he divided the credit with Patrick Sarsfield of obliging King William to raise the siege. Returning to France, he earned distinction in Louis' Army in Flanders, being appointed in 1693 Governor of Charleroi, which had just been captured.[1] He died a few years later.

344. **The Irish Brigade of France.**[2] Reference has been so frequently made in the foregoing sketches under individual names, to the services of the Irish expatriated by the Treaty of Limerick, in the armies of Continental monarchs that a rough summary of the history of that wonderful fighting force, the Irish Brigade of France, will be of general interest.

The origin of the Brigade lay in an arrangement of March 1690 made between James II. and his ally Louis XIV. of France, whereby the latter agreed to supply 6000 veteran French troops for James' coming campaign in Ireland, on condition of receiving an equal number of half-trained Irish troops for his own service in France. Under this agreement, the 6000 French troops commanded by the Count de Lauzun landed in Ireland in April 1690. They were present at the Boyne, but returned to France shortly before the siege of Limerick. The French fleet which brought over these men took back to France the 6000 Irish troops, which were landed at Brest early in May. These troops, under the command of Viscount Mountcashel, consisted of his own, the McCarthy, the O'Brien or Clare and the Dillon Regiments. This force, forming the nucleus of the Irish Brigade under Mountcashel's command, was immediately dispatched to Italy to take part with the French army in the operations against the Duke of Savoy.

While Mountcashel's men were earning a reputation under the flag of France, the Jacobite hopes in Ireland had ended with the fall of Limerick (1691) and under the Treaty of that name another 13,000 Irish troops, electing for service in France, were

---

[1] D'Alton.

[2] Data for which are chiefly derived from O'Callaghan's "Irish Brigade of France," D'Alton's "Jacobite Army List," Harris's "Life of William of Orange," and Macaulay's "History of England."

transported to that country, making a total of nearly 20,000 Irish troops in Louis XIV.'s army.[1] With some few changes and amalgamations of regiments, this force was constituted the Irish Brigade, commanded and regimented under its old leaders, the names of Berwick, Dillon, O'Brien (Clare), Gordon O'Neill (Charlemont), Galmoy, Sarsfield (Earl of Lucan) and Nugent being prominent in the revised grouping. Though paid by Louis XIV., such was the Grand Monarch's delicate consideration that the exiled James had the appointment of the officers. The Brigade was treated as James' army, an *imperium in imperio,* ready at any moment for a descent on any part of the coasts of Great Britain or Ireland.

The first duty of the Brigade was to furnish the Household Troops guarding the Court of St. Germains, and the second to fight for France. These Household Troops of James II. were listed in the Maison de Roi, which accounts for the Duke of Berwick, the Earl of Lucan and others charging with Louis XIV.'s Household Troops at Steinkirk and Landen, as will be seen. In the Flanders campaign of 1692 Louis XIV., at the head of a large army, advanced into that country and laid siege to Namur. He was closely watched by King William, in command of the allied army, which was too weak to raise the siege. Namur fell, and, satisfied with his success, Louis returned to Paris, leaving his most famous Marshal, the Duke of Luxemburg, in command. The Duke held a strongly-entrenched position at Steinkirk, where he considered himself secure. Against this King William hurled his army shortly after dawn on a foggy morning in July 1692. Surprised and driven back at all points, the French fought gallantly, but it was not until Luxemburg had ordered the Household Troops (Maison du Roi), consisting of the noblest blood of France, to charge, that the position was restored and King William compelled to retire, which he did in good order and unpursued. Although Luxemburg held the ground, his losses in killed and wounded were about equal to those of the allies (some 7000 on each side). Among the dead of the allied army were Generals McKay, Lanier and Douglas, who had been prominent in the Irish campaign of 1690–91, and Viscount Mountjoy, who, after his release from the Bastille in exchange for Sir Richard Hamilton, had joined King William's army as a volunteer. In Luxemburg's despatch to Louis XIV. the Duke of Berwick and the Earl of Lucan are specially recommended for gallantry.

In the campaign of 1693 these two great antagonists again confronted each other. At Landen the position was reversed. King William held the entrenchments, which were furiously attacked by Luxemburg. Driven back again and again, at last the Household Brigade carried the position and held it in spite of William's determined efforts to regain it. Although defeated, William's intrepid bravery, leading charge after charge in person, conspicuous with the jewel of the Garter, enabled his army to retire in good order. The carnage had been appalling, the allies losing some 10,000 killed

---

[1] That this is not an over-estimate is confirmed by a French War Office return after the Peace of Ryswick (1697) when the total of the Irish Brigade is given at 18,365.

and wounded and the French some 8000 killed and wounded. On the side of the allies the Dutch General Solms had been killed and the Duke of Ormonde captured. On the French side Sarsfield, Earl of Lucan, had been mortally wounded, while the Duke of Berwick was a prisoner, being next day exchanged for the Duke of Ormonde.

On the opening of the Flanders campaign of 1695, William secretly concentrated his efforts on retaking Namur, captured by Louis XIV. in person in 1692. He felt he could now take risks. The great Marshal, the Duke, had died the previous winter and the French army was under the command of an incompetent Court favourite, the Duke of Villeroy. Advancing rapidly, the King laid siege to the fortress under the command of the able Marshal Boufflers. While Villeroy hung on his flank, refusing to risk battle, William pressed the siege with such vigour that Boufflers, after a gallant defence, was forced to capitulate.

Namur was the seal of William's generalship. Nothing of much further moment occurred in Flanders until 1697, when, owing to the English King's diplomacy and daring, Louis XIV. signed away at Ryswick all he had won in many campaigns. Having secured the temporary peace of Europe, William died in 1702. In the ten years of incessant wars (1692–1702) the Irish Brigade of France had won a great reputation. Of this Brigade Macaulay[1] writes with special reference to the Battle of Marsiglia in the Savoy Campaign (1693):

"This battle is memorable as the first of a long series of battles in which the Irish troops retrieved the honour lost by misfortunes and misconduct in domestic war. Some of the exiles of Limerick showed on that day under the standard of France a valour which distinguished them among many thousands of brave men."

Before his death William had become reconciled to the Earl of Marlborough, taken him into his confidence and appointed him to the command of the British troops in Flanders. The prime favourite of Queen Anne, Marlborough was confirmed in this appointment and shortly afterwards raised to a dukedom by Her Majesty. He was soon recognised as the leader of the European coalition against Louis XIV. His campaigns were phenomenal—victory after victory, with never a defeat. The most famous of his victories was Blenheim in 1704, followed by Ramillies in 1706, Oudenarde in 1708 and Malplaquet in 1709. In all these defeats the Irish Brigade had fought as stubbornly as in the victories of Marsiglia, Steinkirk and Landen. At Malplaquet alone their losses in killed and wounded had been eighty-five officers and 400 men. In 1712 a change in the English political world brought about Marlborough's disgrace and downfall, but he had done his work, as Louis XIV. was obliged to sign the Treaty of Utrecht in 1713. On Anne's death in 1714 George I. came to the throne of England, and on the Grand Monarch Louis XIV.'s death in 1715 his great-grandson Louis XV., a minor, became King of France.

---

[1] "History of England," Vol. IV., p. 428.

In the continental wars 1715–43 the Irish Brigade won fresh honours wherever the banner of France was displayed. But it was at the Battle of Fontenoy in April 1745 that they earned imperishable fame. The Marshal de Saxe, commanding the French army, with Louis XV. present in person, had taken up a strong position at Fontenoy with the main body of his army (say 45,000 men) to cover the siege of Tournai, which another 18,000 of his troops were pressing. To raise the siege the allied army, some 55,000 strong, commanded by the Duke of Cumberland, advanced to the attack. So furious was the onslaught, the English under Cumberland himself penetrating the centre, that the French gave ground, and a retirement was contemplated. The Irish Brigade, consisting of the six regiments of Clare, Berwick, Dillon, Nugent, Lally, and another, had not yet been engaged. It was suggested that they should be given their chance. They were accordingly ordered to charge the advancing English troops under Cumberland while the Household Troops operated on the flank. The order was given. The Irish Brigade, reserving their fire until almost in contact, hurled themselves on their foe, who broke and fled. The day was won. The carnage was terrible, the allies losing 7670 and the French 7139 killed and wounded. The losses of the Irish Brigade were 400 men and ninety-eight officers, among the latter being Col. James Dillon killed, and Viscount Clare (Earl of Thomond) severely wounded. The next morning the King visited the Irish cantonments, thanking the Brigade warmly for their achievement and dispersing rewards and decorations. Viscount Clare was later created a Marshal of France, being known as the Marshal de Thomond.

The next year was memorable for Prince Charles Edward's defeat at Culloden, where several officers of the Irish Brigade of France, sharing in the Prince's ventures, had the mortification of witnessing their Fontenoy antagonist the Duke of Cumberland's success. Luckily for those taken prisoners, their French uniform ensured them honourable treatment and early exchange.

In 1747 the Duke of Cumberland, again in command of the allied army in Flanders, met the French under Marshal de Saxe on the bloody field of Laffeldt. Cumberland, whom the Irish met again, suffered a heavy defeat, but the loss of the Brigade in killed and wounded was no fewer than 1600 men and 132 officers, among the latter being Col. Edward Dillon. Laffeldt (1747) marked an epoch in the history of the Brigade. Up to 1746 recruiting for the Brigade in Ireland, if not actually permitted, had been winked at by the Irish authorities, but in this year the Dublin Legislature passed an enactment making enlistment a penal offence. Henceforth the supply of officers, as before, was maintained by the constant arrival of "wild geese" to fill vacancies in the family regiments, but the rank and file had to depend on the same source of enlistment as other units of the French army. The Brigade did their duty wherever the flag of France was unfurled, particularly in the Colonies, in America, India, and the West Indies. At the revolution the officers almost to a man were loyal to the Bourbon King, but many of the rank and file went over to the Republicans.

Many of the old officers of the Brigade joined the camp of the Emigrés at Coblentz. It is a curious commentary on the changed political position of Europe that, about this time, England, now a staunch supporter of the Bourbons, gave commissions as colonels to six old officers of the Brigade to raise regiments for their service. Notable among these was General Daniel O'Connell, Count of France, an uncle of Daniel O'Connell, "The Liberator," of Derrynane, Co. Kerry, where he was born in 1745. He had a distinguished career in the Irish Brigade. He died at Blois, France, in 1833, aged eighty-eight.

The Irish Brigade was officially dissolved by decree of the National Assembly in 1791. The last Colonel Proprietor of the Dillon Regiment, Col. Arthur Dillon, arrested on the charge of conspiring to restore the Bourbons, died under the guillotine in 1794, with the exclamation "Vive le Roi!" on his lips, as already recorded. On the Bourbon restoration (1814–15) Louis XVIII. presented the surviving officers of the Dillon, Walsh and Berwick Regiments of the Brigade with a "Drapeau d'Adieu" on which was inscribed

1692–1792

SEMPER ET UBIQUE FIDELIS,

thanking them warmly for 100 years' service to France.

O'Callaghan's interesting work closes, not inaptly, with the official death notice of probably the last surviving officer of the Irish Brigade, sent to him by the family, viz. of Louis François Basile Nugent, Comte de Nugent, ancien officier de la Brigade Irlandaise, who died at the Château de Mesnuls, France, on 8th July, 1859.

On the services of the Irish Regiments in Spain and Naples I have not entered, except by an occasional reference under an individual name, having no O'Callaghan from whom to draw the details. I have, however, had the pleasure of reading the publications of the Marquis MacSwiney of Mashanaglass: (i) "Notes on some Irish Regiments in the service of Spain and Naples," (ii) "Notes on Services of 'Irlanda el famoso' in the service of Spain." These two publications, and a letter of the Marquis MacSwiney, fill me with the hope that he will see to the completion of such a work.

The O'Connells of Derrynane, Co. Kerry.

One of the most ancient of the Celtic septs of Ireland.

According to "Burke," Jeffry O'Connell, High Sheriff of Co. Kerry some time during James I.'s reign, died in 1655 leaving two sons:—

(1) Maurice O'Connell of Brentree, Co. Kerry, who left two sons, both officers in James II.'s army, viz.:—

345. (*a*) **Maurice O'Connell**, Lieut.-Col. in James II.'s Guards. Killed at Aughrim, 1691.

346. (*b*) **Lieut. John O'Connell**, of the King's Own Regiment, killed before Derry, 1689. The Brentree line became extinct in 1749.

(2) Daniel O'Connell of Derrynane, from whom descend the line of the great "Liberator." His son and successor at Derrynane,

347. **Capt. John O'Connell**, raised a regiment of his own, with which, embodied with his cousin, Lieut.-Col. Maurice O'Connell's Regiment of Guards, he served at Derry, Aughrim and Limerick. Under the special clauses of the Treaty of Limerick he retained his estates, dying at Derrynane in 1741. He left many sons. His successor was Daniel, among whose descendants was another and more famous Daniel, one of the finest advocates the Irish Bar ever produced, the great Roman Catholic champion, rightly-known in history as "The Liberator." The representatives of this Daniel, still held in affection and reverence for his great services rendered to Ireland, still rule at Derrynane. Among the descendants of other sons of John were two distinguished grandsons:—

348. **Maurice O'Connell**, who, entering the Austrian service, rose to the rank of Baron of the Holy Roman Empire and was Chamberlain to the Empress Maria Theresa.

349. **General Daniel O'Connell**, a Count of France. Born at Derrynane in 1745, he had an extraordinary career. Joining the French army at the age of eighteen, he served in the Clare and Berwick Regiments of the Irish Brigade, so distinguishing himself as to earn the coveted decoration of St. Louis and become a Count of France. The Bourbon downfall and collapse at the revolution so changed the European situation that six old officers of the Irish Brigade received commissions as Lieut.-Colonels in the English army to raise troops in Ireland for their service, General O'Connell being one of them. On the Bourbon restoration, 1814, he was restored to his position in the French army.

He died at Blois in 1833 at the age of eighty-eight, holding the rank of General in the French and Colonel in the English service.[1]

This General Daniel was the uncle of Daniel, "The Liberator," with whom he spent many years when on leave, keeping up a close connection with family and friends.

350. **Capt. James Lally**, of Tollendal (Tullynadaly), Co. Galway, and

351. **Capt. Gerald Lally**, of Tollendal, Co. Galway, two brothers in the Dillon Regiment who served all through the campaign in Ireland, down to the fall of Limerick,

---

[1] See No. 344, The Irish Brigade.

afterwards going to France and continuing officers of the Dillon Regiment of the Irish Brigade.

Both were attainted in 1691 with confiscation of estate. Capt. James was killed in the service of France a few months later. Capt. Gerald was the father of

352. The famous **COUNT LALLY**, born in 1702, a distinguished officer of the Irish Brigade, who fought at Dettingen in 1743, and won a great reputation in command of the Lally Regiment of the Irish Brigade at Fontenoy in 1745.

In 1745 be was one of the officers of the Brigade accompanying Prince Charles Edward in his expedition to Scotland. In 1755 he was sent to command the French troops struggling with England in India. Without adequate support from home he fought out a campaign of five years in which, after many defeats, he was captured at the fall of the last French colony of Pondicherry. Brought a prisoner to England he insisted on returning to France to meet the charges of maladministration brought against him. Tried and found guilty, he was beheaded in 1766.

His son, Gerald, born in 1751, who rose to the rank of Marquis of France, spent years of his life fruitlessly trying to procure a reversal of his father's condemnation. He died shortly after the Bourbon restoration in 1814.

INDEX

57014506R00246

Made in the USA
Lexington, KY
05 November 2016